THE

PRACTICAL

HANDYMAN'S
ENCYCLOPEDIA

THE COMPLETE

ILLUSTRATED

DO IT YOURSELF

LIBRARY FOR HOME & OUTDOORS

VOLUME FOURTEEN

GREYSTONE PRESS/NEW YORK

THE
PRACTICAL
HANDYMAN'S
ENCYCLOPEDIA

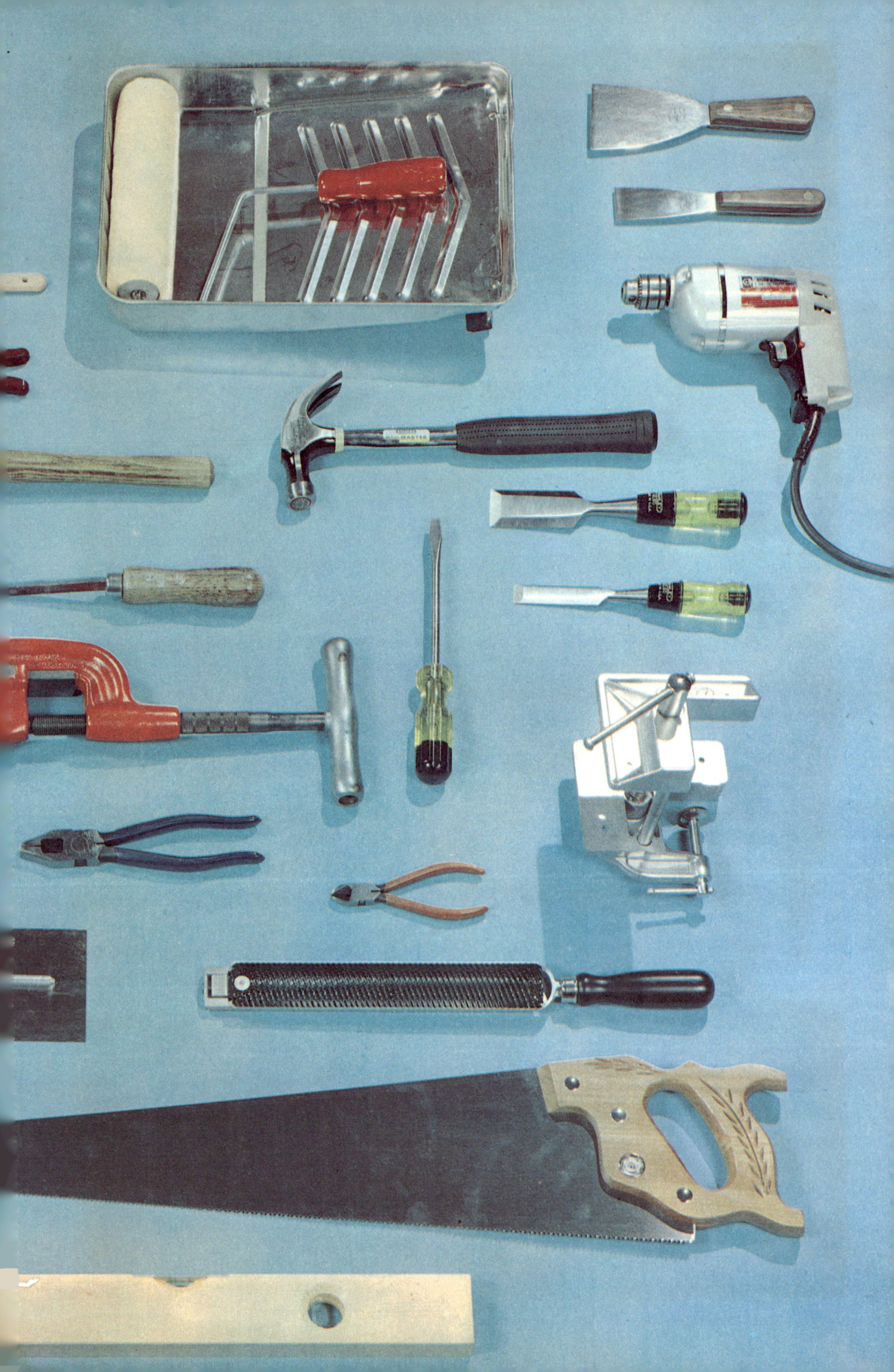

CONTENTS FOR VOLUME FOURTEEN

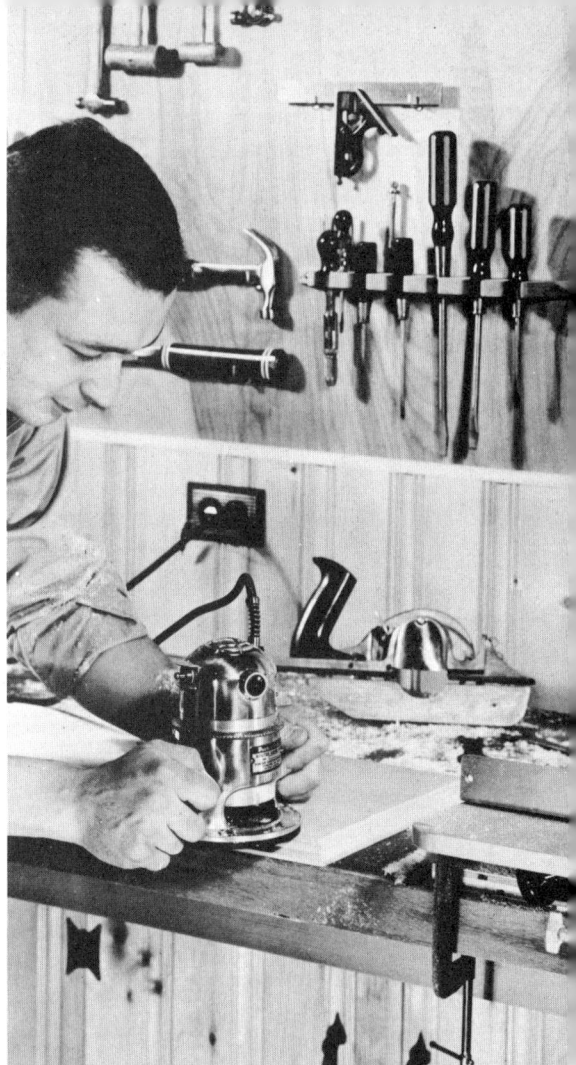

Next to a porch, this large and informal terrace becomes a pleasant sitting room for more than half the year. Roses add the color and fragrance as well as providing a good foundation planting.

Designing the Rose Garden

Landscaping for the amateur is just as interesting as planning the furnishings and colors of the indoor living rooms— especially if roses are the key.

WHEN YOU LOOK at the photographs that illustrate this chapter, you may be inspired to work at designing your own rose garden. Or, you may be a little frightened by the idea of "landscape architecture." You may enjoy looking at the pictures and plans, but say to yourself, "This is too hard for me to do."

It isn't too hard.

It is not as easy as planting one rose bush—but, as a matter of fact, you *can* start that way. If you put one lovely plant of the right size and type in the right place —and anybody can do this—you have done a job of garden designing that will last for years and that will give your family and friends satisfaction.

Nor is the whole subject of rose garden designing one that has to frighten the amateur.

Let's look at it this way: You have seen many natural settings of trees, plants, grass —even including weeds, sand, rocks—that look lovely. There is more chance of doing

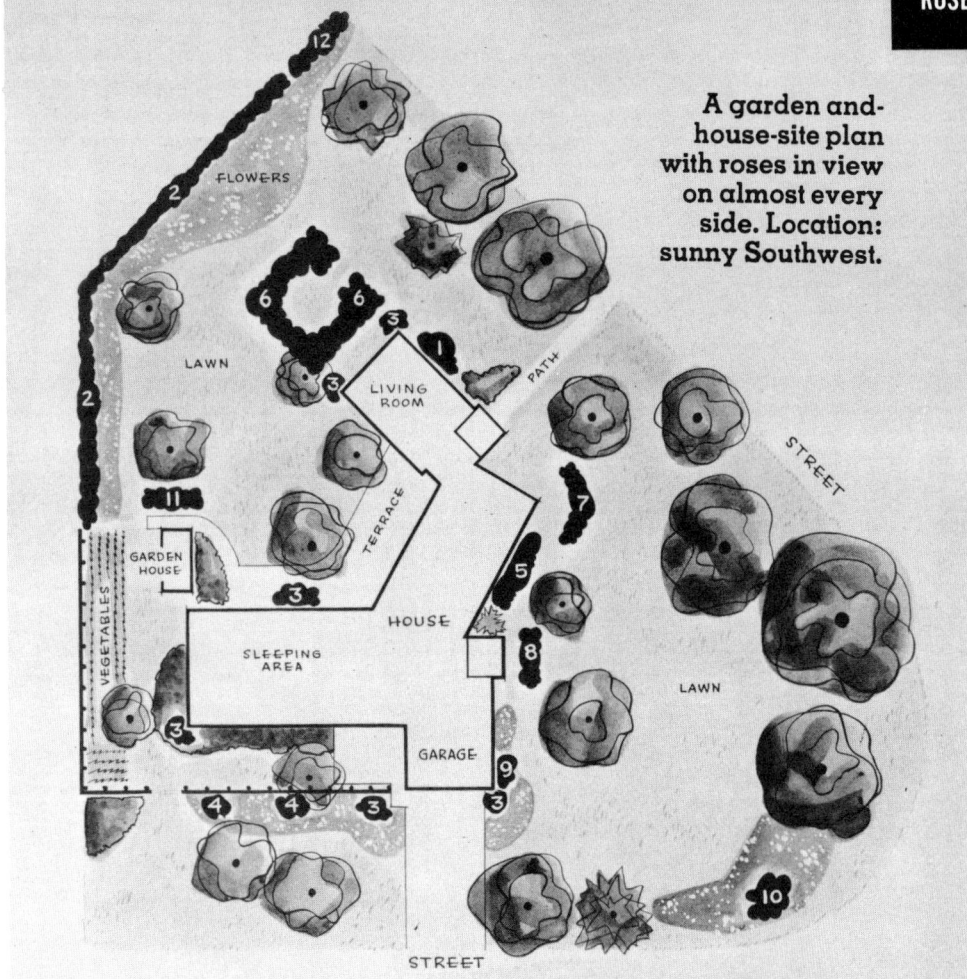

A garden and-house-site plan with roses in view on almost every side. Location: sunny Southwest.

A few colorful floribundas, surrounded by evergreens, have been carefully placed at the house corner and in view of the small open porch.

A gay and friendly hedge of roses serves as a foundation planting as well as a definite edge for covered terrace. Makes house seem larger.

the right thing, if you do it naturally, than of making a mistake. Most mistakes are made by people who get strong opinions, have inherent bad taste, and forget about learning.

Learning some interesting and useful pointers about garden design is fairly simple. It's a question of opening your

eyes and thinking about the things you see.

One time you see a photograph of a goodlooking small garden in a magazine like *Flower Grower*, or in a book like "Landscaping the Small Home." Another time you are visiting a friend, and you make some mental notes about a goodlooking corner of his garden. (It does no

The simplest entrance way can be enhanced with a planting of low floribunda roses—all one color.

If a rock and stream situation has sunlight, you can often find enough good soil for a planting of roses.

A garden seat is surrounded by an arbor, a bed of hybrid teas, and a trellis. Below, a mass of hybrid teas planted along a driveway.

harm to make a sketch or plan, or to take your own picture. You might even start a scrapbook of garden design ideas.)

Still another time you come to the more-than-one-plant-stage and decide to redo part of your own garden. You choose a corner that you have long wanted to plant. You look at it from several different angles —and you try to remember how it looks at different seasons of the year. From the back of your mind (which is your extra scrapbook of garden ideas) you draw out "pictures" of ideas you have had before. How about a group of six low roses forming an "L" in the corner, perhaps with a tree rose to give a little accent, a little change of pace? How about all yellow roses for this corner?

So you put your plan into action.

Doing it is easy. You measure off your space. You know that low floribundas ought to be about two feet apart. Three on each side will come to here—that looks just about right for the size of this corner. Next step: Order six yellow floribundas, one yellow tree rose.

When they come, you can have your planting holes all dug, your manure or compost and fertilizer all spaded into the extra soil and at the bottom of the holes. You plant your special roses carefully. Not only so they'll get a good start in life, but also so they are well lined up, fitting into your setting. Not *too* close to the background—which may be a brick wall, shrubs, or a white picket fence—but with room to grow.

By early June, you'll have a lovely corner of your garden in full bloom, with the

Two more basic home-site ideas using roses are shown at bottom of page. Left, between a walk to a garden shed and the property-line fence. Below, in a structure under a window and in a screened corner. Remember to watch sun areas in planning.

shiny leaves of the plants helping to make them look just right.

What have you done? A little bit of landscape designing. People do it all the time, and seldom incorrectly. It doesn't take an artist or a trained landscape architect to realize that six tree roses and one low shrub rose in that setting would look wrong—your own common-sense artistic taste tells you that.

Yes, you have to avoid some mistakes. Be sure to pick a corner that gets more than half a day of sun. Pick your rose corner for its value as a setting. Can it be seen from your patio, or from the walk?

Of course that isn't all there is to garden design—but it is the beginning approach that we were talking about. This approach, working with one corner at a time, is some-

Containers can be used for tree roses or hybrid teas. Placing them on a terrace or on wide steps when in bloom gives you a movable living garden.

thing that experienced gardeners do—even expensive landscape architects. The results do not look like a beginner's idea.

Now let's look at other ways to approach garden design. The illustrations in this chapter show simple, informal groupings of roses, as well as complete, large formal rose gardens. You can use parts of these ideas, as well as variations. You can make your own plans—it's suprisingly easy. You can plan an expandable garden, and add some roses each year. You can learn about the other flowers that go well with roses. Looking through the pictures is a good way to start.

As you take your walking tour through the pictures, here are some pointers:

1. Don't restrict your thinking and your ideas to things you might do right away

Here are other kinds of containers. If made of solid metal it is best to perforate bottom for drainage, to prevent soil from becoming sour.

A children's garden of Pinocchio roses, at left, in several colors is a happy place. The fence and step treatment help.

A big well-pruned climber near the garage, plus row of graceful Betty Priors makes this an attractive home-grounds setting.

At right, a truly tremendous planting of shrub roses makes a large-scale ending to a large garden. Brick work is also wall.

Gottscho-Schleisner

A flight of stone steps is bare and cold—until you add two dozen rose plants with all their color.

Your own mold for concrete planters is easy to make. Plant three roses, using six blocks, like this.

in your own garden. Think how they might be applied to your neighbor's garden (this is part of the learning process). Learn to see the garden design ideas that even large public gardens have. Eventually they'll affect your own garden, even if only in small ways.

2. Be aware, as you translate picture ideas to actual land situations, of *sunlight*. Where is the shade? Where is the all-day sun?

3. Think in terms of level areas, or ways you can feasibly level a sloping area. Beware of too many rocks and stones. Think of drainage—roses need the kind of soil and the kind of location that does not involve long-standing puddles. (At times you *can* plant on a hillside—if you plan for it.)

4. Think of one other practical aspect of a rose bed: Accessibility for planting, cultivating, pruning, spraying. A bed more than five feet across is usually too difficult to get at for necessary work.

5. Think of the purpose of a rose bed, a row of roses, or a whole garden of roses. If it is purely decorative from a moderate distance, keeping masses of one color is desirable. This affects not only your choice of the roses you buy, but the ideas you get in planning a bed. If, on the other hand, you want a combination of a display of roses, a place to cut flowers for indoor use, and the extra pleasure of growing several new kinds of roses, choose the right kind of location for such a multipurpose bed. A row of low floribundas along a driveway is fine—but the same space devoted to roses of different colors, different heights,

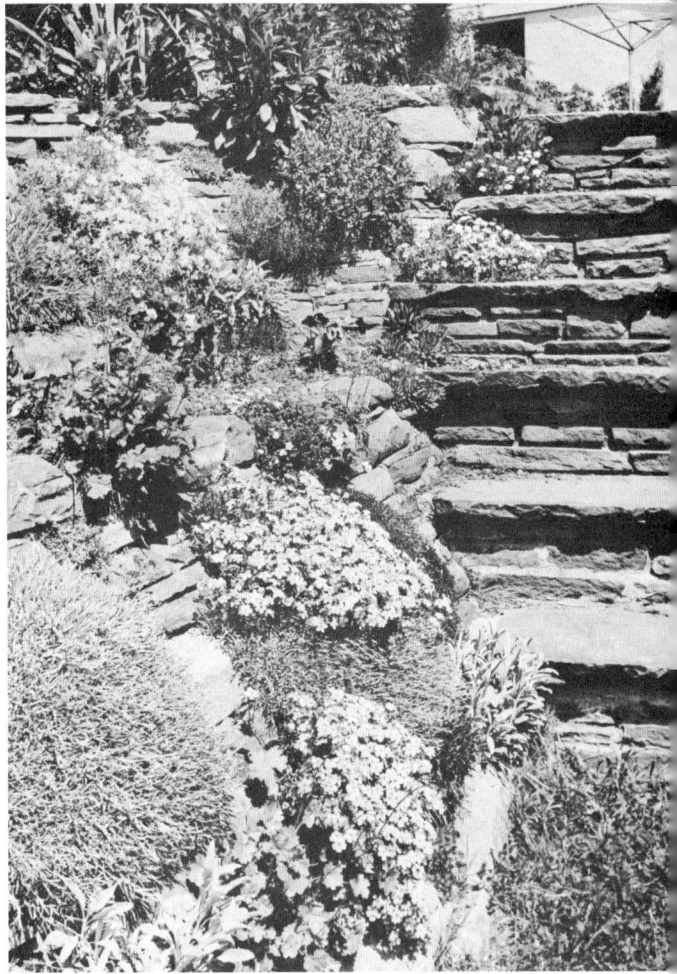

In this wildflower garden, set in rocks on a hillside, are a few miniature roses. They need adequate soil for their roots and some watering.

Here are several ways of laying out a graceful rose garden. A, B, and C are evergreens. Numbers are small beds of same-variety roses. In groupings like this, do not use too many kinds, colors.

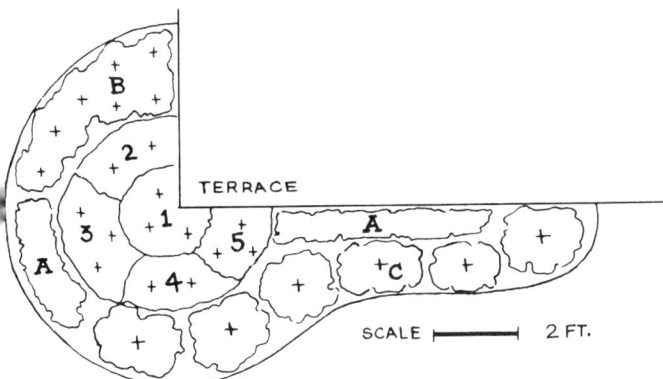

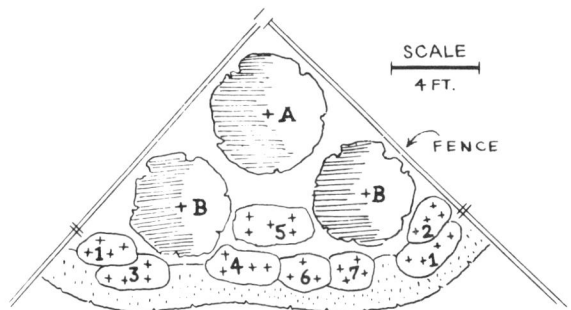

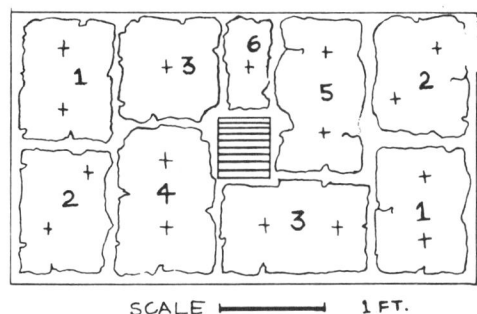

The formal garden should be drawn on paper first, then carefully laid out with stakes and string on the ground. There are many designs to copy from, but careful use of color is the biggest part of it.

Here is a small, traditional design with six tree roses as accents. A gravel walk and shaped evergreen in center are important elements.

and different blooming times would look bedraggled, no matter how beautiful the individual plants were.

6. Think in terms of *Informal*—or *Formal*. You can have both on the same property, but in general it takes skill, practice, and knowledge of just how each kind of plant grows to work out combinations of the two.

These "principles," of course, are ways to approach the whole subject. They're pointers on how to look at a rose garden; as you learn to see the meanings of these pointers in gardens you visit, your mind will be learning how to design—and a very pleasant experience it is. There are other principles of garden design that in time you will learn—a little more arty in sound, and with not so much emphasis on practical points—but these finer approaches work only for someone who knows the practical points thoroughly.

Other ideas that you will get can be

Here are other designs for small formal rose gardens. Each X marks a spot that draws the eye if proper ornament or plant is centered there.

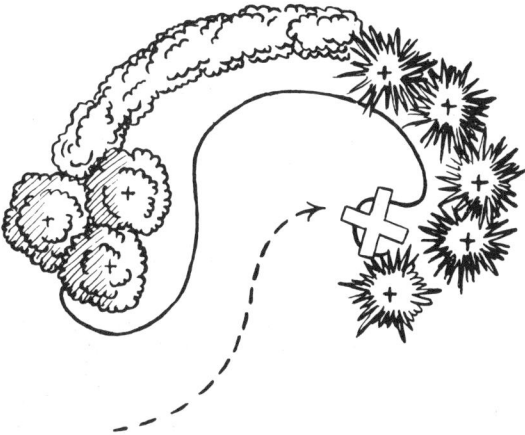

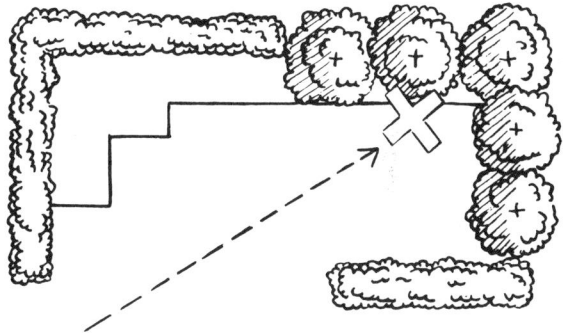

These designs are less formal, but it is just as important to lay them out with proper balance.

Even as an afterthought, roses can be planted along a fence and brighten up a front yard scene.

Two more ideas in children's gardens—a sandbox and a floribunda-bed with bird-bath.

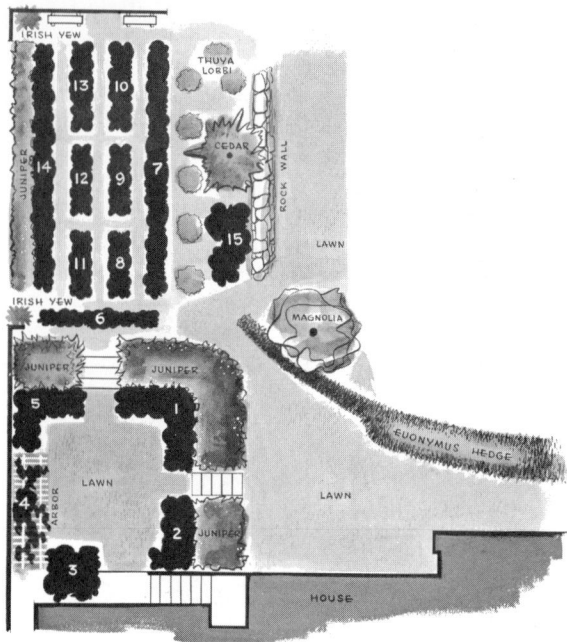

simply larger scale projections of our starting point—the simple corner. For example, think of a small rose garden, or a rose border that's part of a larger garden setting. It doesn't take much thinking to remind you that a table and chairs of attractive garden furniture should be located near the fragrance and the color of the roses—so try to think of that area as outdoor living room space.

One home gardener planned three borders, as edges around a square of grass. In one corner, under a tree, he placed a

Garden at left is in two areas. At top is a formal rose garden, while at bottom you can see a lawn area, making an outdoor living room.

A tree, good lawn grass, a sitting corner, and two informal but well-planned rose beds make this section a gardening family's private joy.

small square—perhaps eight feet by ten—of flag-stones, as the outdoor living room space. One border was full of perennials, the other two were roses. The first rose border had a white fence background—against this a row of pink Robin Hood roses were planted—with their small flowers in spilling-over clusters to complete the background. Hybrid teas were in front of the row of Robin Hood, and they were kept pruned low.

The other rose bed was against the white brick wall side of a garage. Climbers in the back, and both hybrid teas and floribundas in the front row.

The whole effect was pleasant—not completely formal, and not as good from a landscape standpoint as though groups of

all white or all red roses had been used. But the constant bloom, from early June to the end of September, made the "sitting garden" a useful and pleasant place.

Floribundas, as you know, are more informal, give more of a mass effect than hybrid teas. So in garden design, use them for what they are. Use them as an edge for a large rose border. Mary Deputy Cattell, the landscape architect, says, "Use floribundas around the cottage type of house, perhaps as a foundation planting. One variety is enough—usually a floriferous kind of strong color like Fashion, Geranium Red, or Orange Ruffles. Another congenial locale for these roses is around the border of a vegetable or flower garden. The taller growing floribundas used as a hedge or

A garden seat painted white, and a bed of Summer Snow (medium height floribunda) are the focal points of one end of this property.

When a rose garden is this large it needs a boxwood hedge, brick walks, an oak, a holly hedge, and very careful planning of colors.

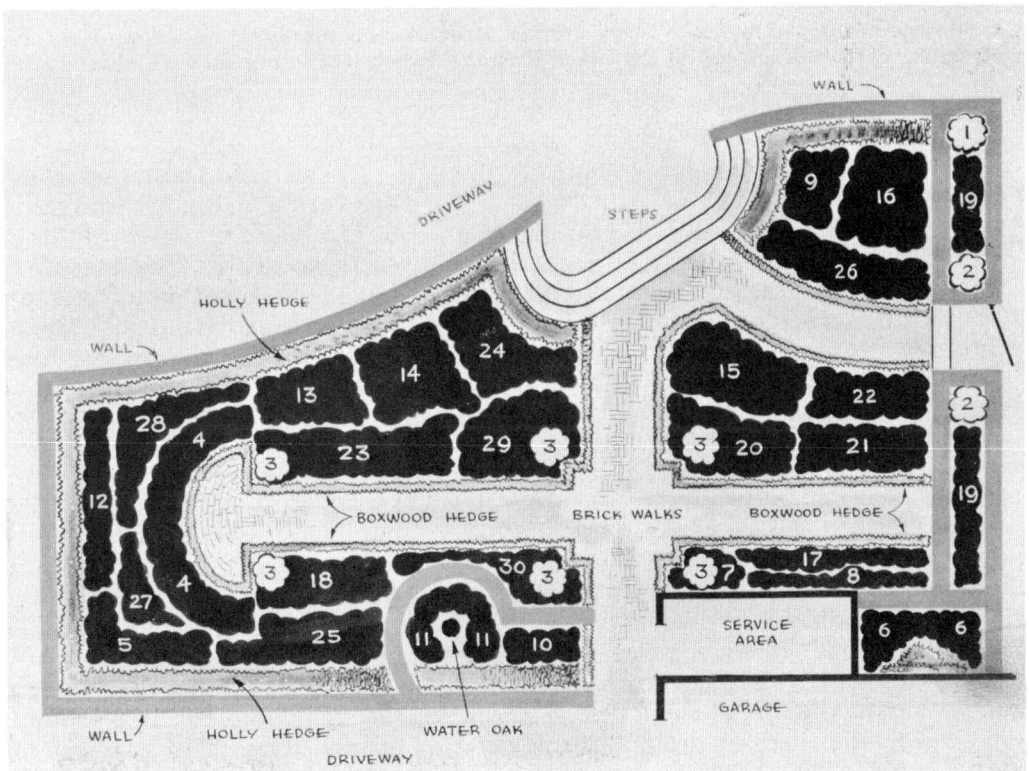

A window that looks out on a large garden gives extra pleasure to the owner. Here the perennial borders are close to the house and the rose gardens are on each side, against evergreens.

trained along a wire fence outline the property strikingly."

As for climbing roses—if you have a trellis, a porch pillar that is suitable, a fence, why of course you think of climbers. Or, to turn the idea around, if you love climbing roses, you must find or create situations for them. You'll get a bigger splash for your money from a few climbers than from any other kind of rose plant, and most times you'll do less caretaking work.

The hybrid tea rose grower has another kind of problem. These are the queen of rosedom, because of perfection of form in the individual blossoms. But this very perfection is obtained at a price—less of a splash of color if you really work at making single blossoms show at their best. So how do you handle them in designing the garden?

Answer: Not so close up as far as plants are concerned, not so prominent, not right out in front of the footlights and spotlight, so to speak. But when cut, for inside the house, you get your closeup back. This means, in garden design, that a hybrid tea specialist's garden is less likely to look as good from a medium distance. You can plant the beds for walking around, to show your guests the choice flowers. You can keep them further away from everyday traffic. You can put edges of splashy floribundas around them to make up for their less dramatic way of life "at the middle distance."

There are other ways of looking at roses in garden design that merit your thoughtful eye. As shrubs, for example, where you can use one plant or a group in a very informal way. You can use old-fashioned roses (e.g. Hermosa, R. Alba, etc.) and

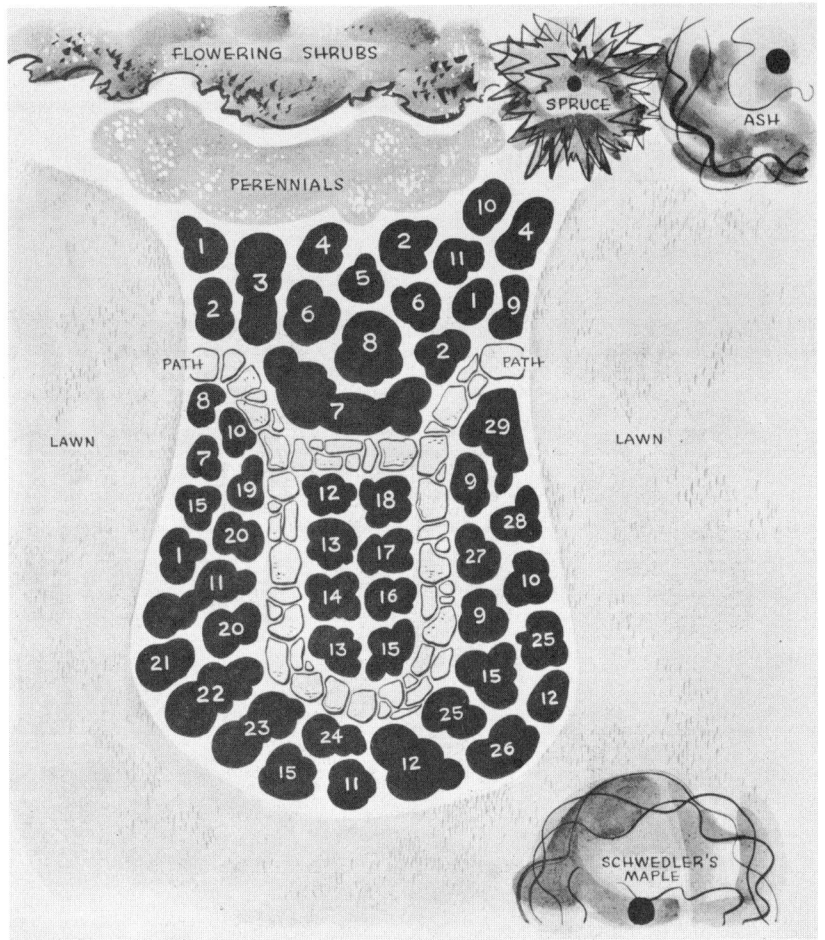

Against a background of spruce, flowering shrubs and perennials, this rose garden projects into the lawn area.

A white ornamental summer house makes a dramatic background. Roses are at the sides, and on the trellis.

Helen Hayes owns this
formal garden, with its
lily pond, yew hedge,
brick walks and perfect
geometrical-type design.

An elaborate-size but
simple-design public
garden can use roses in
tubs to soften straight
lines, modern sculpture.

Drawing from Flower Grower magazine

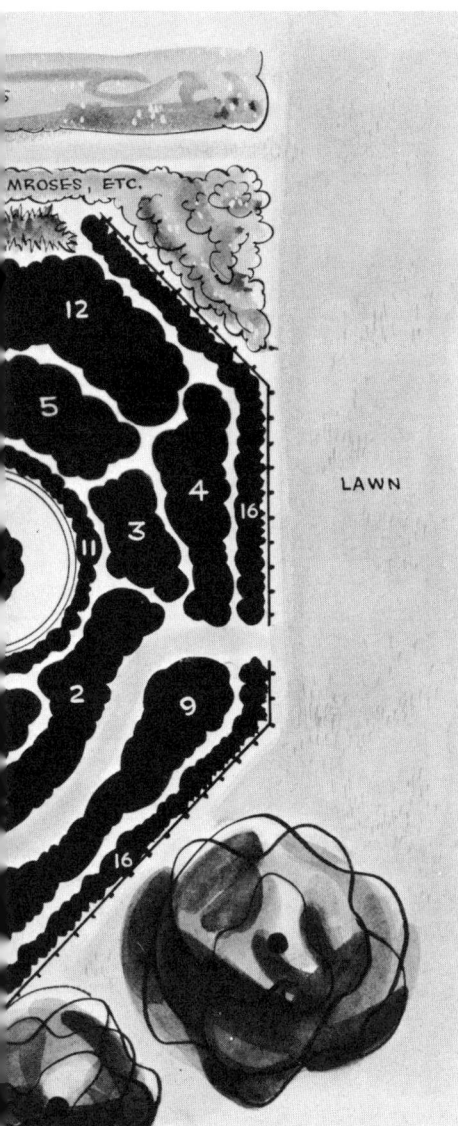

let the plants blend into the landscape when the flowers are not in bloom. You can use many kinds of roses for hedges, for screens, for a change of pace in a distant part of the garden.

Still another variation to keep your eye upon is the rose in a tub or pot. In such a container it can be moved to the patio when you want it. It can be cared for easily and placed just where it ought to be. It will give a special kind of ornamental touch to the architecture of the garden. It can even be used to fill in for a plant that has died.

All in all, your seeing eye gets to look for roses, and for places where roses go well, as you progress further down the gardening path. Recognition of the varieties of roses will be one pleasure; the feeling for the characteristic size and shape of types and even individual varieties will grow in your mind. You'll learn about the glossy, big leaves of PEACE rose, and the delicate, soft green tracery of some moss roses, or the red-to-green variations of CHRYSLER IMPERIALS. You'll get ideas for using this special foliage knowledge in "sculpturing with plants" as you make changes in your garden design.

Most of all, perhaps, you'll learn the eventual "secret" of garden design: That the fun of it is in the fact it never ends. Nature keeps changing the plants; the people who use the garden keep changing; and your own ideas as well as your own design of the garden keep changing, too. It's a growth—just like roses themselves enjoy. So get out your pad and pencil— from here on in it's up to you. •

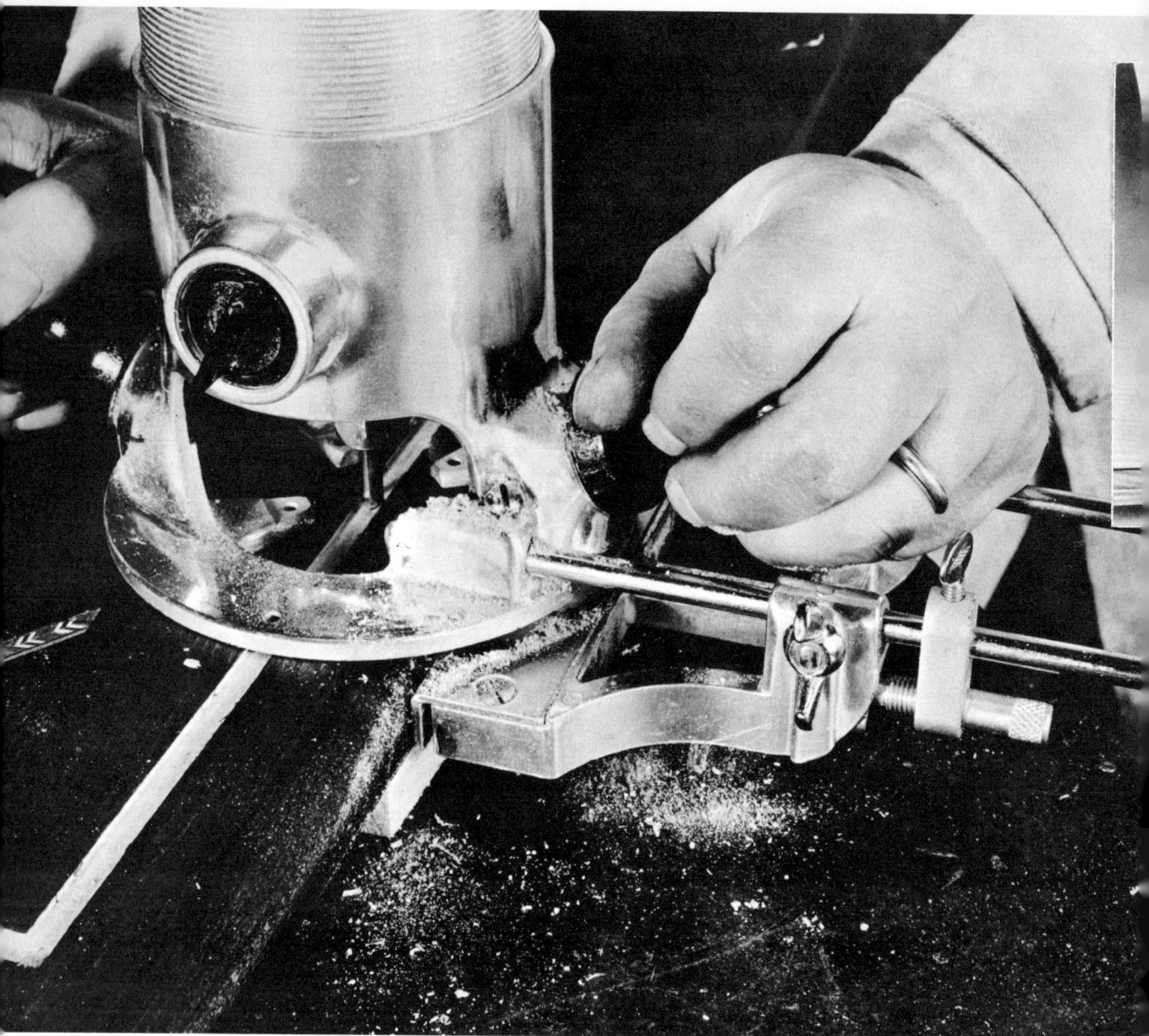

Portable Electric Router

Now the non-professional can turn out work formerly in the domain of the cabinetmaker.

THE manufacturers of the portable electric router make no bones about their claims for this machine. They call it "The most versatile and safest of all woodworking machines."

In this day of power tools geared to perform hundreds of different operations, that's a pretty broad claim. And while there may be some who will dispute it, there's no denying the high place of the router among electric tools with many and varied uses.

As for the safety angle, there is this important fact: there never is any necessity for the operator's hands to get near the spinning bit or any other accessory which is fastened in the chuck.

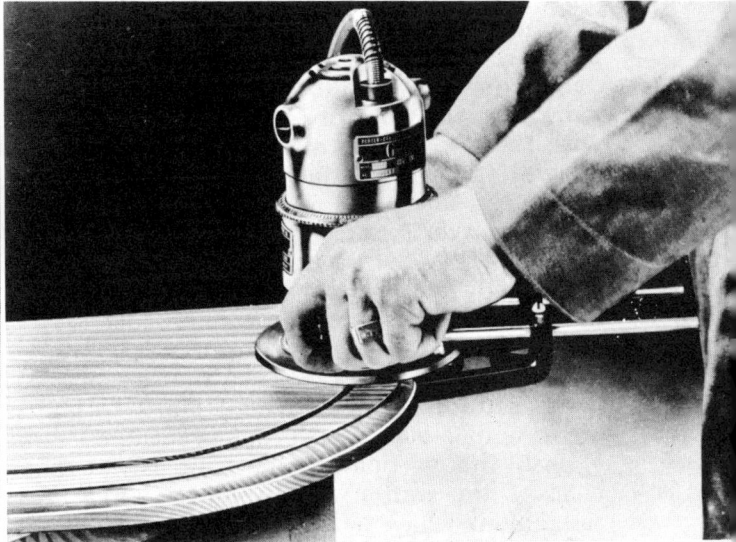

Left, gauge attached to side of router base moves against side of work, keeps the bit at uniform distance from edge.

Above, this operation is simple with the router. Note how operator holds handles at side which aid in guidance.

Top right, the straight and circular gauge has been attached. It works on curved as well as it does on straight stock.

Right, regardless of what operation you are performing, it is always advisable to feed the work quite slowly.

Our own particular satisfaction with the router, aside from the useful functions it performs, has something to do with the creative urge, if you'll pardon this slight deviation from facts and figures. Guiding the router across a piece of wood seems to give a sense of achievement unequaled by any other electric machine. There is almost a feeling that you, and not the router, are doing the cutting.

The router is a high-speed machine, with a speed of from 20,000 to 27,000 revolutions per minute, depending on the model. The most popular sizes for the home workshop craftsman weigh about 6 pounds. It has a universal 115-volt motor, although other voltage motors are available. Manufactur-ers, who had been supplying professional woodworkers with these machines for many years, decided—and rightly—that only light, compact models would satisfy the average person. The result is a tool that is easy to handle even for the novice in the power tool field.

What does a router do?

If that question had to be answered in a single sentence, the reply might run something like this: it cuts into and through wood and many other materials to a desired thickness and depth.

But that would be a simple and not very illuminating explanation of its usefulness. What gives the router a special fascination is that it enables the non-professional to turn out work that once was strictly in the province of the master cabinetmaker. The most intricate joints, decorative cuts and exacting inlays are possible, with just as much accuracy as simple grooves and dadoes for shelf-making. All these wood-working applications are accomplished with the use of dozens of bits and cutters, as well as various attachments for special purposes. There is a plane attachment which converts the router into a high-speed machine for accurate and easy plan-ing of edges; a shaper plate so that the motor unit can be used for spindle shap-ing; an accessory which cuts the recesses for door hinges; and a set-up that enables the heretofore tricky dovetail joints to be made with almost fool-proof precision.

Both the vertical motor unit and the base of the router are threaded, an ar-rangement which permits the depth of cut to be controlled to within 1/64th of an inch. The more the motor housing is turned into the base, the more the bit projects below the base. A clamp screw quickly locks the motor in place. The switch that turns the motor on and off is recessed into the hous-ing so that it can not be moved accidentally. A gauge attached to the side of the base moves against the side of the work to keep the bit at a uniform distance from the edge of the stock. This gauge is shaped so that it can be used for straight or curved work and rides on adjustable rods.

The chuck of the router intended for home use has a capacity of a quarter-of-an-inch. Since much of the work done with the router calls for the use of template, or pattern guides, the base has been cut out so that there can be an accurate alignment of the template guide with the motor spindle.

How fast the router is fed into the stock depends on the type of cut being made and the hardness of the material being used. Feeding too fast will slow the motor and cause an overload. Feeding too slowly will scorch the wood and dull the cutters. Prac-ticing on scrap wood soon will enable the operator to get the feel of the machine and know instantly when the feed is either too fast or too slow. But this practicing should be done on different types of scrap wood

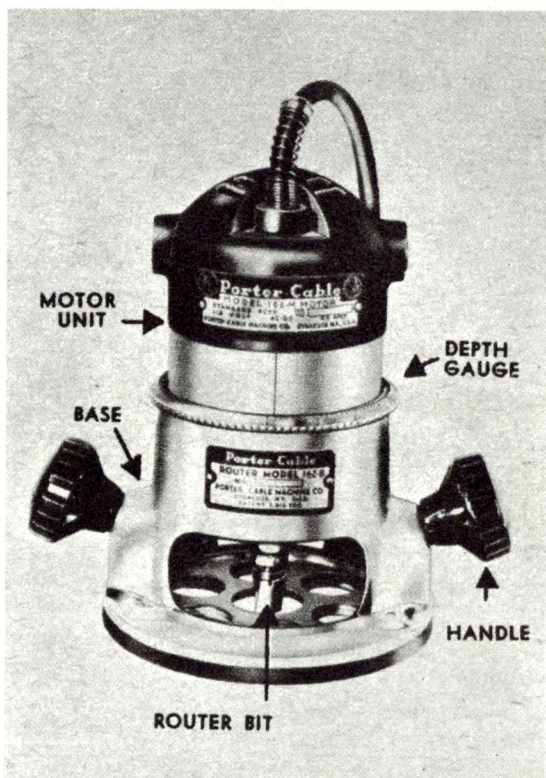

MOTOR UNIT

DEPTH GAUGE

BASE

HANDLE

ROUTER BIT

Above, this model weighs 5½ lbs., has ½ h.p. interchange-able motor, speed of 21,000 rpm.

Right, this craftsman also has a plane attachment and a shaper table attachment for his router.

Left, use of stair template as-sures accuracy on every stringer. This will save a lot of time.

Before you make any adjustments on the router disconnect the motor unit from electric outlet.

Then remove motor unit from base by turning the clamp screw 1½ turns and slipping off base.

and with several different cutter sizes. As with all power tools, an overheating of the motor housing is a sure sign of an overload. Because the router usually is used with both hands on the knobs on either side of it, this overheating may not be detected as quickly as with a machine which is always held in the hand. It is well, therefore, to stop occasionally and touch the motor housing with your fingers to determine whether it is too hot. After using the machine for some time, there will be no necessity for this, as you will be able to tell by the sound of the motor whether it is operating properly, just as you get to know the sound of the motor in your car.

For the most efficient cutting, the direction of feed with the router should be the opposite of the direction of motor rotation. As you look down the motor, the shaft revolves clockwise. The router thus should be moved counterclockwise when cutting circular or curved edges . . . and from left to right when cutting straight edges. Remember this the first few times and habit will take care of it thereafter.

Cutting Grooves and Dadoes

The cutting of grooves and dadoes with the router is a simple operation and forms the basis for the construction of various types of wood joints.

The groove—a channel made with the grain of the wood—usually is made somewhere near the edge of the stock. The straight edge of the gauge is used to guide the machine at exactly the distance you want it. A straight bit is used, with the depth adjustment set in the manner described previously. Whenever possible, it is best to use the proper size bit for the groove being cut; that is, a ½-inch bit for a

½-inch groove, a ¼-inch bit for a ¼-inch groove, and so on. But when the right size bit is not available at the moment, you can accomplish the same result by making more than one pass over the work with an undersize bit. Two passes with a ¼-inch bit, for example, would make a desired ½-inch groove. This means, however, that you must readjust the gauge for the second cut.

Making a groove in the narrow edge of a piece of wood calls for some procedure to prevent the router from tilting as it rides across the work. There is more than one way to do this, but the easiest is to clamp boards on both sides of the piece to be cut. This increases the thickness of the edge so that the router will remain vertical as it does its groove-cutting job.

Cutting a dado—which is a groove across the grain—usually is done with a guide other than the regular metal gauge which is purchased with the machine. That's because most dadoes are cut well across the surface of the wood where the use of the gauge would be impractical. In place of the gauge, a straightedge clamped across the work surface will do nicely. The best straightedge for this purpose is a strip of wood at least ½ inch thick. It should be clamped to the work so that the outside edge of the router base rides against it as the cut is being made. The distance from the straightedge to the cut is exactly the same as the distance from the cutting edge of the bit to the router base edge. The principle of the straightedge in this operation is much the same as the use of a rip fence on a table saw, except that the router, rather than the wood, is moved to make the cut.

There are different kinds of dadoes— the through dado, which goes completely

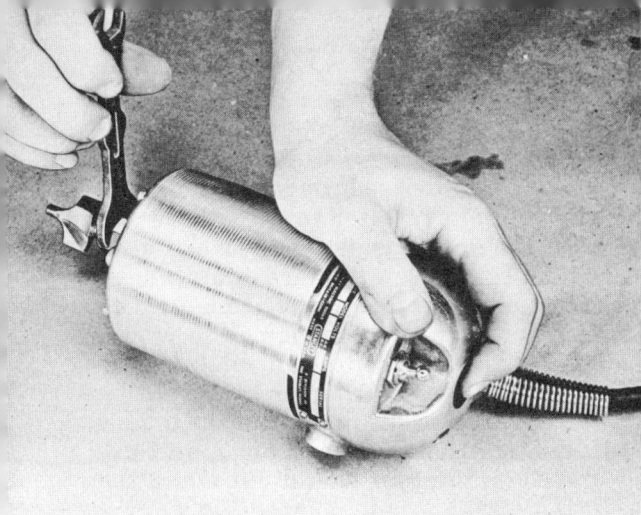

Insert shank of bit at least ½″ into chuck. Then be sure the chuck is properly tightened.

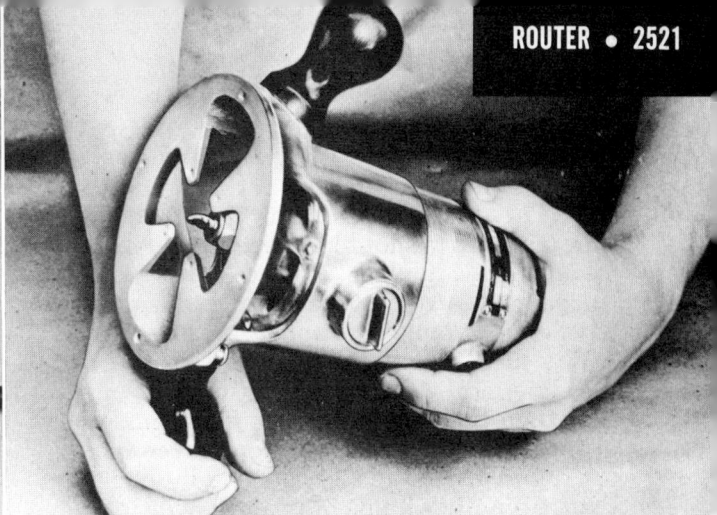

Turn clamp screw three quarters to left, base around motor to right to obtain depth of cut.

across the width of the wood; the half-blind dado, which starts a little in from the front edge and then goes completely across the width; and the blind dado, which does not show on either edge of the board. For extra fine work, a strip of wood should be tacked against each edge of the wood when making a through dado, a practice that eliminates any possibility of marring the work where the bit enters and leaves it. For a half-blind dado, this strip is needed only at the back edge of the wood, and for the blind dado it is not needed at all.

A rabbet cut is a groove on the surface of the work but along the edge. It is made with the gauge, the straight edge of which can be faced with a block of wood for best results. In fact, some workers keep the wood on the gauge for nearly all operations. There are two holes on the face of the gauge so that a piece of wood can be attached with two screws. To guide the router on a curved surface for making veining cuts (narrow grooves for ornamental purposes), the wood block must be curved to fit the contour of the surface on which the cut is to be made.

The Router for Inlay Work

That beautiful inlay work you've probably admired at some time or other can be done with a router. There are many different kinds of inlaying, but the easiest—and the kind that should be attempted first—is called strip inlaying. It's strictly a grooving operation in which the inlay runs in straight lines parallel with the edges of the wood. The gauge is used for this operation, with a spiral bit of the proper size. In making the cuts, any round corners can be quickly straightened out with a small chisel. The inlay is then glued into the

grooves and held there with clamped wood until it is completely dry.

Only when strip inlaying has been mastered should block inlaying be attempted. This is the process known as *marquetry*. The block inlays are purchased intact, the outline cut into the wood with a sharp knife and the routing done with the aid of the gauge or a straightedge. Once the outline has been cut, the router is used free hand

In making adjustments such as this, be gentle with motor and bit, and always take your time.

to remove the rest of the wood inside the outline. The inlay is then set into the recess. This type of inlay has paper on one side. The paper should be face up when the inlay is glued in place. After the glue is dry, the paper is sanded off and the picture you have chosen makes its appearance.

The most intriguing type of inlaying is that in which you cut out the inserts yourself, then make the recesses for them. All of this is done with the router in free hand operation and naturally calls for more skill than with other kinds of routing, where the machine assumes the responsibility for precision results. The practice that brings this skill is well worth the effort when you are able to turn out beautiful inlays of your own design.

It is difficult to make a series of irregular or curved cuts and have them match perfectly in the tiniest detail. That's where the template guide comes in. The template itself is made by you and fulfills the same purpose as a pattern in making dresses. You can use either plywood or tempered hardboard, cutting out the design with a router bit set a fraction of an inch deeper than the thickness of the material. After the template has been sanded to smooth any rough edges, it is used to make the inlay with the assistance of the template guide, which is attached to the router base. The same template and guide serve to cut out the recess for the inlay. You can make any number of identical inlays with this template, and, if desired, put it aside and use it again for similar work weeks, months or even years later.

An interesting result can be achieved with a portable electric router and one of the plastic woods that come in various wood shades. After making decorative cuts in the stock with a veining bit, the recesses are filled with plastic wood, which is allowed to harden. You then sand it flush with the surface. This gives the appearance of an inlaid piece of wood, although it must be remembered that the design will not stand out unless it is either darker or lighter than the stock. A very effective "name" sign for the outside of the house can be made in this fashion, using spar varnish as the finish to protect it from the elements.

Still another effect that can be obtained with the router is the raised design. The pattern is traced or drawn directly on the wood surface. The router bit is then moved along the outside of the outline, which makes the design appear raised, although it really is no higher than the original surface of the stock. The routing of the mate-

rial around the design can be advanced as far outward as desired, depending on the intended effect. A neater result will be obtained if the design is set inside some geometric figure, such as a square or rectangle. Let's say, for example, that you planned to produce the picture of a duck. You would make a square, then draw a duck in the center of it. A small diameter bit would be used to cut around the outside of the duck's outline. Once that had been done, and using the same bit, you would cut along the

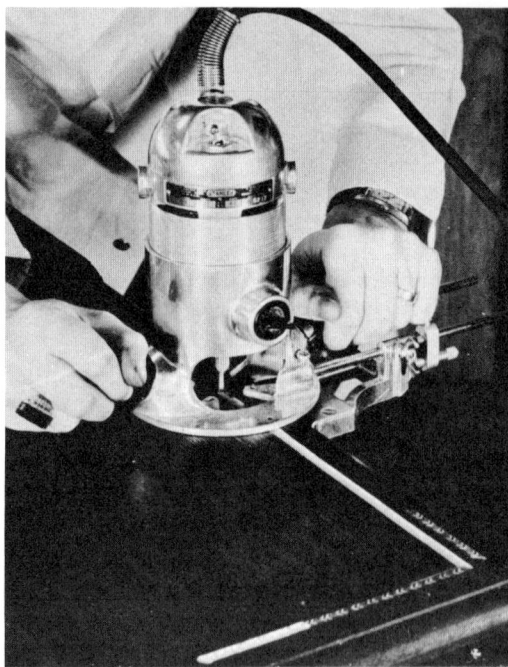

You can make dadoes for an inlay insertion on a table top. Use of guide simplifies this task.

It's fun to make signs like this. Letters are traced, then outlined by router using small bit.

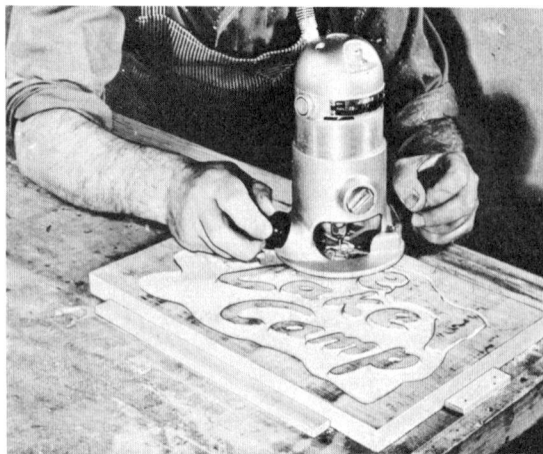

lines of the square, but this time you could use a gauge or straightedge to insure accuracy. The third and final routing step would be to remove the excess wood between the outline of the square and the outline of the duck, using a large diameter bit to speed up the work.

Other Uses for the Router

Just by using the proper bit or attachment you can perform an infinite variety of tasks with the router.

There is no type of wood joint that cannot be made with the router. The mortise and tenon, the cross lap, the end lap, the tongue and groove, the rabbet, all of these and many more are possible with this machine by following the principles mentioned earlier. But that aristocrat of wood joints—the dovetail—would be difficult indeed without the use of the *dovetail attachment*.

Once the attachment has been mounted on the router (and detailed instructions for

Dovetail attachment now permits you to perform work originally done only by master craftsmen.

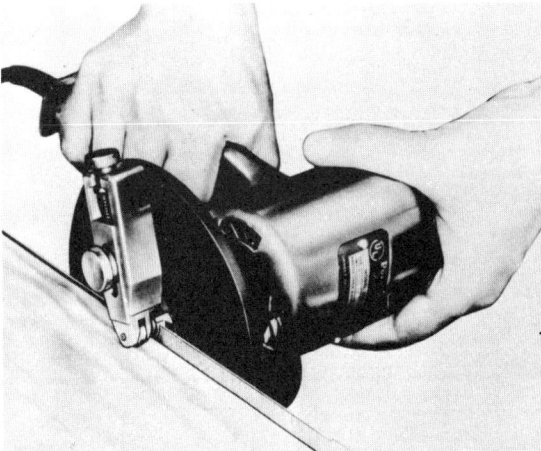

Metal template on door guides router so that hinge mortises are cut to uniform size, depth.

This router has a roller guide assembly so you can accurately edge laminated plastic surfaces.

Cutting dadoes or grooves is a simple job for the router. Note use of guide for straight cut.

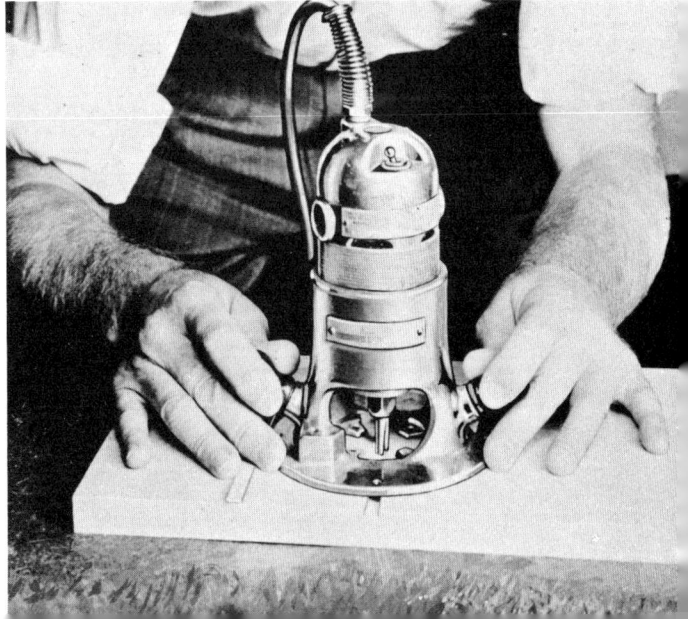

There are bits for every kind of job. You
would be wise to learn just what they are.

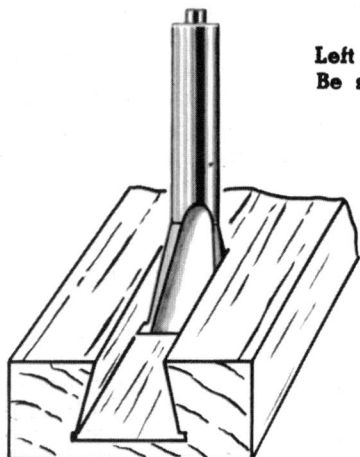

Left is a Dovetail bit. Right, a Rabbeting bit.
Be sure always to keep bits well sharpened.

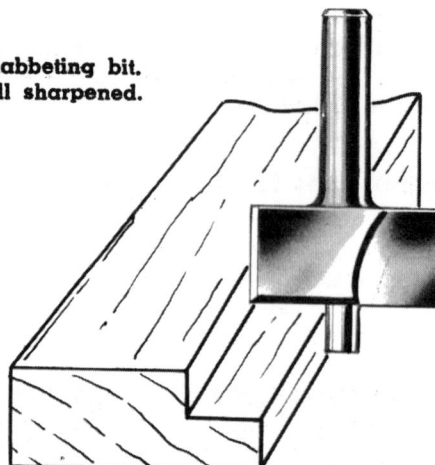

doing this come with the attachment), a
dovetail joint can be cut in about 30 seconds. Perhaps at some time you've cut a
dovetail joint by hand and, if you're lucky,
had the two parts fit perfectly. It's more
likely, though, that the joint had to be
patched up with a little wood putty to make
it tight. With the dovetail attachment on a
router, both members of each joint are cut
simultaneously and so fit exactly.

With a router, you can also make molding cuts, do beading and fluting, cut perfect
hinge mortises, plane wood edges and, with
grinding wheels in the router motor,
sharpen bits and cutters. Because of the
wide variety of bits available, there is almost no limit to the different kinds and
shapes of cuts that can be made.

There is a veneer trimming attachment
for the router that can be used easily for
that heretofore tricky job of slicing off the
edges of plastic laminates. With this handy
attachment you will find that there is no
longer the danger of marring the plastic
edging while you are trimming the top surface flush with the sides.

Left, a Nosing bit. In selecting bits the best
cost less in long run, when properly cared for.

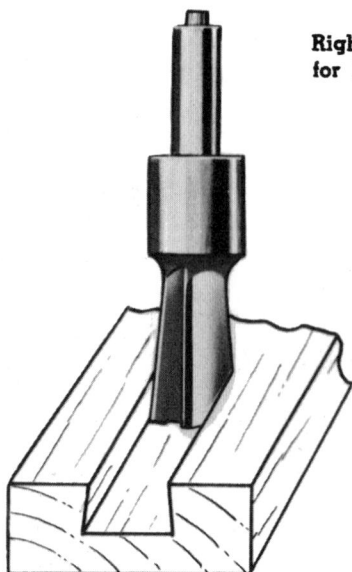

Right, Straight bit. With this bit it is necessary
for beginner to use straightedge as a guide.

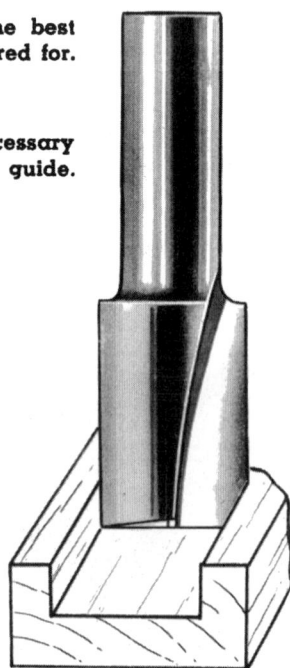

Left, this is a Long shank Straight bit. Right, the Pilot Panel bit. Right below, the Ogee bit.

Insist upon getting high-speed steel bits that have been ground and honed by experts.

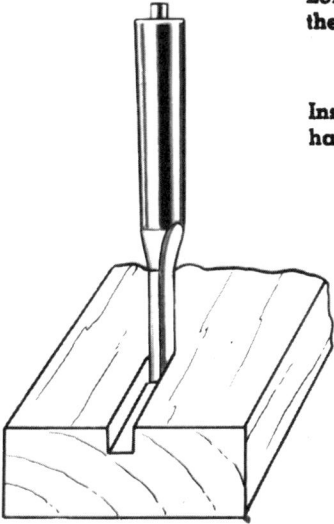

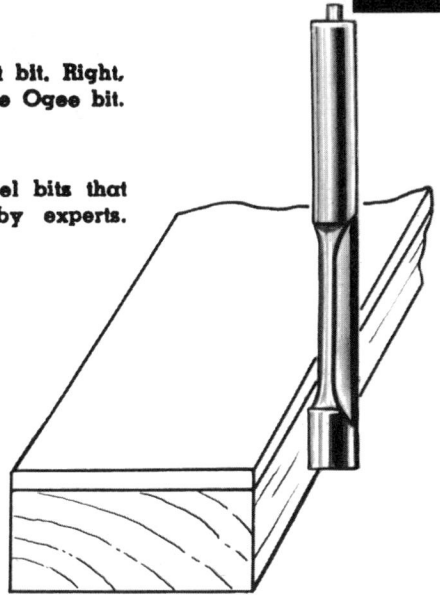

Safety Tips

Disconnect the motor unit from the electric outlet when changing bits or adding attachments.

Never insert anything in the air vents for any reason whatever.

Be sure the bit is inserted at least ½ inch into the chuck, then rotate it by hand to be sure it clears the router base *before* connecting to the power source.

Keep the motor clean, the air holes free from dirt. As with all cutting tools, be sure the bits and cutters are kept sharp. •

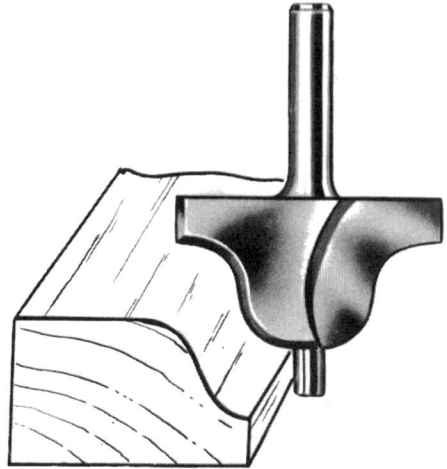

A Cove bit, Chamfering bit, and a Roman Ogee bit. Besides the bits illustrated on these pages there are many others. As you will see, with the router, a simple change of bit permits you to turn out an infinite variety of ornamental cuts including veining, fluting, bevelling, reeding, compound molding.

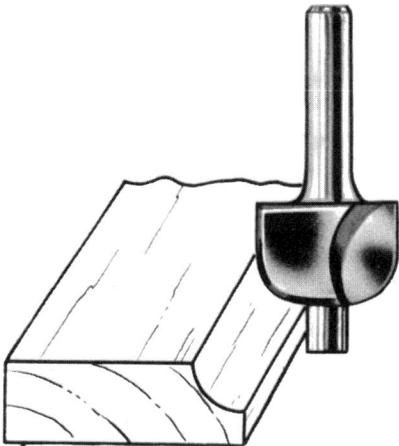

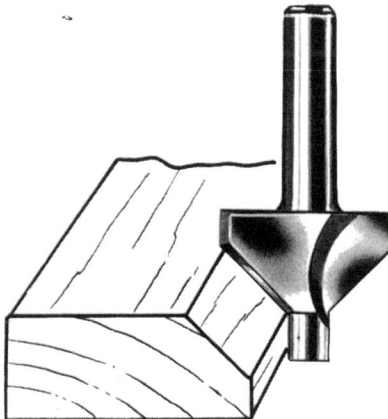

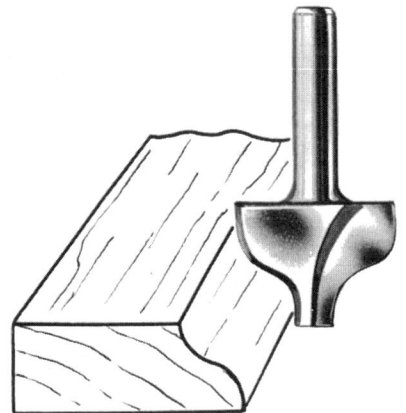

Houdini

By Edwin Monk, N. A.

This 11½-ft. skiff can be taken apart and
stacked to fit into a compact station wagon.

LIKE THE LADY in the vaudeville act, this boat goes on living after she's sawed in half.

THIS BOAT, which is essentially a skiff,
requires no jig or setup stringers.
Only a small amount of material—the
form used temporarily about the middle
of the after section—does not become
a part of the finished product. Even this
can be omitted if care is taken to maintain the width dimension at this point on
the hull.

The photographs are of the completed
boat, except for painting. The boat is *not*
cut in half until everything else has been
completed.

LAYOUT: A clear space about 14' x 16'
is needed. First lay out the starboard side
plank on the 4' x 12' plywood sheet. Put
the bow to the right edge. Use the lower
edge of the sheet as a base line.

Use a batten about 1" x ¾" to outline the
top and bottom lines by springing it

around finishing nails. After drawing the
top and bottom lines, draw in the lines representing the location of the frames and
division pieces.

Cut the side from the plywood, then lay
out the port side, using the starboard as a
pattern. Draw the frame and division piece
lines on the port side.

FRAMES: Lay out and cut the oak and
plywood pieces for Frame No. 1, the two
division pieces and the transom. Cut the
parts for the temporary form from scrap
lumber. The notches in Frame No. 1 for
the gunwales and chines are NOT cut to
the full dimension of the gunwale and
chine pieces. Cut these notches ⅝" x 1½"
instead, because the gunwales and chines
will be tapered at this point. Assemble
Frame No. 1, using waterproof glue and
1" nails on 1½" centers. Drive the nails

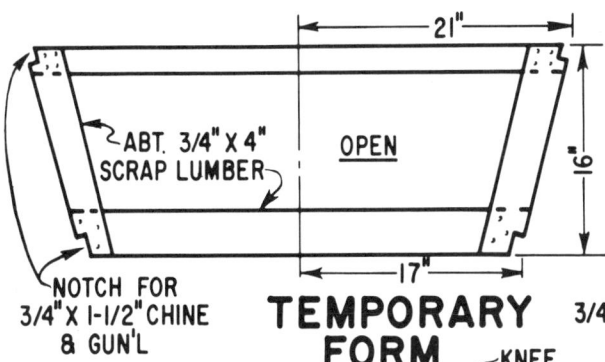

TEMPORARY FORM

ABT. 3/4" X 4" SCRAP LUMBER
OPEN
21"
16"
17"
NOTCH FOR 3/4" X 1-1/2" CHINE & GUN'L

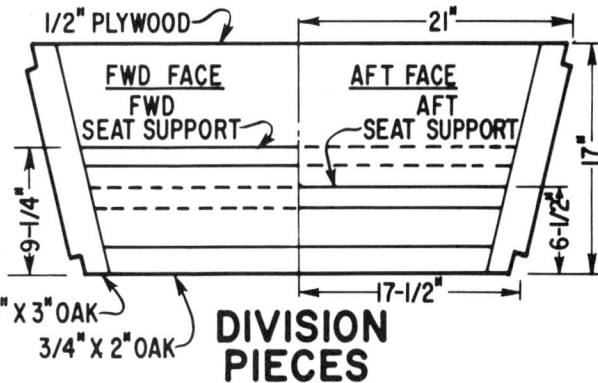

DIVISION PIECES

1/2" PLYWOOD
FWD FACE
FWD SEAT SUPPORT
AFT FACE
AFT SEAT SUPPORT
21"
17"
9-1/4"
6-1/2"
17-1/2"
3/4" X 3" OAK
3/4" X 2" OAK

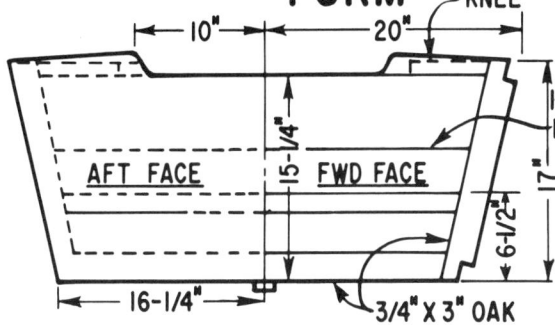

TRANSOM

KNEE
10"
20"
1-1/16" X 5-1/2" MOTOR SUPPORT
15-1/4"
AFT FACE
FWD FACE
17"
6-1/2"
16-1/4"
3/4" X 3" OAK

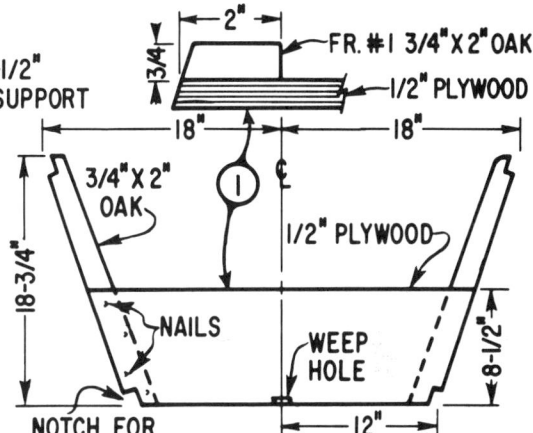

FRAME NO. 1

2"
3/4"
FR. #1 3/4" X 2" OAK
1/2" PLYWOOD
18"
18"
3/4" X 2" OAK
1/2" PLYWOOD
18-3/4"
NAILS
WEEP HOLE
8-1/2"
12"
NOTCH FOR 5/8" X 1-1/2" TAPERED CHINE

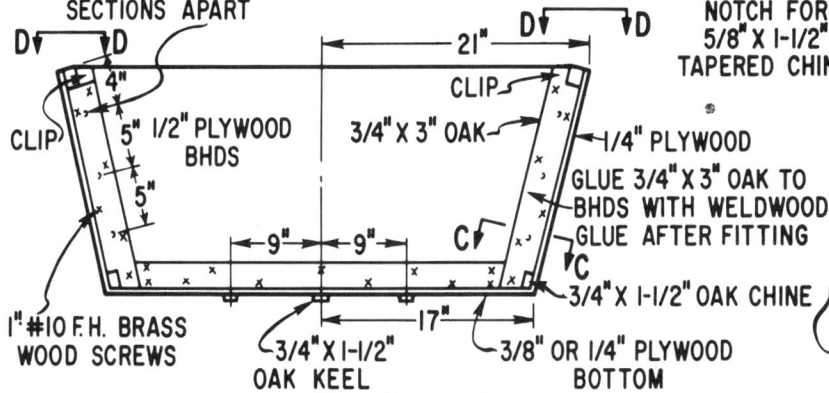

SECTION "AA" & "BB"

DRILL HOLES FOR 3/8" BOLTS BEFORE CUTTING FWD & AFT SECTIONS APART
D
D
D
D
21"
4"
CLIP
CLIP
5"
1/2" PLYWOOD BHDS
3/4" X 3" OAK
1/4" PLYWOOD
GLUE 3/4" X 3" OAK TO BHDS WITH WELDWOOD GLUE AFTER FITTING
5"
C
C
9"
9"
3/4" X 1-1/2" OAK CHINE
17"
1" #10 F.H. BRASS WOOD SCREWS
3/4" X 1-1/2" OAK KEEL
3/8" OR 1/4" PLYWOOD BOTTOM

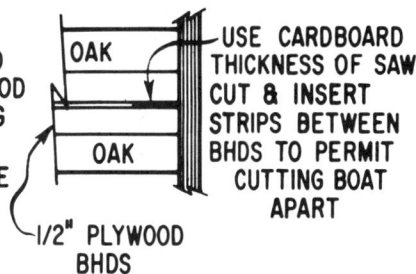

DETAIL "E"

OAK
OAK
USE CARDBOARD THICKNESS OF SAW CUT & INSERT STRIPS BETWEEN BHDS TO PERMIT CUTTING BOAT APART
1/2" PLYWOOD BHDS

through the plywood to the oak, not vice versa. Frame No. 1 must be beveled along the sides to match the inward turn of the hull.

Lay out the two division pieces. Note that the seat support on the forward division piece is higher than the one on the after division piece. Seats in the after half of the boat are lower to accommodate the bow section when nesting it in the stern section for transporting the craft.

Assemble the division pieces, using waterproof glue and 1" No. 10 flathead screws staggered in a double row beside the bolthole marks on the side frames. The bottom frame piece may be fastened with 1" nails on 1" centers, or the screws may be continued. The chine and gunwale notches are cut full size, 3/4" x 1-1/2". This must be done carefully, or trouble will re-

sult later. Study plans before starting.

Assemble the temporary form. Now assemble the transom, using waterproof glue and 1¼" nails on 1½" centers. Cut the side frames that will eventually replace the temporary form. Mark the vertical centerline on Frame No. 1, the division pieces, the temporary form and the transom.

ASSEMBLING THE HULL: Shape the stem and tack the side planks to it, using two nails on each side. Position the stem carefully, then remove the sides and coat the joining surfaces with one of the many modern waterproofing compounds. The previously-driven nail holes will aid greatly in positioning the sides for permanent fastening. This should be done next, using 3/4" nails on 1½" centers.

Pass a rope around the transom ends of the sides and draw them together until

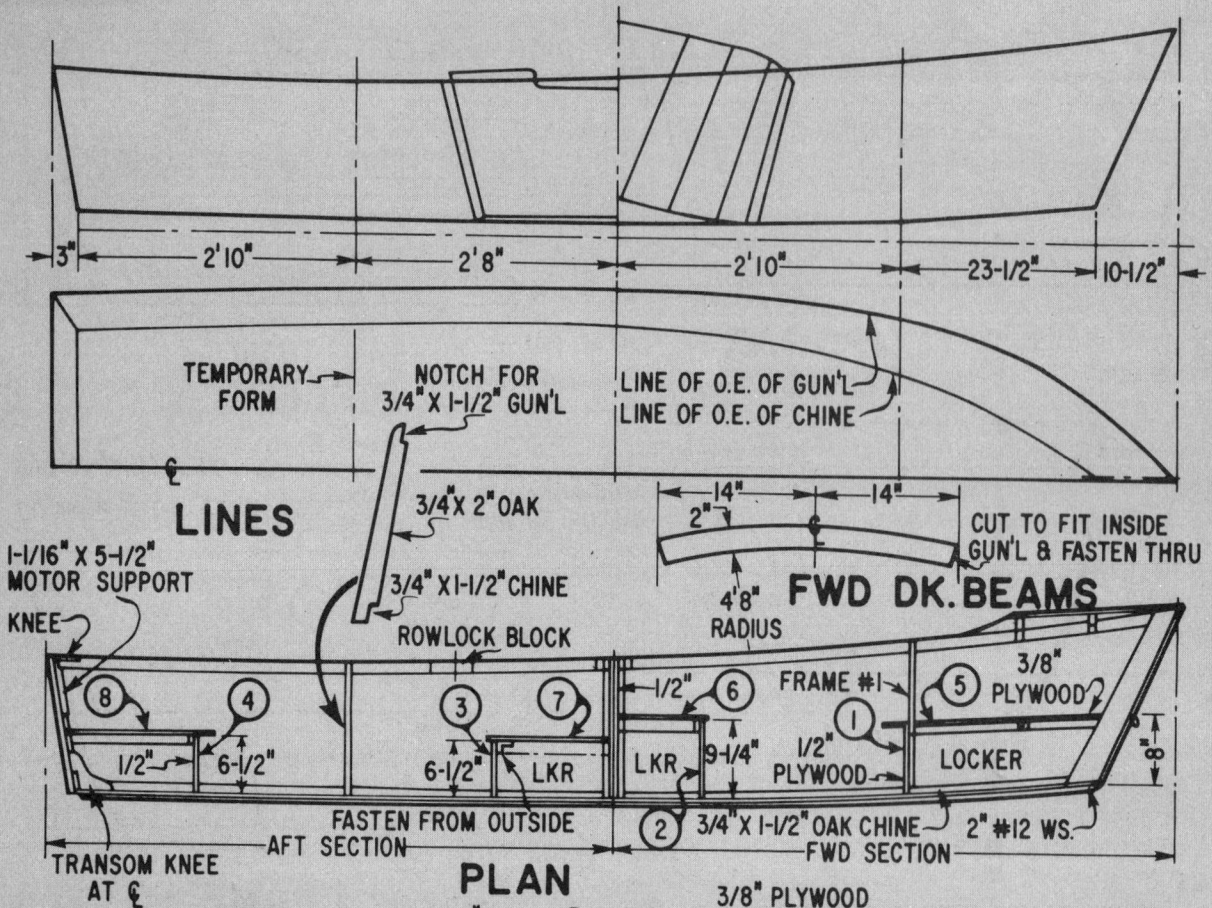

LINES

TEMPORARY FORM

NOTCH FOR 3/4" X 1-1/2" GUN'L

LINE OF O.E. OF GUN'L
LINE OF O.E. OF CHINE

3/4"X 2" OAK

3/4"X 1-1/2" CHINE

FWD DK. BEAMS

CUT TO FIT INSIDE GUN'L & FASTEN THRU

4'8" RADIUS

ROWLOCK BLOCK

1-1/16" X 5-1/2" MOTOR SUPPORT

KNEE

3/8" PLYWOOD

FRAME #1

LOCKER

LKR

LKR

1/2" PLYWOOD

TRANSOM KNEE AT ℄

FASTEN FROM OUTSIDE
AFT SECTION

3/4" X 1-1/2" OAK CHINE
FWD SECTION

2" #12 WS.

PLAN

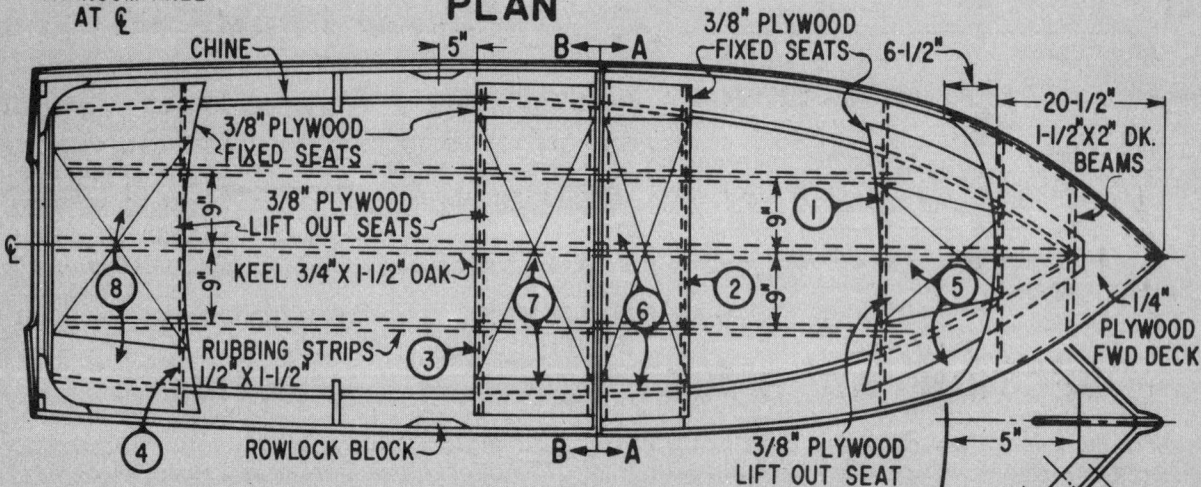

CHINE

3/8" PLYWOOD FIXED SEATS

3/8" PLYWOOD LIFT OUT SEATS

KEEL 3/4" X 1-1/2" OAK

RUBBING STRIPS 1/2" X 1-1/2"

ROWLOCK BLOCK

3/8" PLYWOOD FIXED SEATS

20-1/2"
1-1/2" X 2" DK. BEAMS

1/4" PLYWOOD FWD DECK

3/8" PLYWOOD LIFT OUT SEAT

BREAST HOOK
(IF DECK IS OMITTED)

5 1-1/2" #10 F.H. SCREWS EACH SIDE THRU PLANKING

TOP OF BREAST HOOK & GUN'L TO BE FLUSH

SIDES EXPANDED FOR CUTTING FROM PANEL

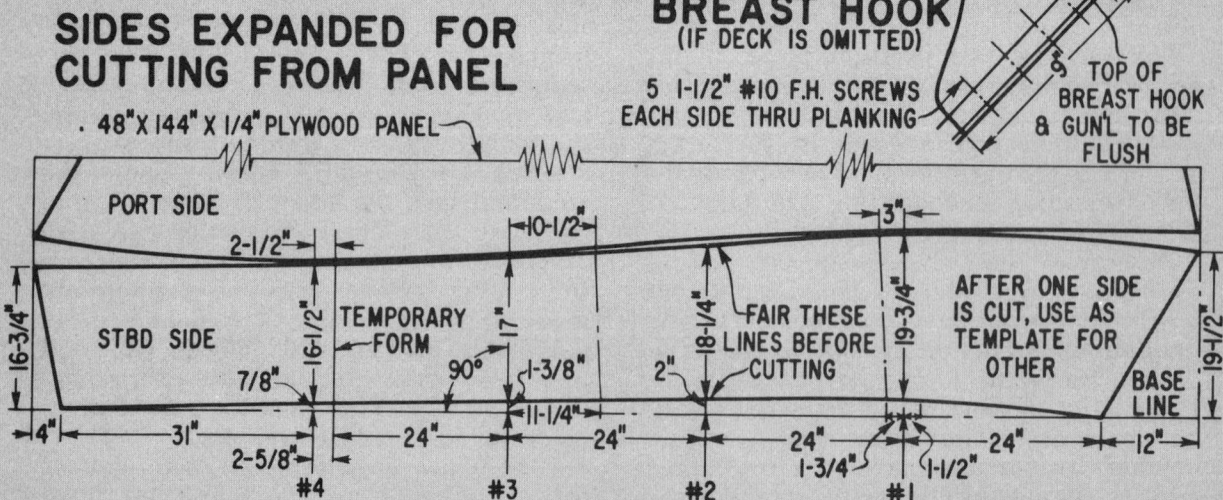

48"X 144" X 1/4" PLYWOOD PANEL

PORT SIDE

STBD SIDE

TEMPORARY FORM

FAIR THESE LINES BEFORE CUTTING

AFTER ONE SIDE IS CUT, USE AS TEMPLATE FOR OTHER

BASE LINE

#4   #3   #2   #1

Frame No. 1 will fit in place. Tack it into position along the station lines drawn earlier, keeping the bottom of the frame flush with the bottom of the side plank. Do NOT fasten permanently yet.

Insert aft division piece at the next station line and tack it in place. Do the same with the temporary form and the transom. Check the structure at this point by lining up the centerlines on the frames and transom. Remove the transom, coat joining edges with waterproof glue and fasten the sides to it with ¾" nails on 1½" centers. Now go back to Frame No. 1 and fasten it permanently with ¾" nails on 1½" centers and waterproof glue.

Take the division piece you did not use, coat it with waterproofing compound and position it carefully, placing pieces of cardboard or linoleum between it and the other division piece. This is to leave room for the saw when the boat is cut in half later. Fasten the division piece with ¾" nails on 1½" centers. Remove the other division piece, coat it with waterproofing compound and fasten it in the same manner.

The chines will be much easier to bend if you have previously soaked them in water for a few days, or wrapped them with water-soaked rags, or soak in hot water just prior to assembly. Taper them to about $\frac{7}{16}$" at the stem from about three feet back. Bevel the forward end to fit against the stem, and force them down into place. If they stick up too high at the frames, notch them out and replace them, driving them hard against the stem. If they do not fit tight against the sides, they must be clamped. When you have them shaped to fit exactly, cut them off at the transom end. Use waterproof glue between the chine and the plank, and fasten permanently with ¾" nails on 2" centers.

Place the ⅜" plywood on the bottom, mark around the sides and transom and cut it. Tack the bottom on (using the blocks of scrap wood again) and mark both edges of the division pieces. Remove the bottom and drill holes about two inches apart for the fastenings to the division pieces. (The bottom is *not* fastened to Frame No. 1.) Be sure the holes lead to the oak frames on the division pieces, not to the plywood. Coat the chines, division pieces, stem and transom with waterproofing compound, position the bottom with the aid of the tack holes previously made, and fasten the bottom, using 1¼" nails on 1½" centers around the border.

The boat can now be turned right side up and the gunwales inserted in the same manner as the chines. Taper them at the

DO NOT cut boat in half until after it is completed. Photo, above, shows front half.

AFT SECTION. Use a rubber washer on each of the machine or stove bolts for tight fit.

BORE HOLES for bolts before cutting the boat in half. Make corners tight with tape.

1/2" PLYWOOD TRANSOM

1-1/2" #12 F.H.WS.

3 PC. 1/2" PLYWOOD GLUED & CUT TO FIT

NOTCH OVER 3/4" X 3"OAK

2" #12 F.H.WS.

1-1/2" #12 F.H.WS.

1/4"

4"

KEEL

3/8" OR 1/4" PLWOOD BOTTOM

TRANSOM KNEE AT ℄

1/2" PLYWOOD TRANSOM

1/4" PLYWOOD SIDES

3/4" X 1-1/2" GUN'L

1/4" X 1-3/4" CARRIAGE BOLTS

2" #12 F.H.WS.

KNEES-2 PC. 1/2" PLYWOOD GLUED & CUT TO FIT

CLIPS CAN BE ALUM., WROUGHT IRON OR ANGLE IRON NOT LESS THAN 1/8" THICK

PLAN AT "DD"

1-1/2" #12 F.H.WS.

TRANSOM KNEE

3/4" X 3" OAK

1/2" PLYWOOD BHD-FWD SECT.

3 3/8" MACH. BOLTS EA. SIDE. WING OR HEX NUTS WITH 2 RUBBER WASHERS

1/4" PLYWOOD SIDES

1/2" PLYWOOD BHD-AFT SECTION

1" #10 F.H. BRASS WOOD SCREWS ON 3-1/2" CENTERS

SECTION "CC"

STEM

FALSE STEM

HALF ROUND STEM BAND 3/8"

3/4" X 1-1/2" GUN'L

GALV. OARLOCK SOCKET

2 3/16" CARRIAGE BOLTS

COUNTER SINK

1/16" X 1" ALUM.

1" X 1-1/2" X 7" HARDWOOD

ROWLOCK BLOCK

STEM OAK

1"

1/2"

2-1/2"

RABBET LINE

2 3/16" X 4-1/2" STOVE BOLTS

1/4" PLYWOOD SIDE

STEM

FALSE STEM

NOTCH OUT FALSE STEM FOR RING

1/4" X 2" INSIDE DIAMETER TOWING & MOORING RING

23-1/2"

STOVE BOLTS

7"

2-1/4"

1/2"

22-7/8"

2-1/2"

1/4"

1"

1/2"

8-7/8"

BEARING LINE

3-3/8"

2-1/8"

STEM

FALSE STEM

KEEL

STEM DETAIL

3/8" OR 1/4" BOTTOM (IF A LIGHTER BOAT IS DESIRED A 1/4" PLYWOOD BOTTOM IS ACCEPTABLE)

forward end and use waterproof glue. Fasten with ¾″ nails on 3″ centers. Take out the temporary form and replace it with the side-frame pieces. There is no bottom member on this frame. Now is the time to bore the six holes for the bolts that will hold the two sections of the boat together.

Cut the seat tops from ⅜″ plywood, measuring the fore-and-aft dimension from the seat supports. After the tops have been cut and beveled to fit, cut them into three sections. (Except for Top No. 5, which is in four sections.)

All that remains is cutting and fitting the transom side knees, the false stem, with its ⅜″ half-round metal band stem and towing ring, and the rowlock blocks.

The last step is to saw the boat in half between the bulkheads. This is the most vulnerable section of the structure. It would be wise to use 3″ or 4″ glass-fiber tape at each corner, covering the ends of the chines and running it up the sides. If possible, run tape along each side at the chine for protection against chafing as well as for watertightness. If glass-fiber tape is not available, soak a small strip of muslin in waterproof glue and pass it over the ends of the chines. Be sure to soak this area with paint when finishing the boat. •

BILL OF MATERIALS

LUMBER AND PLYWOOD

ITEM	NO. PCS.	NET SIZE	LENGTH	KIND OF MATERIAL
Sides (planking)	1	¼″ x 48″	144″	EXT-DFPA A-A Grade fir plywood
Transom	1	½″ x 20″	40″	EXT-DFPA A-A Grade fir plywood
Bhds.	2	½″ x 22″	44″	EXT-DFPA A-A Grade fir plywood
Seat front Mark ①	1	½″ x 9″	31″	EXT-DFPA A-A Grade fir plywood
Seat front Mark ②	1	½″ x 9¼″	40″	EXT-DFPA A-A Grade fir plywood
Seat front Mark ③	1	½″ x 6½″	40″	EXT-DFPA A-A Grade fir plywood
Seat front Mark ④	1	½″ x 6½″	36″	EXT-DFPA A-A Grade fir plywood
Bottom (planking)	1	⅜″ x 36″	144″	EXT-DFPA A-A Grade fir plywood
Seat top Mark ⑤	1	⅜″ x 33″	28″	EXT-DFPA A-A Grade fir plywood
Seat top Mark ⑥	1	⅜″ x 11″	40″	EXT-DFPA A-A Grade fir plywood
Seat top Mark ⑦	1	⅜″ x 15″	40″	EXT-DFPA A-A Grade fir plywood
Seat top Mark ⑧	1	⅜″ x 20″	40″	EXT-DFPA A-A Grade fir plywood
Forward deck	1	¼″ x 36″	27″	EXT-DFPA A-A Grade fir plywood
Frames (side only)	4	¾″ x 2″	21″	Fir, oak or mahogany
Gunwales & chines	4	¾″ x 1½″	12′-0″	Oak or mahogany
Motor support	1	1-1/16″ x 5½″	40″	Fir, oak or mahogany
Forward deck beams	1 to cut	1½″ x 5½″	30″	Fir, spruce or mahogany
Seat stiffeners & supports	30 lin. ft.	¾″ x 2″	Random	Fir to cut
Stem	1	2½″ x 3⅜″	25″	Oak or mahogany
False stem	1	1¼″ x 1″	24″	Oak
Keel	1	¾″ x 1½″	10′-6″	Oak
Rubbing strips	2	½″ x 1½″	9′-0″	Oak
Bhd. borders at sides	4	¾″ x 3″	24½″	Oak
Bhd. borders at bottom	2	¾″ x 2″	41″	Oak
Transom border at sides	2	¾″ x 3″	18″	Oak
Transom bottom frame	1	¾″ x 3″	33″	Oak

FASTENINGS

ITEM	NO. PCS.	NET SIZE	LENGTH	KIND OF MATERIAL
Patent nails (sides to chine) "Annular ring"			¾″	F.H. silicon bronze nails
Patent nails (sides to gunwale) "Annular ring"			¾″ 1 lb.	F.H. silicon bronze nails
Patent nails (sides to stem) "Annular ring"			1″ ½ lb.	F.H. silicon bronze nails
Patent nails (transom) "Annular ring"			1¼″ 1 lb.	F.H. silicon bronze nails
Stem band	1	⅜″ half R.D.	33″	Brass, bronze or iron
Stem band stove bolts	2	3/16″	4½″	Bronze or iron
Towing ring	1	¼″ by approx. 2″ D.		Bronze or iron
F.H. brass wood screws	1 doz.	No. 8	¾″	Brass
F.H. brass wood screws	4 doz.	No. 10	1″	Brass
F.H. brass wood screws	1½ doz.	No. 10	1½″	Brass
F.H. brass wood screws	1 doz.	No. 14	1½″	Brass
Machine bolts	6 only	⅜″	3½″	Bronze or steel
Clips—2 R.H., 2 L.H.	4	1¼″ x 2″ x ⅛″	About 2¼″	Brass, aluminum or steel
Carriage bolts	8	¼″	1¾″	Brass or steel
Aluminum sheer moulding	2	1″	144″	Extruded aluminum
Brass F.H. wood screws	12 doz.	#6	¾″	Brass or steel plated
Brass F.H. wood screws	3 doz.	#12	1½″	Brass
Brass F.H. wood screws	2	#12	2″	Brass
Carriage bolts	4	3/16″	2″	Brass or galvanized
Glue	2 lbs.			Weldwood waterproof

SHOP SAFETY

**You have but two eyes—two hands—10 fingers.
Can you spare them?**

By Robert Hertzberg

HOLD up your hands in front of you and count your fingers. Now ask yourself, "How many of these can I afford to lose?"

Go look into the nearest mirror. . . . Look closely. . . . Get your nose right up against the glass and stare directly into your eyes. Now ask yourself, "Can I spare one of these?"

Repeat these performances daily for about a week. By that time you should have convinced yourself that your fingers and eyes are practically indispensible. Then you'll be careful every time you pick up a tool or flip on a motor switch.

The important thing is to acquire good shop habits—you might check your's against those shown in the accompanying pictures.

Safety in the shop—like safety when swimming, driving, or shooting—is a matter of common sense. I was going to say "horse sense," but no horse in his right mind would dream of using a power grinder without wearing a pair of blinkers. . . . Oops, beg pardon! I mean a pair of well-

fitting shatterproof glasses with sideboards.

The steel particles that are ground off a lathe bit or chisel by a carborundum wheel turning 57 revolutions per second are hot and sharp. You can comb 'em out of your hair and shake 'em out of your clothes, but you can't blink 'em out of your eyes. So the first rule of shop safety is to wear shatterproof glasses for all grinding, buffing, polishing, and similar high-speed operations.

If you wear glasses for correction of vision, perhaps you'll prefer a hood of the type made popular by girl welders during the war—they're available from most tool and hardware dealers.

Protective glasses are usually not needed for woodworking operations—wood chips are relatively light and soft. The safety problem with woodworking machines is a matter of everlastingly keeping out of the way of the high-speed cutting surfaces.

Study these pictures carefully. If your initial reaction is, "This is beginner stuff," again count your fingers and eyes. 'Nuff said? •

RIGHT

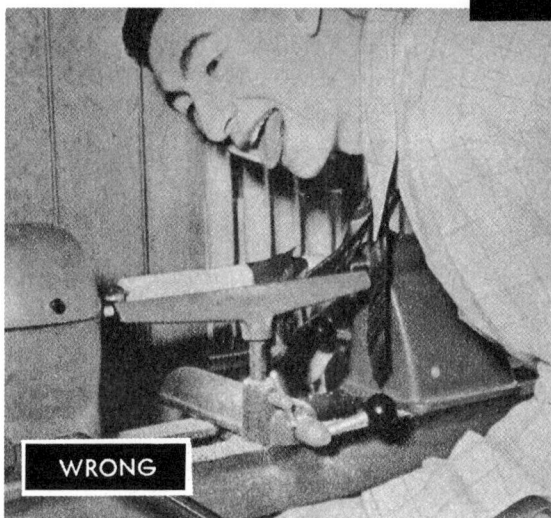

WRONG

Proper stance for wood turning: no loose clothing to get caught, left hand guides chisel, right swings tool, shavings fall to the machine bed.

Funny? Not if it happens to you. This is what comes from turning while wearing regular clothes. Before you know it, you're tied up in your work.

Ready for an evening of shop enjoyment: no tie or jewelry, sleeves rolled up to the elbow, an apron adequately protects good shirt and pants.

You look sharp for a party, chum, but not for a workshop session. The tie, key chain, sleeves, and wrist watch are easily snagged accessories.

RIGHT

WRONG

With safety glasses, you can really get up close to see how a tool is biting—you'll just blink a bit when the hot chips hit against the lenses.

He thought a quick look wouldn't do any harm; so he didn't put on his glasses. The result? A hot chip in the eye. NEXT time he'll wear glasses.

RIGHT

WRONG

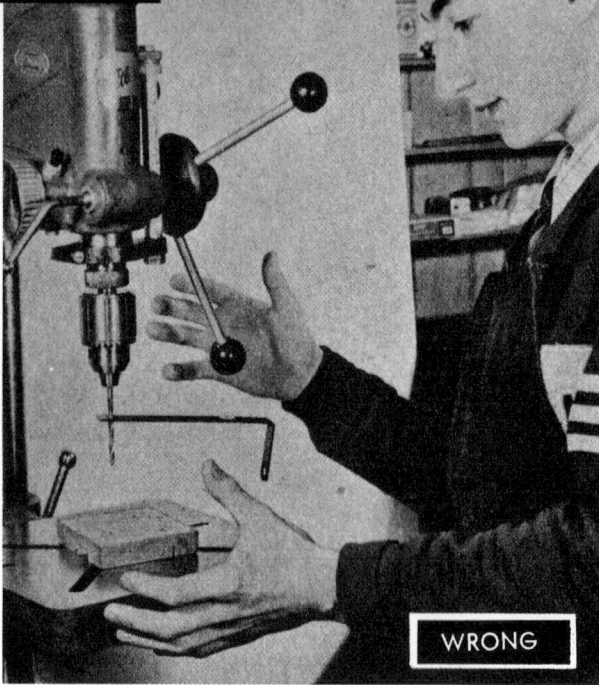

WRONG

The whole trick in drill-press safety is adequate clamping of the work. If work isn't held down, it'll surely slip and become a flailing weapon.

RIGH

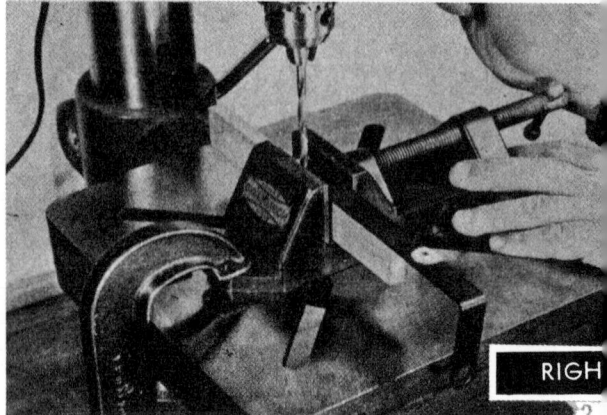

RIGH

Special drill-press vises and common clamps will prevent acident shown at left. Scrap wood under job lets drill go through without nicking table.

WRONG

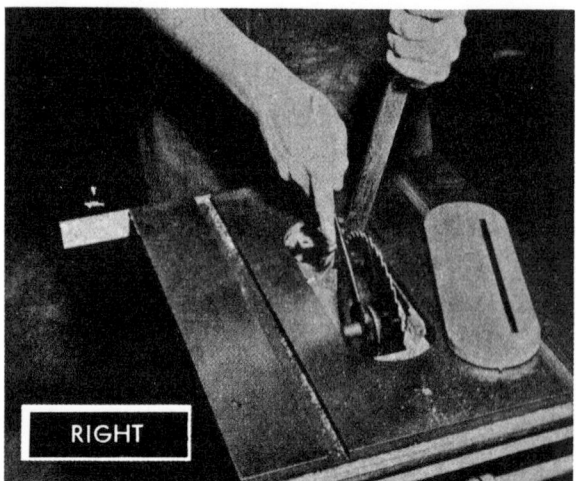

RIGHT

RIGHT

Above: Changing circular-saw blades takes care because the teeth are sharp. Jam a stick between teeth and table frame to keep saw from turning.

Above left: We admit MI is fascinating, but this character is making two mistakes that may cost him a couple of fingers. First, he's paying no attention to that rapidly revolving saw blade. Second, he's holding the work incorrectly. Left: The right way to hold a crosscut job: hands well away from blade, body not in front of machine.

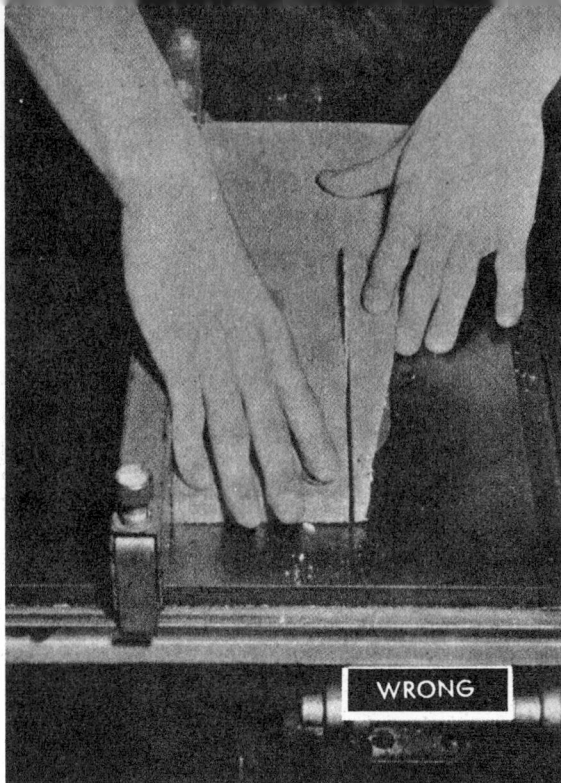

WRONG

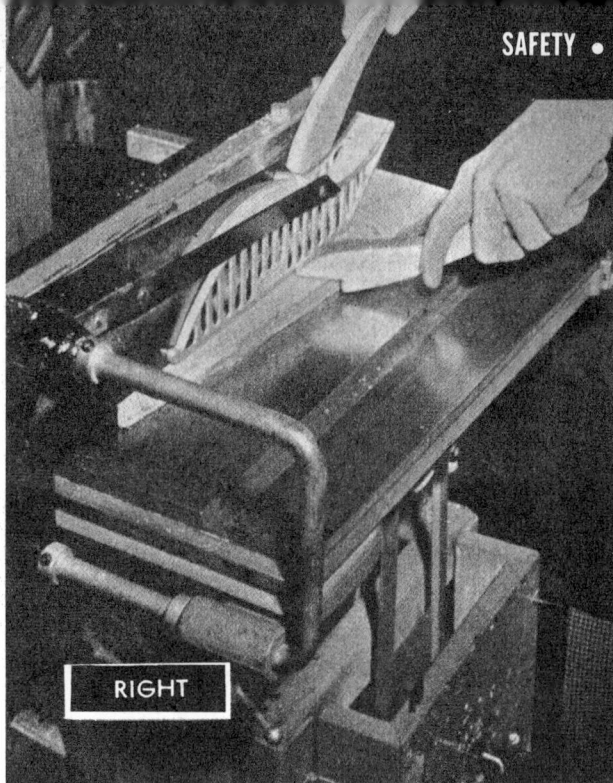

RIGHT

Quick way to lose a fingertip or a thumb. And never, never stand directly behind the work when ripping—wood, when kicked back, can cripple you.

When ripping, always use the guard with its kerf splitter and anti-kickbacks. Stand to one side of work. Use push sticks to guide the material.

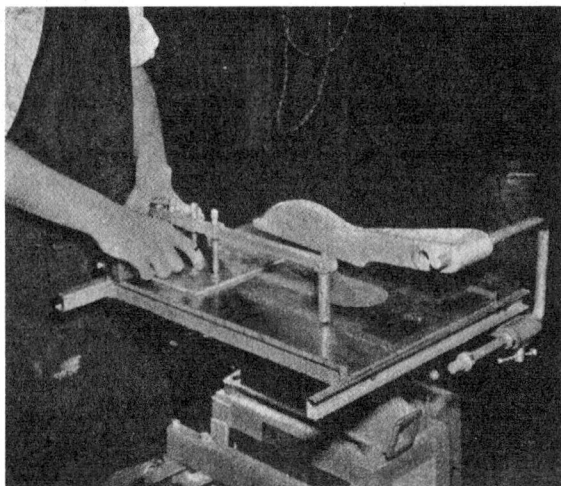

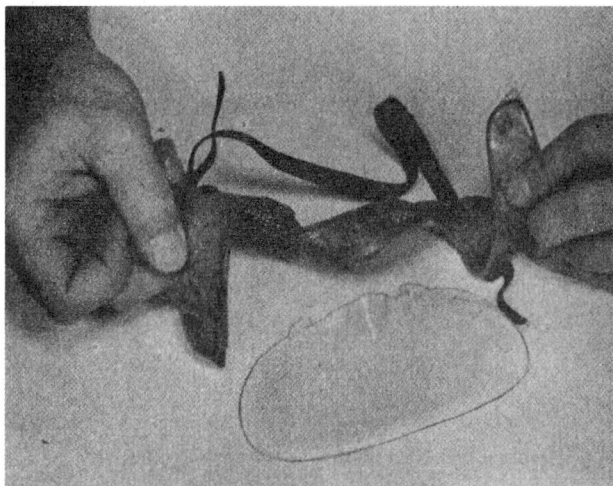

Using an abrasive wheel to cut metal calls for a pair of tight goggles, a holddown attachment on the miter gauge, and a guard over the abrasive. Above right: Here is a new type of eye protector.

The Willson MonoGoggle combines the unobstructed vision of a hood with the convenience and light weight of spectacles. The one-piece goggle fits in a flexible headband. Right: The goggle-type protector can be worn over ordinary eyeglasses, so good sight with safety is allowed everybody.

SAFETY BOMBS

Burnt-out electric bulbs are not as useless as you thought —if you convert them into easily fabricated firebombs.

By Emil Brodbeck

GAIN extra fire protection where you need it with these simply made extinguishers. Carbon tetrachloride, which is handled by many hardware stores, is the ideal fire-fighting liquid used. When it strikes a fire, the chemical begins vaporizing, immediately forming a heavy gas blanket which chokes the flames to death. One drawback of carbon tet is the fact that the vapors sometimes give off unpleasant odors that may be toxic. If fire breaks out in a badly ventilated room, therefore, your job is to throw the bombs around the fire area and waste no time in getting out of the place.

With the bulb clamped tightly at the base, bore a small hole between second and third threads.

Once through the metal, drive a nail through glass portion of base. Base rests on table.

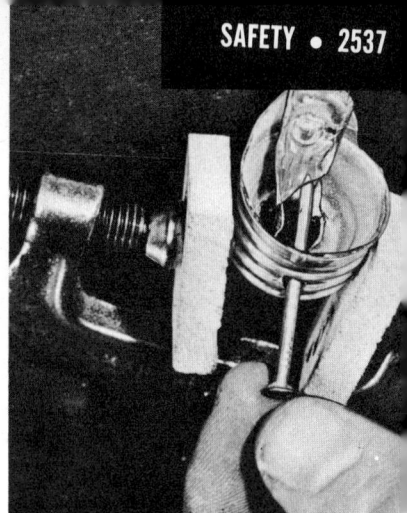

The nail breaks through the stem that holds the filaments. Note that base is still intact.

Roughen the area around the hole so that it will hold adhesive seal. Use a file or No. 1 sandpaper.

You'll find that this method is quickest for filling the bulb with the carbon tetrachloride.

A good tight seal is important. Use plastic body solder. Seal the joint at the base if needed.

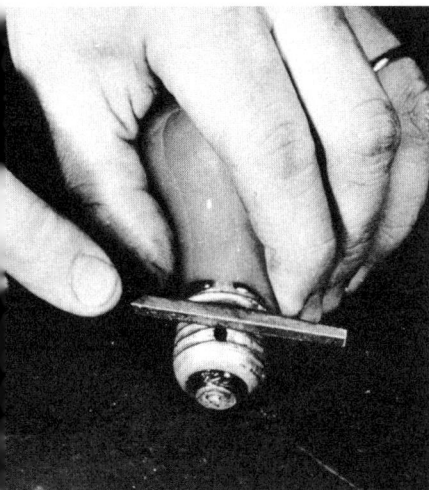

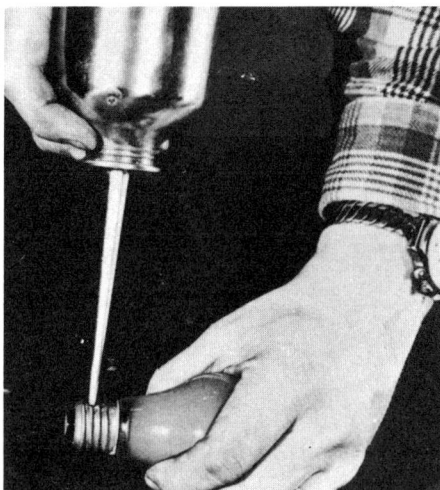

This heating installation looks safe enough, but if any trouble occurs, that trio of handy firebombs makes an inexpensive and thoughtful bit of fire insurance.

The bombs are made of discarded electric bulbs—40-watt sizes are fine. These require about 4 ounces of liquid, so that one or two quarts of carbon tet will fill all the bombs you may care to make.

It's a good idea to make racks or small containers from which the units are easily accessible. They should be placed in spots around your house where the danger of fire is most likely: in the attic and cellar, garage, kitchen, workshop, and so forth.

The photos on this page fully explain the step-by-step construction details. Just make certain that you seal the finished unit tightly to prevent evaporation. •

Lincoln's windshield wiper operates from the pressure created by the pump for power steering system.

Your Safety Slaves
This equipment helps safeguard your life

BECAUSE so much of the special equipment now standard on cars bears directly on safety it has become essential to have an understanding of how they work and what should be done if trouble develops. Of all these devices the turn signals can be the most puzzling because they involve four light bulbs, two telltale lights on the instrument panel, a flasher and the switch with its manually controlled lever on the left side of the steering post. Lamps at the front are often combined with the parking lights, and at the rear they are part of the stop lights.

While there have been several different hook-ups, including the three-wire parallel circuit used on older cars, we will consider only the basic six-wire circuit. Here the first wire goes from the accessory post of the ignition switch to the flasher and the signal switch, often passing through a fuse. There is one wire each from the turn signal switch to the front and

rear signal lights on the left side, and one wire each from the switch to the lights on the right side of the car. A sixth wire runs from the signal switch to the "cold" side of the stop-light switch. The indicator lamps (telltale) are in the circuits to the left and right front turnlights. There's a wide variation in the location of the flasher as well as the fuse, and some cars do not have the latter. Incidentally, the flasher should wink the lights about 90 times a minute. If the turn lights flash too fast or too slow the flasher should be replaced. It can be damaged by high current.

For simplicity's sake the lamp bearing the number 1034 is used for both front and rear. It has two filaments. Up front, its 32 cp filament is used for the signal while the 4 cp filament serves for the parking light. In the rear the brighter filament is for the signal and also for the stop lights, while the other is for the taillight. Thus if the stop lights operate, you know that the

At right is standard horn equipment on General Motors cars, and below is the horn wiring diagram showing the horn relay with (1) lead to battery; (2) the horn button switch; (3) lead to horns.

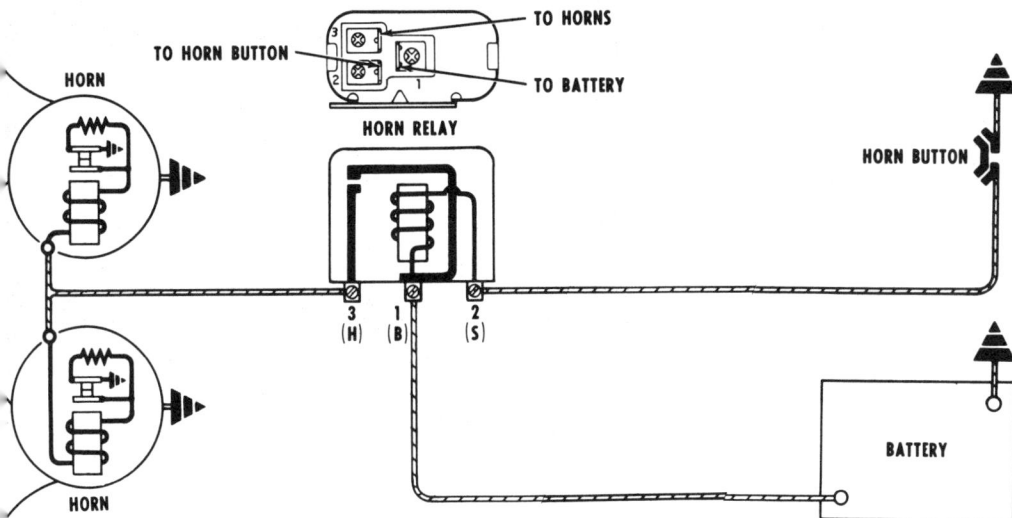

rear lamp bulbs are all right. This goes for the fuse as well. But if the signals for both turns fail you will start looking for a blown fuse, or a flasher that has failed. The usual cause of failure is merely a burned-out bulb.

You have a neat guide to a burned-out bulb by the fact that the indicator light will burn steadily on the side affected. However, if the park and the stop lights work, the flasher is the culprit. Now and again the indicator light on one side or the other may fail. This usually means that its little bulb has burned out. But if both indicator lights fail a faulty flasher is again the answer. There can, of course, be trouble with the switch itself. Most common in this field is failure to cancel when the steering wheel is moved back to the straight-ahead position. This calls for a check on the switch mechanism which is located in the top of the steering column. The steering wheel must be removed for this.

Something that worries motorists is having the stop lights fail to go off when the brake pedal is released. This doesn't always mean need for replacing the switch, but can be the result of brakes dragging or the brake pedal not having enough clearance. Where the stop-light switch is located in the rear of the brake master

cylinder, and is operated by fluid pressure, a clogged compensating port in the master cylinder will cause a pressure build up and force the stop-light switch to stay on. Many of the switches are now independent of the hydraulic system and are operated mechanically by the brake pedal.

One of the most important safety slaves is the windshield wiper system which may be vacuum or electrically operated. Many motorists still do not realize that in most of the vacuum systems there is booster action provided by a dual type fuel pump, and in some cases by the oil pump. If the diaphragm of the booster side of the pump springs a leak, not only will the wiper blades slow down when the engine is accelerated, as well as when the car is climbing a hill, but oil will be sucked up from the engine, drawn into the intake manifold and burned off. The engine will also idle roughly because the mixture is then leaned out too much.

Control is simpler with the electric type wiper, but there are the added complications of the wiring. Vacuum wipers have a simple control knob which provides for a wide range of wiper speeds whereas even the newest electric wipers have only slow and fast options. With both systems there is mechanical linkage for operating the wiper arms. There can be binding here.

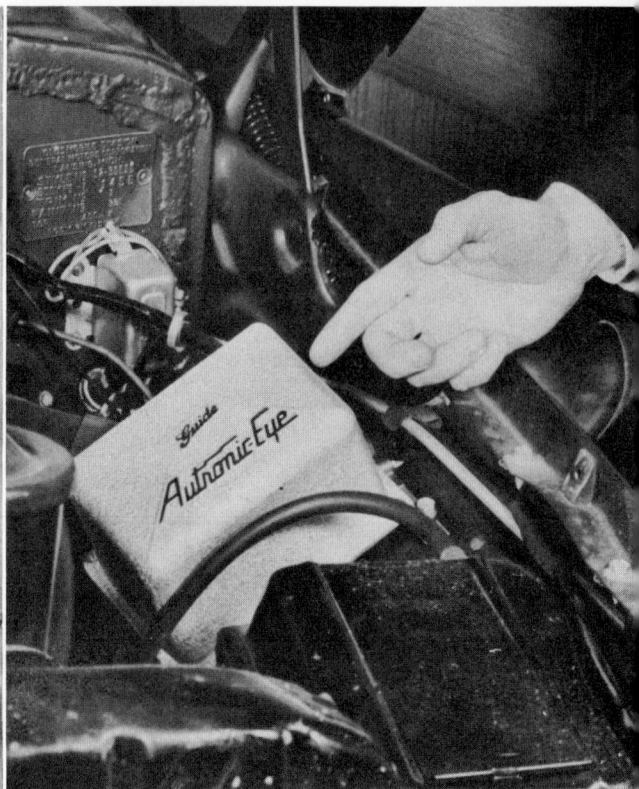

There must also be an arrangement for parking the blades when the system is switched off. If an electric motor continues to run after the switch is turned to the "off" position, there's trouble with the relay. Parking the blades, with this system, is obtained electrically through the grounding of the contact points acting like a brake. In the vacuum system, parking is done by means of a differential valve that is built into the cover of the motor. Connections in the vacuum line to the manifold or oil pump should be checked occasionally. Keep the rubber hose away from hot parts of the engine or any moving parts that might damage it. If the fitting at the intake manifold becomes clogged with carbon, it should be removed and cleaned. The motor is lubricated at the factory and needs no additional servicing.

In the electrical system the gearbox contains special gear lubricant, and is only three-quarters filled. Also the cross shaft for the crank is lubricated with this same kind of grease for its entire length. Trouble can be expected if any lube is allowed to get on the motor's commutator. If relay points become dirty, they can be cleaned with a little carbon tetrachloride applied to a narrow strip of clean cloth and pulled between them. Point trouble will likely blow the fuse and prevent the motor from starting. But there are other causes of a

blown fuse, and oddly enough, owners often forget that if the battery is too weak voltage will not be high enough to operate the relay.

Much of the trouble motorists have with scratched windshields is due to the habit of operating wipers at full speed when conditions call merely for minimum clearance. Wipers should be switched off when parking, when driving into a covered bank drive-in or into a garage. Glass damage is especially likely to occur if the wipers are operated without first manually cleaning the windshield or turning on the automatic washers, if the car is so equipped. Many washers are not working simply because their nozzles at the base of the wiper arms are clogged with road dirt. Clean these out with a pin or a piece of fine wire just about as often as you can remember to do it.

Looking into an early type vacuum-powered washer we find that intake manifold suction released through a simple control valve provides power for a little diaphragm-type pump which sucks washer fluid from a glass jar under the hood and sends it to the nozzle jets at the windshield. Later a coupler for actuating the washer was designed to slide into the wiper motor housing, and an adjusting screw provided to lengthen or shorten washer operation period. Button control for the vacuum

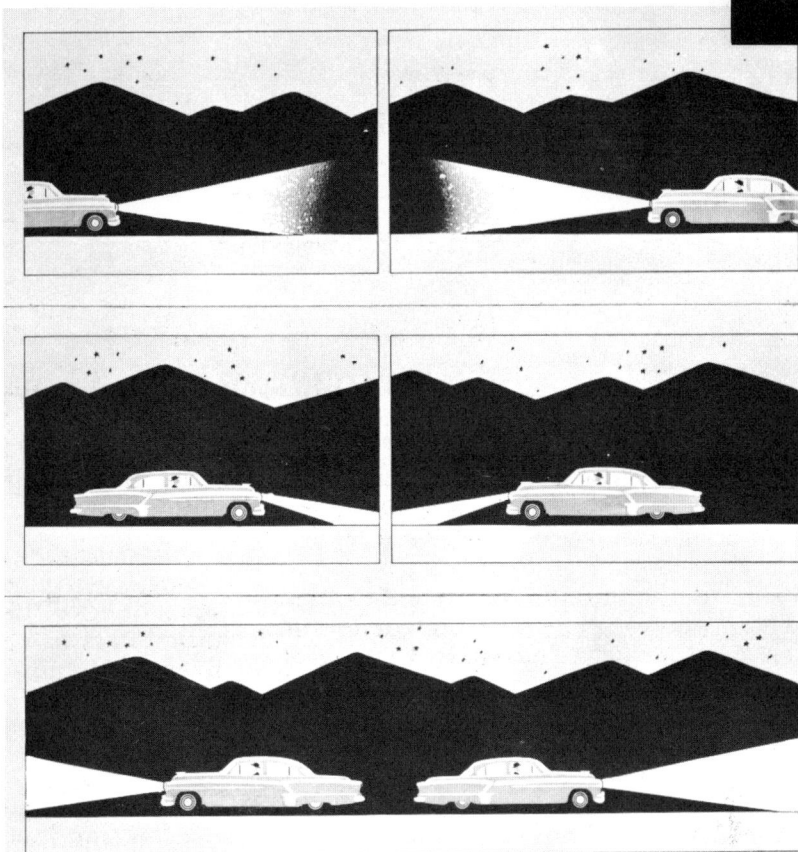

At far left on the opposite page is the Autronic Eye, optional on General Motors cars. It is mounted on the left side of the instrument panel just back of the windshield. It is a device which automatically dims the headlights of the car on which it is installed when it catches the light of an oncoming vehicle. The amplifier and power relay is found under the hood. At right is illustrated the effect on beams of passing cars.

operated windshield washer may be electrically controlled.

Washers are also electrically operated, and in combination with an electric wiper motor. In fact while the wiper motor is in action the cam of the washer rotates but there is no pumping of washer fluid until the driver presses the control button. Then a little relay coil is energized, the relay armature and ratchet are raised and the plunger arm is allowed to move forward to collapse the bellows. That, in turn, forces fluid out through the outlet valves to the nozzles. There are four intake and four pumping strokes for each turn of the wiper motor gear and the washer cam. The washer pump returns to idle automatically.

In addition, there are manual washer systems which require use of a fluid container in the form of a bag which can be located on the toeboard to the left. To actuate this the driver presses on the bag with his foot when the windshield needs cleaning. In all the systems, special washer fluid is needed, not only to provide for easy removal of the accumulated dirt but also to insure against freezing in cold weather.

Because they are so faithful, the car's horns are likely to be quite a puzzle if they fail, or especially if they start blowing of their own accord. Failure of horns to operate usually means trouble in the horn button circuit and sometimes in the grounding of the horns themselves. And when the horns "toot" of their own volition there is likely to be a short in the horn button circuit where the wire runs down the steering column. But first always consider stickage of points in the horn relay because if you know where the relay is located you can lift the hood and rap its cover with your clenched fist. That may be enough to stop the racket. If this doesn't help, all you need do to stop the horns from blowing is to disconnect the wires to the horns at this little relay box.

Horns are mostly of the vibrator type utilizing an electromagnet. Tone adjustment is obtained by removing the horn's cover and turning a screw which is held in position with a lock nut. This should be a last resort, however, because often horns do not sound right merely because they are not securely mounted or need to have their bolts or screws tightened. A weak battery will also adversely affect the horns.

Horn button trouble is not uncommon. Not all buttons are reached by pressing the medallion at the center of the horn ring and turning it slightly. Some rings are held in place with screws which are reached from the underside of the steering wheel. Horns usually are paired for a high as well as a low tone, but you can add a third horn to provide a very distinctive E, G and B chord of the musical scale. •

Teena

By Edwin Monk, N. A.

This classic 15-ft. sailboat is well designed, easy to build and will take auxiliary power.

GENEROUS freeboard and clean lines distinguish this simple, well-designed knockabout. Though its performance delights experts, the craft is a safe, stable sailboat for family fun on inland water.

When you've collected the materials you'll need, make a full-sized drawing of each hull frame. You can use one of the plywood panels ordered for planking as a layout board, with one of the long edges of the sheet serving as a baseline. Lay out a centerline at right angles to this edge with a large steel square. Then draw a setup line 22″ in from the edge, parallel to it.

After locating dimension points for each frame, pencil the straight sides along a straight edge. To establish bottom curves, tack brads at chine and centerline and a third brad midway between, but offset the fraction of an inch noted in the plan. Springing a light batten around the brads gives a true curve.

Layouts completed, transfer the lines to the framing lumber. Simply lay the hard-

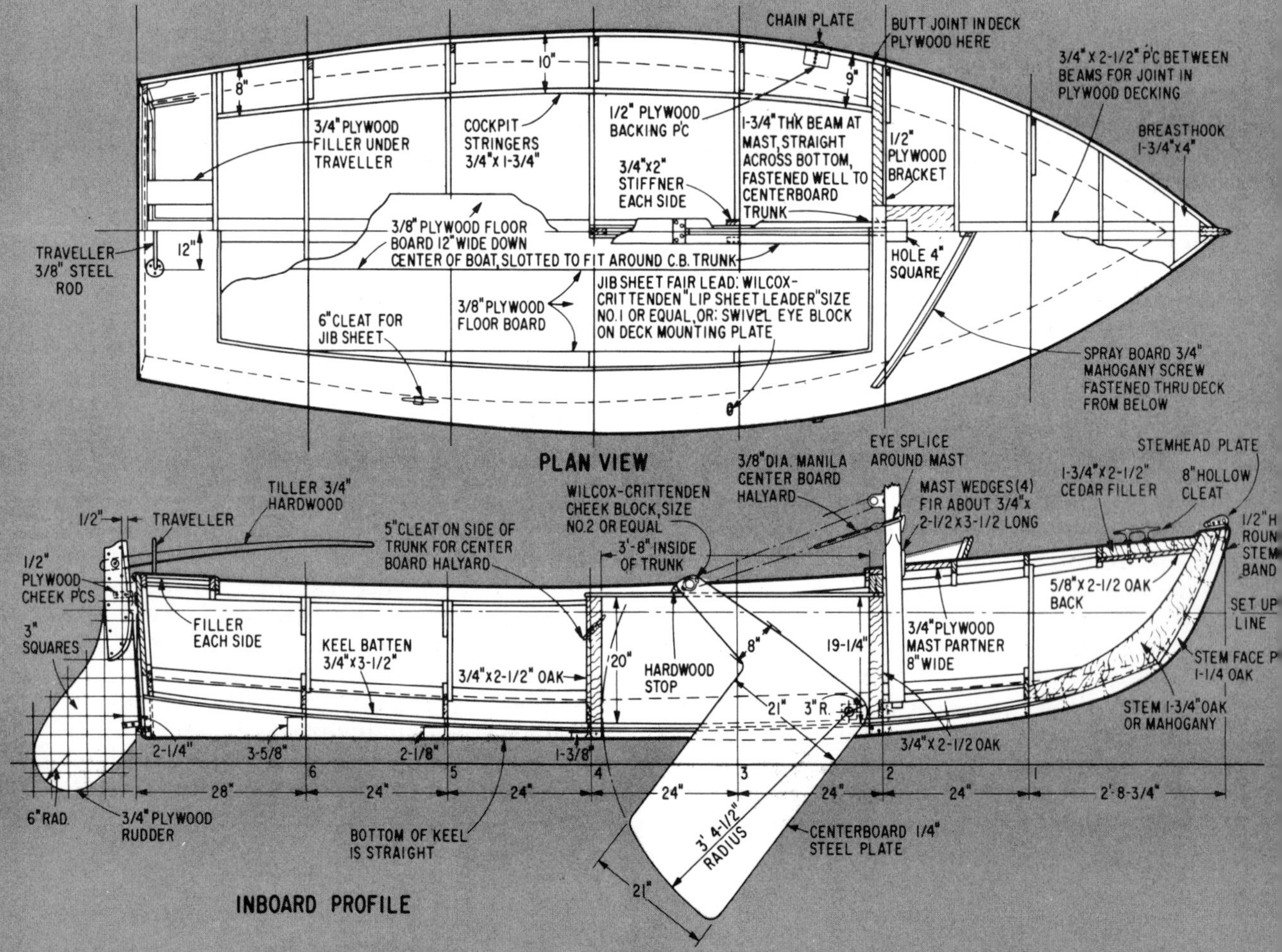

PLAN VIEW

INBOARD PROFILE

1-1/2" DIA. SHEAVE IN MAST

5'

1/4" RUNNING RIGGING

3/16" WIRE

LEECH 19'-0" TO TOP OF SHEAVE

LUFF-TOP OF BOOM TO TOP OF SHEAVE 17'-3"

JIB LEECH 10'-10"

LUFF 12'-0"

87 SQ. FT.

115 SQ. FT. TOTAL SAIL AREA

28 SQ. FT.

BOOM 1-3/8" DIA.

BOOM 1-7/8 DIA.

FOOT 10'-4"

BOOM 1-1/2 DIA.

3/16" WIRE

5/8" TRACK ON MAST

FOOT 5'-1"

JIB SHEET CLEAT

4" CLEAT EACH SIDE

FAIRLEAD

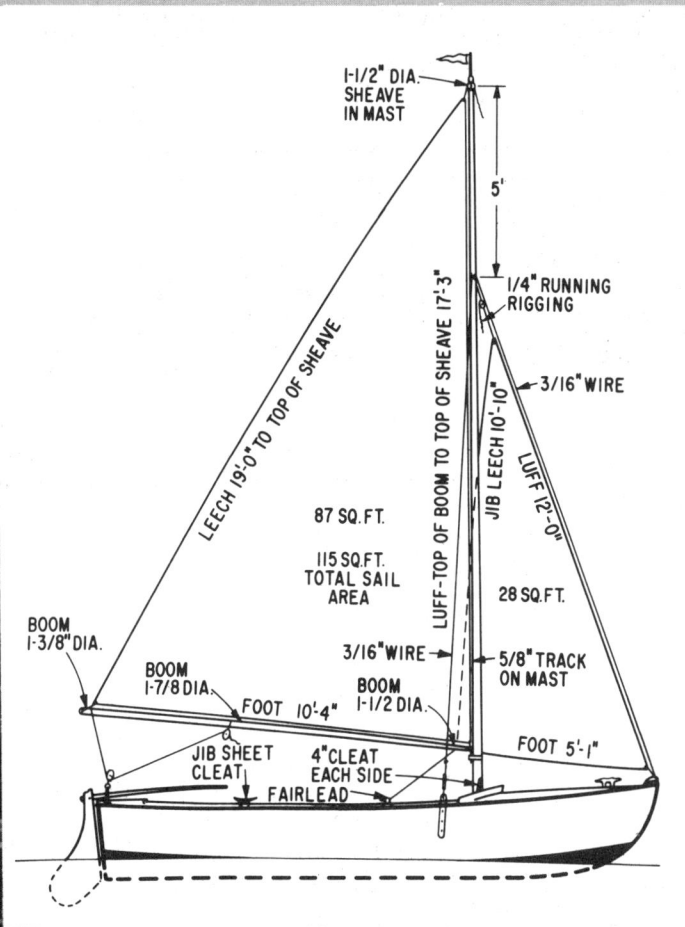

PERFECT for inland waters, Teena handles well, will really perform in a good breeze.

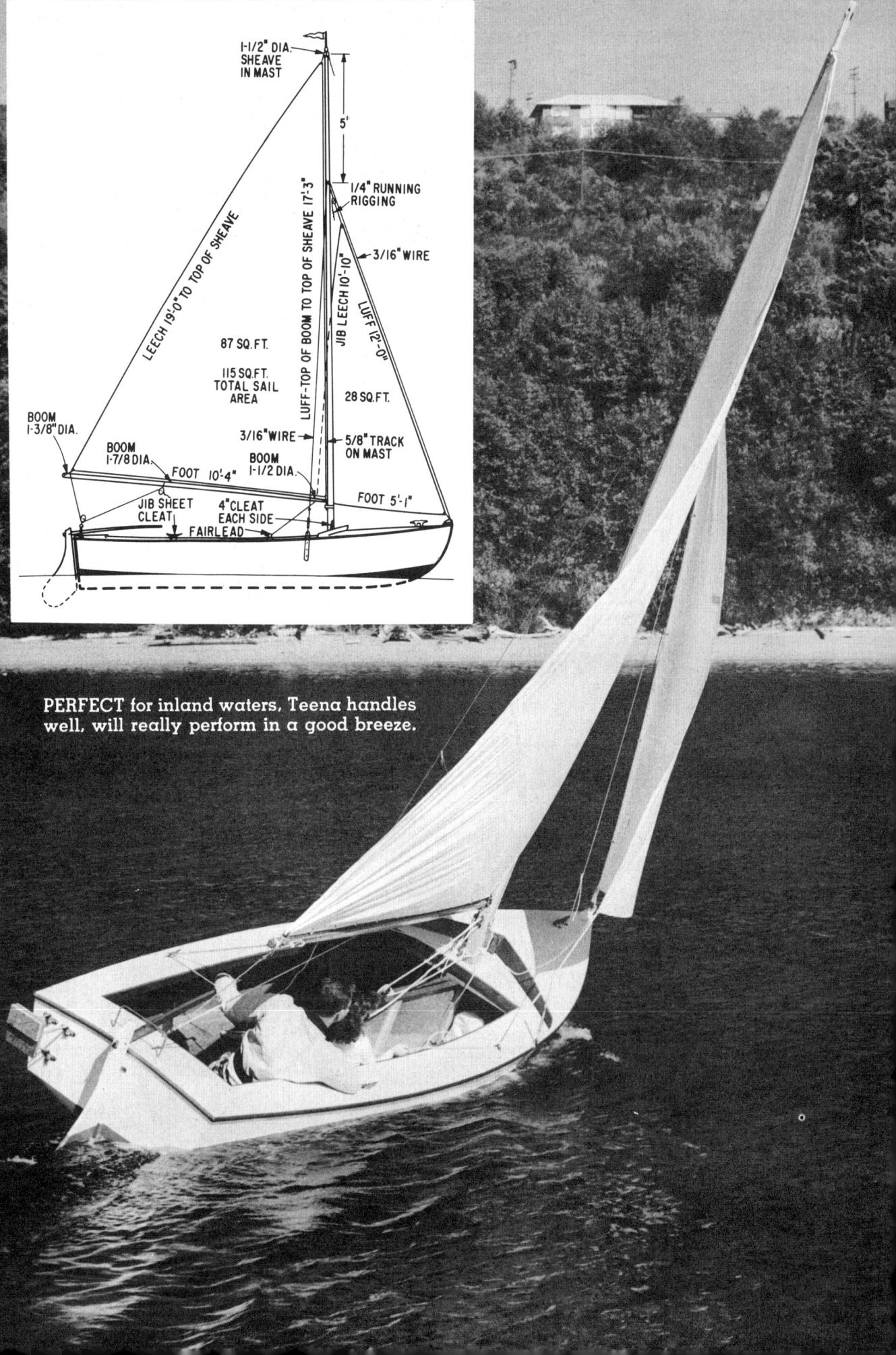

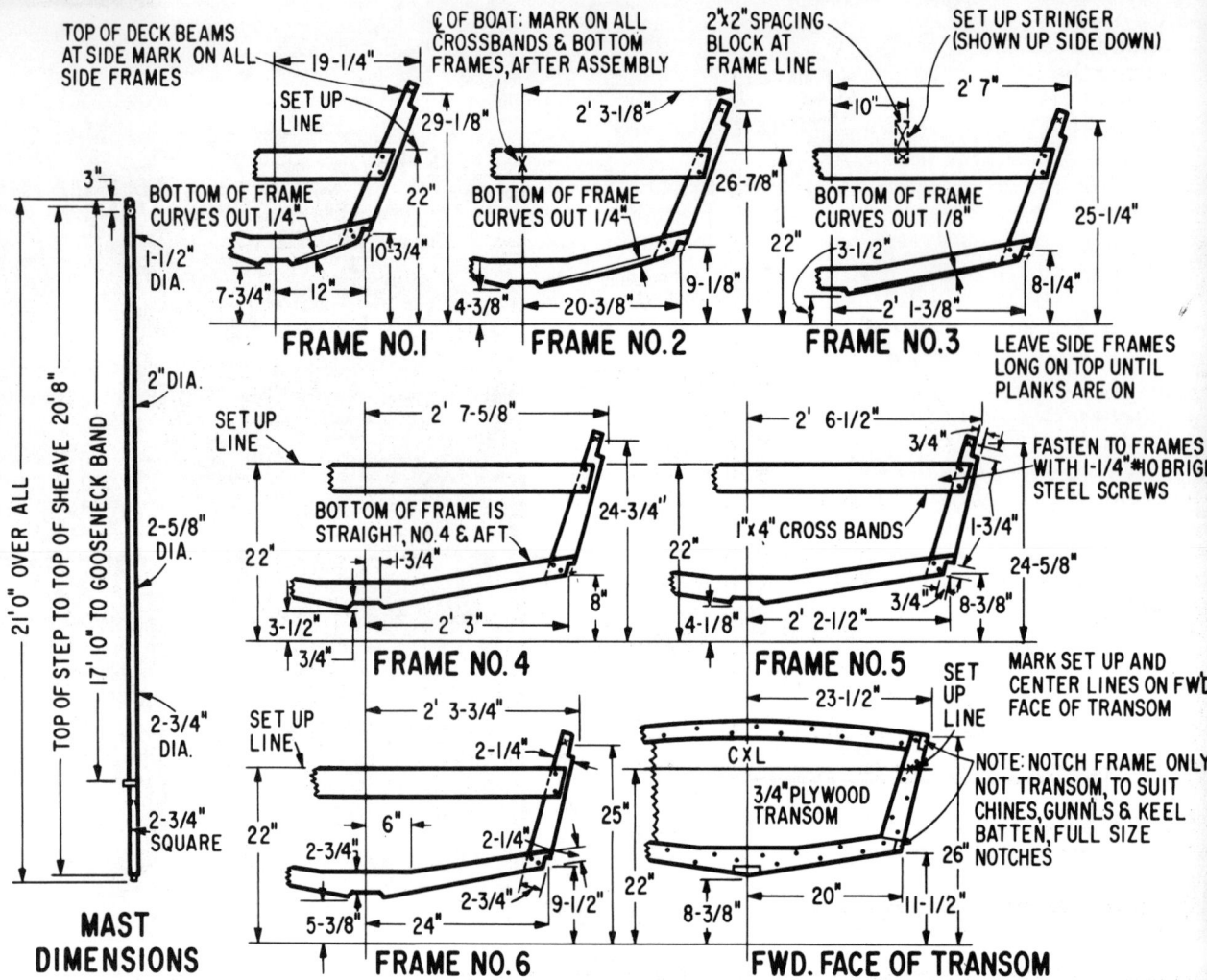

FRAME NO.1

FRAME NO.2

FRAME NO.3

LEAVE SIDE FRAMES LONG ON TOP UNTIL PLANKS ARE ON

FRAME NO. 4

FRAME NO.5

MARK SET UP AND CENTER LINES ON FWD FACE OF TRANSOM

FRAME NO.6

FWD. FACE OF TRANSOM

FRAME LAYOUTS

MAST DIMENSIONS

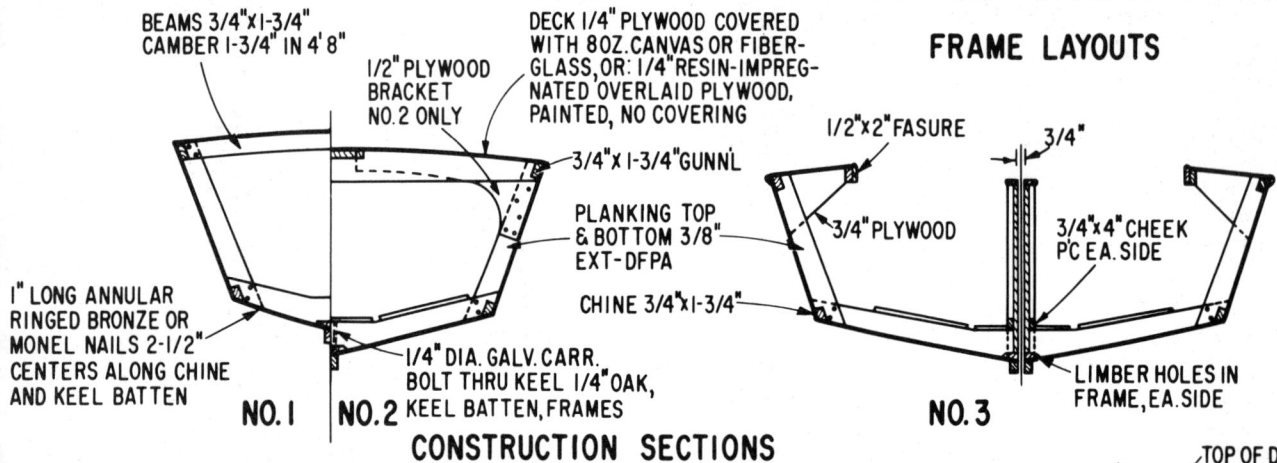

CONSTRUCTION SECTIONS

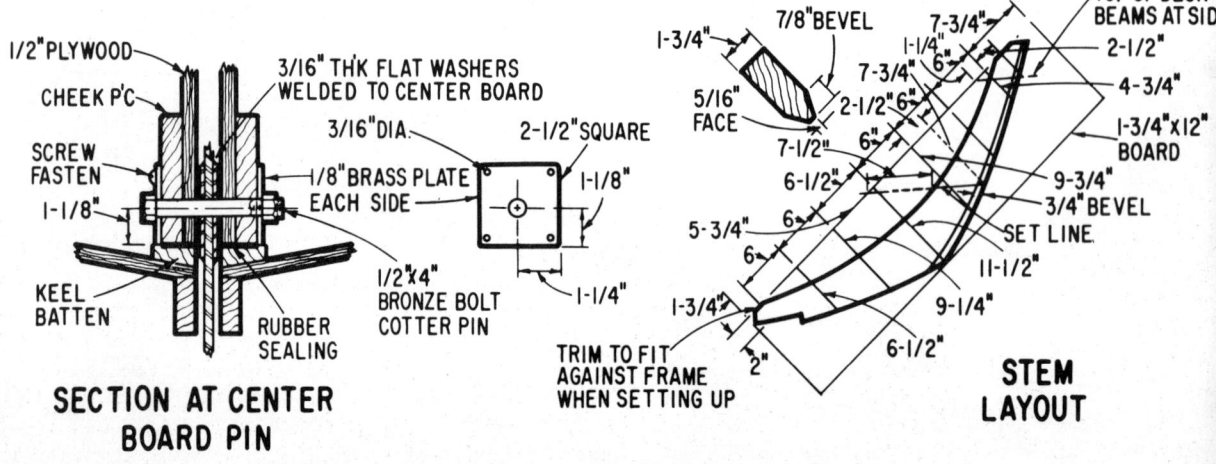

SECTION AT CENTER BOARD PIN

STEM LAYOUT

wood over the appropriate layout and re-draw the lines. All frames are symmetrical. When you've cut one side member for a frame to shape, turn the piece over and use it as a pattern for the other side.

Line up the parts for each frame in turn directly over the corresponding layout. Drill screw holes, countersinking for the heads, spread the joints liberally with waterproof glue and drive screws.

Fasten a crossband across each frame, lining the top edge of the band with the setup line. Mark the centerline and the position of the setup stringers on each crossband.

Next take approximate angles directly from the plan with a small carpenter's bevel and bevel edges of each frame roughly with a jack plane. Also notch each frame for the keel batten, chines and sheer battens. Saw these notches somewhat undersize to allow for trimming. Be sure to notch the transom framing members before fastening them to the ¾" plywood transom, for these notches are cut through the frame only, not through the plywood.

You can lay out the stem directly on the hardwood. Bandsaw this piece to shape and bevel it with a plane or drawknife. Mark the sheer line and setup line.

Assemble the jig—the temporary backbone on which you'll build the hull—on sawhorses toenailed securely to the floor. See that the stringers are parallel before spiking them to the horses. Then saw off the after ends and mount transom brackets. Lay off frame locations along these stringers with a square, nailing cleats for the frame crossbands on each stringer at these marks.

Nail the transom to the stringer end brackets with the setup line lining with the tops of the stringers. Drive the nails through small blocks of scrap wood to make it easier to pull them later.

Now mount the frames in order, checking each for alignment and plumb before nailing the crossband to the stringer cleats. Then set up the stem, blocking one end to the floor and butting the foot against

ASSEMBLE the temporary backbone (on which you will build hull) on sawhorses.

MAST STEP and centerboard box are shown here to explain why keel must be built up.

WORK from bow to transom when installing chines and sheer battens. Rough-cut sides.

CLAMP bottom panels in place. Trim away planking at centerboard slot for good fit.

OUTER KEEL is now built up after bottom planking is installed. See detail on p. 2544

BILL OF MATERIALS

PLYWOOD AND LUMBER

ITEM	QUANTITY—NET SIZE	MATERIAL
Planking	3 Panels 3/8"x4'x16'	EXT-DFPA·A-A Grade Fir Plywood
Centerboard Trunk Sides	1 Panel 1/2"x4'x6'	EXT-DFPA·A-A Grade Fir Plywood
Transom, Rudder, Brackets	1 Panel 3/4"x4'x6'	EXT-DFPA·A-A Grade Fir Plywood
Decking	2 Panels 1/4" x4'x8'	EXT-DFPA·A-A Grade Fir Plywood
Floorboards	2 Panels 3/8"x4'x6'	EXT-DFPA·A-A Grade Fir Plywood
Frames, Trunk Ends	36 Lin. Ft. 3/4"x3"	Oak
Bottom Frames	28 Lin Ft. 3/4"x7"	Oak
Stem	1 Piece 1 3/4"x11 3/4"x4'	Oak or Mahogany
Keel Batten	1 Piece 3/4"x3 1/2"x14'	Oak
Trunk Cheek Pieces	1 Piece 3/4"x4'x8'	Oak
Chines and Sheer Battens	4 Pieces 3/4"x1 3/4"x16'	Oak
Stem Facing	1 Piece 1 1/4"x4'x5'	Oak or Mahogany

Plus Oak or Mahogany Trim Molding as Needed

LUMBER FOR JIG

ITEM	QUANTITY—NET SIZE	MATERIAL
Stringers	2 Pieces 2"x4"x14'	Fir or Pine (Low Grade)
Crossbands	2 Pieces 1"x4"x14'	Fir or Pine (Low Grade)
Cleats	1 Piece 2"x2"x6'	Fir or Pine (Low Grade)
Keel, Skeg	1 Piece 1 1/4"x6 1/2"x12'	Oak
Centerboard Slot Edging	1 Piece 1"x1 1/2"x9'	Oak
Beams	1 Piece 3/4"x12"x10'	Fir or Spruce
Cockpit Beam	1 Piece 1 3/4"x6"x5'	Fir or Spruce
Cockpit Stringers	2 Pieces 3/4"x1 3/4"x10'	Fir or Spruce
Cockpit Facing	2 Pieces 1/2"x2"x10'	Fir or Mahogany
Cockpit End Facing	2 Pieces 1/2"x6"x4'	Fir or Mahogany
Tiller	1 Piece 1"x3"x4'	Oak or Mahogany
Breasthook	1 Piece 1 3/4"x4"x1'	Oak or Mahogany
Spray Boards	1 Piece 1/2"x4"x6'	Oak or Mahogany
Mast	1 Piece 3"x3"x21'	Spruce
Boom	1 Piece 2"x2"x11'	Spruce

FASTENINGS

For salt water use, bronze or monel metal fastenings are recommended.

SCREWS

SIZE	QUAN. (Approx.)	USE
1" No. 8 Flat Head (or Patent Boat Nails)	4 Gross	Planking, Decking
1 1/4" No. 10 Flat Head	1 Gross	Frames, Brackets, etc.
1 1/4" No. 10 (Bright Steel)	2 Dozen	Crossbands
2" No. 10 Flat Head	1/2 Gross	Battens, Chines
2 1/2" No. 12 Flat Head	1/2 Gross	Stem, Keel, etc.

Plus Other Sizes in Small Quantity

BOLTS

SIZE	QUAN. (Approx.)	USE
1/4" diam. x 6" Carriage	3 Each	Skeg, Stem, Keel
1/4" diam. x 8" Carriage	2 Each	Skeg, Breasthook
1/4" diam. x 10" Carriage	1 Each	Skeg
3/8" diam. x 2" Carriage	1 Each	Rudder
3/8" diam. x 5" Carriage	1 Each	Mast Step
1/2" diam. x 4" Machine	1 Each	Centerboard

Plus Miscellaneous Bolts For Fittings

ROLL HULL right side up and remove setup stringers. Leave crossbands on the frames.

REMOVE CROSSBANDS when deck is framed; lay on decking, canvas and trim.

Frame 1. A triangular positioning piece notched for the stem and nailed to the stringers helps brace the stem in place. Lay the keel batten in the notches across stem, frames and transom, trimming out the notches as necessary. Slope the sides of these notches to form limber holes.

Fit chines and sheer battens similarly. Work from bow to transom when fastening these battens, screwing them to both sides of each frame in turn to avoid warping the hull out of alignment. Miter the forward ends of the battens to butt against the stem and secure them with heavy screws.

Now fair the assembled framework, which is an important step. First plane bevels along the keel batten conforming with the line of the frame bottoms. Then bevel the chines similarly and fair the sheer batten. Also correct the bevels on the frame edges themselves, carefully smoothing off the irregularities with a plane. Bending a strip of ⅜" plywood across frames and battens at various angles will show the exact bevels required.

Slot the keel batten for the centerboard before fitting the centerboard trunk. Assemble the trunk as shown first mounting hardwood cheek pieces and stiffeners to the side pieces, then gluing and screwing the sides to hardwood end pieces. Bore the centerboard bolt hole before installing the trunk in the hull.

Frame 3 must be cut in order to fit the trunk against the keel batten. Gluing the joint liberally, fit the assembly in place and drive heavy screws through the keel batten into the cheek pieces.

Fit the side planks first. To make a pattern for them, lay building paper over the hull framework and pencil around the stem, battens and transom. Rough-saw the plywood to shape, allowing material for trimming after fastening, and clamp the planks in place to check fit.

Before fastening each plank, spread waterproof glue liberally along the frame edges, chine and sheer battens and transom. Lay a glue-soaked thread of candle-wicking along stem and transom joints.

Use patent bronze or monel boat nails instead of screws to fasten the planking if you prefer.

When you've planed the side planks flush with the chines, fit and fasten bottom planks. Then plane the bottom flush with the sides.

If necessary trim away the bottom planking at the centerboard slot. Then plane the ridge of the V-bottom flat for the skeg, centerboard slot molding and keel. Fill the seam between the bottom planks with rubber-base sealing compound before fastening keel pieces.

Fair the beams if necessary with a plane before laying plywood deck panels. When you've trimmed the deck, overlay the plywood with resin-saturated canvas.

Finish the hull with suitable hardwood molding and screw a hardwood sprayrail on the foredeck. Then fit removable plywood floorboards. Assemble the rudder as shown in the plan and mount it with standard pintles and plate gudgeons.

Try to find reasonably straight lengths of lumber for the mast and boom. After rounding and tapering the mast above deck-level with a plane, mortise a small sheave into the masthead. Also taper the boom slightly. Use a standard gooseneck fitting to hang the boom.

It's a good scheme to make a plywood pattern for the centerboard and try it in place—to be sure you'll be able to pull it all the way up—before having one burned from ¼"-thick steel plate. Bolt a small cheek block to the arm of the plate.

A sailmaker or tent-and-awning firm will be glad to give you estimates on cotton and nylon sails in various weights. •

shaded sandbox

Protection from the hot sun is provided by the collapsible canvas-covered roof.

Your youngster will be delighted with this sandbox.

It's big enough to hold three or four kids at once.

By Stanley Lehrer

WHEN a child is about 12 to 15 months old, the desire to dig—in the ground, in the garbage, or on the living-room rug—becomes very strong. It happened to our youngster last spring and up went the cry, "The baby needs a sandbox!" So we looked over several store models and decided we could do as well, or perhaps better, by building our own. The result was a large, sturdy affair with a collapsible canvas-covered roof that can be erected or lowered by one person. When lowered, the roof keeps the sand perfectly dry, even in the most prolonged downpours.

To duplicate our project, make the sandbox of 1-in. pine boards assembled with 1½-in. No. 10 flathead wood screws. Build the sides in the form of a frame and add a 2x2-in. wooden block in each corner to act as a reinforcement. After the frame is made, attach the floor boards. To prevent sand escaping, edge-lap these boards as shown in a detail. Install a 2x2-in. center support across the underside of the floor to prop it and to insure that the floor boards lay evenly. The seats are triangular pieces of either ¾-in. plywood or 1-in. pine. If pine is used, the grain should run parallel to the hypotenuse of each piece. Complete the box by attaching the legs.

The roof consists of a light wooden frame and a striped canvas cover. To provide adequate rigidity, the frame is both nailed and glued together. Begin by assembling the four 1x2-in. horizontal members. These are butted together and the corner joints are reinforced with triangular pieces of ¼-in. plywood or Masonite. Next, attach the 1x3-in. studs and follow by installing the ridge pole and the four rafters. Com-

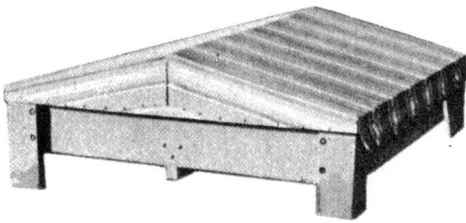

When lowered, the roof, which can be handled by one person, keeps the sand perfectly dry in even hardest rains.

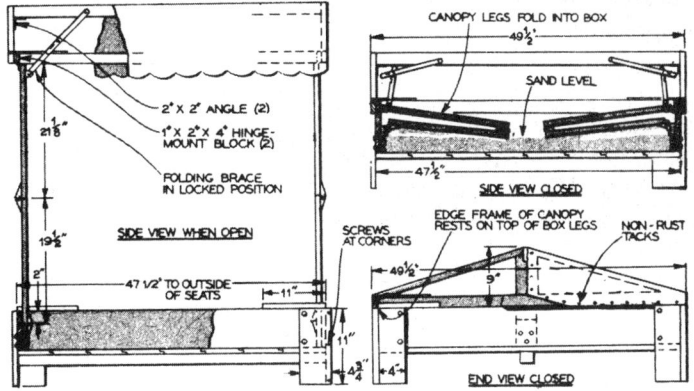

2" X 2" ANGLE (2)
1" X 2" X 4" HINGE-MOUNT BLOCK (2)
FOLDING BRACE IN LOCKED POSITION
SIDE VIEW WHEN OPEN
47 1/2" TO OUTSIDE OF SEATS
SCREWS AT CORNERS

CANOPY LEGS FOLD INTO BOX
SAND LEVEL
SIDE VIEW CLOSED

EDGE FRAME OF CANOPY RESTS ON TOP OF BOX LEGS
NON-RUST TACKS
END VIEW CLOSED

plete the assembly of the frame by adding the hinge-mount blocks.

Attach the canvas with rustproof round-head tacks. Care should be exercised to insure that the canvas is pulled evenly so that the straight stripes remain straight. Because the frame is wider than the canvas rolls ordinarily available, a center seam will be required. However, even a hand-sewed seam will present no difficulties in assembly and will be rainproof. To add a finished touch to the job, bind the scalloped edges.

The support for the roof is made up of 1x4-in. vertical struts, two pairs of heavy-duty spring-loaded screen-door hinges, a pair of ordinary 3-in. butt hinges, and a pair of bridge-table leg braces. The drawings show all necessary assembly details. Make sure that the vertical struts *are* vertical when viewed face-on. The purpose of the bridge-table leg braces is to lock the roof in its raised position.

To obtain a lasting finish, coat all wooden parts with a high-grade exterior enamel, scrupulously following the undercoat directions on the paint can. We used green enamel throughout except on the triangular seats, where Chinese red was employed to add a touch of color. •

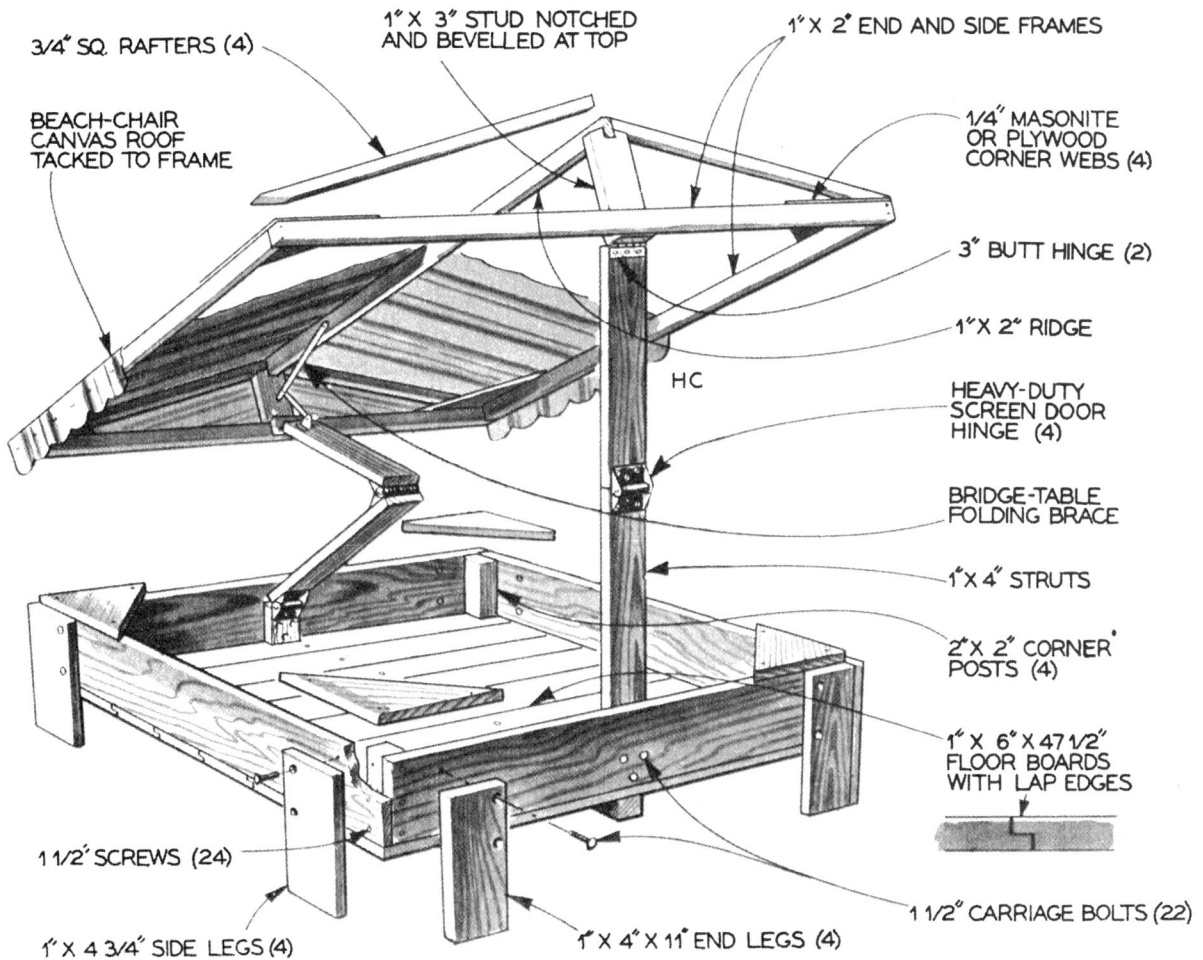

3/4" SQ. RAFTERS (4)
1" X 3" STUD NOTCHED AND BEVELLED AT TOP
1" X 2" END AND SIDE FRAMES
BEACH-CHAIR CANVAS ROOF TACKED TO FRAME
1/4" MASONITE OR PLYWOOD CORNER WEBS (4)
3" BUTT HINGE (2)
1" X 2" RIDGE
HEAVY-DUTY SCREEN DOOR HINGE (4)
BRIDGE-TABLE FOLDING BRACE
1" X 4" STRUTS
2" X 2" CORNER POSTS (4)
1" X 6" X 47 1/2" FLOOR BOARDS WITH LAP EDGES
1 1/2" SCREWS (24)
1" X 4 3/4" SIDE LEGS (4)
1" X 4" X 11" END LEGS (4)
1 1/2" CARRIAGE BOLTS (22)

TOY STORAGE SANDBOX

There'll be no more sandy trails over newly polished floors when toys are kept in the capacious storage chests of this easy-to-build sandbox.

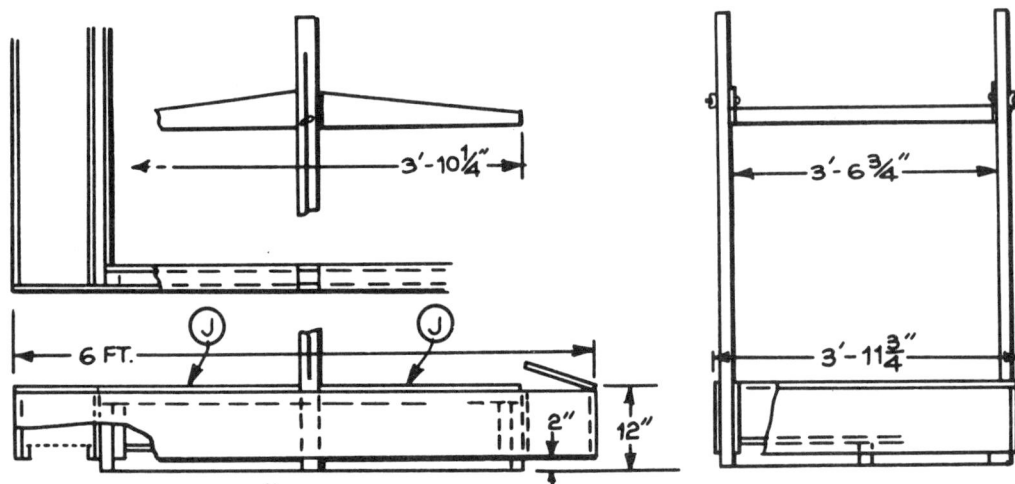

A MONG pre-schoolers, a sandbox is invariably the favorite back-yard play center. It is also the gathering point of their toys. This design features toy storage chests at each end—so that sand-covered toys need not be brought into the house each evening—and screen bottoms that will keep the toys dry outdoors. Also, this sandbox is of generous size; several children can use it at the same time. Its canopy supports will slip out of the box frame, for easy removal of the canopy when desired. And it features strength. The large box will withstand a full load of sand, as well as romping feet and the canopy will withstand any tug-of-war!

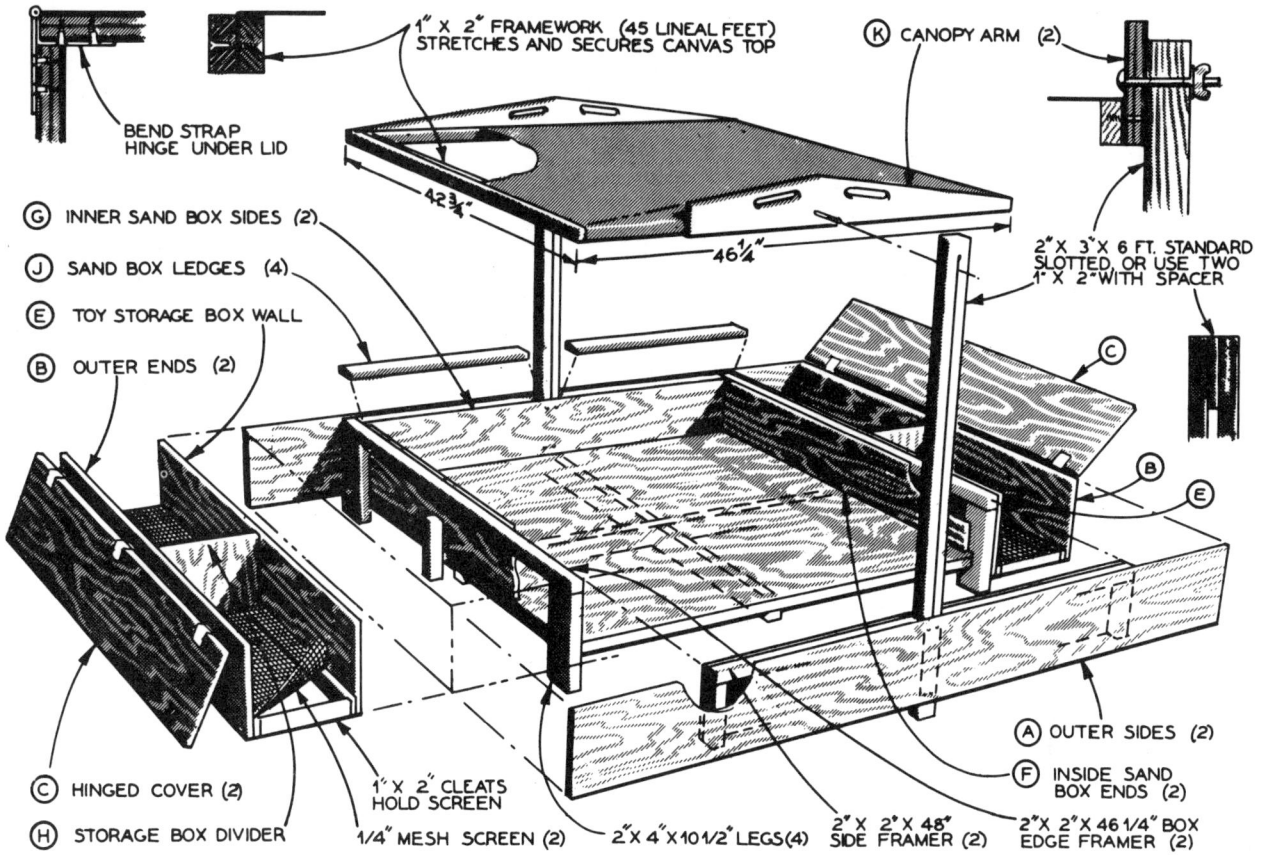

BEND STRAP
HINGE UNDER LID

1" X 2" FRAMEWORK (45 LINEAL FEET)
STRETCHES AND SECURES CANVAS TOP

K CANOPY ARM (2)

42¾"

46¼"

2" X 3" X 6 FT. STANDARD
SLOTTED, OR USE TWO
1" X 2" WITH SPACER

G INNER SAND BOX SIDES (2)

J SAND BOX LEDGES (4)

E TOY STORAGE BOX WALL

B OUTER ENDS (2)

C

B

E

C HINGED COVER (2)

H STORAGE BOX DIVIDER

1" X 2" CLEATS
HOLD SCREEN

¼" MESH SCREEN (2)

2" X 4" X 10½" LEGS (4)

2" X 2" X 48"
SIDE FRAMER (2)

A OUTER SIDES (2)

F INSIDE SAND
BOX ENDS (2)

2" X 2" X 46¼" BOX
EDGE FRAMER (2)

When cutting a heavy plywood sheet, clamp 6-ft.
length of scrap in bench vise to support free
end. Homemade extension stand serves well, too.

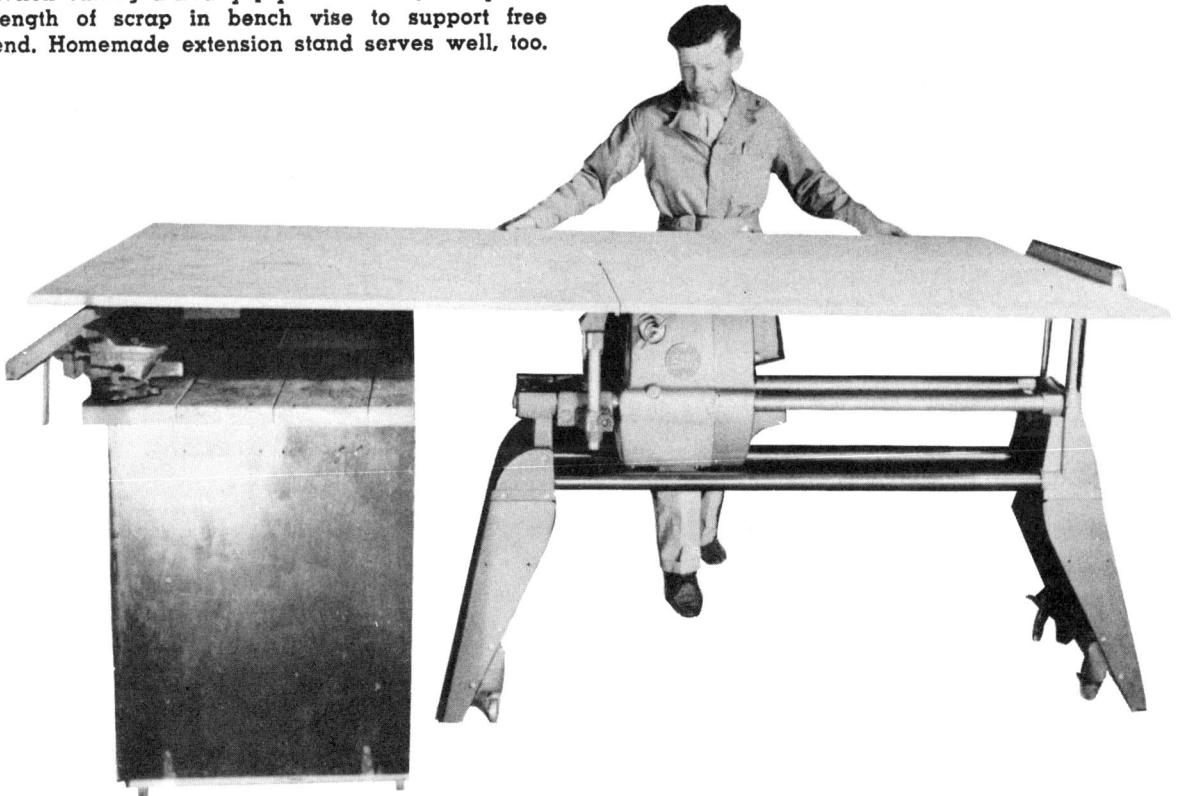

CUTTING SCHEDULE

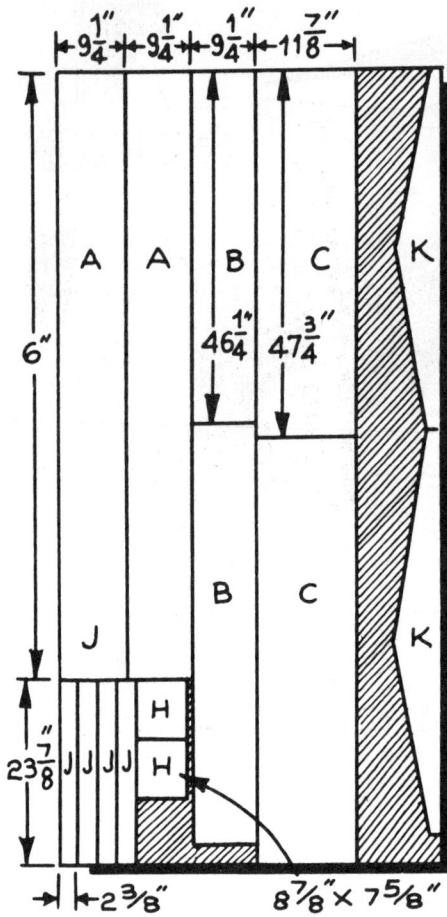

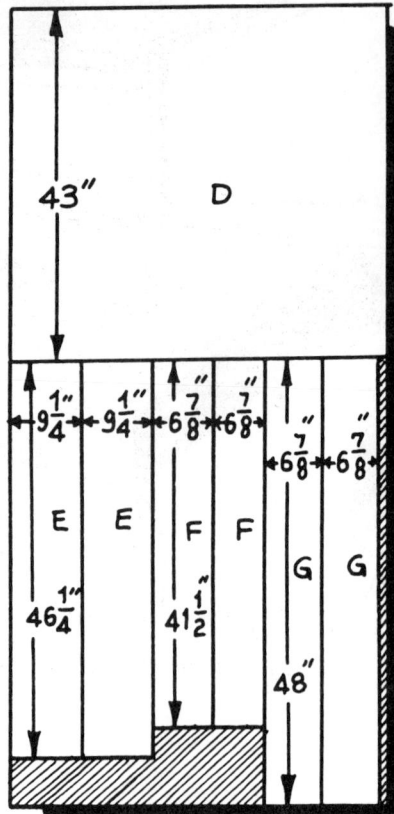

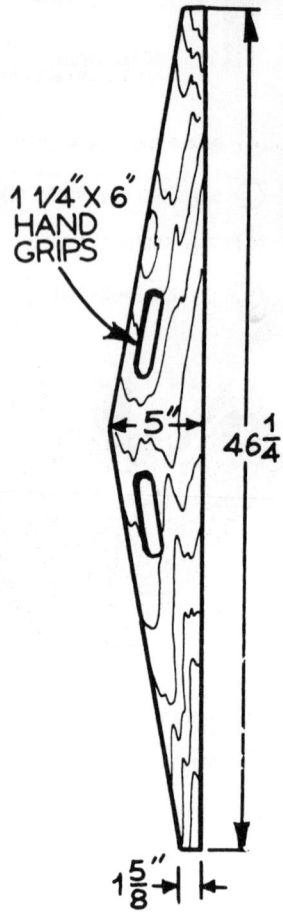

9¼"   9¼"   9¼"   11⅞"

A   A   B   C   K

6"

46¼"   47¾"

B   C   K

J

23⅞"

J J J J   H   H

2⅜"

8⅞" X 7⅝"

3/4" X 4 FT. X 8 FT. EXTERIOR A-C FIR PLYWOOD

43"   D

9¼"   9¼"   6⅞"   6⅞"

6⅞"   6⅞"

E   E   F   F   G   G

46¼"   41½"   48"

1 1/4" X 6"
HAND
GRIPS

5"

46¼"

1⅝"

CANOPY ARM

(D) BOTTOM (FLOOR)

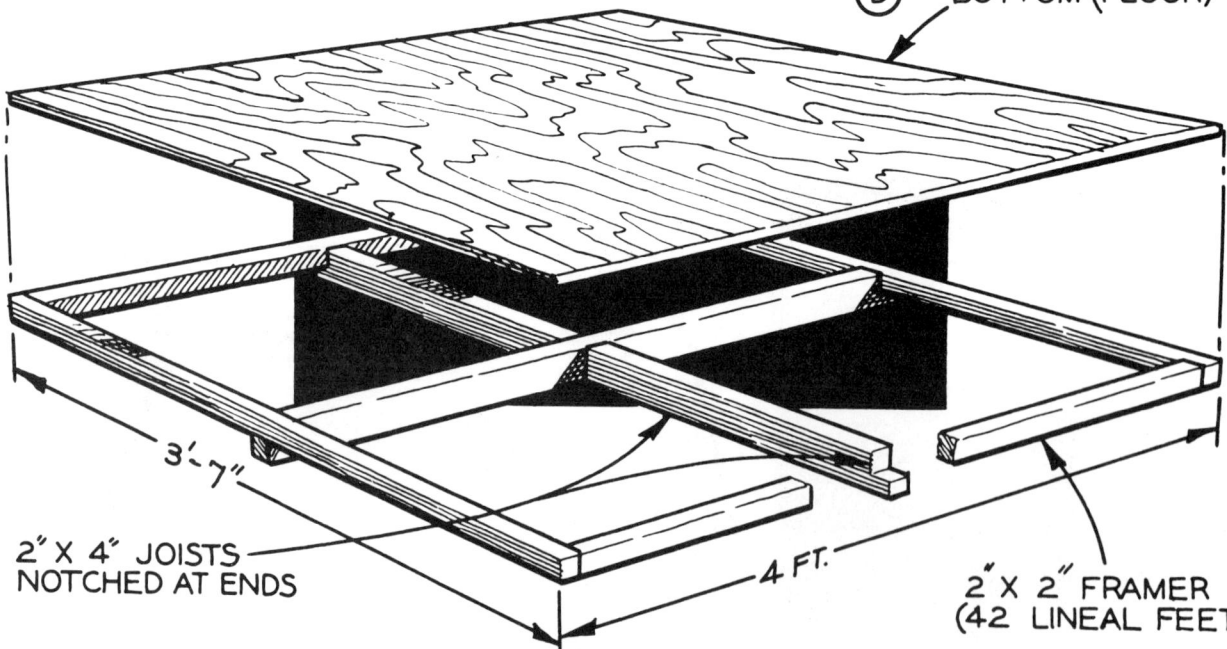

3'-7"

2" X 4" JOISTS
NOTCHED AT ENDS

4 FT.

2" X 2" FRAMER
(42 LINEAL FEET)

FLOOR FRAME ASSEMBLY (MADE FIRST)

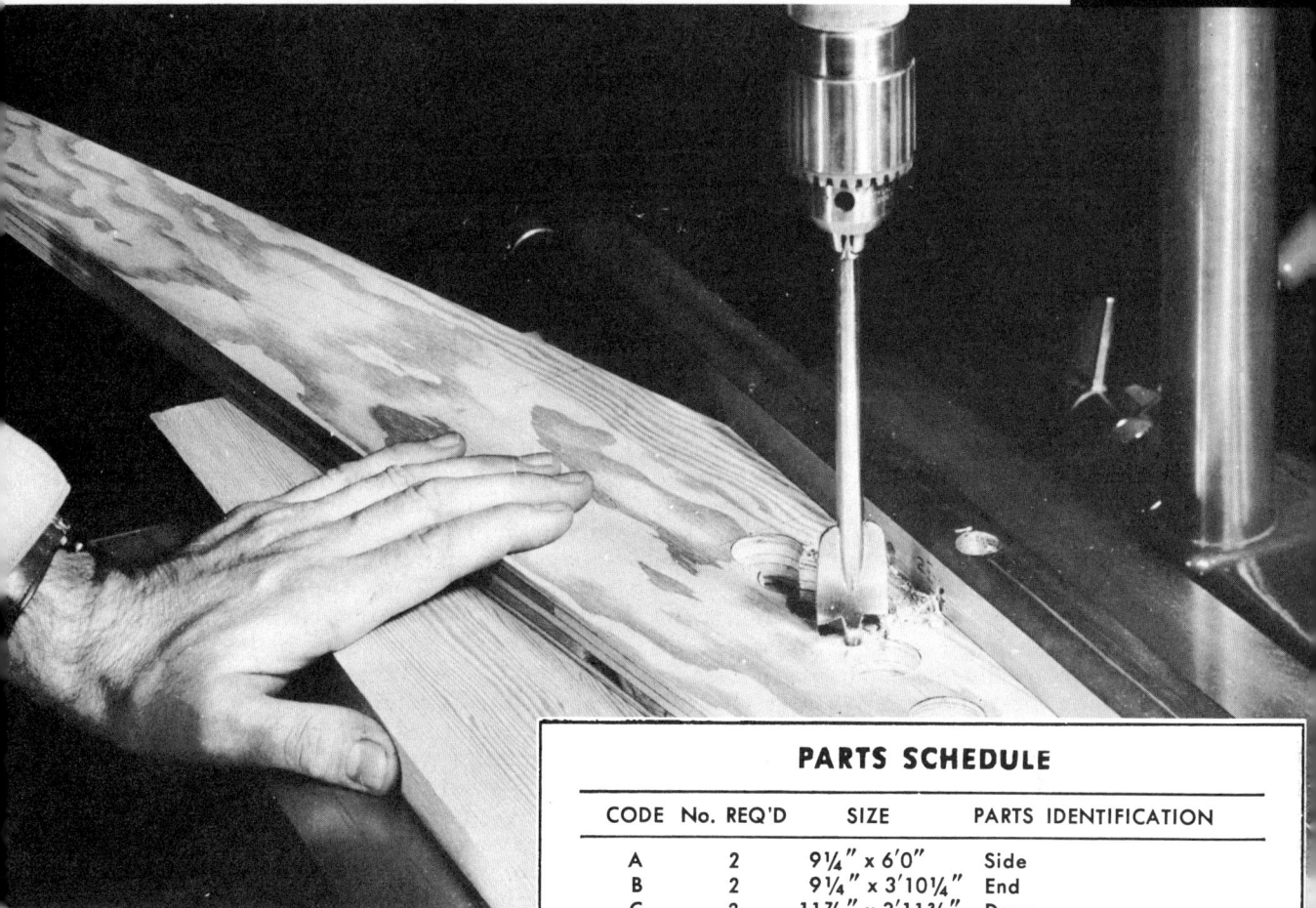

Cut handholds in cover arm with 1-in. bit, finishing with fine wood rasp, or cut 1-in. holes at ends and finish with router bit. Here, rip fence as backrest eliminates need of clamping.

PARTS SCHEDULE

CODE	No. REQ'D	SIZE	PARTS IDENTIFICATION
A	2	9¼" x 6'0"	Side
B	2	9¼" x 3'10¼"	End
C	2	11⅞" x 3'11¾"	Door
D	1	4'0" x 3'7"	Bottom
E	2	9¼" x 3'10¼"	Side — toy storage
F	2	6⅞" x 3'5½"	End — sand box
G	2	6⅞" x 4'0"	Side — sand box
H	2	8⅞" x 7⅝"	Divider — toy storage
J	4	2⅜" x 1'11⅞"	Trim — sand box
K	2	See det. "A"	Canopy arm
	6 ea.	—	Strap hinges
	2 ea.	⅜" Φ	Carriage bolts
	2 ea.	—	Washers & wing nuts
	8 sq. ft.	¼" x ¼"	Wire screen
	12 lin. ft.	2" x 4"	Framing
	42 lin. ft.	2" x 2"	
	45 lin. ft.	1" x 2"	Canopy & toy storage frame
	12 lin. ft.	2" x 3"	Canopy support

Miscellaneous — waterproof glue
4d & 6d galvanized finishing nails

You will note from the cutting schedule that all plywood parts can be obtained from two 4 x 8 ft. panels of ¾-in. exterior fir plywood. You build the bottom frame of 2 x 4s and 2 x 2s first, and then cover it with the plywood floor (D). Next, attach the four 2 x 4 legs and their 2 x 2 crosspieces to the two ends of the box. The inner box sides (F) are next attached, and then the sides (G). The side frames of 2 x 2s that hold the canopy supports are now attached, followed by the toy chest assemblies at each end. The sturdy ¼-in. mesh galvanized screen used for the chest bottoms is also called hardware cloth. Outer sides (A), chest lids (C) and trim (J) complete the sandbox proper.

The canopy consists of an inner 1 x 2 frame, to which the canvas is attached by tacks, and an outer frame of the two sides (K) and two 1 x 2 end pieces. By using screws to secure these two frames together, the canvas can easily be replaced. The ½-in. slots in the 2 x 3 canopy supports can be cut with a ½-in. router bit in the drill press or can be cut on the table saw, finishing the ends with a chisel. Or you can build each support of two $1\frac{1}{16}$ x 1⅝ x 72 in. pieces (ripped on the table saw), with ½-in. spacer blocks between. •

Portable Electric Sander

NO finishing material is ever better than the surface to which it is applied. That's not a new or startling statement, yet it's something that each new entrant into the field of woodworking has to discover for himself. Rare indeed is the person who, on his first project, smooths all the surfaces so perfectly that he has no pangs of regret after the finish has been put on.

This seeming reluctance to obtain the best possible surface undoubtedly is a throwback to the days when all sanding operations were done by hand. Then, it was a tedious process that called for as much patience and elbow grease as skill. But there's no excuse for it these days. Power sanders have taken over—and the home craftsman who has yet to be initiated into the benefits of the modern way of surfacing materials is far behind the times. Whenever someone says he does not think that electric sanders can do the job as efficiently as hand sanding, it's a pretty fair bet that he does not own one and never has used one. This is not to say that, occasionally, some particular operation might not be performed more conveniently with a piece of sandpaper over a sanding block than with a power sander. But by and large, the home workshop enthusiast will find that he can do 95 percent of his sanding tasks with one or more of the electric sanders now available. With so many dealers now renting such machines on a daily or weekly basis, even the fellow who does not have a workshop can enjoy the speed and efficiency of portable sanders for a particular project.

Portable electric sanders come in a wide variety of sizes, styles and prices, not to mention dozens of different names—but they fall pretty much into three categories —(1) belt sanders (2) finishing sanders and (3) disc sanders.

The Portable Belt Sander

The portable belt sander is a power-plus machine. It has an abrasive belt which runs continuously over pulleys or drums at both ends. The average "home" model weighs between 9 and 15 pounds. Its size usually is designated by the size of the sanding belt—such as 2x21 inch or 4x27 inch. Most operate with 115-volt AC-DC motors so they can be used with the electrical systems common to the large majority of houses.

Belt changing is a simple operation, although varying slightly with each different make. All sanding belts are spliced and have an arrow on the inside to show which way the installation should be made so the splice will not break. There is always some kind of screw arrangement on the machine to keep the belt running in a straight line. When using a belt sander, check this alignment every once in a while to be certain the abrasive is not rubbing against the frame.

Before turning on the belt sander switch, be sure the machine is in your hands, not on the work surface. The belt should be allowed to gain momentum before being used. Lower the machine slowly so that the back part of the belt touches first, then quickly bring it to a horizontal position as you move it forward. From there on it's a case of guiding the sander back and forth in a sort of stroking motion. Hardly any pressure is needed. If you decide to stop for any reason, lift the sander from the wood to prevent taking off an excessive amount in one spot. The belt should go only a little over the edges of the surface being sanded. When it is pushed over too far, the machine will begin to tilt and cause rounded edges where you might not want them. Extra caution is necessary at the corners of the wood.

The belt sander will really prove a blessing when you have to sand a large, flat surface, such as a piece of plywood or a table top. When a lot of wood must be removed or when the surface is very rough, the first sanding should be diagonally across the grain. This is done by keeping the sander on a diagonal course but moving your hands in the same direction as the grain of the wood—not as difficult as it sounds! A coarse abrasive belt is used for cross-grain sanding, after which it can be replaced with a finer abrasive belt. The final sanding is always with the grain.

Open-grit belts will enable your sander to be used for removing paint and varnish. There is a tendency for the old finish to become gummy and clog the abrasive. A

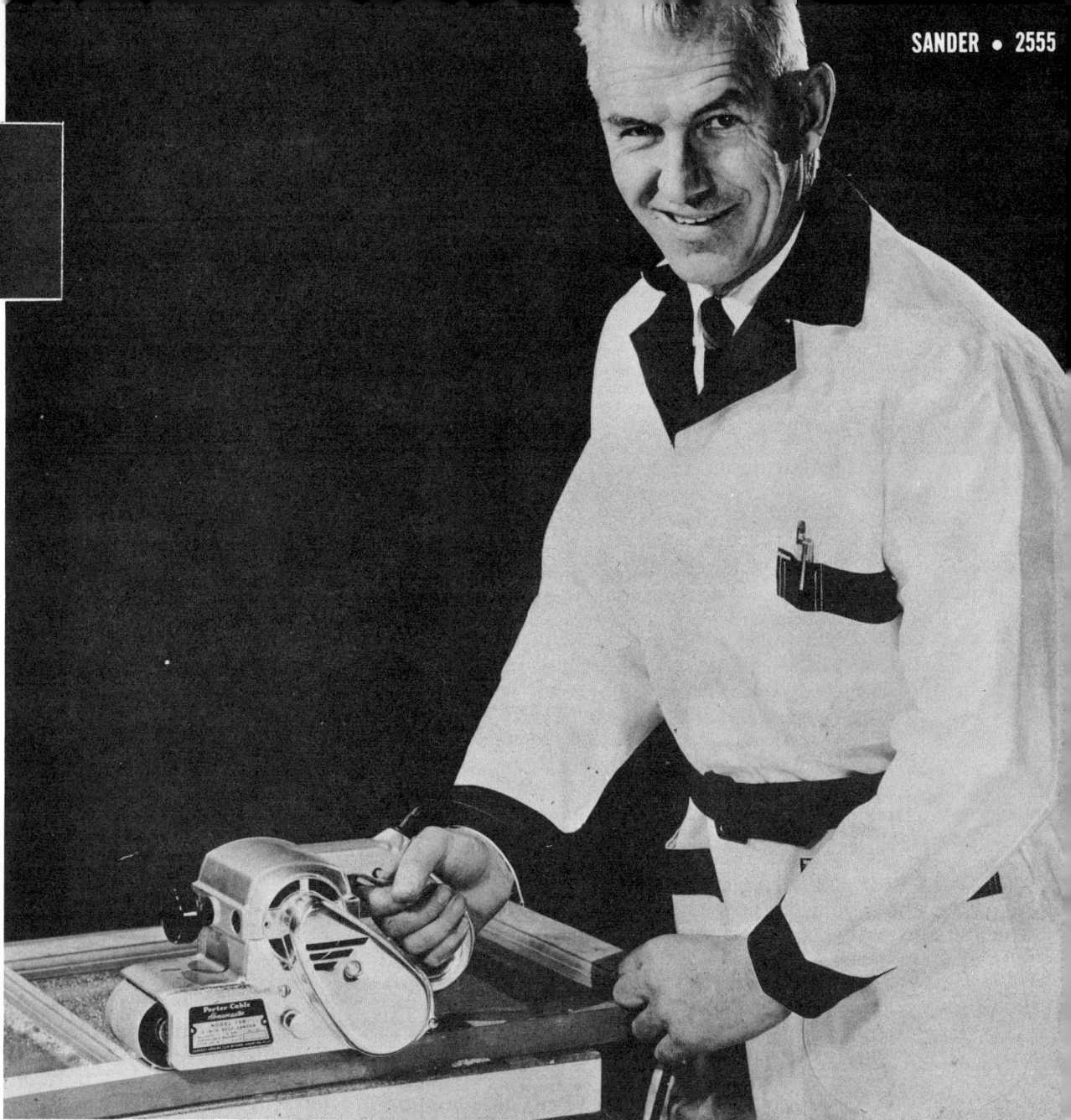

Three-inch belt sander weighs 10 lbs., can be used in any position—horizontal, vertical, even overhead.

minimum amount of trouble will be encountered if you use shorter strokes than usual and if you begin at the far end and work toward you. The machine should be lifted at the end of each stroke so that it is not immediately placed down again on a spot that has started to soften.

Some authorities feel that belt sanders should never be used on thin surfaces, such as veneer. It is difficult to be arbitrary about this, as there are decidedly different thicknesses of veneer. But it's well to remember that belt sanders are, as we said before, power-plus machines. They are intended for rugged work and, until you are fully aware of what they can and cannot do, it might be wiser to refrain from sanding veneer. When you feel ready to try out your skill in that direction, use only the very finest of abrasive belts.

Aluminum oxide and silicon carbide abrasives are generally considered best for belt sanders, with garnet a third choice, and flint unsatisfactory. The first two cost more, the third does a good job on wood but will not last as long, and the fourth will not stand up under high-speed use. Some of the abrasives still come in grit sizes designated by those mysterious numbered symbols that very few people understand, but most manufacturers, happily, are beginning to use plain words like "coarse," "medium" and "fine" to say what they mean.

The regular sanding belts may be replaced by various types of belts for polish-

Sander saves valuable time in chamfering, rounding edges, surfacing wood, metal and plastics.

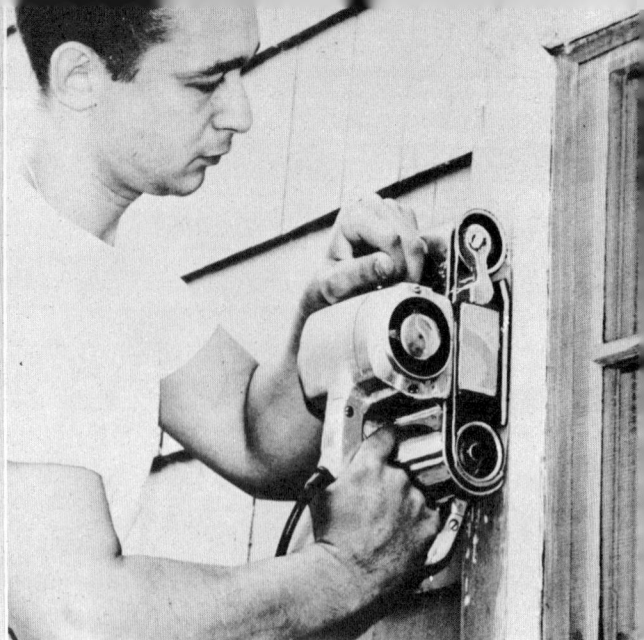

With correct abrasive this tool handles any surfacing job from rough sanding to fine finishing.

ing plastic and other special operations.

You can make or buy a bench stand that will enable the belt sander to be mounted on its side and held in place. Stock can then be pushed into the moving belt in the manner of a stationary belt sander.

Finishing Sanders

Finishing sanders is the over-all name for the numerous portable electric machines designed to perform the final finishing operations on wood or metal. There are many different kinds, with many different names, but they fall into two general classes—the *orbital sander,* which has a fractional horsepower universal motor and operates on either AC or DC current, and the *vibrator sander,* which has a magnetic power unit and operates only on AC because it is activated by the pulsations of alternating current. All have one thing in common which distinguishes them from the belt sander: they use flat pieces of sandpaper, attached in one way or another to the bottom of the machine.

The orbital sander costs more than the vibrator-magnetic sander, but usually is larger, will handle bigger jobs faster and is definitely more of an all-purpose unit. The vibratory machine performs well within its limitations of light sanding and polishing.

An orbital sander gets its name from the motion of the flat pad or foot at the bottom of it. The pad moves back and forth in a slight orbit, permitting sanding in any direction. You'll run across some different names for sanders of this general type—oscillating is one of them—and find some minor differences in design and means of

transmitting the power, but we'll use the term orbital for the purposes of discussion.

Because the abrasive pad extends slightly beyond the frame, the orbital sander can be moved flush up against square corners, a highly desirable feature in many operations. Another advantage, from the standpoint of economy, is the size of the pad to which the sandpaper is attached. Nearly all manufacturers make the pads in sizes which enable you to use standard sheets of sandpaper and so avoid any waste. There is one size for which a standard 9x11-inch abrasive paper will provide four sheets for your sander; another which calls for tearing the paper in three parts; and a heavy-duty model which takes half of a standard abrasive paper. That makes it a simple matter to provide sandpaper for your machine when it is inconvenient to get the special size sheets made especially for the model you have purchased.

Clamps or locking levers are used to hold the abrasive paper in place. A few models call for removal of the pads themselves. In either case, the changing of the paper is so easy that there is no reason for failing to switch to a finer grade of abrasive when the occasion demands. The sheet which is removed can, of course, be used at a later time. IMPORTANT: always be sure the abrasive paper is stretched tightly across the pad if you want it to perform properly.

Unlike the belt sander, the orbital sander may be used safely on veneered surfaces. Its cutting action is comparatively slow, ideal for producing high quality finishes but hardly practical for rough chores like removing paint. Light in weight, it can be

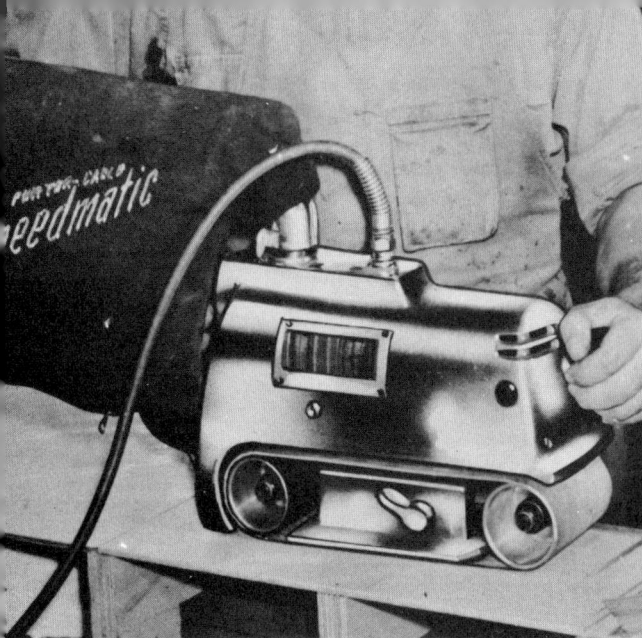

Big problem in sanding is dust. This heavy-duty model with vacuum system solves that difficulty.

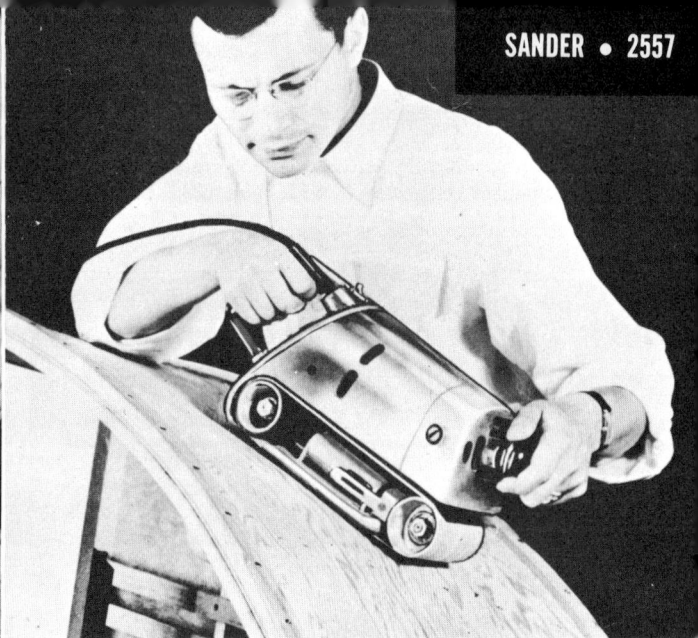

If you've ever had to sand a boat or the side of a house by hand then you know how long it takes.

used for sanding wall surfaces preparatory to applying either clear or pigmented finishes. Most sanders of this type weigh between 5 and 8 pounds.

The orbital sander must be allowed to do nearly all the work by itself. The weight of the tool is usually sufficient to permit it to operate freely. Your pressure must be confined to the handle and, where there is one, the front knob. If you exert a downward pressure, you slow the cutting action and, at the same time, cause undue wear on the abrasive paper.

It is possible to use the orbital sander for "wet" sanding, which some professionals contend is the best way to obtain a so-called super-finish. In this operation, the wood is wiped with a cloth or sponge moistened with water. When the wood has dried, its surface will be rough, caused by a lifting of the grain. Sanding over this surface with extra-fine abrasive paper will result in a glass smooth finish. The same procedure is followed between coats of the finishing material, except that in this case the sanding is done before the lubricant, either water or oil, is dry. For this between-coats wet sanding, waterproof sandpaper is used. It is known by various names, such as wet-or-dry, speed-wet, rub-wet and so on. Some experienced finishers also use the wet-sanding method after the final coat has hardened for a few days, but this should not be attempted by the amateur on quality work until he has first learned the knack of it on scrap material.

The vibrator-magnetic sander is sometimes called an oscillating sander, but there

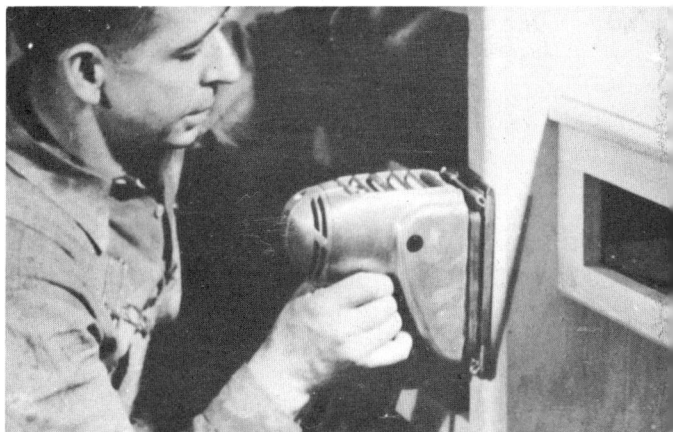

For finishing the orbital sander is the right tool. This handy new model weighs between 5 and 8 lbs.

is an overlap of terms here because some oscillating machines have direct-connected motors which drive the pads. The manufacturers of sanders with what is called straight-line action say this is preferable to the orbital movement even though it makes with-the-grain sanding a necessity. From this observer's viewpoint, either is satisfactory for home workshop use, with whatever difference there is being detectable only to the expert.

In general, the sander driven magnetically is a light-duty machine which, as we said earlier, operates only on AC. It is easy to handle, weighing as little as two pounds in one model, and produces a satin smooth finish on a surface from which the irregularities have been previously re-

When preparing sandpaper for sander be sure never to cut sheet with scissors. Use file.

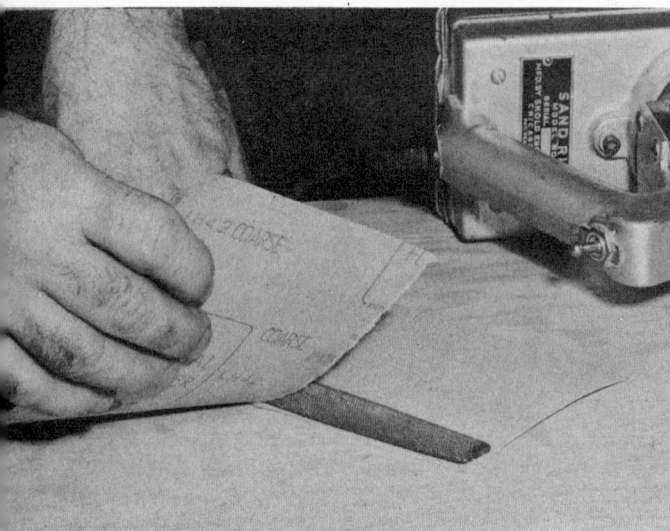

Sandpaper must be stretched taut over sanding pad, as you see worker doing in this picture.

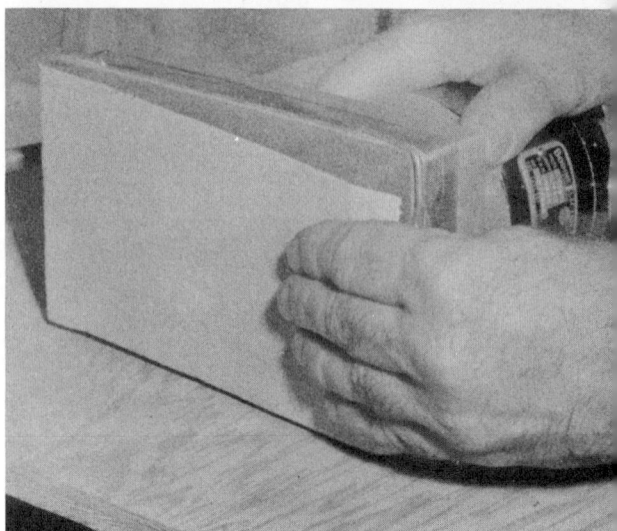

On this particular model a screwdriver blade is used as lever to tighten sandpaper clamp.

Edge sanding. Be careful not to exert downward pressure or you will slow cutting action.

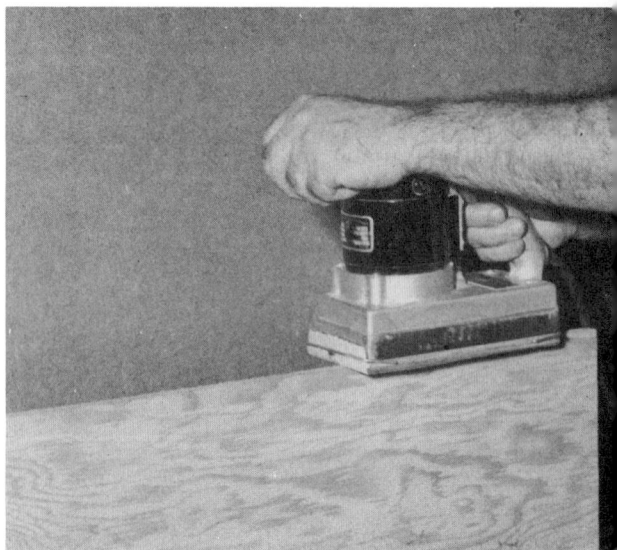

Here is an illustration of how not to allow the sander to tip over the edge of the wood.

On belt sander check alignment to make sure abrasive is not rubbing against the frame.

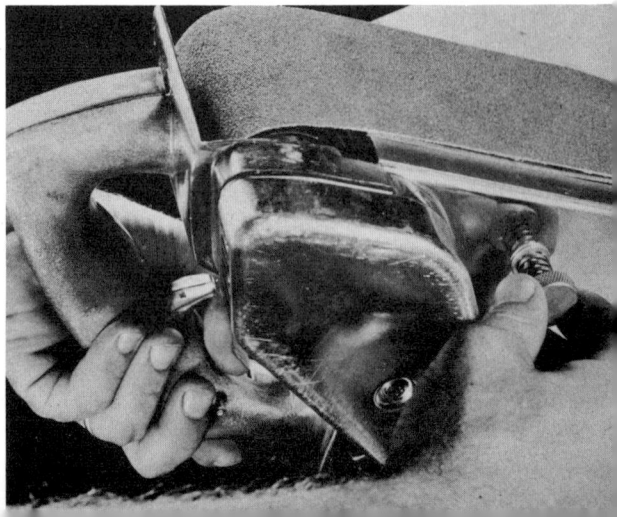

Surface sanding is a simple job. Note how worker uses both hands to guide sander slowly.

moved. Careful preparation is important.

All finishing sanders make fine polishers for metal, plastic and wood surfaces which have been lacquered, varnished, shellacked, enameled or waxed. Special pads are available for this purpose.

Disc Sanders

The disc sander is like the portable electric drill used with a disc-sanding attachment—meant for the rapid removal of stock where an extra fine finish is not essential. Used with a special chuck, it will perform all the duties of a drill. But whereas the drill is designed to give maximum performance when used as a drill, with sanding an auxiliary function, the disc sander is powered to do its best work as a sander and polisher, with drilling in the secondary area of capability.

The handle of the disc sander is parallel to the surface of the work and usually has a second handle or knob at the side of the motor housing. This makes it easier to move around when a lot of sanding has to be done. A circular flexible pad is mounted at right angles to the drive spindle. The size of the pad determines the size of the sander. Most sanders take abrasive discs of 5, 6, 7 or 9 inches, with the net weights of the machines varying between 4 and 15 pounds. The discs usually are attached with a special screw which fits into a recess in the center so it will not interfere with the sanding.

Disc sanding, as explained in the section on the drill used as a disc sander, must be done with the abrasive tilted so that most of it, but not all, is in contact with the surface. It must be kept moving back and forth while it is being advanced. Do not push the disc into the stock; rather, sweep it along in a kind of glide. The manufacturers of disc sanders are making every effort, with new design features, to prevent the disc from making swirls and scratches, but it still takes practice to achieve reasonable smoothness. This cannot be considered an indictment of the tool, any more than you can condemn a snow shovel because it fails to dig post holes efficiently. Disc sanding is for rough, heavy work.

There is one place where the disc sander really shines, both literally and figuratively. It is a real giant when used as a polisher. Many machines of this type are, in fact, known as sander-polishers and are becoming increasingly popular with the ladies. Equipped with a lambswool bonnet, the disc sander is excellent for polishing furniture and performing other household tasks of a similar nature. Special waxes are available to use with electric polishing tools. Adding a long extension handle to the sander enables it to be used for waxing and polishing floors.

Converting a disc sander into a drill with a drill chuck also sets it up for use with grinding wheels, wire brushes and dozens of other accessories.

Floor Sanders

Floor sanding machines are not generally considered in the portable class, yet if we accept the word portable in its true meaning, they fall into that species. Nobody is likely to buy one of them in order to refinish his living room floor. But these days it is easy to rent one for any such project. If and when you get around to an undertaking of that sort, you'd be smart to consider it as a big time and labor saver. And when you do, also rent an edger to get into places which the big sander will not reach, unless you have a small sander of your own that will do the job equally well.

A room must be stripped of all furniture, drapes, pictures, etc., before sanding the floor. All windows should be opened and the doors to all adjoining rooms closed.

A close inspection of the floor must first be made. Remove all loose nails and replace them with nails driven close by, *not* in the same holes. Nailheads should be driven below the surface, using wood putty or plastic wood to fill the openings. Only when the floor is completely ready for the sanding operation should the sander be

Disc sander can be used for reducing rough surfaces. But drill with attachment is capable, too.

Vibrator sander should be used only on surface from which irregularities have been removed.

Orbital sander's abrasive pad extends slightly beyond frame, permits it to go flush into corner.

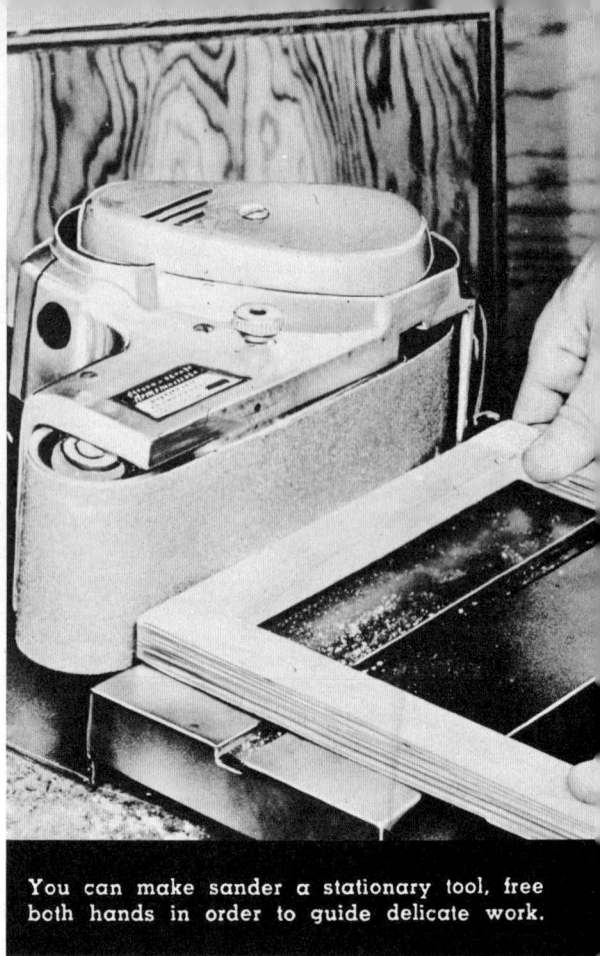

You can make sander a stationary tool, free both hands in order to guide delicate work.

rented, otherwise you will be paying for an idle machine.

Three sanding operations are recommended for old floors. The majority of professional floor refinishers believe that all three sandings should be lengthwise with the floor boards, although there are some who say that the first sanding should be at a 45-degree angle to the boards. This diagonal cutting is particularly effective when the floor is cupped, warped or otherwise in very bad condition.

Coarse grit paper is used on the sanding drum for the first cut, medium for the second cut and fine for the finishing operation. On a new floor, or one in good condition, the first sanding, with the coarse grit paper, may be skipped.

On some sanding machines, the drum is raised and lowered by tilting the base. On others, a lever located on the handle does the raising and lowering. In either case, the vital thing is to keep the machine in motion when the drum is in contact with the floor. If the machine is allowed to rest in one spot, indentations may result that will be extremely difficult to remove with further sanding. It is important that when a run is finished in one direction, the drum is raised quickly and kept off the floor until the return pass is started. However, be sure the drum is operating before it is lowered

See how this craftsman is cutting down a flat surface with belt sander. This is the first step.

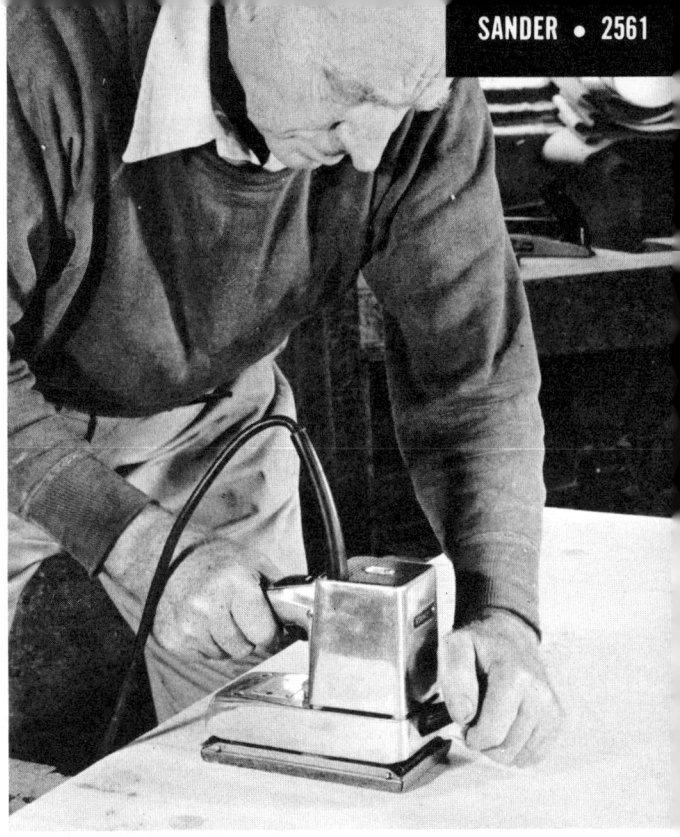

He finishes with orbital sander, not exerting heavy pressure, but letting tool do the work.

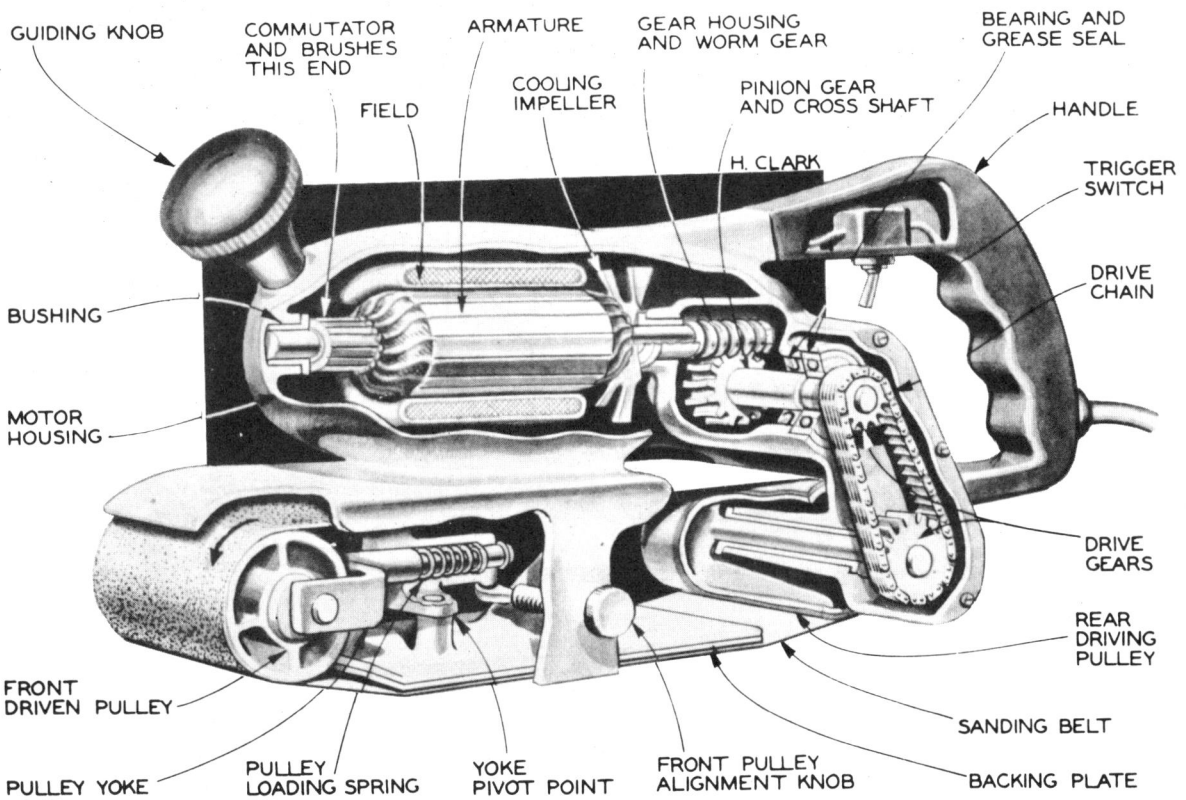

GUIDING KNOB

COMMUTATOR AND BRUSHES THIS END

ARMATURE

GEAR HOUSING AND WORM GEAR

BEARING AND GREASE SEAL

FIELD

COOLING IMPELLER

PINION GEAR AND CROSS SHAFT

HANDLE

H. CLARK

TRIGGER SWITCH

BUSHING

DRIVE CHAIN

MOTOR HOUSING

DRIVE GEARS

REAR DRIVING PULLEY

FRONT DRIVEN PULLEY

SANDING BELT

PULLEY YOKE

PULLEY LOADING SPRING

YOKE PIVOT POINT

FRONT PULLEY ALIGNMENT KNOB

BACKING PLATE

With any machine maintenance is important. The better you know your machine the better it can work.

This craftsman has thoroughly prepared the surface of this wood frame before starting to sand.

again. Starting the power while the drum is on the floor will result in scratching and gouging.

Each pass along the floor boards should overlap the previous one by a couple of inches. On the first sanding, use a slow rate of walking speed. On the second, use a slow to medium walking movement. The final pass can be made much quicker.

After you have finished the second sanding, the floor may appear perfectly smooth and in excellent shape for application of the finish. Do not allow this to mislead you into passing up the final sanding with fine grit paper. No matter how many times the floor is sanded, you will not get the necessary satin smooth finish unless you use fine grit paper for the last cut.

The small edge sander is used for sanding along baseboards and in other areas which the drum sander cannot reach. The same grade of paper should be used for each cut as was used in the drum sander. After the first sanding with the drum, use the edger; after the second sanding with the drum, use the edger; and so on. In other words, don't do all the drum sanding, then all the

Housewives can easily use the sander around the house because it is so light and maneuverable.

Be careful never to hold the sander in one place but keep it moving, to insure an even surface.

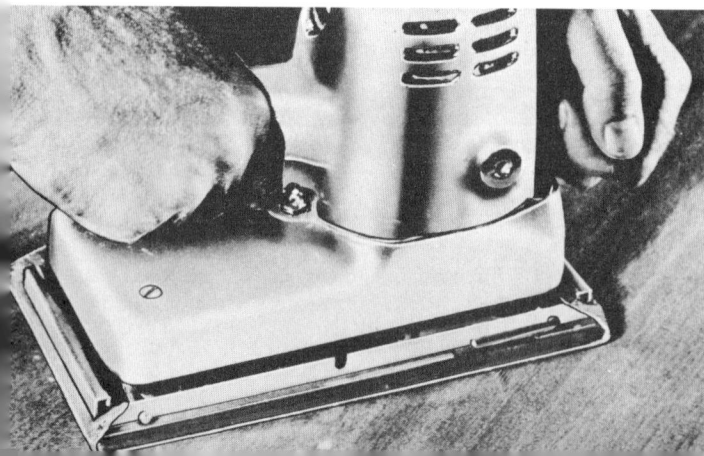

Although operator is holding sander at an angle, he is nevertheless moving machine with the grain.

Special pad makes sander perfect polisher for waxed, varnished, enameled, lacquered surfaces.

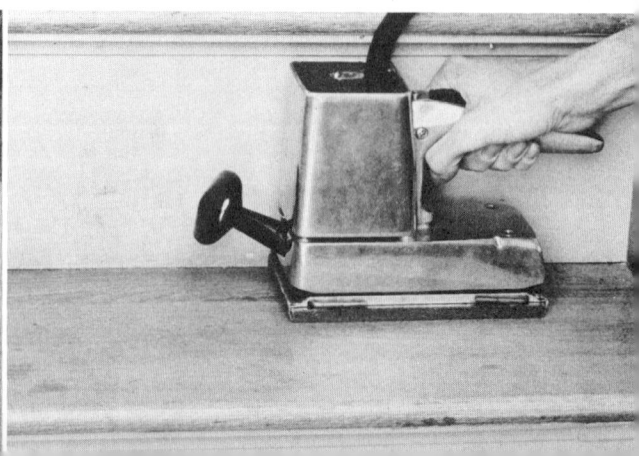

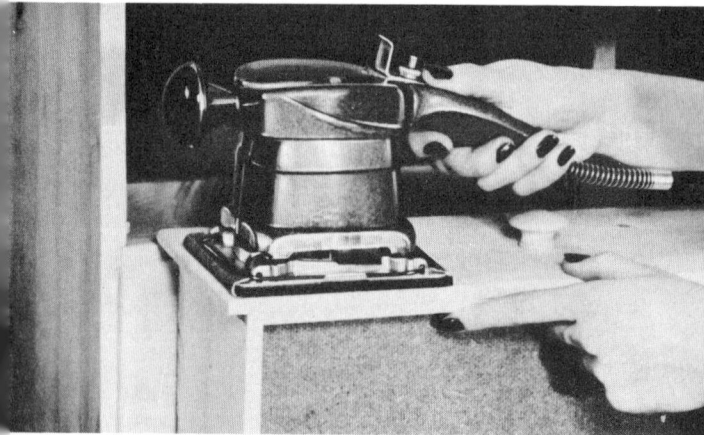

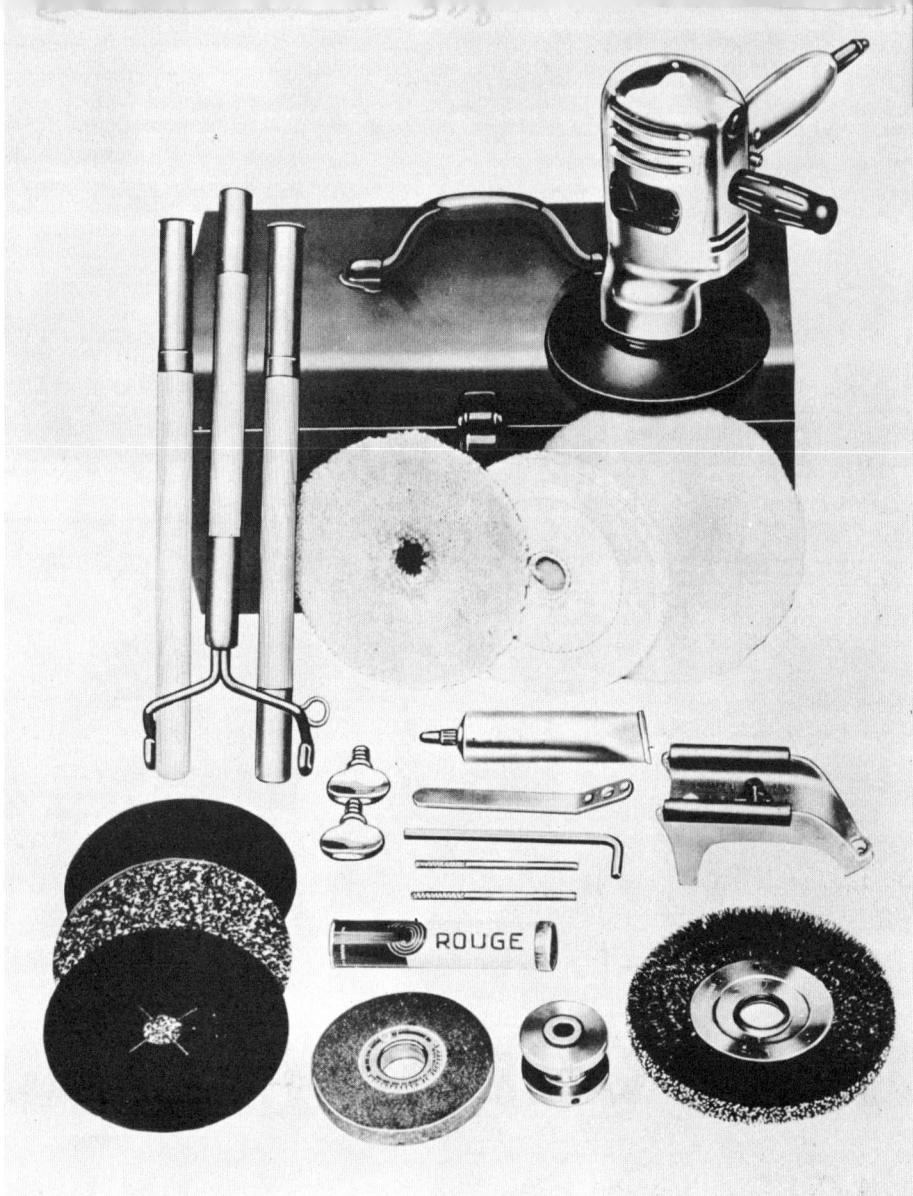

One of many types of sanding kits. This one is put out by Porter-Cable. It has discs, brushes, polishing bonnets.

edging. In sanding always take lots of time.

Although all floor sanding machines have dust bags, a certain amount of dust will be spread around the room. Use a vacuum cleaner or dry mop to remove this dust, being certain to include baseboards, window ledges and doorways as well as the floor. If this is neglected, the dust eventually will find its way onto the finishing material used on the floor, possibly spoiling the job.

The dust in the sanding machine bag should be kept in a metal container until it can be disposed of. The bag should be emptied when it is less than half full. And the dust should never be burned in a furnace or incinerator.

Safety Tips

Get into the habit of picking up your portable electric sander before you plug in the cord. An alternative is to be certain that the switch on the machine is turned off. But the really safe way is to take the machine by the handle, then put in the plug. In this way, if the switch should be on, nothing will happen except that the sander will start to jiggle or, in the case of a belt sander, the belt will revolve. If, on the other hand, the machine is resting on a table or other work surface, and you plug it in while the switch is on, it may quickly crawl away and wind up on the floor with almost certain damage.

You may recall we mentioned "wet" sanding as a possibility with finishing sanders. Fine—but *don't* do it unless your machine is equipped with a ground wire which you have properly connected, as explained in the section on the portable electric drill. •

Build Your Own Sauna

A Centuries Old Scandinavian Heat Bath Has Provoked Some Red-Hot Converts Here Who Find High Heat And Low Humidity More Stimulating Than Steam

FIFTY mile hikes? For some, it's a great way to stay fit. But others have found they can have the equivalent of an hour's physical exercise in 15 minutes without moving a muscle! The secret is Sauna Bathing, a traditional Finnish bath which has made its way across the ocean to the U. S. where it has enjoyed instant success.

A Sauna is a small, wooden room heated with a powerful stove, usually electric, to around 200 degrees. The heat is comfortable, because the humidity is kept very low—under 6 per cent. The dry heat bath is some 80 degrees hotter than an average steam room, with none of the discomfort sometimes associated with bathing of this type.

The high heat sets into motion three powerful body forces—profuse perspiration, cleansing the skin and pores; in-creased circulation (the same as you get from running around the block a few times); and increased body temperature, which burns off germs much like a fever. The Finns ascribe their good health to regular Sauna baths. Americans have found them to be a great relaxant and an excellent drugless way to relieve tension.

There are Saunas installed at SAC bases to keep the pilots physically fit. They can be found at health clubs, athletic stadiums, motels, apartment buildings, and even beauty shops. But the trend is toward their use in private homes.

Architects are using them to create unusual affects. Bathrooms are designed as Sauna-Baths; rec rooms serve a dual purpose, and they are even being built into master bedrooms. Designers and decorators are using Sauna to create unsual decorative effects.

Among the larger national firms is Viking Sauna Corporation with headquarters on both coasts (18 East 41st St., New York, and 2095 Union Street, San Francisco), along with offices in many U.S. cities.

Viking imports its Sauna heater from Sweden. The unit can heat a room to 200 degrees in 15 minutes, a far cry from the old wood burning stoves in use centuries ago. The Sauna unit also circulates the air and removes moisture from the room.

There are two ways to build a Sauna room, either utilizing pre-cut rooms of various sizes manufactured by Cascade Industries, Inc., Edison, N. J., or custom building a room to fit a particular site. The costs of either method are comparable. The pre-cut unit is simpler to assemble at the site.

Installation of the Cascade room is an uncomplicated affair and requires no special skills. A fascia is positioned into place on the floor, using 1" by 4" boards. The corners are secured by placing corner

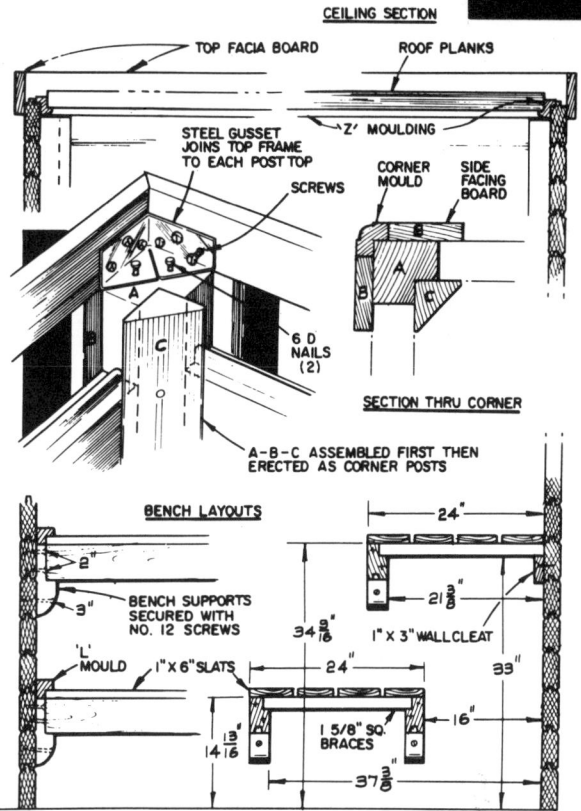

CEILING SECTION

TOP FACIA BOARD   ROOF PLANKS

STEEL GUSSET JOINS TOP FRAME TO EACH POST TOP

SCREWS

'Z' MOULDING

CORNER MOULD   SIDE FACING BOARD

6 D NAILS (2)

SECTION THRU CORNER

A-B-C ASSEMBLED FIRST THEN ERECTED AS CORNER POSTS

BENCH LAYOUTS   24"

2"

3"

BENCH SUPPORTS SECURED WITH NO. 12 SCREWS

21 3/8"

34 9/16"   1" X 3" WALL CLEAT

'L' MOULD   1" X 6" SLATS   24"   33"

13 13/16"   1 5/8" SQ. BRACES   16"

37 3/8"

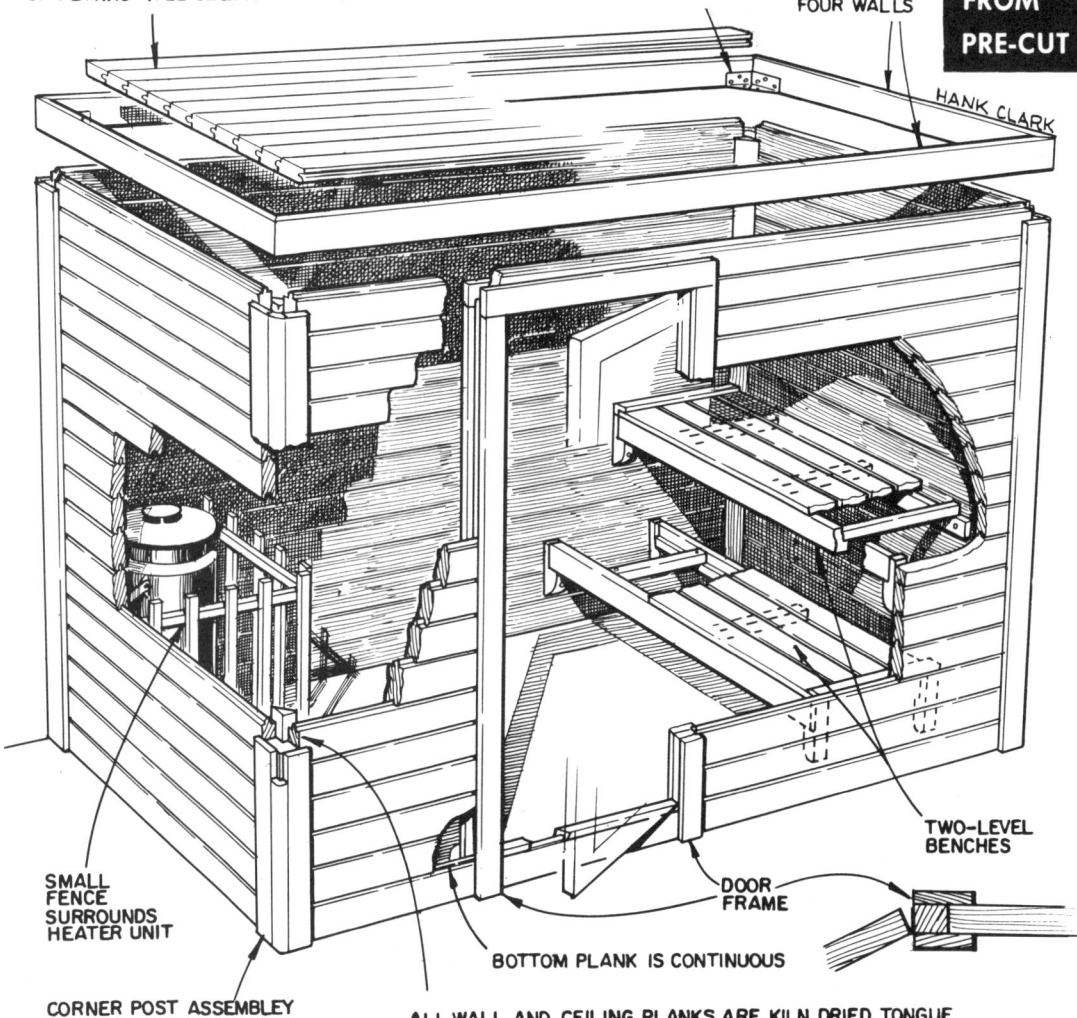

SAUNA ROOM FROM PRE-CUT KIT

CEILING PLANKS REST ON 'Z' SHAPED MOULDING NAILED TO INSIDE OF TOP PLANKS (SEE CEILING SECTION)

STEEL GUSSETS (4)

TOP FASCIA BOARD ON FOUR WALLS

HANK CLARK

TWO-LEVEL BENCHES

SMALL FENCE SURROUNDS HEATER UNIT

DOOR FRAME

CORNER POST ASSEMBLEY

BOTTOM PLANK IS CONTINUOUS

ALL WALL AND CEILING PLANKS ARE KILN DRIED TONGUE AND GROOVED CEDAR PLANKS SET INTO CORNER POSTS

The fascia boards are positioned to the area required for the Sauna. Size is about 8 x 8 feet.

The three inch red cedar beams fit into channels in support beams. Note planks are not nailed.

Three sides of the Sauna are enclosed. Door frame is positioned. Door is solid cedar.

With the door in place, remaining beams are cut to size and installed. Installation is quick, easy.

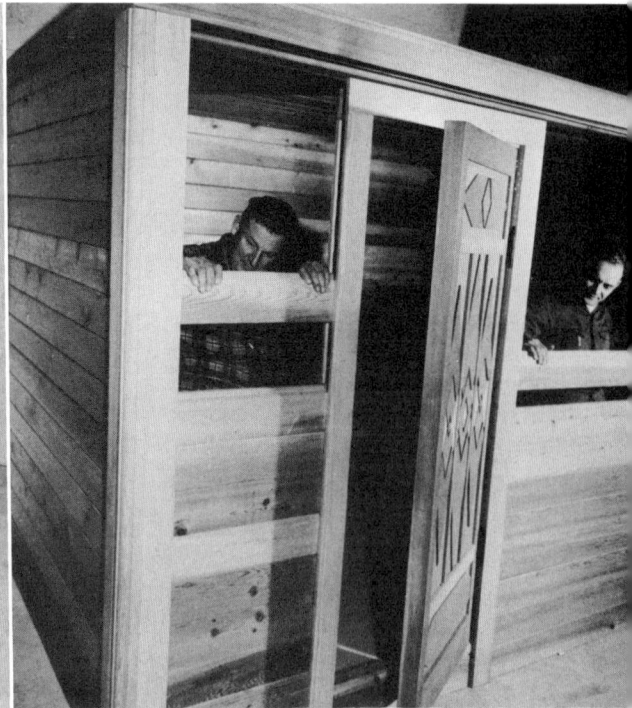

brackets flush with the bottom of the fascia boards.

Corner posts are then inserted, and a rooftop fascia is erected in a similar manner and secured to the corner posts. This skeleton provides the outside binding that will give the room its structural strength.

The room then goes together like Lincoln Logs. Three inch thick boards of Western Red Cedar are inserted into grooves in the corner posts. A tongue-in-groove arrangement locks them securely into place on top of each other.

This is an excellent method of construction for several reasons. The thick cedar needs no further insulation. This property also means it will not burn the skin when sat on, despite the high heat inside the room. Since it is not a rigid structure, the expansion and contraction of the room from heating the room up and cooling it down will not cause cracking or warping. There are no nails to pull loose.

After completing three sidewalls, a "Z" molding is placed on the top beam. This serves as a receptacle for the ceiling boards, which are then placed on top of the lip of the "Z" molding.

Now, we are ready to install the door.

One red cedar beam is placed on the floor of the open side. The pre-cut door assembly is fitted on top of this beam in a track provided on the bottom of the assembly. This can be placed in any desirable location, in the middle or on either side. The door can be made to open in or out, or from either side. This gives great flexibility to the kit.

Once the door is in place, the remaining cedar beams are cut to size on each side of the door, completing the structure.

Inside the Sauna, a corner is selected for the heater, and the unit is bolted to the wall. For the protection of the bathers, a heater guard is provided which is placed around the unit and fastened to the inside walls. In the event that it is decided to put the heater in the middle of a wall, rather than a corner, an extra guard rail must be constructed to close in the third side.

Two tiers of benches are the most popular method of construction. Since heat rises, it is always about ten degrees hotter on the upper tier. This is for the more hardy bathers, or the old-timers.

Supports are erected and bolted to the room on a line with the third beam from

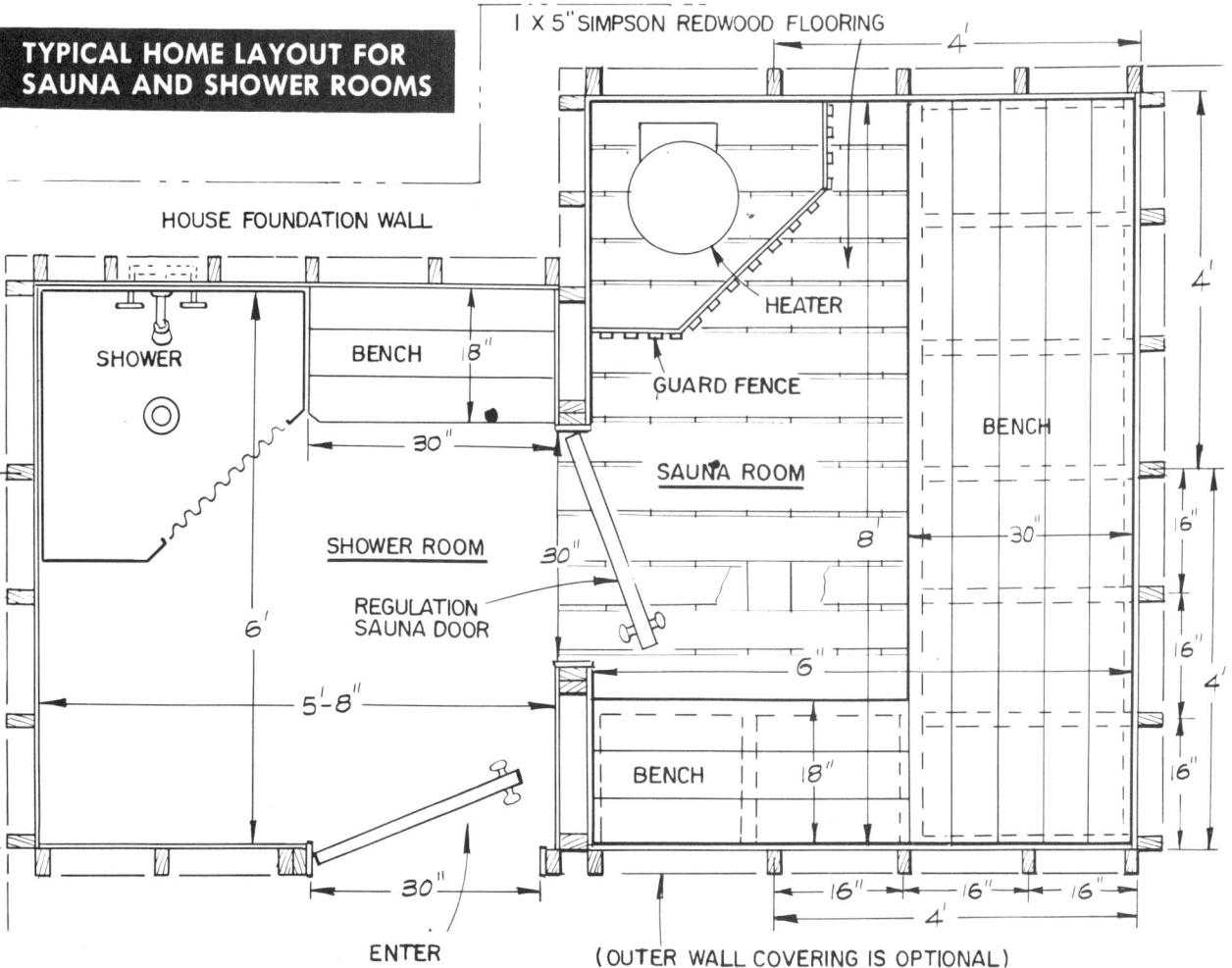

TYPICAL HOME LAYOUT FOR SAUNA AND SHOWER ROOMS

the floor. The main beams of the bench are anchored to the supports with a toe-nailing effect. The upper bench is constructed in a similar manner.

The Viking heater can be equipped with a pre-wired control panel, which includes Honeywell controls and thermostat. It can be hooked up easily to any 220 volt circuit. However, since it operates on 9 KW and draws 40 amps, it is wise to check on available amperage before contemplating a Sauna installation. A smaller 5 KW, 26 amp heater is also available.

It is not expensive to operate, since it turns itself off when it reaches the desired temperature, usually in 15 minutes.

A room 8' x 8' or slightly less is ideal for the 9 KW heater. The room is framed with 2" x 4" studs, in much the same manner as the walls of a home are constructed. The walls are then insulated with 3" thick Fiberglas batts and the inside wall and ceiling covered with ½" sheet rock. The joints are taped in the conventional manner and then the walls and ceiling covered with an aluminum foil-faced vapor barrier which is stapled in place. Overlap the joints no less than 3 inches.

The walls and ceiling are then planked with tongue and groove redwood as shown in the drawings. Simpson 1 x 6 tongue and groove planks, prepacked in waterproof packages (to prevent the boards from absorbing moisture during the time the planks are cut and dried until they are sold) are ideal. They come in handy 8' lengths. Finishing nails (8 penny) driven into the tongue, through the sheetrock and into each stud hold the planks in place.

The floor is constructed of 1 x 6 Simpson redwood planks laid over ¾ x 6 inch sleepers. The ceiling is insulated with vermiculite or rockwool poured 6" deep.

It is best to vent this type of room in order to assure low humidity. The vapor barrier does not permit the air moisture to force itself out through the wood planks. Therefore, other provisions must be made.

The recommended method is construction of a 4" x 10" duct which is attached to the ceiling. You should build a redwood duct cover in keeping with the over-all

DESIGN FOR CUSTOM-BUILT SAUNA ROOM

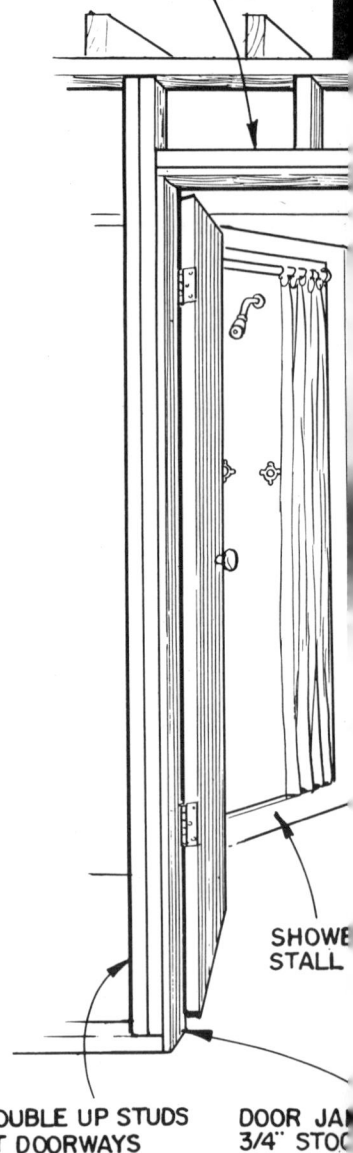

CEILING IS SAME AS WALLBOARD-ALUMINUM FOIL AND 1 X 6" SIMPSON REDWOOD

2 X 4" HEADER

SHOWER STALL

DOUBLE UP STUDS AT DOORWAYS

DOOR JAM 3/4" STOCK

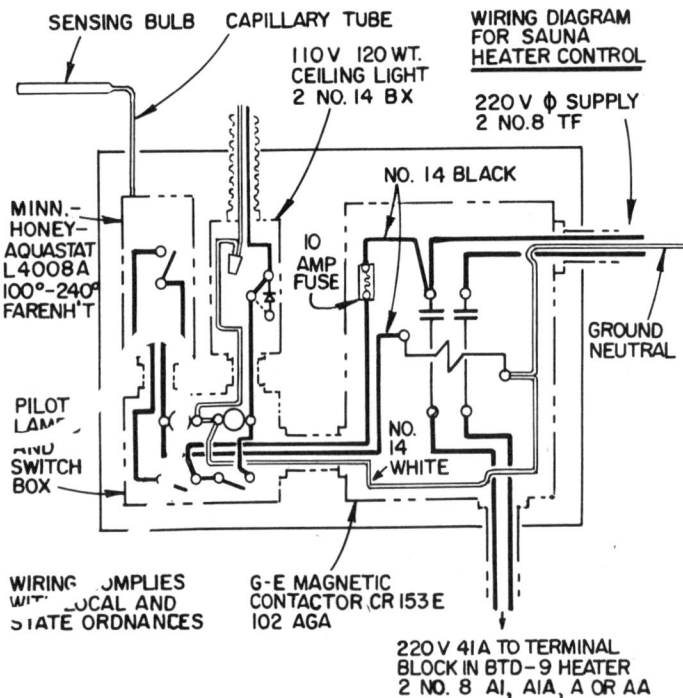

SENSING BULB   CAPILLARY TUBE

110 V 120 WT. CEILING LIGHT 2 NO. 14 BX

WIRING DIAGRAM FOR SAUNA HEATER CONTROL

220 V ϕ SUPPLY 2 NO. 8 TF

NO. 14 BLACK

MINN.- HONEY- AQUASTAT L4008A 100°-240° FARENH'T

10 AMP FUSE

GROUND NEUTRAL

PILOT LAMP AND SWITCH BOX

NO. 14 WHITE

WIRING COMPLIES WITH LOCAL AND STATE ORDNANCES

G-E MAGNETIC CONTACTOR CR153E 102 AGA

220 V 41A TO TERMINAL BLOCK IN BTD-9 HEATER 2 NO. 8 AI, AIA, A OR AA

design. The duct is attached to a blower motor which will exhaust the hot air and humidity when use of the Sauna is completed.

Once you have built your Sauna, the important thing to remember is that Sauna bathing is not designed to be an endurance test. A bather should set the timer at 10 minutes and come out of the Sauna after that time whether or not he is perspiring. He should then take a shower (as cold as possible) and return to the Sauna for a second 10 minute stint. He then takes another cold shower and relaxes in a rest area for at least 15 minutes. This final relaxation phase is very important, and no effort should be made to plunge back into daily activity without this rest.

Since the shower is an important part of Sauna bathing, when laying out your Sauna area, you must make provision for this, as well as a small rest area.

As you become accustomed to taking Sauna baths, you may wish to increase your time inside. Some bathers like to follow the old Finnish tradition of beating themselves lightly with birch leaves to further stimulate blood circulation.

Anyway you prefer to do it, you are likely to join the ranks of those who have adopted this bathing ritual as their own and enjoy its many physical benefits. •

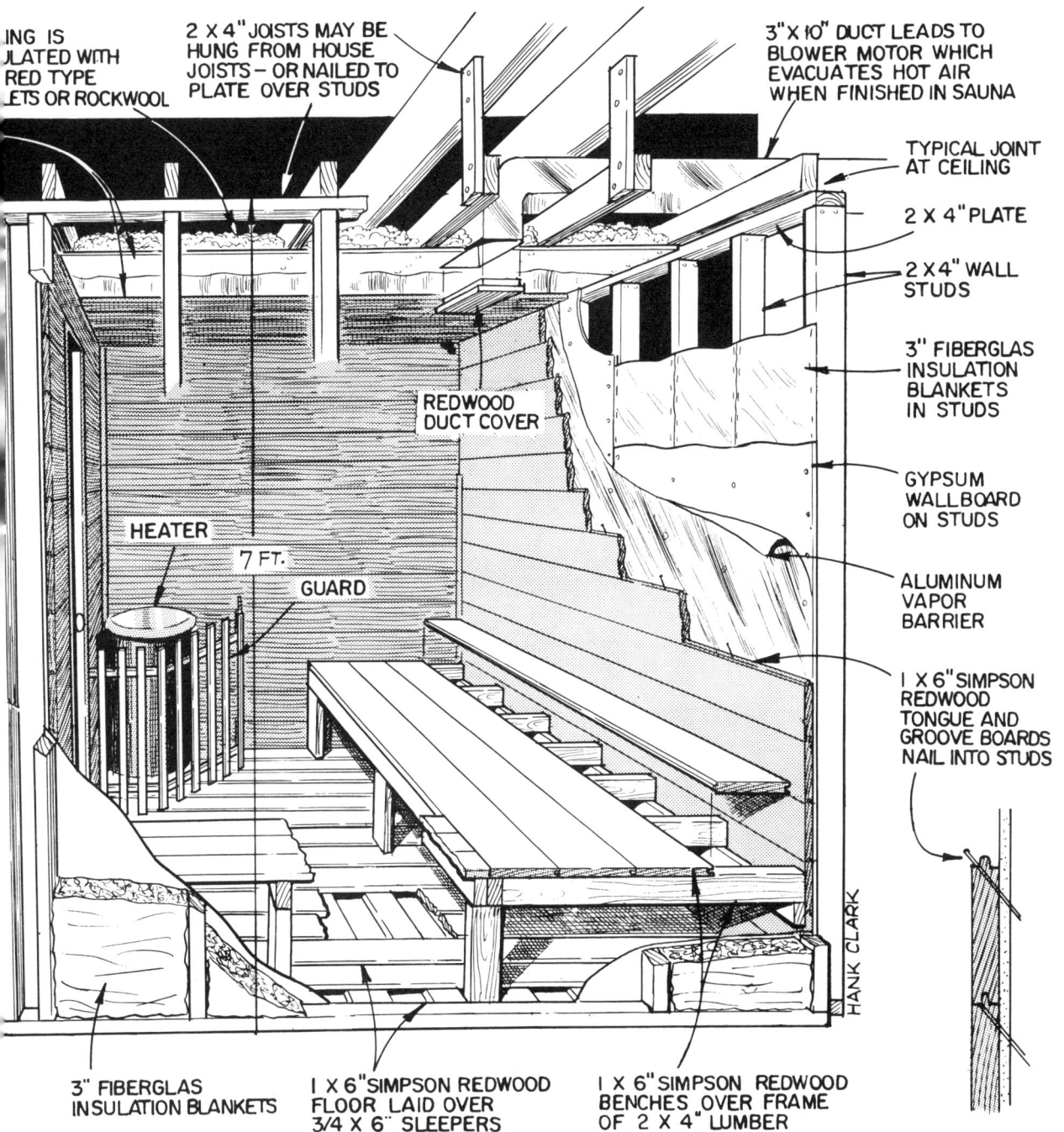

ING IS
ULATED WITH
RED TYPE
ETS OR ROCKWOOL

2 X 4" JOISTS MAY BE HUNG FROM HOUSE JOISTS — OR NAILED TO PLATE OVER STUDS

3" X 10" DUCT LEADS TO BLOWER MOTOR WHICH EVACUATES HOT AIR WHEN FINISHED IN SAUNA

TYPICAL JOINT AT CEILING

2 X 4" PLATE

2 X 4" WALL STUDS

3" FIBERGLAS INSULATION BLANKETS IN STUDS

GYPSUM WALLBOARD ON STUDS

ALUMINUM VAPOR BARRIER

1 X 6" SIMPSON REDWOOD TONGUE AND GROOVE BOARDS NAIL INTO STUDS

REDWOOD DUCT COVER

HEATER

7 FT.

GUARD

HANK CLARK

3" FIBERGLAS INSULATION BLANKETS

1 X 6" SIMPSON REDWOOD FLOOR LAID OVER 3/4 X 6" SLEEPERS

1 X 6" SIMPSON REDWOOD BENCHES OVER FRAME OF 2 X 4" LUMBER

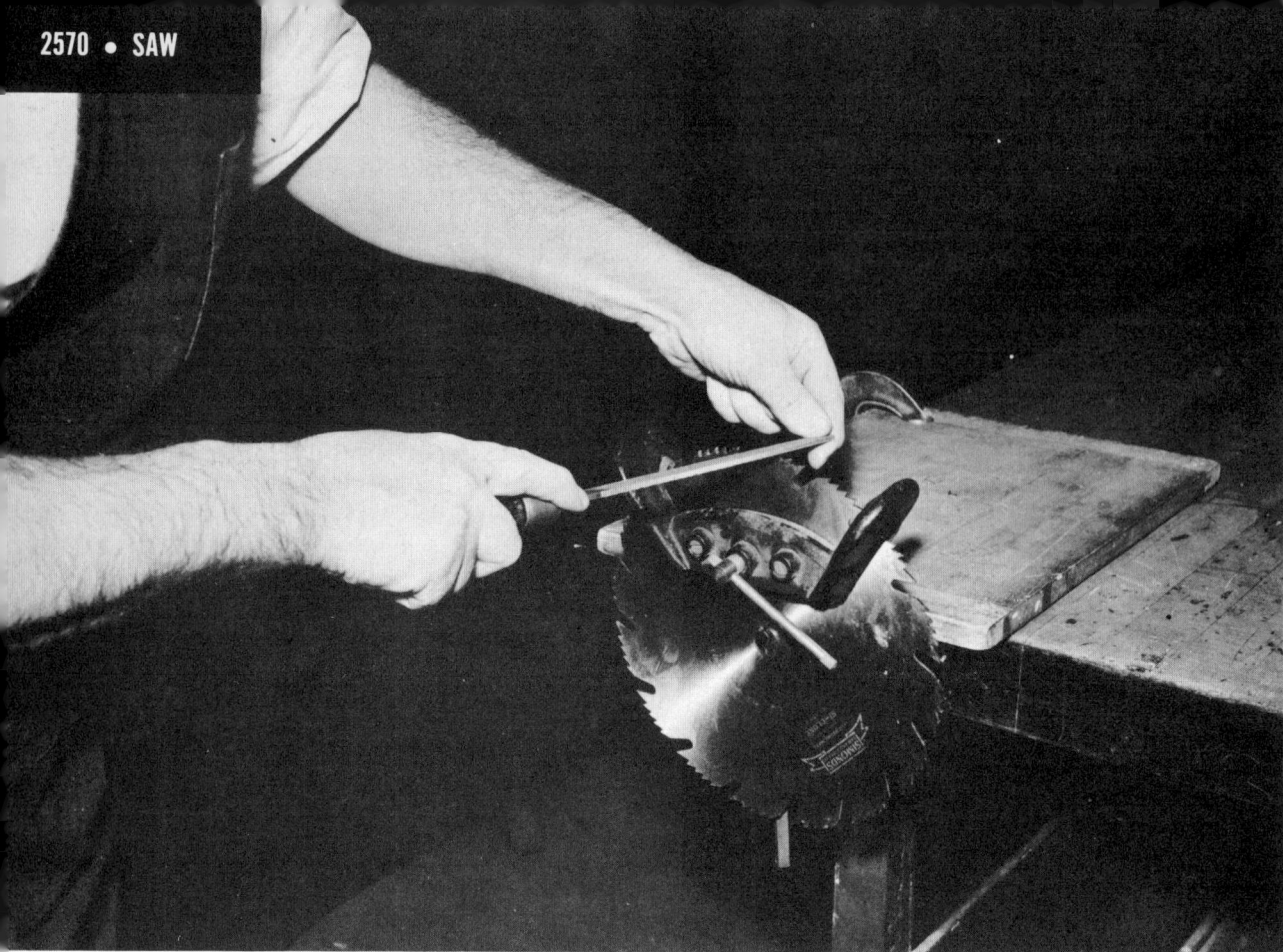

The Circular Saw

This number one power tool is basic equipment in any home workshop. It will save you time,

energy, money because it can produce more work than any other electrical power tool.

ON August 7, 1777, Samuel Miller of Southampton, England, was granted a patent for a circular saw, a saw similar to models that had been in use in Holland for quite some time. Early records seem to indicate that the first circular saw in this country was built about 1814 by Benjamin Cummins in Bentonville, New York.

While circular saws in general include the electric hand saw, the radial arm, even the farmer's buzz saw, the home carpenter is primarily concerned with the bench saw equipped with an 8 or 10-inch blade.

This bench saw, one of the most useful of all woodworking tools, will perform a great variety of sawing operations, perhaps more than 75 percent of all that are required in cabinet making. It is probably the first large power tool that most people will want in their home workshop. The various illustrations shown as part of this article give just one example of the type of saws made. For a complete listing, price and description, write to each manufacturer.

Basically, there are two kinds of bench saws. One has a tilting arbor and the other a tilting table. The tilting arbor type is used with the table always in a horizontal position and is therefore easier and faster to use in making angle or bevel cuts and is more adaptable to the use of an extension table.

The tilting table saw is generally less expensive but is just as good as the tilting arbor type for making straight cuts. These cuts represent the majority of all sawing operations performed.

Other refinements that are built into a saw must also be considered when comparing cost. Some have more accurate controls and scales for the tilt and lock of the table or blade and also for the adjustment to alter the depth of cut. The fence and the miter gauge may be more accurate and easier to adjust. Arbor bearings may be either bronze or sealed ball bearings. These, and other factors enter into the value of the machine.

The circular saw should be placed in a central location in the shop and with plenty of room on all sides. Floor model saw tables are usually about 34 inches above the floor. It is advisable to have bench tops at about this same height.

A saw should be lubricated before being put into service. Sealed bearings require no attention. Bronze bearings, however, must be greased according to instructions, care being exercised not to over-lubricate. In addition, all parts subject to rust should be given a protective coating of oil or wax.

The circular saw can be one of the most dangerous of all the woodworking machines especially when operated by one who is careless or nervous. Two kinds of guards are available and should be used whenever possible. One is a splitter, located behind the blade. This serves to keep the saw kerf open to lessen the possibility of binding and kickbacks. The other, a basket type affair, fits over the blade and may be made of either plastic, metal, wire mesh or wood. Sometimes both of these anti-kickback fingers are combined in one complete unit.

In addition to the guards, other safety precautions should be observed. The blade should be sharp, properly set and securely mounted on a saw that is in perfect working order. Tools or other materials must never be on the saw table nor should the operator ever reach across the running saw to pick up pieces that have been cut. The saw blade should never project more than one inch above the work. Adjustments of any kind are never made with the saw running. Stock must lie flat on the table, have one straight edge that can be held against the fence or guide. Gloves should never be worn and sleeves must always be rolled above the elbows. Above all else, the operator should stand slightly to one side of the saw, be alert, keep his eyes on his work, and should never talk to anyone nor permit himself to be distracted in any manner.

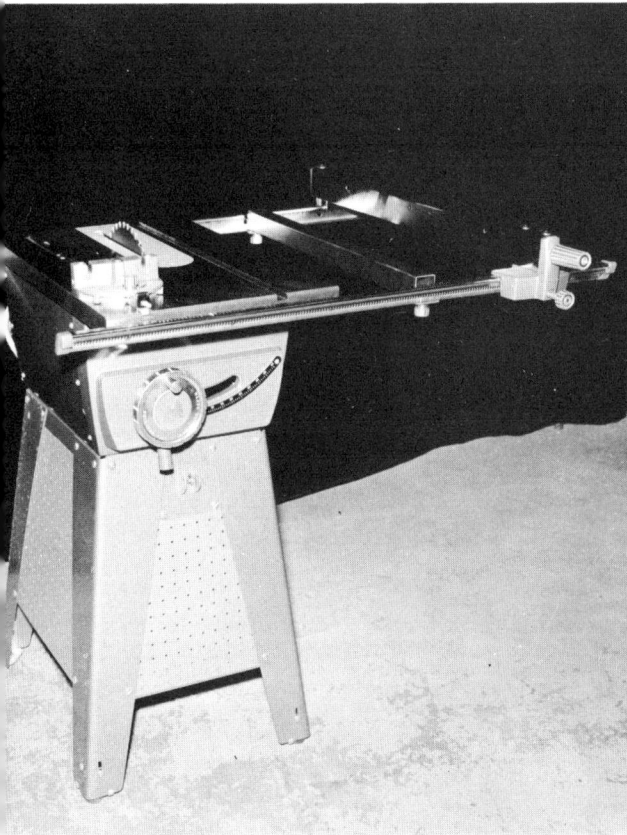

This is a Magna 9-inch tilting arbor bench saw mounted on its matching stand. The table with extensions is 24x36, depth of cut is 2¾ inches. Depth of cut at a 45-degree angle is 1⅞ inches.

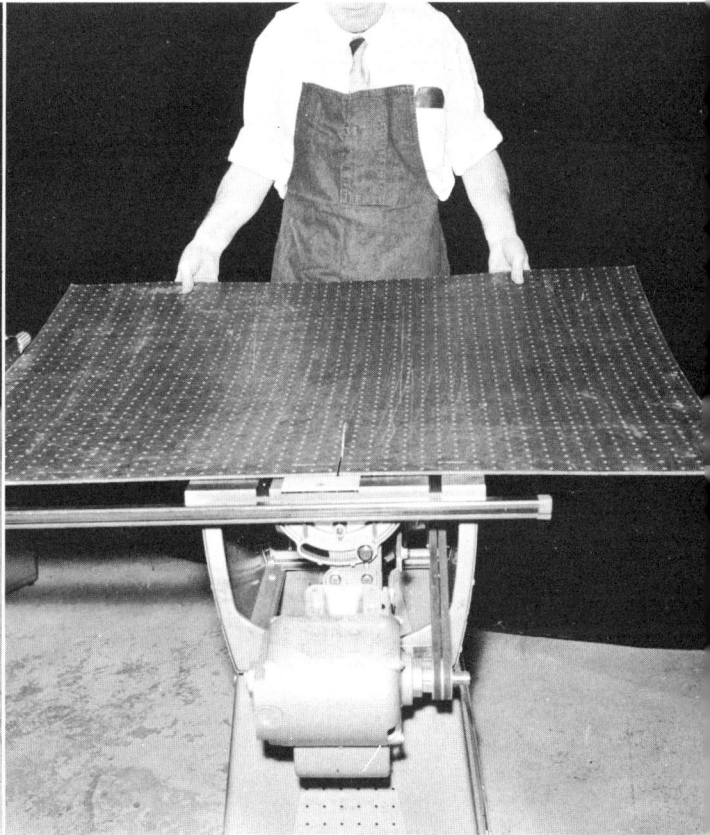

A wide panel being ripped with the fence set at its maximum 26-inch width. Note the operator's apron, worn for protection against clothes catching on saw. And note how he has sleeves rolled.

Circular saws for cutting wood are made from four inches to over 84 inches in diameter. Those for use in the home workshop naturally are the smaller sizes, usually eight or ten inches in diameter. There are also a great variety of special blades but four or possibly five types are in common use.

The combination saw is used to rip, crosscut or miter. One model looks similar to a rip saw except that the teeth are finer and are beveled on the back. Alternate teeth are set, their faces are filed square, and their backs are beveled at a 5° angle.

The crosscut, or cut-off blade, is used for squaring or trimming to length. Its teeth tips are set in alternate opposite directions for clearance or shear to enable them to sever the wood fibers. The front of the face is usually filed at 15° and the back at a 10° bevel. These angles may be increased to 25 and 15° for fine cutting.

The ripsaw cuts with the grain, each tooth acting as a small chisel. The teeth are filed square across to obtain this cutting effect.

The hollow ground planer saw requires no set, and will cut three ways; rip, crosscut, or miter. It has sets of four cutting teeth to sever the fibers and one raker tooth to clean them out from the kerf. This blade leaves a smooth edge and will stand fast feeding without gumming or overheating. The raker teeth are less than 1/32nd of an inch shorter than the cutting teeth. Cutting teeth are beveled on alternate sides.

A new blade recently placed on the market has only eight teeth. It is claimed that the blade lasts longer, eliminates kickback, cuts smoother and faster, and is more efficient in operation.

The dado head is used to cut grooves from 1/8 to 13/16 of an inch wide. It has two outside cutters that are filed similar to a combination hollow ground blade and can actually be used individually. Inside cutters, 1/16, 1/8, and 1/4-inch wide are filed square. If necessary, paper spacers or washers may be used to obtain the exact width groove.

A molding head may be used to cut a great variety of shaped, beaded or grooved designs by fitting it with various cutters or knives. Straight knives may be ground to a desired shape if a particular pattern is needed for some specific job.

A few of the hundreds of shapes which can be cut are those for corner moldings, picture frames, table edges, railings and panel strips. Others include spiral turn-

Before starting work the operator is attaching table extension rails that greatly expand capacity of machine by providing an ample support.

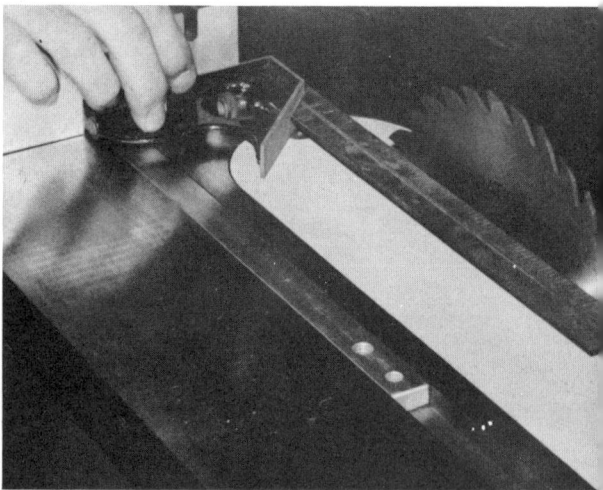

Operator checks the miter gauge for accuracy. In case there is any misalignment it is easy enough to correct with a simple adjustment.

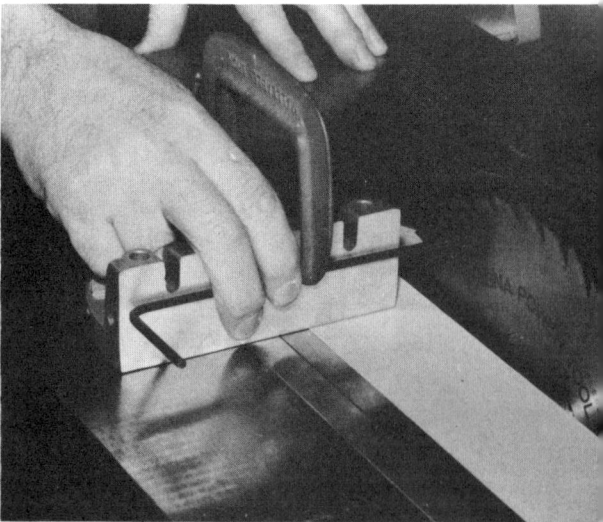

Miter gauge may also be checked for accuracy by using Allen wrench clamped to it in order to check with front and rear edge of blade.

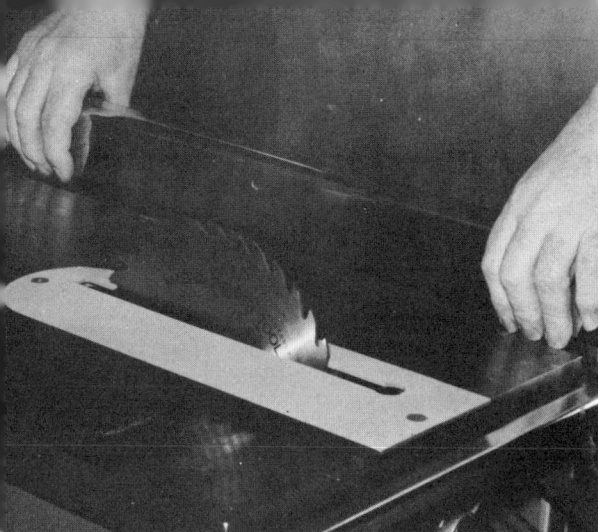

You can check the parallelism of the fence to the blade by measuring to blade, or by using fingers to see that fence is parallel with slots.

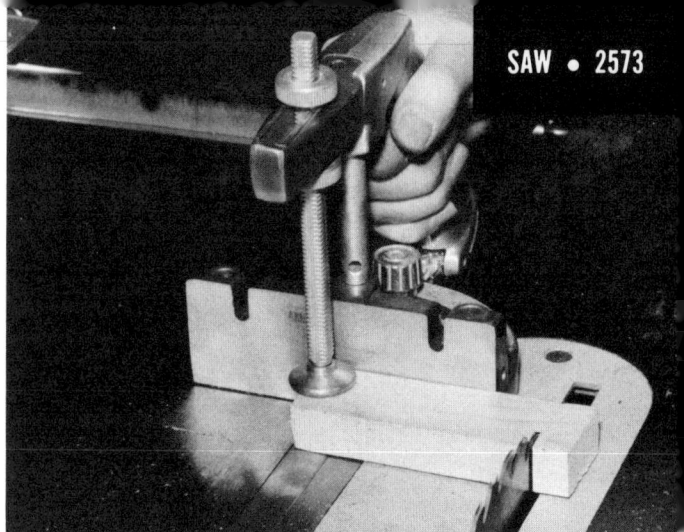

Miter gauge safety grip keeps fingers away from blade when crosscutting short pieces. Blade must not project more than inch above work.

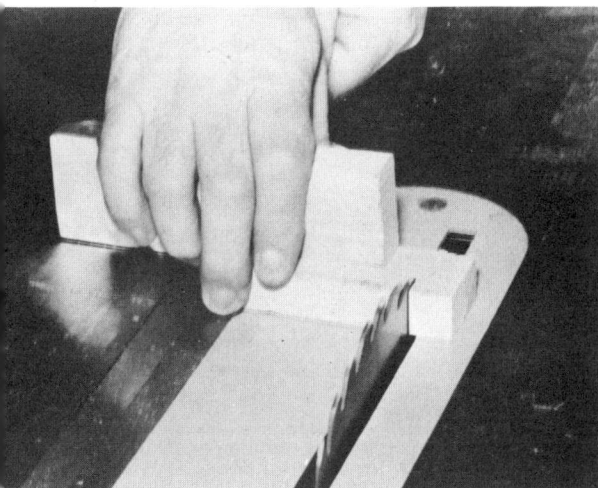

When sawing short piece of stock it's wise to support it by another block of wood. Remember that saw is sharp, and you've only ten fingers.

Additional support is given to work by means of a board that is screwed to the miter gauge. This extension simplifies crosscutting operations.

You can cut stock to exact lengths by inserting stop rods into the miter gauge. Never reach across running saw to pick up pieces already cut.

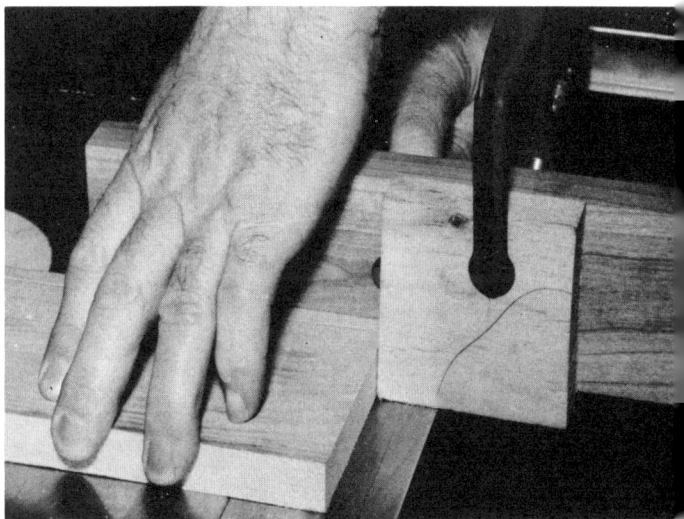

A block clamped to the miter gauge extension may also be used to cut stock to exact length. Always remove any extra tools or equipment on saw table.

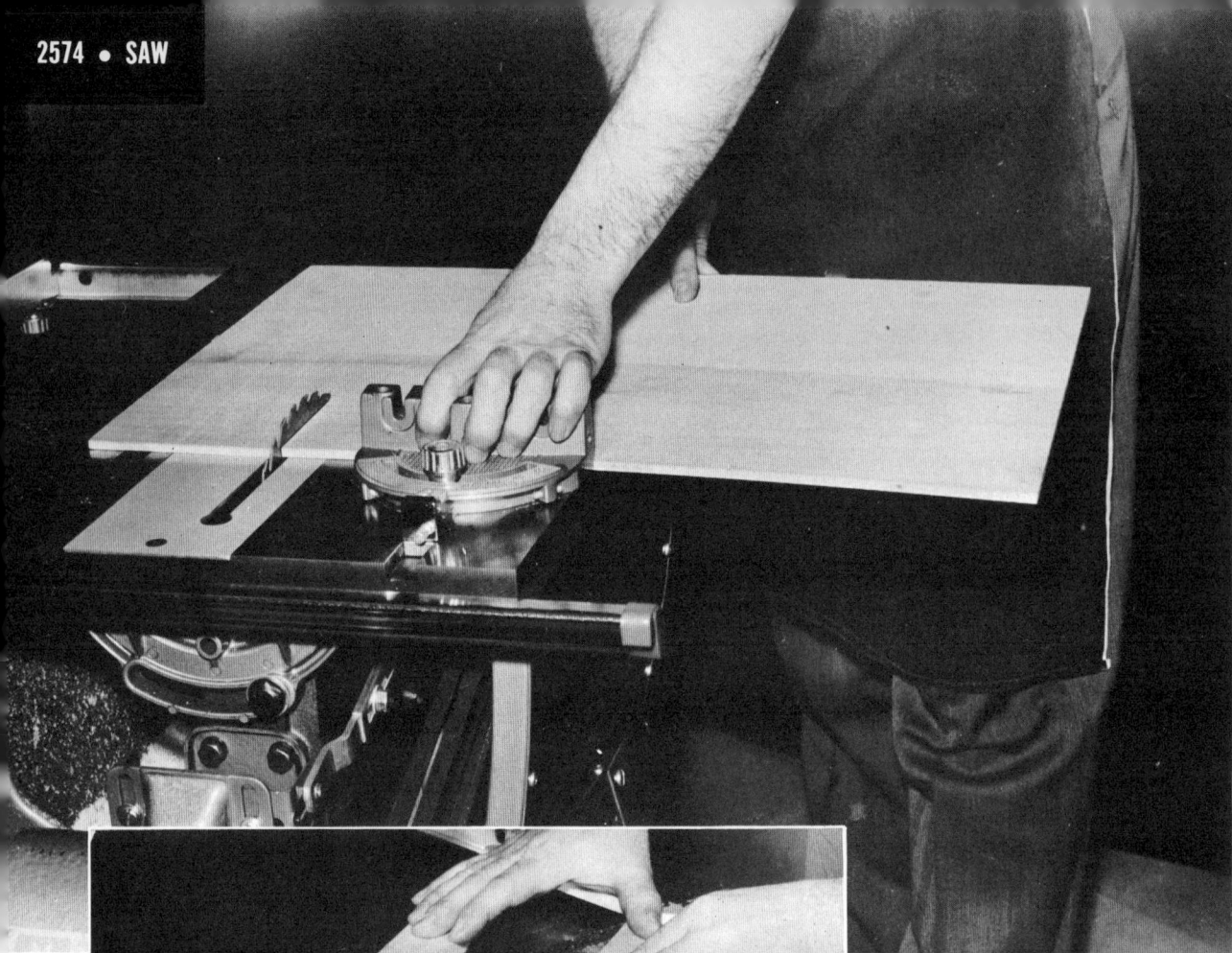

Problem of crosscutting wide stock is simplified if you just use the miter gauge backwards, as operator is demonstrating above.

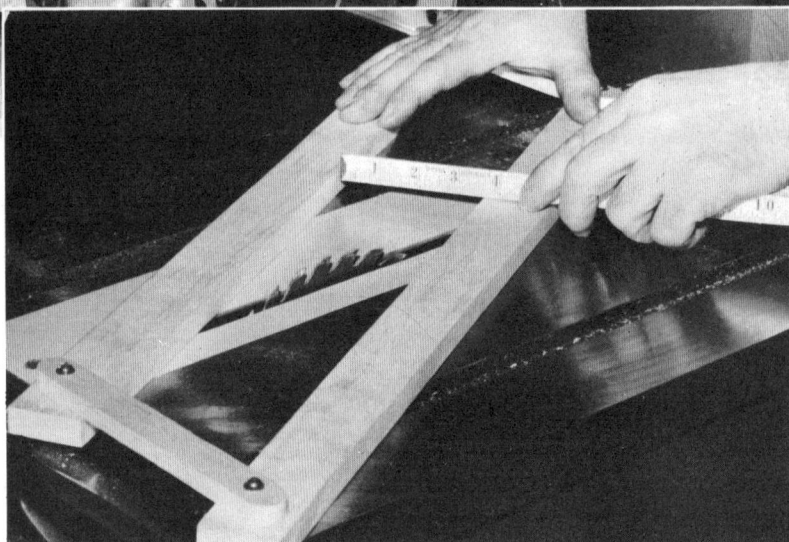

To set the saw for a cove cut use parallel rule. The inside measurement being taken equals diameter of the desired cut.

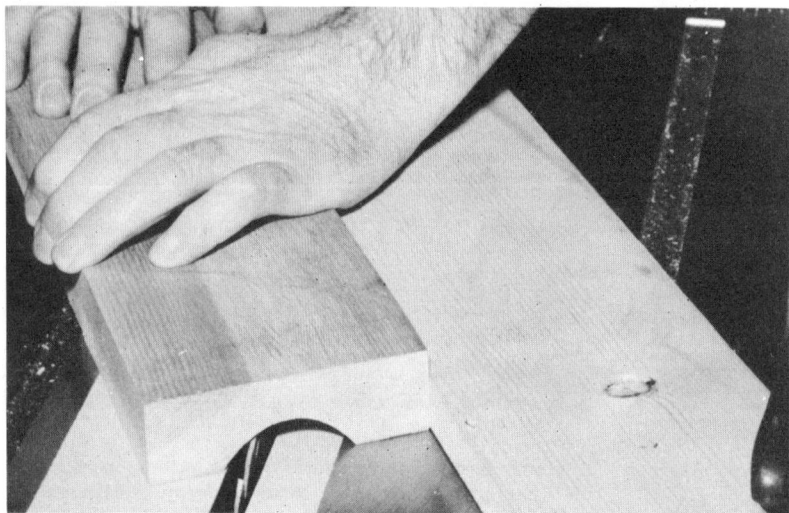

Make cove cut by feeding work across blade at angle guided by board clamped to table. Tilt and angle determine other shapes.

Use adjustable jig to cut wedges. Same jig may be used for cutting other tapers.

Center, a dovetail taper is being cut in wide board, so that it may be fitted with dove-tail key to prevent warping.

You will need a tenoning jig when cutting this joint. You can buy, or make it yourself.

ings, ornamental moldings, coves, rabbets and tenons.

Abrasive wheels may be mounted in place of the regular saw blade, but they should always be backed with heavy paper washers. Aluminum oxide is used to cut steel and non-ferrous metals. Silicon carbide cuts glass, porcelain, plastics and hard rubber. Sanding may also be done by means of a steel sanding wheel on which an abrasive disk is cemented. A guard should always be used.

Ripping, crosscutting, cutting miters and resawing are probably the basic fundamental operations that are performed on the circular saw. They are easily and quickly mastered. In ripping, or cutting lengthwise with the grain, the stock should have one straight or planed edge which is held snug against the fence while the wood is fed through the saw. If the work is wide and has a raw edge, it may be successfully ripped by clamping a straight-edge cleat to the under side in such a manner that it will ride against the edge of the table. A narrower board may be held to a wider baseboard with anchor pins, then both fed through, the base and the board being held snug against the rip fence.

Long boards should be run over some kind of roller support or a helper, or "tail man," should hold it as it leaves the machine. Work less than three inches wide should be fed with a push stick.

Crosscutting is used for the squaring or trimming of ends, the cutting of stock to

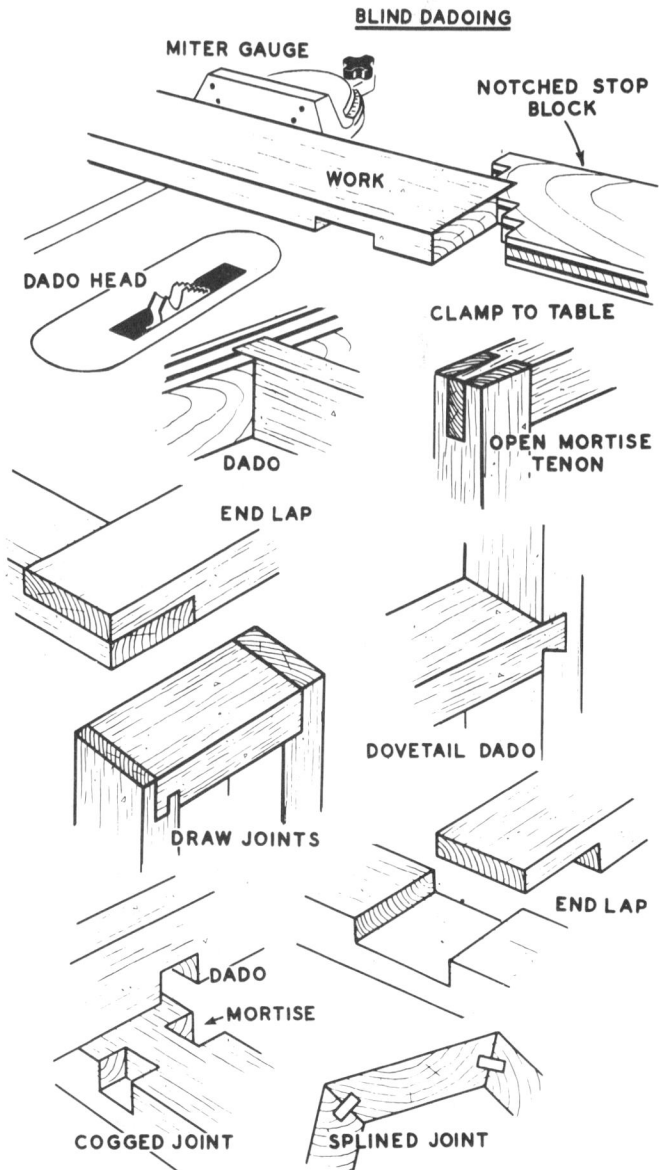

BLIND DADOING

MITER GAUGE

NOTCHED STOP BLOCK

WORK

DADO HEAD

CLAMP TO TABLE

DADO

OPEN MORTISE TENON

END LAP

DOVETAIL DADO

DRAW JOINTS

END LAP

DADO

MORTISE

COGGED JOINT

SPLINED JOINT

MITER GAUGE

WOOD FENCE
3/4" x 3-1/2"

SLOT FOR SAW

SHARP SCREWS AS
ANCHOR POINTS

MITER GAUGE

FENCE

45° BLOCKS

WORK

MITER JIG

BRACKET

3/4" STOCK

CLAMP WORK
TO JIG

CUT OUT
FOR FENCE

3/8" STOCK

1/8"

TENON JIG

ANGLE

3/4" STOCK

STOP

FENCE

CUT OUT FOR FENCE

BRACKET

TENON JIG

OUTSIDE
MOULD

CLAMP

WOOD FENCE

GUIDE

WORK

POINT OF CONTACT

CIRCLES

MOULDING CURVES

FENCE

FENCE

SAW BLADE

WORK

WORK

CUTTING CURVES

COVE CUTTING

CLAMP FENCE TO TABLE

WORK

BLADE TILTED

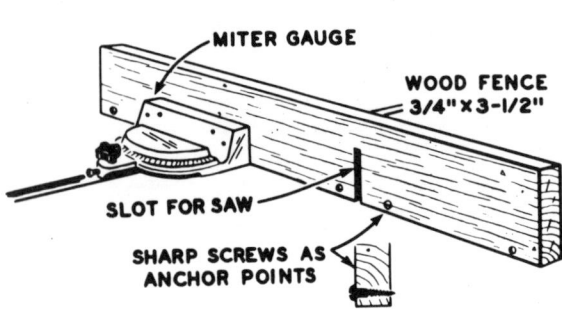

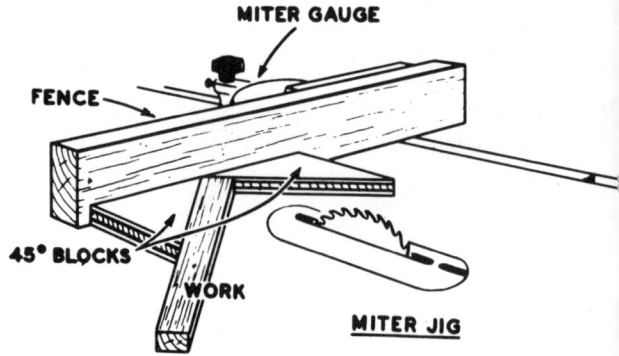

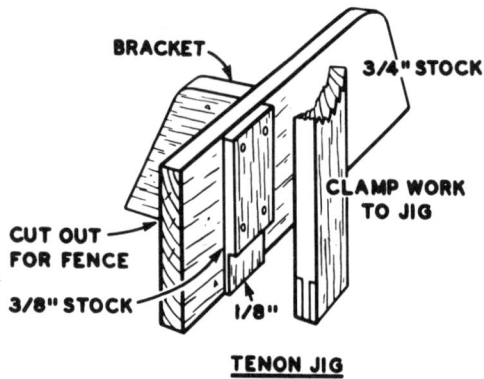

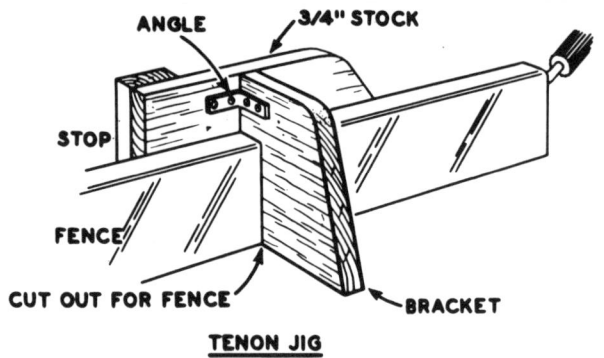

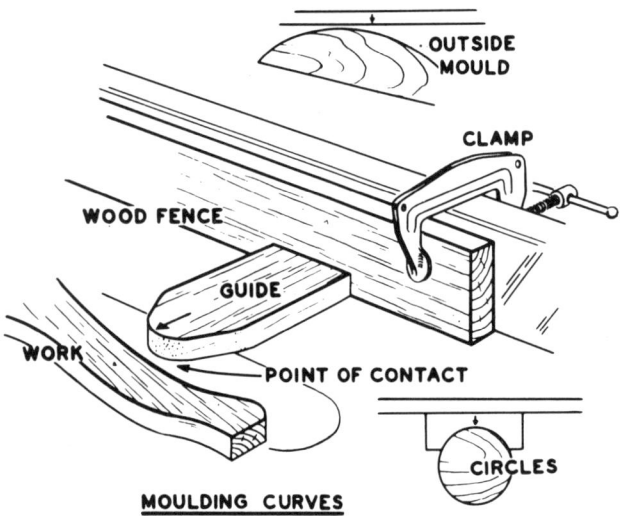

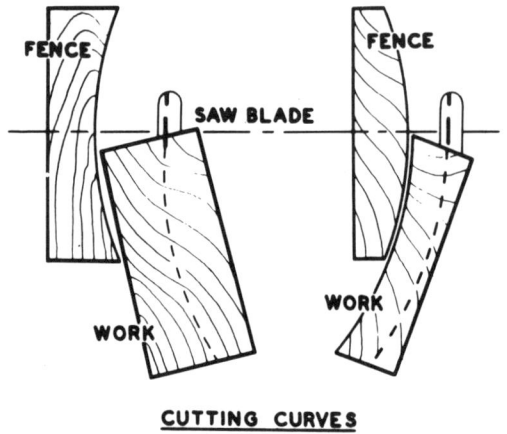

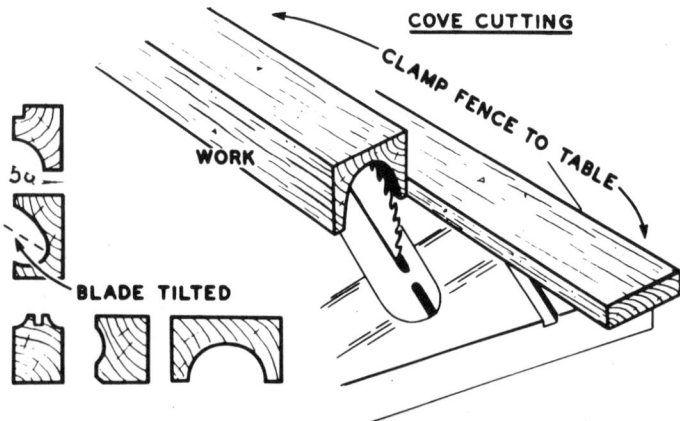

Diagrams on this page show you how to make certain needed accessories such as tenon jig, miter jig, which will help you in a number of operations. Often you can use scrap stock for these constructions. Also illustrated are methods of molding, cutting curves, and cove cutting. Be sure everything is securely clamped before starting work.

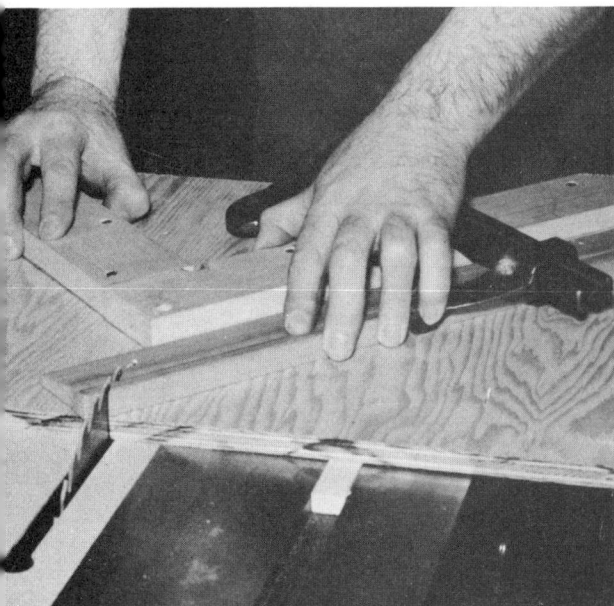

Mitering jig, in form of sliding table, permits molding to be cut at any point along its line.

When cutting thick board into thinner boards make maximum depth cut from opposite side.

length or for cutting duplicate lengths. All make use of the miter gauge set at right angles to the blade. In some cases, a wood facing is screwed to the face of the gauge to simplify the operation or to make it safer. Short work may be cut more safely with a hold-down, and wide stock may be cut with the miter gauge reversed.

Duplicate lengths are cut by clamping a short clearance block to the front end of the ripping fence, then setting the fence so that the block stops the work at the correct length but is not in contact with it as it reaches the blade. Another method is to use a metal stop rod fitted into the miter gauge. Still another is to clamp a stop block to the miter gauge or to the edge of the table.

Miter cuts are also made with the miter gauge or with one of several jigs that can be made. Either a clamping device for holding down work or small anchor pins in the wood facing on the miter gauge will help to prevent the stock from creeping.

A "featherboard" will be of great assistance when resawing. It is made from a board about four by ten inches, with parallel six-inch long cuts ¼ inch apart made in one end and with this ripped end cut at a 60° angle. The featherboard should be clamped to the saw table slightly in front of the blade so that its "fingers" or "feathers" hold the board firmly against the ripping fence. This same aid will prove useful for many other sawing operations.

Rabbets, grooves and dadoes may be

Block of wood clamped to fence, or extension, is used when making blind saw cut or groove.

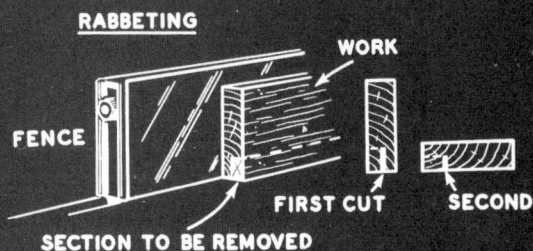

RABBETING

FENCE   WORK

FIRST CUT   SECOND

SECTION TO BE REMOVED

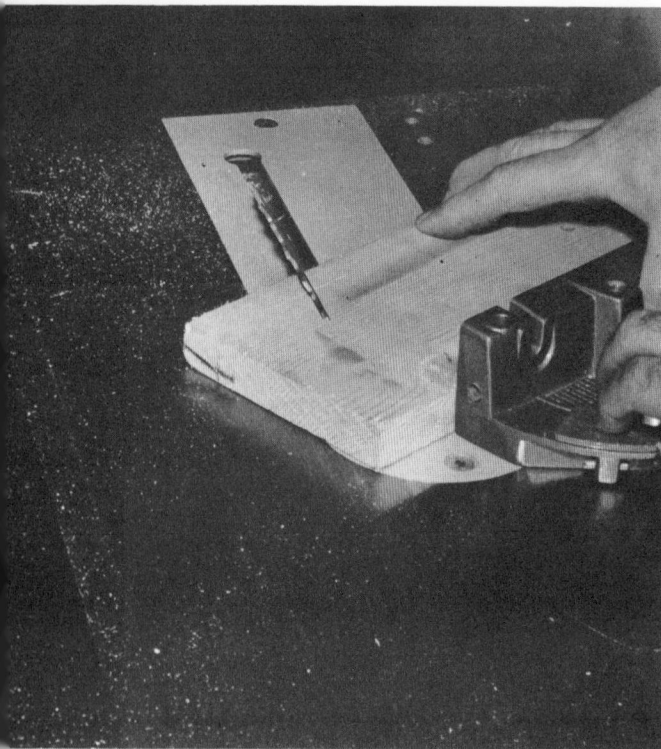

You can make a compound angle cut by setting the miter gauge at an angle with blade tilted.

Second cut in making rabbet should clean the corner. But never stand right behind blade.

Step board attached to guide board may be used for taper ripping, as needed for table legs.

made with two or more cuts with the regular blade or with one using the dado head. A groove, partially cut lengthwise or crosswise in a board, is known as a blind dado. Here, stops are used to locate the beginning and the end of cut.

A tenon, cut with the dado head is a safe, simple operation. When using a regular blade, shoulder cuts can be made using the miter gauge, but some type of jig to clamp the work is essential in making the cheek cuts. This can be a manufactured tenoning jig or one improvised with a "C" clamp.

Many special, more advanced operations may also be performed by the use of other accessories or jigs. These operations include tapered legs for tables, chairs or other furniture; dovetailed tapered grooves in the underside of a table; spline grooves for butt joints or for a miter joint, as used in boxes or chests, and multiple cutting with patterns.

Other advanced jobs are cove cuts for rounded corners or for molding, both made by passing the stock obliquely over the saw.

When you stop to think of it, you get an awful lot for your money when you spend it on a good circular saw. •

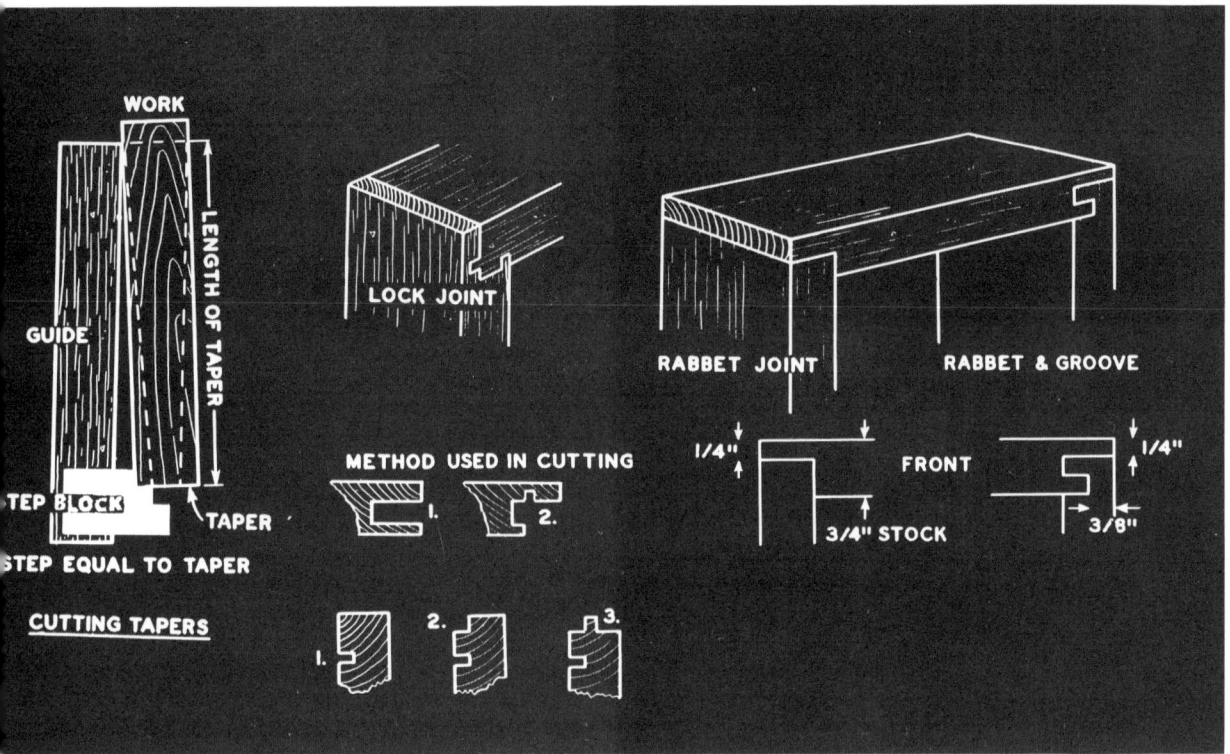

WORK

GUIDE

LENGTH OF TAPER

STEP BLOCK

TAPER

STEP EQUAL TO TAPER

CUTTING TAPERS

LOCK JOINT

METHOD USED IN CUTTING

1. 2.

1. 2. 3.

RABBET JOINT

RABBET & GROOVE

1/4"

FRONT

1/4"

3/4" STOCK

3/8"

Some of the more advanced, special operations which you can perform with the circular saw are here illustrated. The diagram shows you how to cut tapers, make lock, rabbet joints, rabbet and groove.

Box joint is usually cut with the dado head and a stop for accurately spacing the cuts.

Molding head, for use in finer cabinet work has interchangeable blades, can make decorative cuts.

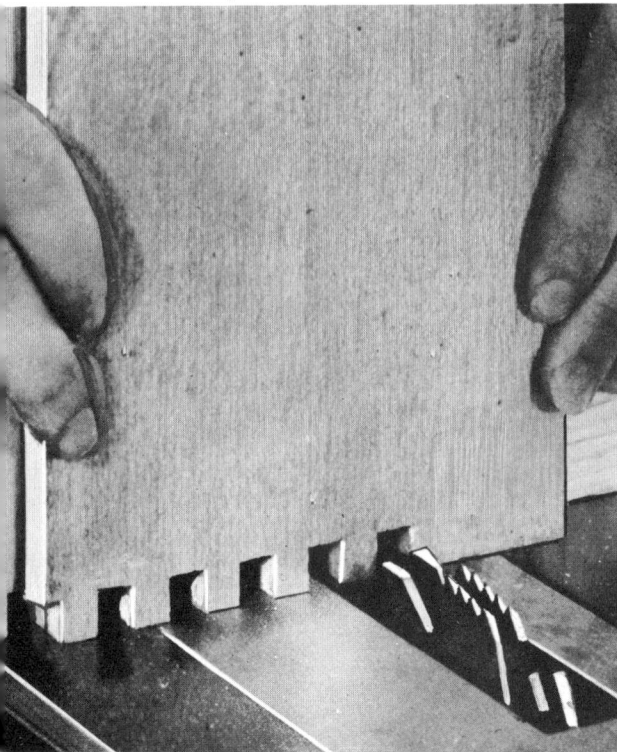

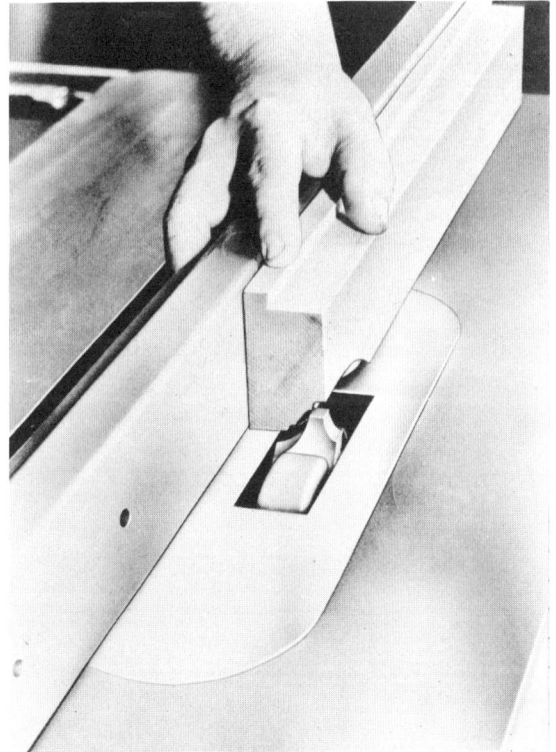

The Electric Hand Saw

You will find new uses for this wonderful tool every day. It will cross-cut, rip, bevel, and miter. For speedy, accurate cutting the portable electric hand saw is a shop essential.

THE full meaning of the word "power" is brought home to the user the first time he operates any kind of electric saw with a circular blade.

This is true whether it be a stationary saw of the table or radial arm type or the electric hand saw. There's something about the whizzing sound of a circular blade and the way it slices through a 2 by 4 that seems to proclaim unlimited capacity. It has a sort of "get out of my way, here I come" authority. As long as its power is given the proper respect, it will perform wonders in the saving of time and effort with no threat to the safety of the operator.

While the stationary power saw holds on to its acclaimed position as the work horse of the home or industrial shop, it has certain limitations because of the very fact that it is stationary. Where the saw must be brought to the work, rather than the work to the saw, the portable electric hand saw steps in to take over with its own brand of power.

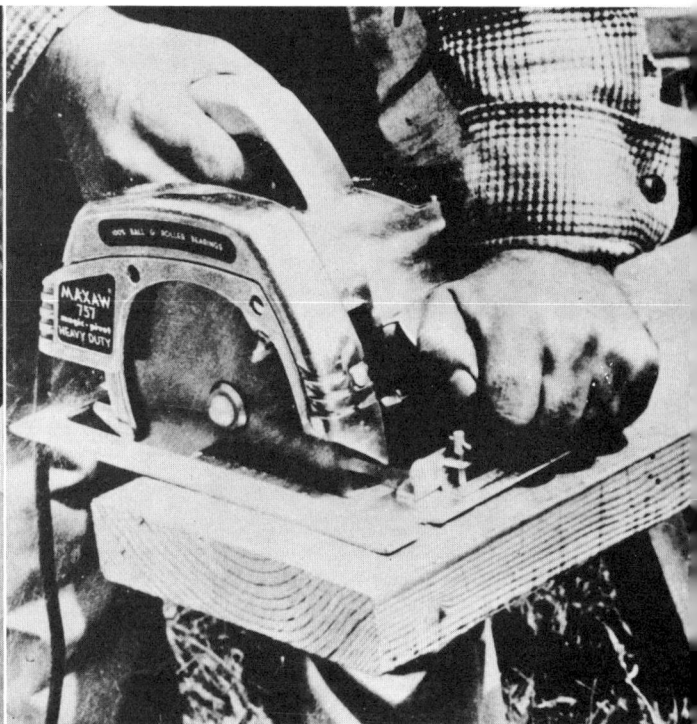

Left, this portable electric hand saw has guide attachment so that operator can rip a straight line. Right, crosscutting. Guide saw through work slowly, but steadily, with firm pressure, but not forcing.

It was the building trade which first discovered the cutting marvels that could be accomplished with the electric hand saw. It could be brought right to the building site and used for many different cutting operations, making difficult tasks easy and reducing the flow of perspiration to a minimum. The general public got an introduction to it when it was discovered that this labor-saving machine could be rented by the day or the week for tough construction projects. Before long, manufacturers put out models within the reach of the average pocketbook until finally, electric hand saws found resting places in home workshops and on farms throughout the country.

Where once the portable power saw would cut only wood, it now can be used for slicing ceramics, slate, marble, tile, nonferrous metals, transite, corrugated galvanized sheets and almost every kind of building material — provided that the proper blade or abrasive disc is used. There is even a special type of blade for cutting through flooring or sawing reclaimed lumber where nails might be encountered.

The diameter of the maximum size saw blade that can be used establishes the size of the machine for purposes of convenience. The blade sizes range from 4" to 12", with anything under 8" considered suitable for home use. The small machines weigh as

Electric saw zips through board 28 times faster than hand method. Light streak shows hand moves only 10 inches, and uses 87 times less effort.

little as 4 pounds, the large ones as much as 40 pounds. Most of the popular models are in the 6 to 12 pound range. Nearly all have universal motors for use on AC and DC and operate on the usual house voltage of 115, with larger voltages available in some stores or on order. The motor speed ranges from 1,800 to 5,500 rpm, the latter figure being about average for machines that take 6-inch and 7-inch blades.

Different manufacturers use different types of guards on their saws to decrease the possibility of accidents. Some tools have special clutch arrangements designed to eliminate kickbacks. More and more safety factors are being added to these saws and it is quite possible that several new devices will have been added between the time you read this and the time you look over any new models which reach the market.

Electric hand saws operate with the use of a trigger switch so that a relaxation of pressure will halt the motor immediately. The handle may be on top of the housing or, occasionally, at the back or somewhere between the two. With some saws, the cutting depth of the blade is regulated by adjusting a wing nut at the rear of the machine. With others, there are both front and rear adjustments, which can be used separately or together.

Heavy boards that are used so widely in garage, tool shed, greenhouse and other outdoor construction yield quickly to the electric hand saw.

Bevel cutting can be done at any angle between 45 and 90 degrees. Stock can be turned over and sawed a second time when single cut is not sufficient. For beginner work must be clamped, not held by hand.

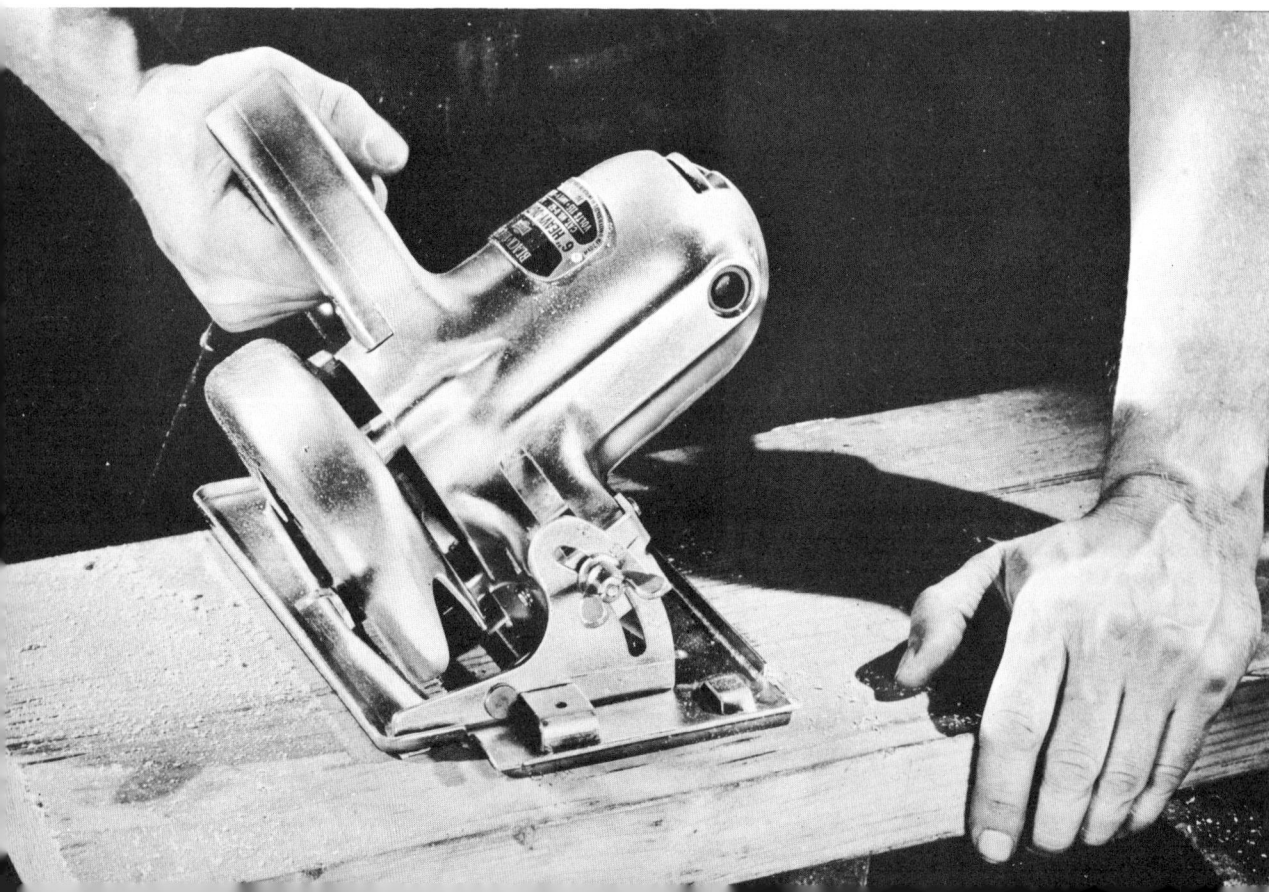

Left, miter cut. Be sure adjustments are secure. Right, bevel cuts require lower setting of blade.

The teeth of the blade should project a fraction of an inch below the work being cut. In this position the blade will make a smoother cut and is highly recommended even though some professionals permit the blade to project more than an inch below the material. While it is true that the deep blade makes a slightly faster cut, it has a tendency to kickback the work and must be regarded as a dangerous practice. After adjusting the blade to the proper depth, be sure that the wing nut is tightened securely.

Only after this blade adjustment has been made should the cord be plugged into the electric supply. The front of the saw base is then placed on the edge of the work so that the blade is lined up with the cutting line *but the blade teeth should not be touching the stock*. Now press the trigger and allow the motor to run freely a few seconds before starting the cut. The saw is guided through the work slowly but steadily, with firm pressure but without forcing. Too much force will slow the blade, cause undue wear on the motor and produce a rough cut.

We now come to what is one of the most important points in the operation of the electric hand saw to prevent sending it to the service shop for repairs. If the saw stalls while you are making a cut, do not

Note how operator keeps his right arm in line with blade, minimizing need for pressure to make cut.

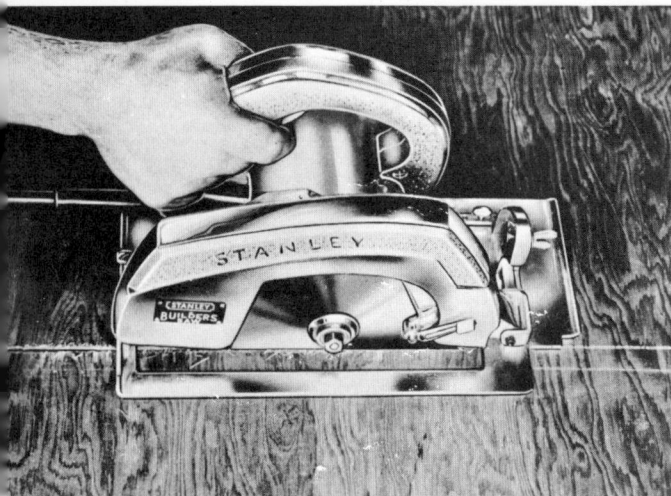

For pocket cut rest front of base against work, lower saw, then continue along the scribed line.

You can cut through a cinder block easily enough just by fitting your saw with an abrasive wheel.

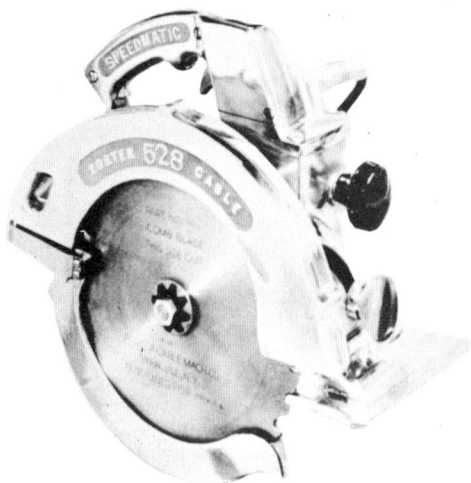

Porter-Cable's 8¼-in. saw with KickProof Clutch.

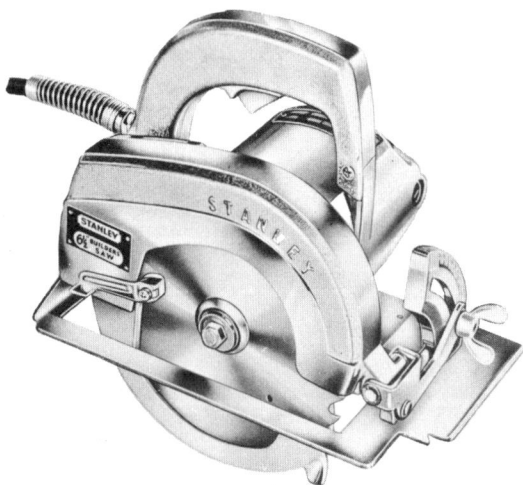

Stanley's 6½-in. saw with inverted reading scale. Both above will give excellent use to hobbyist.

release the trigger switch. While you are still pressing the switch, back up the saw a little, which will allow the blade to regain its momentum. You can now resume cutting or you can lift the saw, shut off the motor and stop for a moment. The thing to remember is *not to release the trigger switch while the saw is stalled in the stock.* Failure to observe this step may cause damage to the switch, dull the blade or put severe pressure on the motor—or all three at the same time.

The material being cut should be firmly anchored. Production workers often neglect this precaution, sometimes using knee support to hold the work steady and sometimes using hand pressure. This kind of cutting should be avoided by the beginner, who should see that the stock is clamped in place or otherwise attached securely.

When cutting any material which has one good side and one "bad" side, the good side should be face down. In that way, if there should be any splintered edges, they will occur on the "bad" side. This is the opposite of the standard procedure in making cuts with a table saw.

Always be certain to allow for the saw kerf when making measurements and then make the cut on the waste side of the scribed line. It is well to bear this in mind when buying lumber. If you need two pieces of 2 by 4, each 6 feet long to the fraction of an inch, you will not get them by cutting a 12-foot length of 2 by 4 in half. The saw cut will take up from ⅛ inch to ¼ inch, depending on the blade being used. This kind of precision calculation may not be necessary on some projects, yet it may be vital on others.

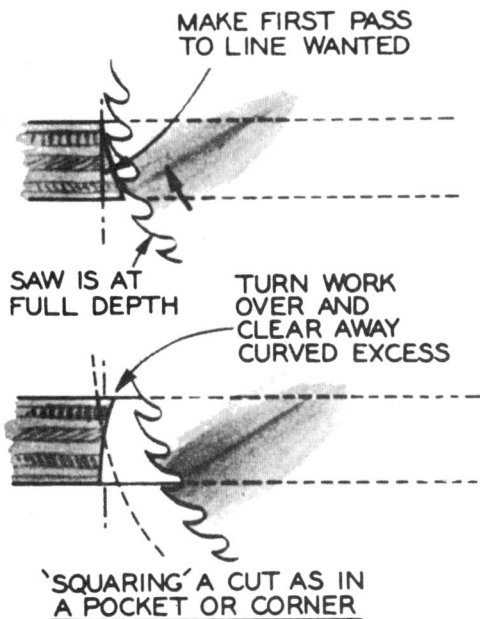

MAKE FIRST PASS TO LINE WANTED

SAW IS AT FULL DEPTH — TURN WORK OVER AND CLEAR AWAY CURVED EXCESS

'SQUARING' A CUT AS IN A POCKET OR CORNER

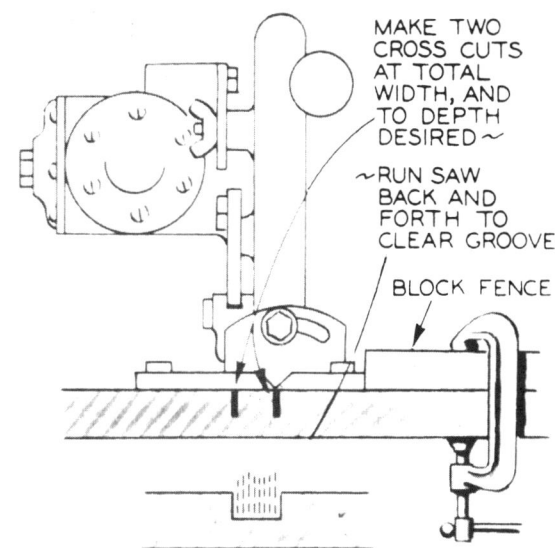

MAKE TWO CROSS CUTS AT TOTAL WIDTH, AND TO DEPTH DESIRED~

~RUN SAW BACK AND FORTH TO CLEAR GROOVE

BLOCK FENCE

CUTTING DADOS, GROOVES, DOVETAILS, ETC

Most saw guards are designed so that the guard swings back into safety position the second a cut is completed. To tie back the guard for any reason is courting trouble.

Learn to make similar types of cuts in bunches when working on a project. This, of course, is good practice in any kind of shopwork, eliminating much needless readjusting that can add a considerable amount of over-all time to the job. It's especially important when cutting materials of different thicknesses and when some will be straight, others bevel cuts. If your saw cuts to a depth of 2 inches, it will not cut that deeply when beveling. To take as an example, one popular model which does have a 2-inch depth cut will make a maximum cut of 1⅝ inches when set at 45 degrees. Another which cuts to $2\frac{13}{16}$ inches in straight sawing will go to a maximum depth of $2\frac{1}{16}$ inches at 45 degrees. In either straight or bevel cutting, the stock can be turned over and sawed a second time when a single cut will not suffice. Bevel cutting can be done at any angle between 45 and 90 degrees.

Making a Pocket Cut

A pocket cut is made within the interior of a board or, more often, a piece of plywood. It is made when you do not want to have any saw cut between the edge of the wood and the area being removed. After making certain that the blade is at the desired cutting depth, rest the front of the shoe, or base, against the work, gradually lowering the saw until it makes the first cut. Then, as the saw base is flat against the surface, continue along the scribed line

as in normal cutting. This will take a little practice in order to get sharp, clean corners and you occasionally may have to do a bit of finishing with a hand saw, but you soon will be able to do it neatly. Be sure both the saw and the stock are well supported for this operation.

Guided Ripping

In ripping long work, the best results will be obtained with the use of some sort of guide, either homemade or ready-made. Almost any straightedge that is tightly clamped will do, after you have first determined its proper position in relation to the cut being made. The saw is then moved along the straightedge with a firm but not excessive pressure. Accessory guides are available in different designs but all fulfill the principle of guiding the saws at pre-determined distances from the edges of the boards. They are adjustable for cutting widths up to 6, 7, 8 inches and sometimes more, with those which can be mounted on either side of the saw being more practical. Even when you have a rip fence guide, you sometimes may have to use a straightedge of your own (as, for instance, when the edge of the work piece is not straight), so it's a good idea to have one handy at all times. Over the long run, however, the manufactured rip fence guide will make your work a lot easier.

Rabbeting

Cutting a groove on the edge of a piece of wood, called a rabbet, is done in two operations. A saw cut first is made along the edge of the stock to the proper

A carbide-tipped blade is best when it comes to tough materials. It costs more but lasts longer.

Sensible craftsman always starts motor and lets blade come to full speed before starting to cut.

Cutting plastic to make a porch roof. Note use of guide to conduct saw blade along straight line.

depth. A second saw cut is made on the face of the board to remove the amount of wood necessary to complete the rabbet. This second step is a simple cutting motion similar to that previously explained in making ordinary saw cuts, except that the blade does not go all the way through the work. But the first operation may require a little ingenuity in order to give the saw enough support. You may find it possible to make the cut in the edge of the wood if the thickness of the stock is 2 inches or more. But the edge will not be sufficient support if it is less than 2 inches. In that event, you must, in one way or another, increase the thickness of the edge being cut. You can do this by nailing another piece of wood to the work piece to increase its thickness. Or you can nail the work piece itself to the side of a work table so that the extra thickness is developed that way. Any other method you use will suffice as long as you provide the saw with some support as it is making the cut.

Should you have to make a number of similar rabbets, make all the edge cuts first and all the face cuts second. There will be no necessity then to keep setting and resetting the projection adjustments.

Cutting Groves and Dadoes

Cutting a groove in the edge of stock is the same as the first step in the rabbeting operation; cutting a groove in the face is similar to the second step. A groove wider than the width of the blade, however, must be done gradually. One cut is made to a scribed line which will be one side of the groove; another cut is made to a scribed line which will be the other side of the groove. The wood in between the two is then removed with several successive cuts. The procedure is the same for making dadoes, or grooves against the grain. In all cuts of this type—even more so than when doing ordinary sawing—rip fence guides or guide jigs of some sort should be used.

Blades for Purposes

The most widely used of all saw blades is the *combination,* as it can be used equally well for crosscutting and ripping and thus eliminates frequent blade changing. Many persons who have had electric saws for years have never used any other type of blade.

For those who do a lot of ripping, there is a special ripping blade—and for those who do a lot of cross cutting, a special crosscutting blade. In each of these cases,

HANDLE

TRIGGER SWITCH

POWERCORD

MOTOR

TILT ADJUSTMENT

BLADE GUARD

BLADE

SAW TABLE

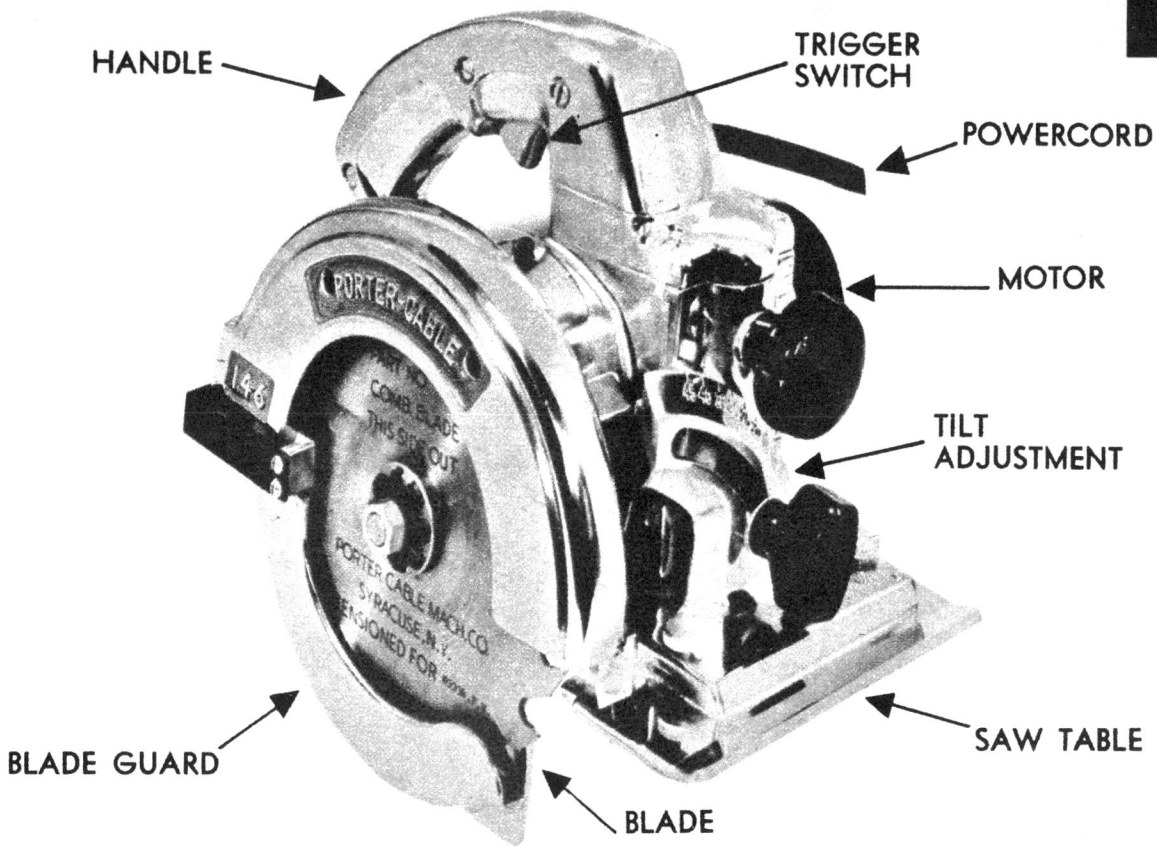

Anyone can quickly learn to operate this typical electric hand saw. Major adjustments are few, simple.

the special blade for the special purpose makes a slightly smoother cut than the combination blade. And for the smoothest cuts of all, there is the planer blade, used by craftsmen who must obtain the finest possible saw-cut finish.

Flooring blades are for use on jobs where occasional nails might be encountered. Abrasive discs are available for cutting through ceramics, slate, marble and materials of that nature and can be used for cutting thin gauge, non-ferrous metals, although metal-cutting blades can be obtained for that purpose. Abrasive discs also will cut corrugated galvanized sheets, but friction blades will do the same thing faster.

A carbide-tipped blade is the ultimate when it comes to handling tough materials. It costs more but will last longer than the ordinary blade because of the diamond-like hardness of the tips, which are brazed into a special alloy steel blade.

Attachments

Besides the rip fence guide mentioned earlier, there are many other attachments designed to make it easier to operate your portable electric hand saw with precision. There is a cross-cut guide, a bevel attachment, a protractor and numerous others. In addition, most saw manufac-

turers also make special saw tables so that the utility of the machine can be increased. These tables are made so that the saws can be attached underneath the table surfaces and used in the manner of stationary power saws.

Safety Tips

Follow the grounding procedure outlined in the section on the portable electric drill.

Never change a blade or make any adjustments or inspection of the saw while the electric plug is in the power supply.

Keep blades sharp. Dull blades may cause the saw to swerve or stall under pressure.

Make maximum use of the saw guard.

When working on hard materials or making deep cuts, hold the machine with both hands.

Always wear goggles when using the abrasive discs or metal-cutting blades.

Most shop accidents occur as a result of overconfidence. This seems to be even more the case with the professional than the amateur craftsman, who is more apt to be just a little afraid of the new power tool. In the case of working with a power saw it is well to be afraid. The important thing in operating any tool is always to keep your attention on what you are doing. •

This fence uses ¼" tempered Masonite in an off-balance pattern. Horizontal members are set to show through on side not covered by the panels.

Fences and Outdoor Screens

Decorate your property, give yourself privacy and mark the boundary lines

BOUNDARY fences, screens and dividers should be pictured as part of the overall plan of the house and lot. Many rush jobs in these areas have resulted in much wasted time, effort and money. For example, one family bought one of a few homes that had been constructed on an old walnut orchard. Their lot had about a dozen trees. They planned a patio near the house to be edged by a six-foot screen, figuring wisely that this would cut out the ground view and just leave the pretty, upper part of the trees visible. But then they ignored this fact and went ahead and put up a six foot, solid, boundary fence. There didn't seem much

point in putting up what amounted to a private fence within a private fence. They could have saved a lot of money had they used a simple rail fence to establish the boundary and they would have accomplished all their objectives.

Before you do any fencing make a scaled plan view of the property. Establish areas such as patio, storage yard, laundry yard and the place you'll keep the garbage can. Some of these areas you'll want accessible from both sides. Some of them you'll want to hide from your own eyes as well as your neighbor's. You'll want to think in terms of the traffic pattern you'll establish after you've moved in: garage to house, washing

Aluminum panels, framed by posts and rails, form an inside screen. Boundary fence on the property is a low economical rail fence. It would have served no purpose to put a high fence on the boundary, also.

ESTABLISH HEIGHTS AT FIRST POST

WITH LINE AND LEVEL MARK HEIGHT ON OTHER POSTS AFTER SETTING THEM UP

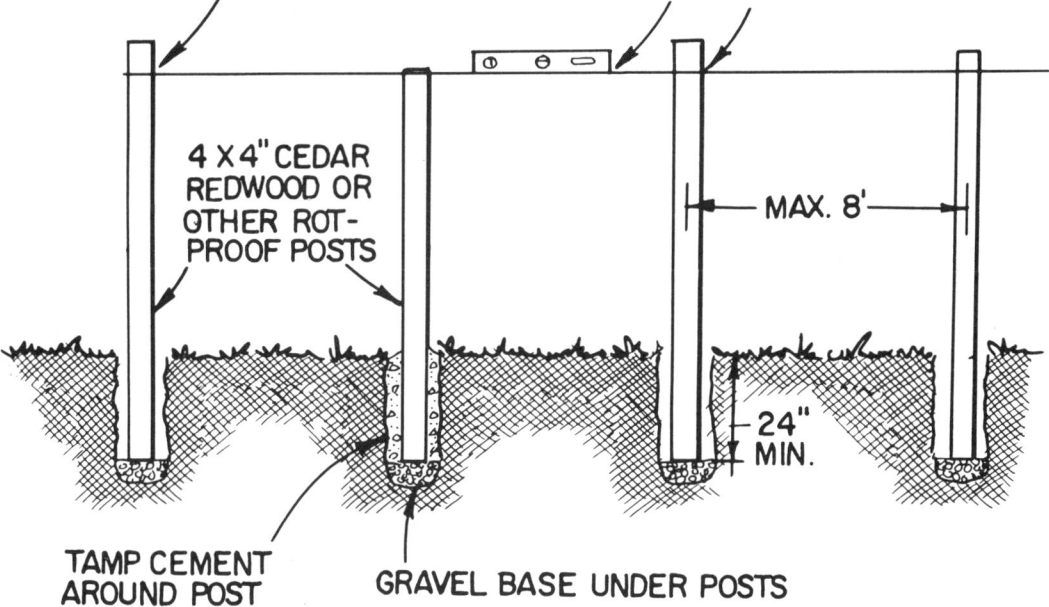

4 X 4" CEDAR REDWOOD OR OTHER ROT-PROOF POSTS

MAX. 8'

24" MIN.

TAMP CEMENT AROUND POST

GRAVEL BASE UNDER POSTS

FENCE ON A HILL

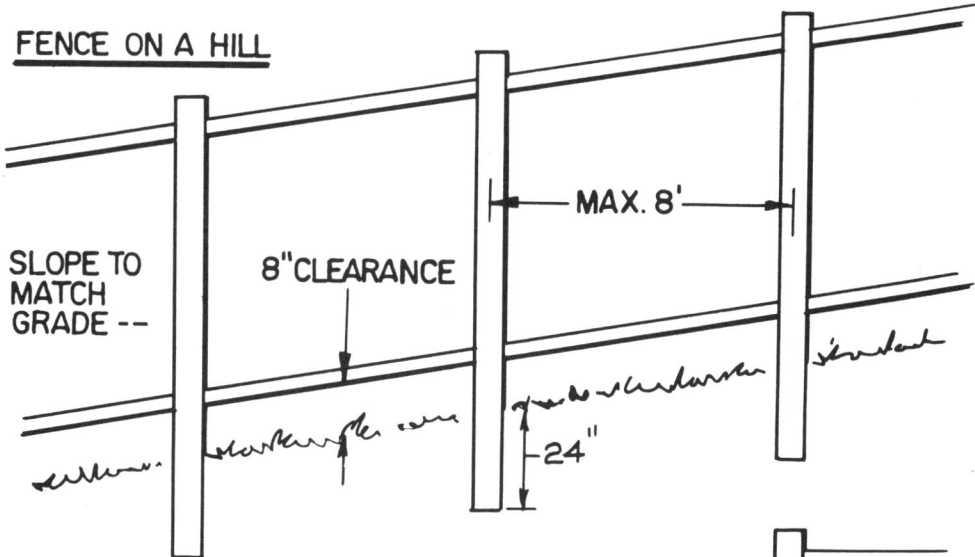

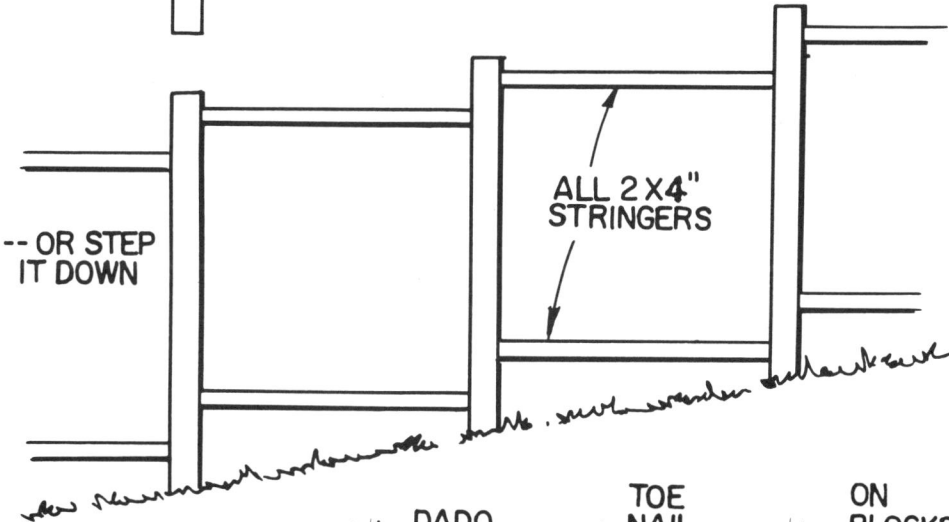

MAX. 8'

SLOPE TO MATCH GRADE --

8" CLEARANCE

24"

-- OR STEP IT DOWN

ALL 2 X 4" STRINGERS

JOINING STRINGERS TO POSTS →

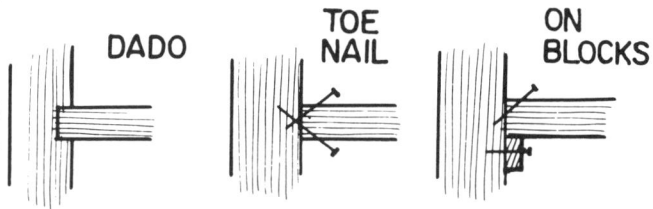

DADO

TOE NAIL

ON BLOCKS

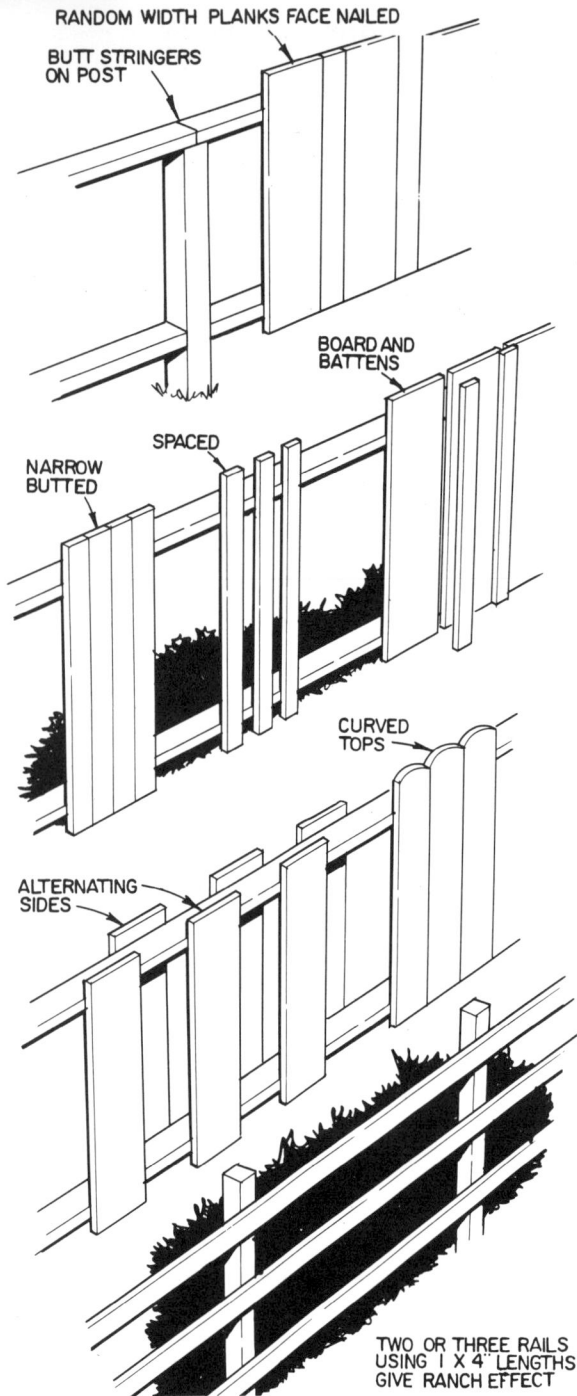

RANDOM WIDTH PLANKS FACE NAILED

BUTT STRINGERS ON POST

BOARD AND BATTENS

NARROW BUTTED

SPACED

CURVED TOPS

ALTERNATING SIDES

TWO OR THREE RAILS USING 1 X 4" LENGTHS GIVE RANCH EFFECT

machine to clothes line, kitchen to garbage can, and so on. If you'll be using garden tools and a wheelbarrow a storage yard for these will keep them handy, safe and unobtrusive, but since you'll want to move them easily, the gate into the storage yard should be wide enough to permit easy passage.

A fence or a screen should have a reason, and, often the reason will help decide placement of the fence, its size and its design.

Always check local codes before doing any designing. They will have some bear-

ing on fence height and even location. For safety reasons, a fence across your front yard will seldom be permitted as high as a fence you can build elsewhere. Equally important, be sure you know your property lines before digging that first hole. Build a fence on your neighbor's property and it will legally belong to him. Build it too far over on your own property and some-day you may have trouble re-establishing your true boundaries.

Be a good fence-neighbor. Many fence styles have a "good" and "bad" side. You can plan the bad side so your neighbor has

The Masonite fence above was planned so that air and light could pass through the frame to the children's play yard beyond.

Powered post-hole digger with a six-inch auger is the best and fastest way of forming holes that are perfect for 4x4 posts.

A fence is started by laying out a line inside boundary of your property. Stakes driven in soil will mark post locations.

This is a handsome, good-neighbor fence because it affords privacy, but doesn't look bad on the other side. Alternate panels of Ridgeline and Peg-Board Masonite are spaced to provide free air passage.

THESE POST TOPS WILL SHED WATER

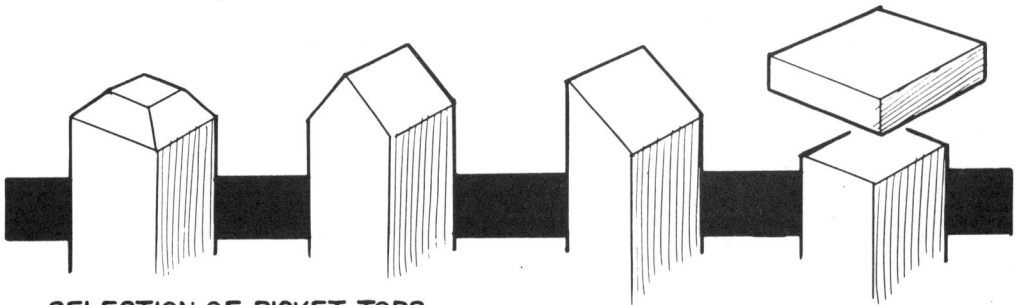

SELECTION OF PICKET TOPS

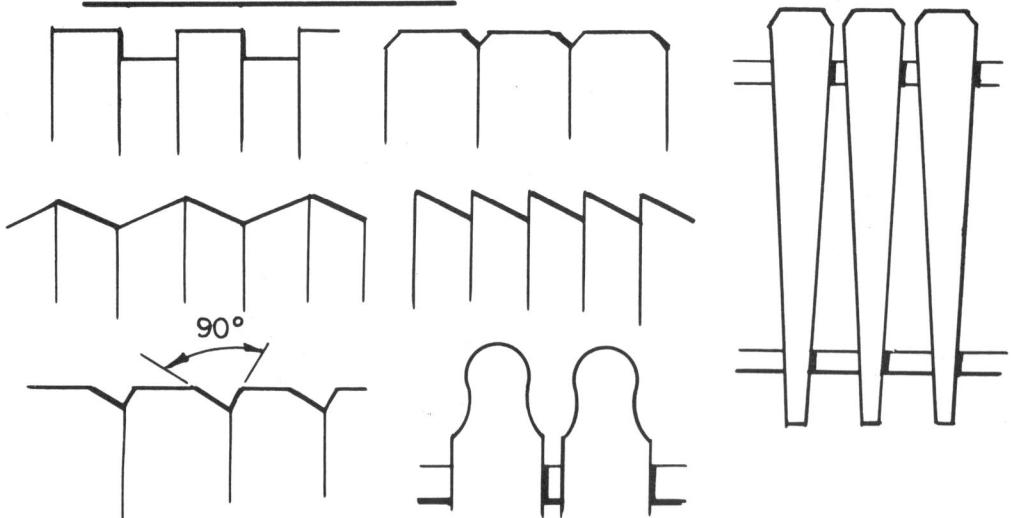

90°

The delightful patio, at left, is screened with Kaiser aluminum panels inset in 2x4 redwood frames. At right, the aluminum panels are used on both patio cover and screen. Note the swinging panels which can be closed should a breeze become annoying. Glamor treatments like these are not difficult projects.

3/8" EXTERIOR PLYWOOD

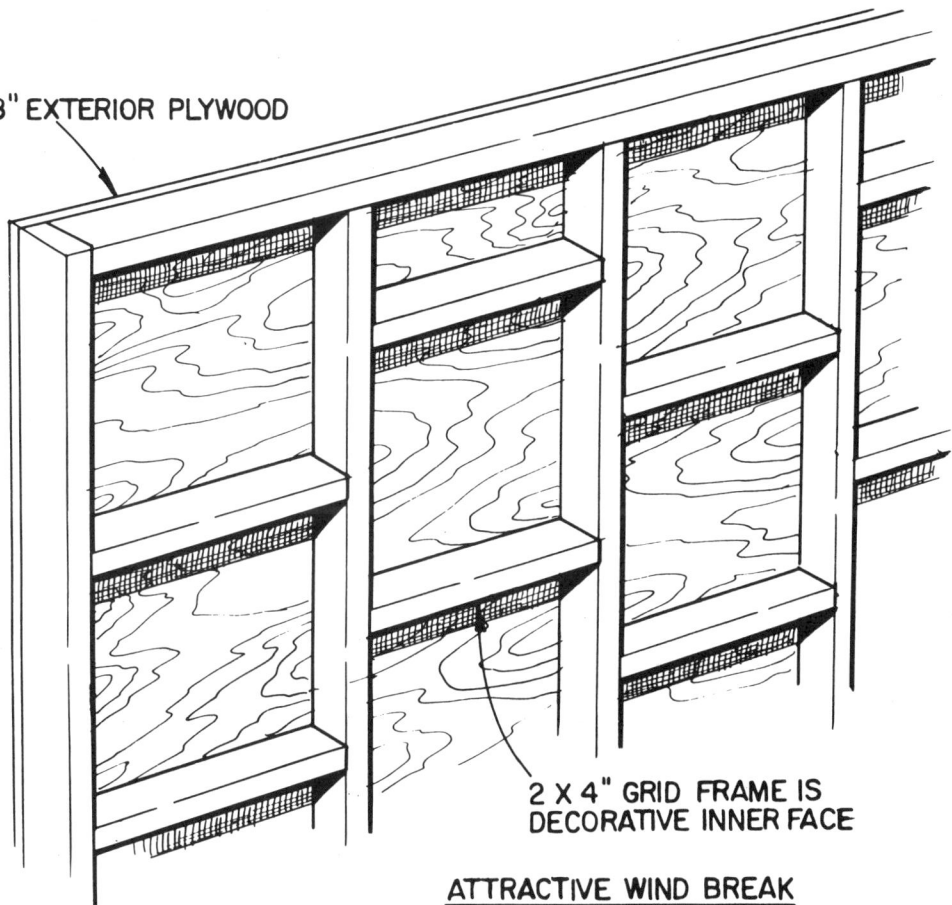

2 X 4" GRID FRAME IS DECORATIVE INNER FACE

ATTRACTIVE WIND BREAK

to look at it, but don't forget that the bad side becomes part of your over all property appearance. One way to get around this is to build a fence that looks good on both sides. One basic difference is this— a fence skeleton on which you hang a facing material. If you nail over the facing on one side, you have the exposed frame on the other. If you plan it so the facing is set inside the frame, then the fence will have a similar appearance on both sides.

This can cost more money and/or time and effort, but can sometimes be offset by working *with* your neighbor, each chipping in, with the understanding that the fence belongs to both of you.

A fence is a frame to which you attach a facing material. The material is usually wood, but it can be aluminum, Masonite, fiberglass, reeding, bamboo, etc. Regardless of what material you use to build it, all fences have three things in common—holes for posts, posts, and horizontal members between posts (rails).

Holes for the posts can be dug with a shovel (a small round-nose type is good) or with a special tool called a clamshell. They can also be bored with a powered post-hole digger. The latter is by far the best and fastest way to get the holes done, especially in quantity. You can rent a powered digger at reasonable cost, but don't expect to put your wife on one end of it. This machine requires two huskies.

Posts are set in the holes on a shallow gravel bed. Sometimes they are back-filled with the same dirt that was removed. If you do this, be sure to use a wood preservative on the post.

A post will be substantially firmer if you fill the hole with concrete instead of dirt.

Don't attempt to dig each hole to an exact depth or to precut the posts to exact height. Dig the holes reasonably close in depth and leave the posts oversize. After they are set, you can stretch a line from the first one to the last one and cut off excess at the top. Use a level to assure plumbness of each post, and use temporary braces to hold the alignment until the concrete sets. Many times posts and rails are assembled before the post holes are refilled. This is okay but it seems like a lot more trouble.

Rails come next and these should be cut to exact size between each set of posts. It isn't likely that your post spacing will be so accurate you can precut all the rails. If the post tops are not covered with a rail, be sure to cut them in one of the ways suggested in the drawings so water will drain off. •

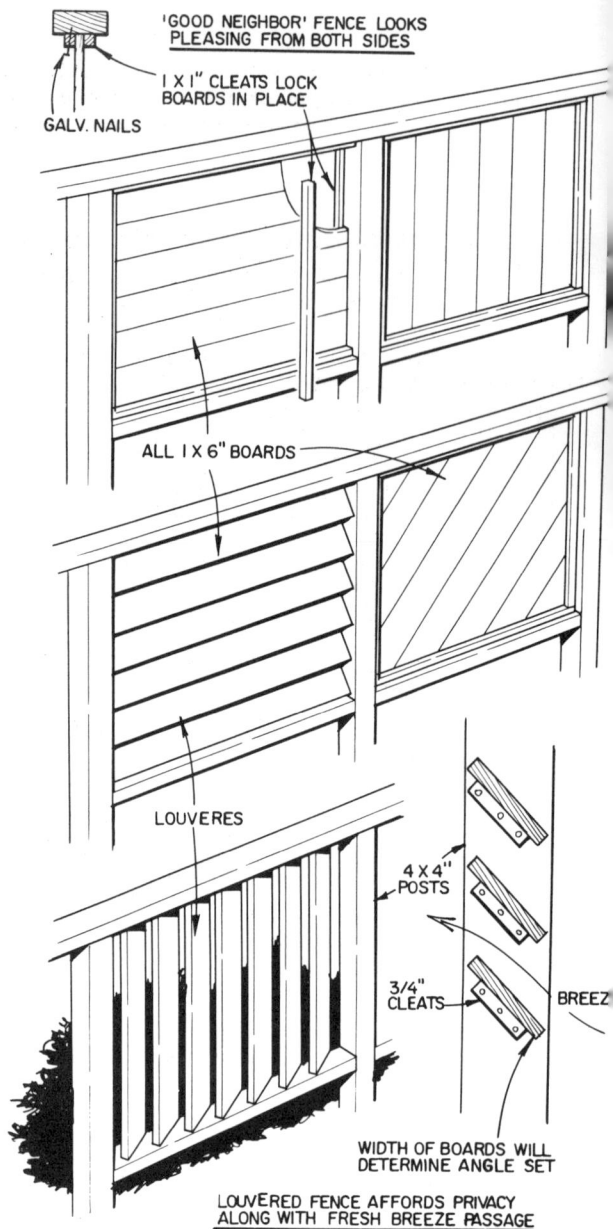

'GOOD NEIGHBOR' FENCE LOOKS PLEASING FROM BOTH SIDES

1 X 1" CLEATS LOCK BOARDS IN PLACE

GALV. NAILS

ALL 1 X 6" BOARDS

LOUVERES

4 X 4" POSTS

3/4" CLEATS

BREEZ

WIDTH OF BOARDS WILL DETERMINE ANGLE SET

LOUVERED FENCE AFFORDS PRIVACY ALONG WITH FRESH BREEZE PASSAGE

Fences and gates don't always have to match, as effectively demonstrated here. Filon gate provides an interesting break in an all-wood fence.

You can't beat this style of fence for neatness. Simple framing, set in the lawn off the concrete area, permits the utilization of the entire patio.

To cut out an uninteresting part of the yard from your own view, consider a screen. Translucent fiberglass does the job without cutting out any light.

Indoor Screens

They can be stationary or movable; used as a wall or to divide a room

WALLS and partitions are erected to close off an area and to provide privacy. Screens and dividers are visual barriers, and in a sense, traffic directors. A screen in a large room can direct traffic from an entry to the bedroom end of the house without destroying the spacious feeling of a room like a wall would do.

Screens are usually light in feeling even though the materials used to make it may be opaque. The screens can be fixed or movable, decorative and functional. They should not look like another wall even

Left, sculptured screen is used to form a private entrance into the house. Screened-in passageway has now literally become part of the actual house.

Rather than build a wall to separate this small music area from the rest of the room, a divider-screen was used for better acoustical qualities.

In the above photo, four panels of Sculptureboard, made by Terminal Industries, are seen set between vertical division strips. At left, another unusual effect is created by using outdoor materials for indoor decorating purposes. The screen partition here is made out of Diamond Rib aluminum panels which add dramatic metallic luster.

In photo, top right, a wall of Sculptureboard makes this patio a screened-in outdoor area while maintaining a mood of indoor privacy. The open lattice work of the screen allows a free flow of air and light whereas a solid wall would forbid an atmosphere of outdoors. The photo, bottom right, shows the wall from outside—very attractive.

SCULPTURE BOARD

CONTINUOUS PANELS

EDGE FRAME

4" X 4" POSTS

DIVIDE!

A — A

TYPICAL CORNERS

RABBET   MITER

SEC. A-A

CABINET DOOR

1" X 2" FRAME IS DADOED

BUTT FIT HERE

BULLET CATCH

HOLE

NOTCH INTO POSTS

DOWEL

STOP BLOCK GLUED ON AS LEG BRACE

TABLE LEGS STORE HERE

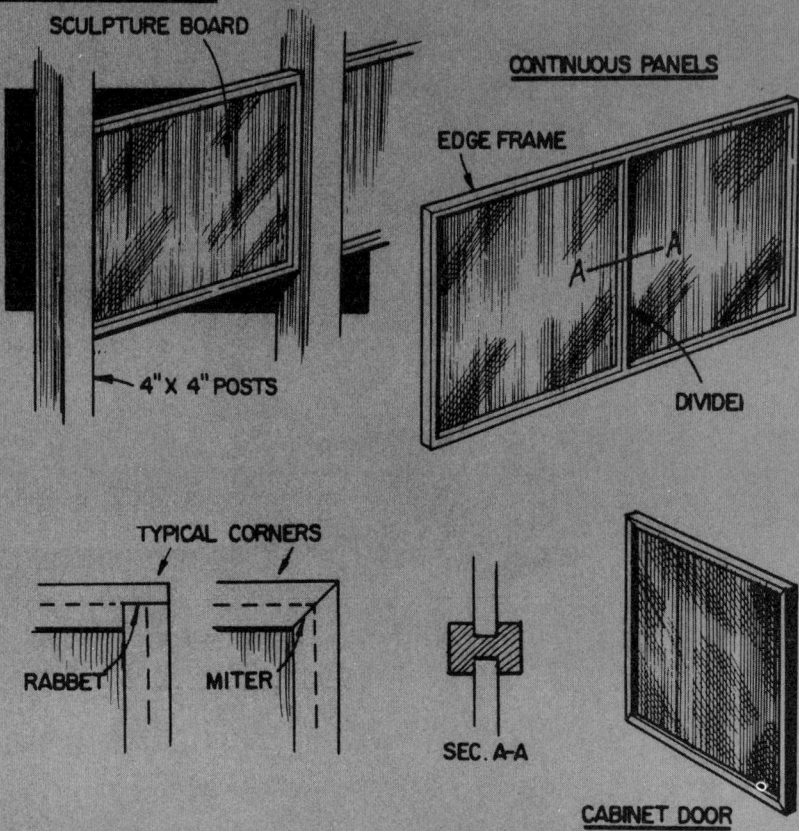

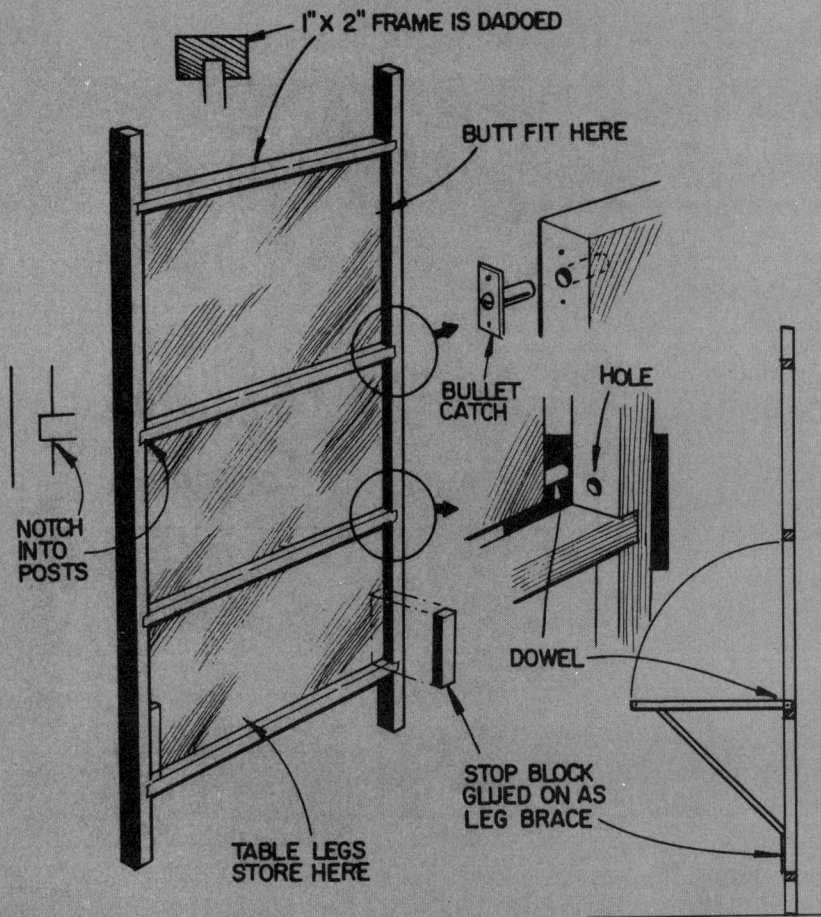

Notice how even a small screen such as the one above can make two rooms. Screen uses same material used on walls, Celp-Rok wallboard. The construction details are at left.

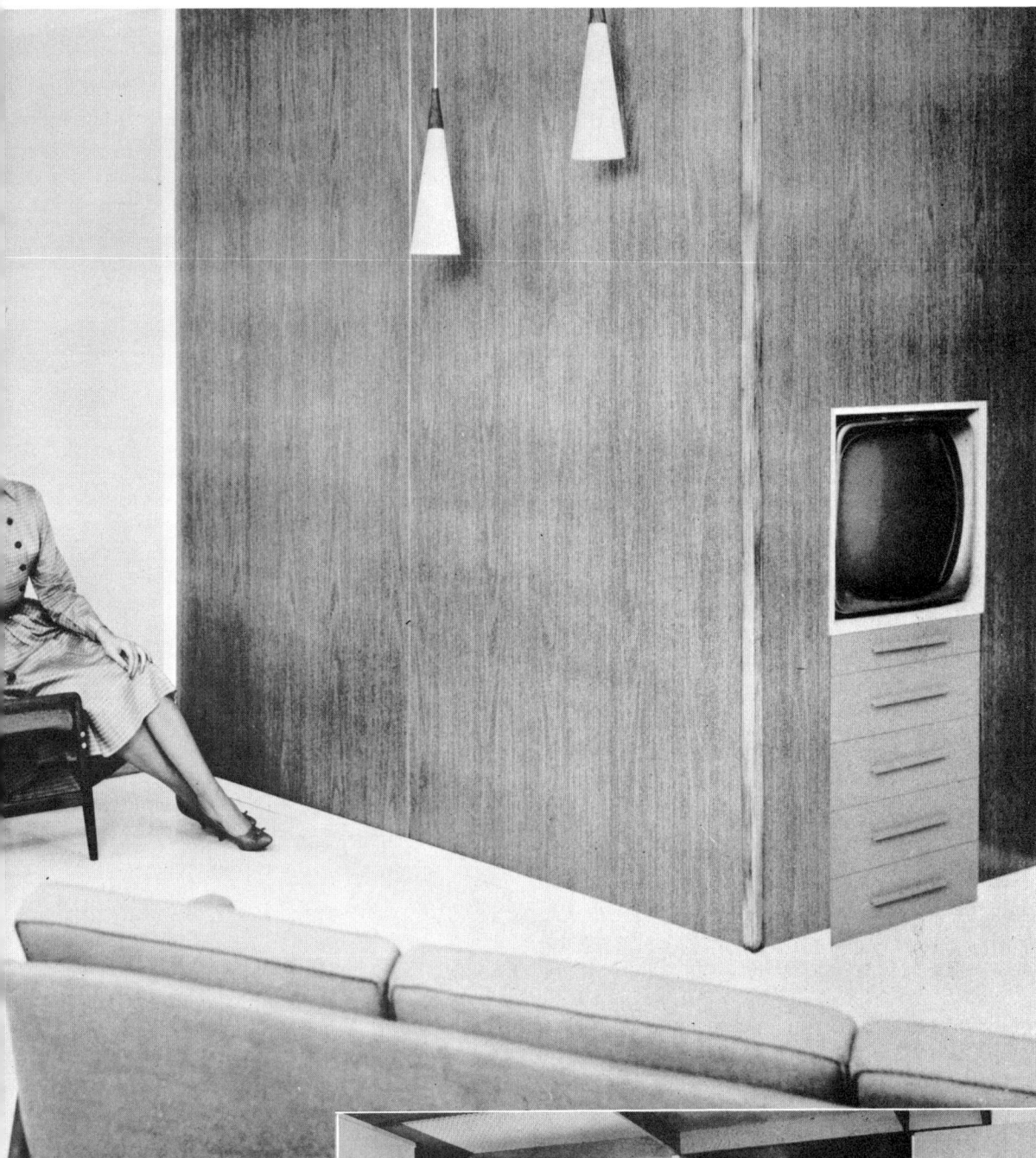

This easy-to-make screen, designed by Architect Edward H. Ficlett, combines solid fir plywood panels and perforated hardboard to define the breakfast nook, just off a kitchen.

Photo on opposite page shows how decorative and functional a screen can be even in the kitchen. Tempered hardboard panels withstand rough usage.

When constructing a three-panel hinged screen it is best to paint the perforated hardboard before attaching it to the frame. Each frame is made of two 6-foot lengths and two 12½-inch lengths of 1x2 stock. Put frames together on an even floor. Next, lay a strip of canvas or heavy press cloth for the hinge along one side of the frame, leaving half of it draped over for the next frame. Now tack a panel of the prepainted ⅛-inch perforated hardboard over the hinge and frame with decorative upholstery nails leaving one half of the canvas hinge exposed for the next panel.

A second frame, duplicating the first one (see top left) is positioned, next. Place the remaining half of canvas hinge over the second frame and attach a second sheet of hardboard, nailing through the canvas into the frame. With one side of two panels finished, turn completed part of the screen over to install the remaining part of the second hinge to the reverse side of the third frame. Screen will be reversible since a covering of hardboard goes on both sides. Above, the back side of two panels is shown completed and final frame is being formed with hinge in place. If preferred, a different type of hardboard can be used on reverse side of screen, perhaps a solid type in place of a perforated one, or perhaps one of different color.

though wall covering materials can be utilized in their construction. Usually, there is an open space between the top of the screen and the ceiling, and many times there is also an opening at the bottom.

A screen can be an extensive storage wall, but this would fall more into the category of "dividers".

There are many materials that can be used to make distinctive screens. Sheet plastics are used extensively for Shoji-type screens. Perforated hardboards are functional as well as decorative. Plywoods can be used solid, or cut to provide patterns. Plastic-covered rope (modern clothes line) can be strung to provide interesting effects. There are ready-made plastic panels that hook together so you can size a screen to suit.

"Sculptureboard" is a pierced hardboard, manufactured in many patterns and designs, that is available in large panels, will permit light and air to pass through, yet provides privacy.

The ideas offered here are to spark your own imagination since a screen should be designed and constructed to suit surrounding decor. The three-panel hinged screen is an exception since a project of this type can find a use in many rooms.

But the important thing is to select materials carefully. Since there is such a great variety you should have no trouble getting exactly what you want. •

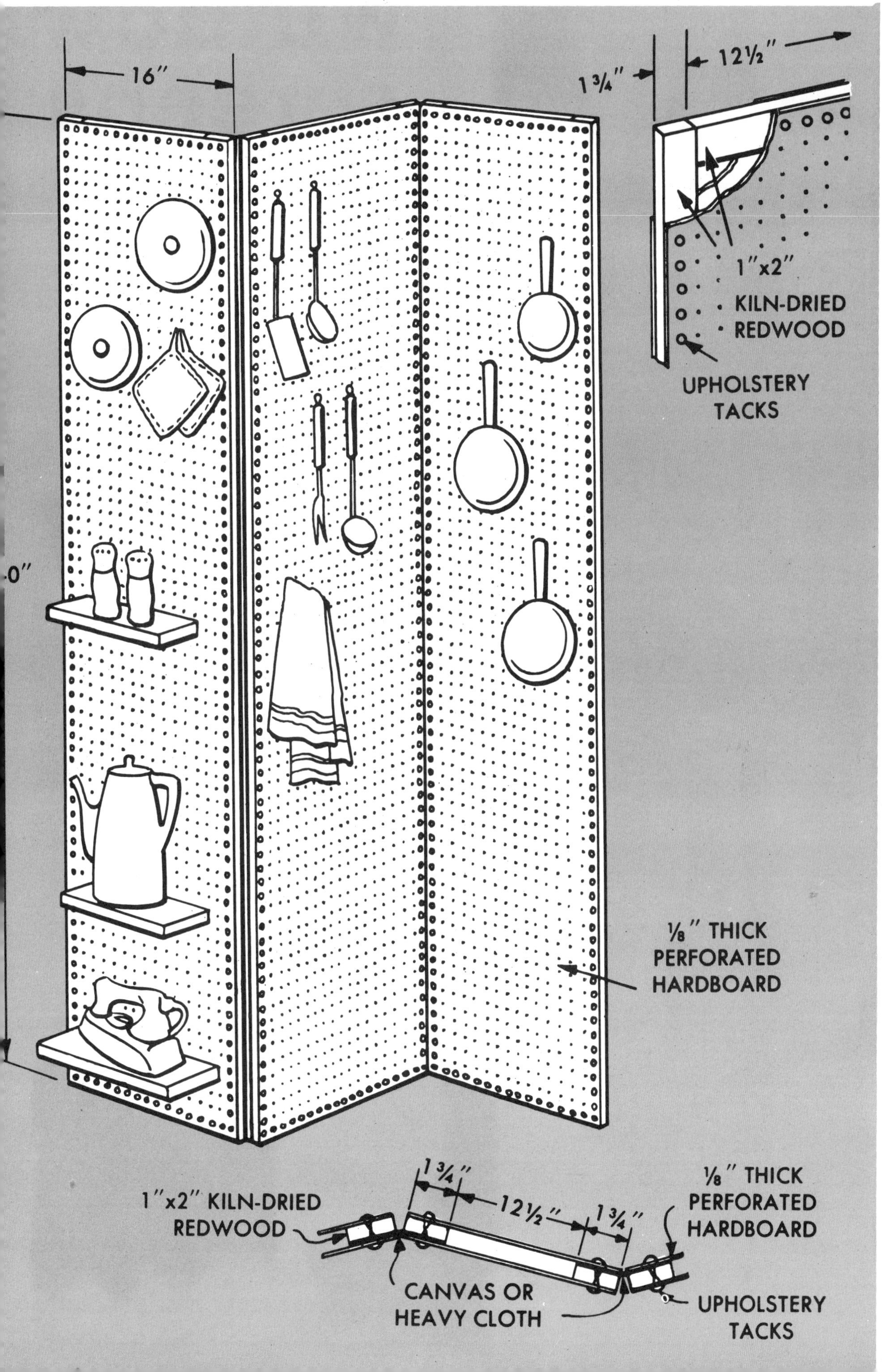

16″

1 3/4″

12 1/2″

1″x2″
KILN-DRIED
REDWOOD

UPHOLSTERY
TACKS

-0″

1/8″ THICK
PERFORATED
HARDBOARD

1″x2″ KILN-DRIED
REDWOOD

1 3/4″

12 1/2″

1 3/4″

1/8″ THICK
PERFORATED
HARDBOARD

CANVAS OR
HEAVY CLOTH

UPHOLSTERY
TACKS

window screens

New developments in screening materials and improved designs in manufactured units make it easy for you to protect your home against insect invasion.

By Clarence Martin

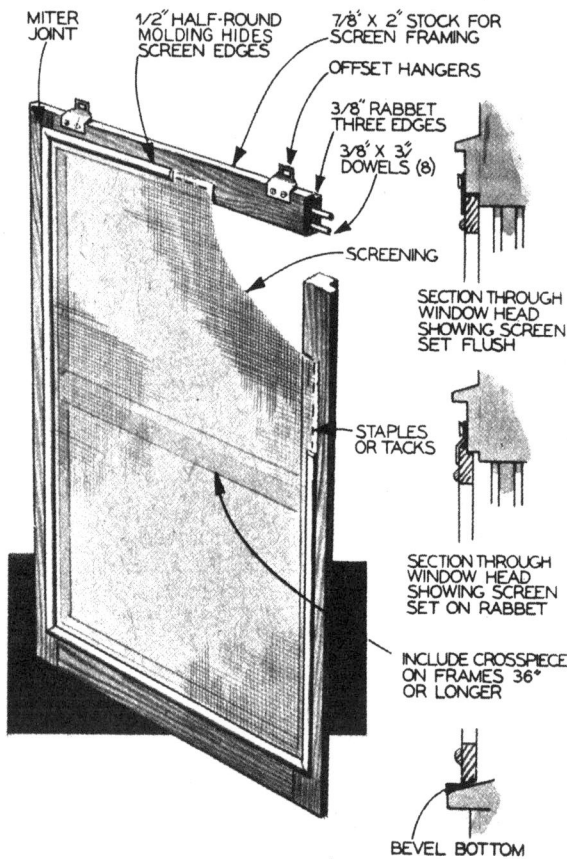

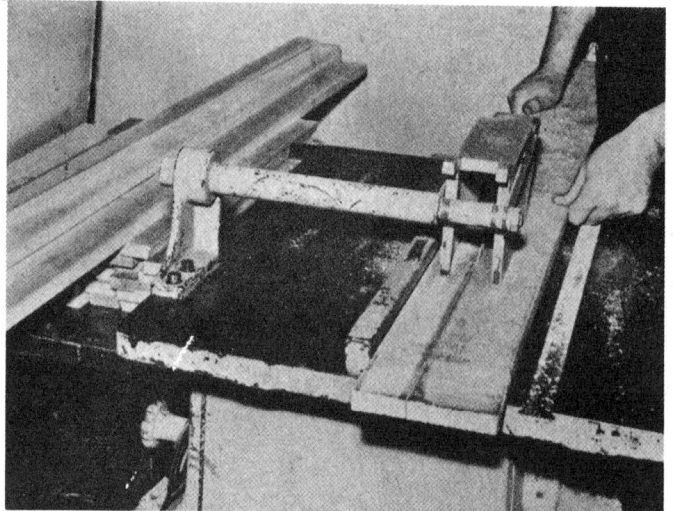

MITER JOINT

1/2" HALF-ROUND MOLDING HIDES SCREEN EDGES

7/8" X 2" STOCK FOR SCREEN FRAMING

OFFSET HANGERS

3/8" RABBET THREE EDGES

3/8" X 3" DOWELS (8)

SCREENING

SECTION THROUGH WINDOW HEAD SHOWING SCREEN SET FLUSH

STAPLES OR TACKS

SECTION THROUGH WINDOW HEAD SHOWING SCREEN SET ON RABBET

INCLUDE CROSSPIECE ON FRAMES 36" OR LONGER

BEVEL BOTTOM

Stock for screens may be purchased at a local lumber yard or ripped on your circular saw.

Dowels are used for reinforcement at all corners. Apply glue and use a wooden mallet for driving.

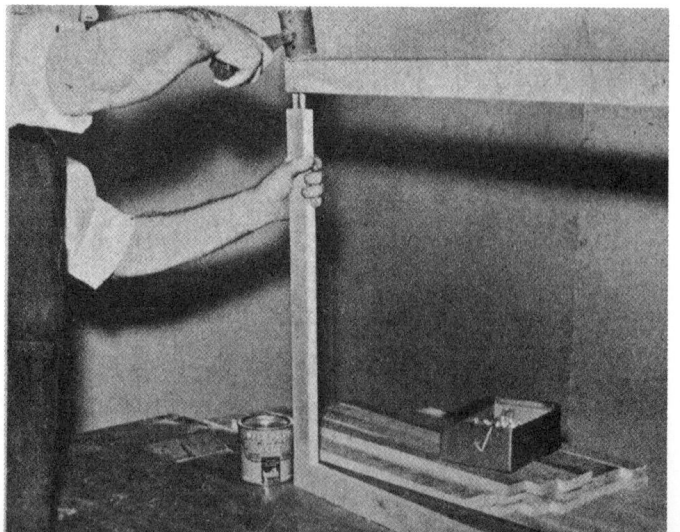

INSECTS are fine in their place and most people agree that their place is outside of the home. The best way to make sure that they stay outside is to protect open windows with adequate screening.

Conventional screens include half-screens that slide up and down metal channels, they are most frequently found in large apartment buildings. Another type is the sliding adjustable kind, which is clamped in place by means of the lower sash and of course the full length screen.

The newest style of window screen is the type which operates very much like a roller blind. Still another screen increasing in popularity is the frameless tension type which uses the bottom sill and upper blind stop of the window in lieu of the framework. They are comparatively inexpensive and can be readily stored by rolling them up.

Still another kind of screening is made by the Kaiser Aluminum Co. of Oakland, Calif. This screening resembles a Venetian blind. The slats, however, are very fine and closely spaced so that flies and mosquitoes cannot get through. You can look through it, from inside a room but an outsider cannot look in. Because of the slanting slats rain drains off to the outside and not into the room.

Screening includes galvanized iron, aluminum, bronze or copper, and plastic. Each has its own advantage, either in a lower initial cost or in length of service. While screening may be obtained in different size meshes, the fine 18x14 is common. It comes in various widths and should be purchased at least one inch longer than the length of the rails or the width of the opening in the frame.

Galvanized wire has a low first cost but must be painted every year or it will not last very long. It is not recommended for damp climates or for coastal areas. Aluminum on the other hand never needs painting or varnishing and will not stain light-colored paint or masonry. It is light

A square and a sharp pencil should be carefully used to mark the corners for the doweled joints.

Corrugated fasteners are used to hold joints so that bar clamps can be removed for next screen.

The rabbet for the center reinforcing bar is being cut with a dado head on the circular saw.

A professional looking job is the result if you use a portable belt sander to smooth the joints.

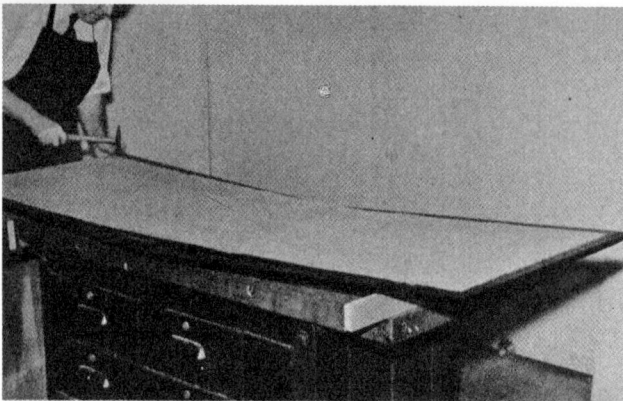

Stretching material by placing two screens in tandem with blocks of wood to raise the ends.

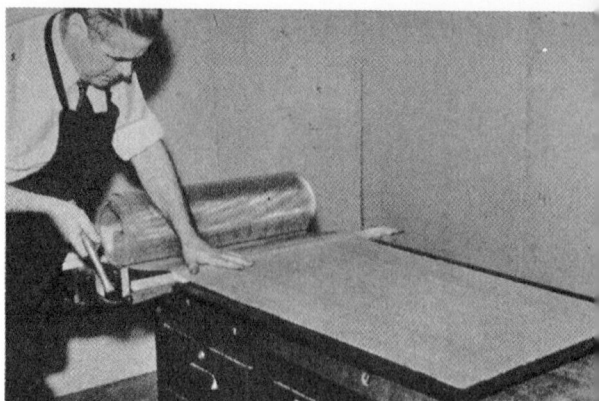

Wedge driven between scrap (to which fabric is temporarily tacked) and frame tightens fabric.

Third method uses a toothed stretcher to pull fabric to frame.

Molding is accurately mitered by cutting it in place on the screen.

Screwing screen hangers in plac Don't forget to number screen

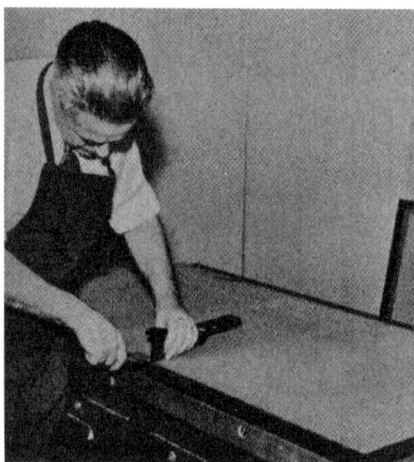

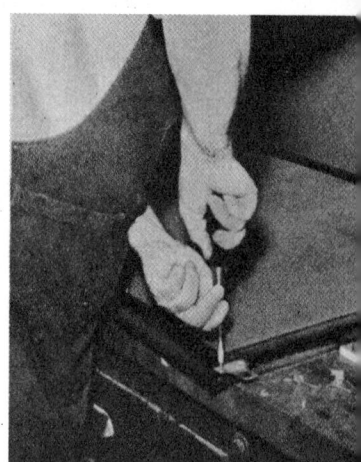

in weight and is much more resistant to rain, salt air, smoke, and extreme temperature changes than galvanized wire.

Bronze screening is said to cost less per year of service than either galvanized or aluminum. With ordinary care it should last indefinitely but it does require a yearly coat of clear lacquer or varnish if you want to keep the finish bright and to prevent it from staining.

The newcomer, plastic screening, is elastic and will return to its original shape if slightly dented. If a hole is burned in it or if it should become torn, it may be mended with a patch of screening fastened in place with Duco-type cement.

Window screens are very simple to make, so simple that one wonders why so many are sold ready made to home owners who know how to use tools. Only a few basic tools are needed but if machinery is available it will help in getting out the stock and in doing some of the work.

The screens described here are full length and are planned so that they will fit "bug tight" regardless of any shrinking or

expanding of the wood. This unique featur is made possible by a $\frac{3}{8}$-in. rabbet cut o the top and the two sides. The screen wi fit tightly all around regardless of an irregularities in the window frame. Th

Columbia aluminum frameless screens utilize t and bottom window sills for their framewor

Frameless screens are easily detached from inside of window.

Below: How they are rolled up for storage during the winter.

Window screen and storm window combinations in kit form are now made by the Buckeye Screen Company in Columbus.

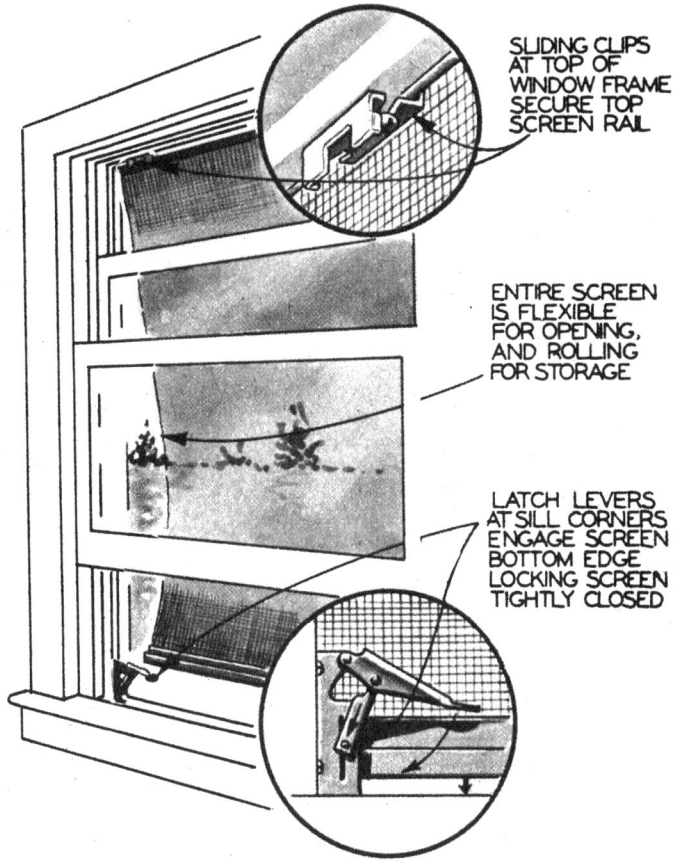

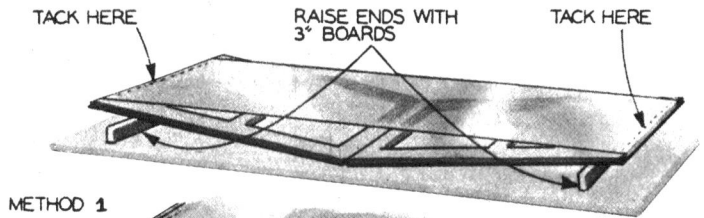

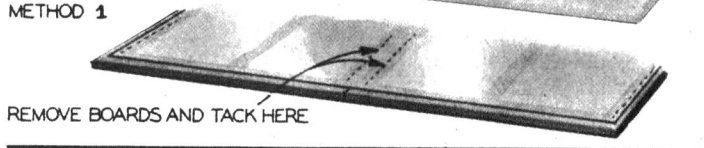

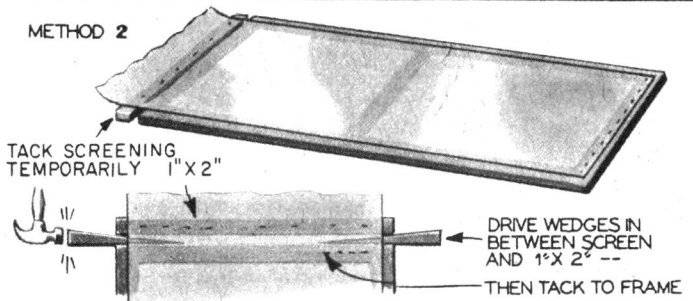

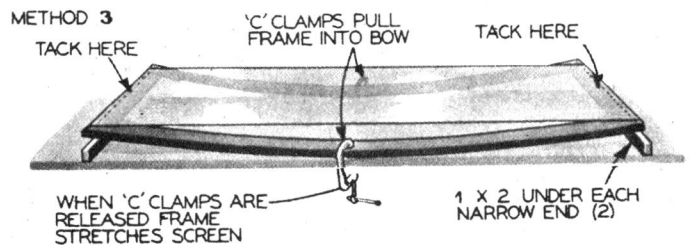

SLIDING CLIPS AT TOP OF WINDOW FRAME SECURE TOP SCREEN RAIL

ENTIRE SCREEN IS FLEXIBLE FOR OPENING, AND ROLLING FOR STORAGE

LATCH LEVERS AT SILL CORNERS ENGAGE SCREEN BOTTOM EDGE LOCKING SCREEN TIGHTLY CLOSED

TACK HERE   RAISE ENDS WITH 3° BOARDS   TACK HERE

METHOD 1

REMOVE BOARDS AND TACK HERE

METHOD 2

TACK SCREENING TEMPORARILY 1" X 2"

DRIVE WEDGES IN BETWEEN SCREEN AND 1" X 2" --

THEN TACK TO FRAME

METHOD 3   'C' CLAMPS PULL FRAME INTO BOW   TACK HERE

TACK HERE

WHEN 'C' CLAMPS ARE RELEASED FRAME STRETCHES SCREEN

1 X 2 UNDER EACH NARROW END (2)

Newest type of screen material is made by Kaiser Aluminum. It has miniature downward slanting louvers, resembles a Venetian blind. The picture below is an actual-size photograph of the screening.

same feature will also solve the problem of fitting screens to old type homes whose windows contain no blind stop.

The first step is to measure the size of the windows. Don't be surprised if you find that many of the windows do not measure the same at all points. This is the reason that regulation screens and storm windows require so much fitting. Take the smallest or narrowest measurements only and forget about the fitting. The ⅜ rabbet on the top and the two sides will take care of any unevenness.

The next step is to decide on the kind of joints to be used. They may be simply nailed and reinforced with angle irons or corner plates or they may be glued and doweled. They may be made with a lap, butt or notched butt, mortise and tenon, or a mitered joint. The joint selected here was a plain butt joint, doweled and glued, and reinforced with corrugated fasteners. It was chosen because it is strong and is easily and rapidly constructed.

Stock may be purchased at a lumber yard or it may be cut to size on the circular saw. For the average size window it should be about ⅞ in. thick and two inches wide. When purchasing the stock, do not forget the molding. This may be the regular screen molding or may be ½-in. or ¾-in. half-round. The amount should equal the total in linear feet of the top and bottom rails plus the sides and cross-pieces.

The stiles or sides are ¼ in. longer than the window opening measured at its shortest point. They may be left somewhat longer to prevent splitting when making the joints but these "horns" will have to be cut off before the frame is rabbeted.

The top, bottom, and cross rails are 3⅜ in. shorter (for 2-in.-wide stiles) than the window opening measured at its narrowest point. This size allows ⅛ in. for possible expansion. The edge of the bottom rail may be cut at a 15° angle so that it will make a better fit with the window sill. The center brace cross rail may be omitted on screens less than 36 in. long.

Mark the corners for the dowels, number each corner, and bore ⅜-in. holes accurately and at least 1¼ in. deep, using a doweling jig. Mix a small amount of waterproof glue and assemble the frames. Use a mallet to drive the dowels home and pull up the joints tightly with bar clamps. Check for squareness with a steel square, then secure each joint with a ⅜-in. corrugated fastener. The clamps may then be removed and used on the next screen. A neat job will result if all joints are sanded even and smooth after the glue has had a chance to dry overnight.

At this point the ⅜-in. rabbet should be cut on the top and the sides. A dado head on the circular saw will do it in a short time. One coat of priming paint should be applied before all screening is installed. The molding should also be given a primary coat on the underside if maximum protection is desired.

The wire screening is fastened by any one of the following three methods:

1. It may be tacked on two sides and stretched in place with a special screen wire stretcher, then tacked down. This stretcher is also good for replacing worn out screening.

2. It may be stretched tight by placing two frames, bottom to bottom, and raising the far ends about two inches on blocks. The screening in one piece is then fastened to the tops of the two frames. When the blocks are removed and the screens pushed down flat, the wire will be stretched tight. After it is tacked down the screens are cut apart.

3. It may be fastened to one side, then tacked to a strip of scrap wood that is at

least two inches wide. Wedges driven between this scrap and the bottom of the screen frame will stretch the wire cloth.

After it is tacked in place, the surplus is cut off. A stapler makes tacking easier. Still another method is shown in the drawings on page 26 09 .

If you are planning to use Lumite plastic screening it is not necessary to stretch it taut. This material has a tendency to tighten up after it has been exposed to the weather.

Molding dresses up the job and protects the hands from the sharp wire ends. Corners should be mitered for neatness. These miters may be cut on the saw, in a box, or may be cut directly on the screen. To do this, nail the molding in place with the corners loose and lapped over. Place a thin piece of wood under the joint to protect the saw and the screen and saw the miter right in place with a thin saw. The fit will be perfect. Complete the paint job and your screens are ready to be hung. No fitting should be necessary if your measurements were accurate.

The screens may be held in place on the window frame with turn buttons on the outside or with hooks and eyes on the inside. An easier and better method is to use a hanger set consisting of two hanger eyes, two hooks, and a regular hook and eye for the bottom.

As these screens will project out from the frame by about 3/8 in., the hanger hooks will have to be flattened. This can be done by clamping them between the jaws of a large vise.

The following suggestions for the care of screens will prolong their life.

1. Wash them thoroughly before putting them up on the windows.

2. Make necessary repairs to the frames as soon as discernible.

3. Patch holes immediately.

4. Clean rusted areas with a detergent then brush the section with turpentine.

5. Paint, if necessary, with a good grade of screen enamel and do it on both sides.

6. Store your screens in a dry place and make sure that they are all upright or else on edge. Build a storage cabinet if it is at all possible.

7. Be sure that the screens will be hung on their matching window by using small number tacks, or by stamping or marking a number on both screen and window.

By the way—don't get out the ladder to hang up the upper story screens. Lower the top sash, pull up the screen on a rope, reach out and hook the eyes over the hooks, pull closed, and secure with the bottom hook and eye. •

This joint uses 1/4x5-in. dowels

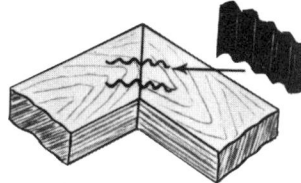

A mitered joint and fasteners

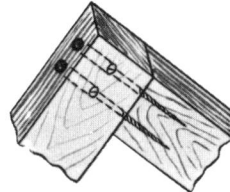

Butt joint uses screw or nails

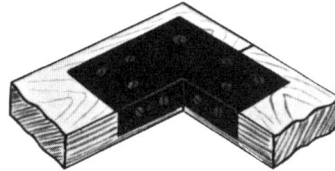

Recess metal corner braces flush

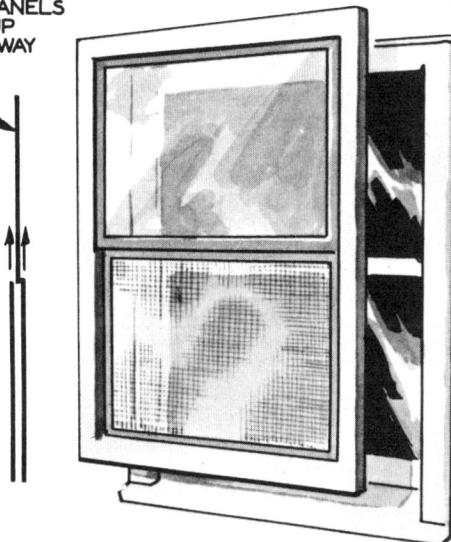

SCREEN OR GLASS PANELS STORE UP OUT OF WAY

COMBINATION STORM SASH AND SCREEN UNIT IS PLACED INTO DOUBLE HUNG WINDOW, SAVES TROUBLE OF SEASONAL REMOVAL

Screening-in a Porch or Breezeway

Screen-in your porch or breezeway and add an outdoor living room to your house with screen panels made from easy-to-work aluminum.

OUTDOOR living is in style these days. Whether you already have a porch to be screened-in or you want to add an outdoor living room to your present house, you can quickly build screen panels from Do-It-Yourself Aluminum screen sections with hand or power woodworking tools. When you build your screen panels from Do-It-Yourself screen sections, there are no tricky joints to make. Corner locking clips join side and end frames with built-in accuracy. With aluminum woven screen cloth, you can build your own panels for about one-third the cost of custom-made screens.

Plan screen panel sizes, meeting rails and door location before picking up materials from your local hardware dealer. Whether your present porch already has a partial stub wall around it or is open from floor to roof beams, plan equal width panels at sides and end. Draw a plan of your porch to scale, using graph paper. Keep in mind while planning that woven screen cloth is available in 24, 26, 28, 30, 32, 36, 42 and 48 inch widths. Also consider that screen section comes in 6, 8 and 12 foot lengths. If possible, plan to cut one side and one end or two ends out of one length of screen section using a screen cloth width that will minimize waste. If your porch already has a stub wall or railing around it, the doorway location is already established. However, if you have a choice, locate the doorway as one of the regular panels. Your porch will look better if panels are evenly spaced around the porch. Fig. 13 shows common porch shapes with vertical meeting rails and doors planned for a minimum number of screen panels.

CONSTRUCTING FRAME AND SCREEN PANEL

1. Measure screen panel openings. Side frames should equal the opening's height less ⅛ inch. End frames should equal opening's width less ⅛ inch.

2. Splines are furnished with the screen

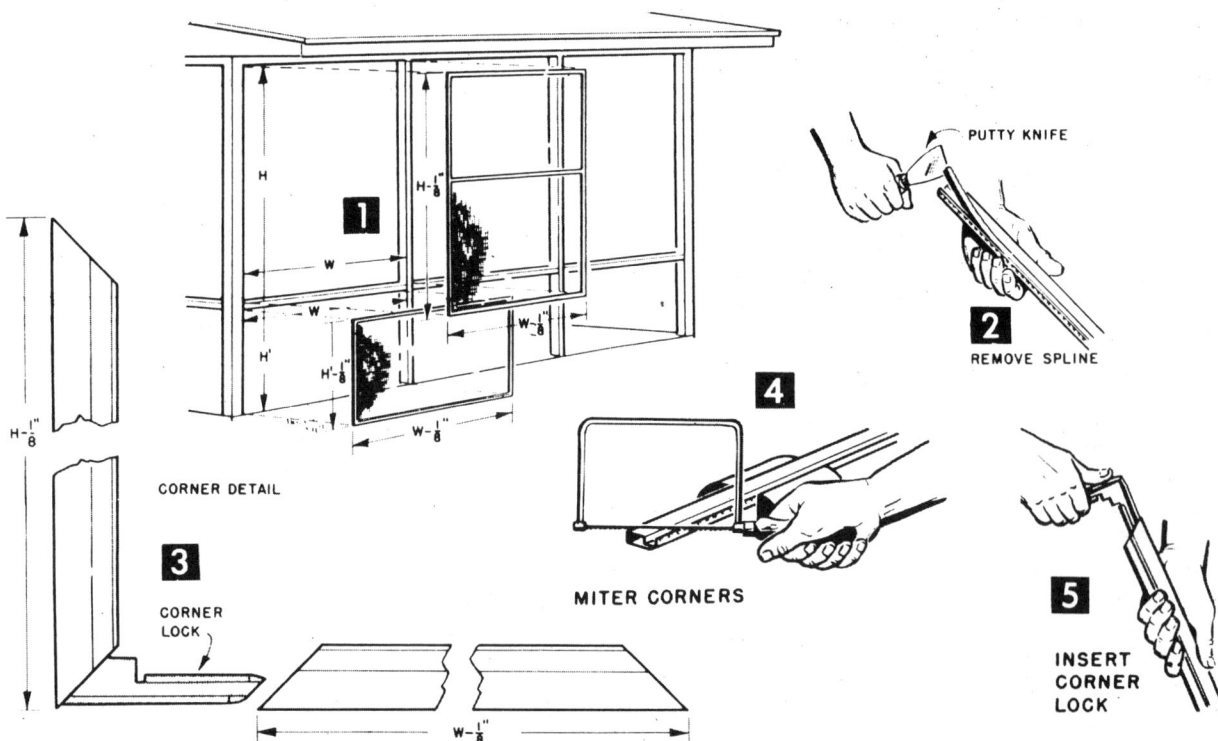

CORNER DETAIL

1

2 REMOVE SPLINE — PUTTY KNIFE

3 CORNER LOCK

4 MITER CORNERS

5 INSERT CORNER LOCK

sections and are removed with a putty knife. Lay splines aside until later.

3. Mark frame members for cutting according to measurements obtained from Step No. 1. The ⅛-inch clearance permits easy installation. Scribe 45° angles at ends of frame members. Spline groove is along inside of frame and faces out when screens are in place.

4. Mitre corners by cutting mitres with fine-toothed coping or hack saw. Smooth end cut with a small file or garnet paper.

5. Start assembly of frame by pushing corner locks into ends of frame member. A gentle tapping with a hammer seats corner locks.

6. Assemble end member with corner locks to side members. Push corner locks into remaining end member and complete frame assembly. Cut splines for end frame members to full length of groove. Splines for side frame members butt-joint against end frame splines (see Fig. 12).

7. Large screens may require a reinforcing channel between side frame members. Trim channel to fit frame members and drill hole in end. Position channel brace parallel with end frame members and punch hole in side frame member with 6-penny nail. Screw channel to frame with No. 6 x ⅜-inch aluminum tapping screws. Screen section may be used instead of channel as the reinforcing brace for greater rigidity where screen panels are wider than 30 inches.

8. Roll woven screen cloth over frame and square cross wires with end frame members. Cut screen cloth to length between two screen wires.

9. Lay frame on cleared bench top, floor or ping-pong table. Check corners of frame with a carpenter's steel square to make sure they are square before lining up edge of screen cloth with outside edge of spline groove along one side. Wood blocks across corners help to keep screen cloth from rolling up and moving about.

10. Form the edge of the screen cloth into the spline groove with a putty knife. A block of wood on top of screen cloth and along inside edge of spline groove helps to form a sharp bend in screen cloth's edge. Scrap pieces of screen section keep surface level with frame members. Start forming screen cloth at one end of groove and work down full length. CAUTION: Screen cloth fits down *inside* edge of spline groove only. Follow the same screen wire along edge to prevent pulling too much of the edge into groove and bowing frame. Short pieces of scrap spline pressed temporarily in place help to hold screen cloth from moving about as work progresses.

11. Stretch screen cloth across frame and trim edge of screen cloth even with outside edge of spline groove. Form edge of screen cloth into spline groove as you did along first side. Align ends of screen cloth with frame and temporarily fasten both sides in place with short scrap sections of spline. Trim ends of screen cloth along outside edge of spline groove. Form ends of screen cloth into spline groove.

12. Drive both end splines into grooves of frame end members with a block and hammer. Remove short temporary splines along sides and replace with full-length splines, butt-jointing corners of splines as shown.

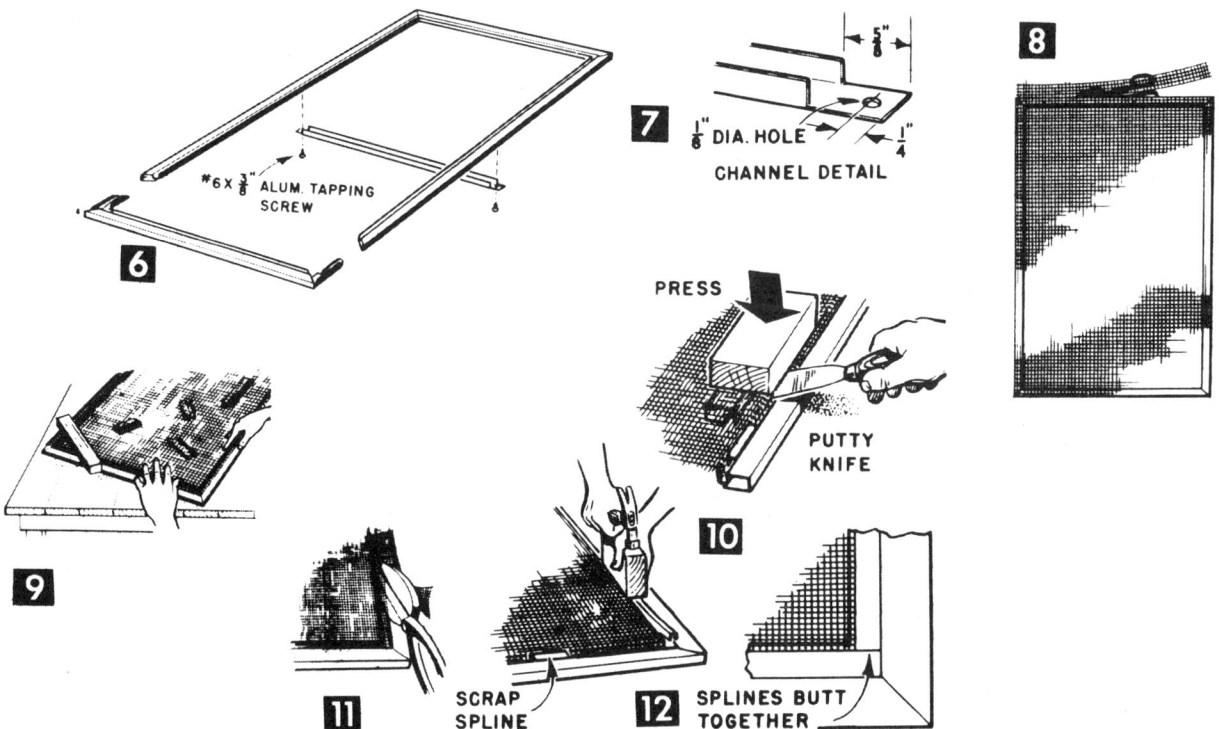

#6 X ¾" ALUM. TAPPING SCREW

⅛" DIA. HOLE

CHANNEL DETAIL

PRESS

PUTTY KNIFE

SCRAP SPLINE

SPLINES BUTT TOGETHER

SUPPORTING THE SCREEN PANELS

Vertical meeting rails divide porch areas into uniform areas, support the screen panels and hold them in place. For a porch that is largely masonry, you may want to use an all-aluminum T-section formed by riveting two ⅛ x ¾ x ¾-inch angles back to back (Fig. 14). Angle clips riveted to the back of the T-section fasten the meeting rail in place at top and bottom. A simple method for holding the screen panel in place is to slip the panel up into a recess along the top formed between an angle and quarter-round mold. The recess is deep enough to hold the screen panel as it slips down to rest in a ½-inch channel across the bottom (Fig. 14A). Attach matching angles at the posts. If your porch is high off the ground, locate the open side of the angle in toward the porch so you can slip the screen panels in from the porch side.

For full-height openings, 2 x 4's with rabbeted edges or with a recess formed by nailing quarter-round molding back of the edge are easy-to-make meeting rails. Horizontal meeting rail at chair height helps to prevent damage to screens and divides the vertical height into more manageable panel sizes. Vertical 2 x 4 meeting rails can also be used between the top of a wood railing or stub wall and underside of porch roof. Common screen hooks will hold screen panels in place (Fig. 15A). To install hooks, punch a hole through the screen section close to the spline groove with a 4-penny nail. Screw a small screen hook into the hole until it begins to dimple the opposite side. Chisel or rasp away part of the quarter-round molding to let hook past. Locate hook eye where it will hold screen panel securely.

Another method for holding screen panels in place is to make turnbuttons from ⅛ x ¾-inch aluminum bar stock (Fig. 16A). The off-center hole permits screen panels to be removed along one side and then the other of the narrow meeting rail left between rabbeted edge of 2 x 4.

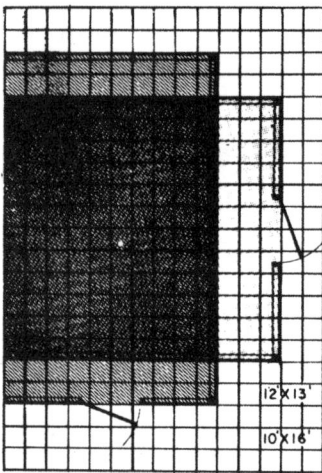

13 PORCH LAYOUT

12'X13'
10'X16'

14

⅛" DIA. RIVET 8" ON CENTERS

⅛" X ¾" ALUM. ANGLE

14 A

⅛" RIVETS

INSERTING SCREENS

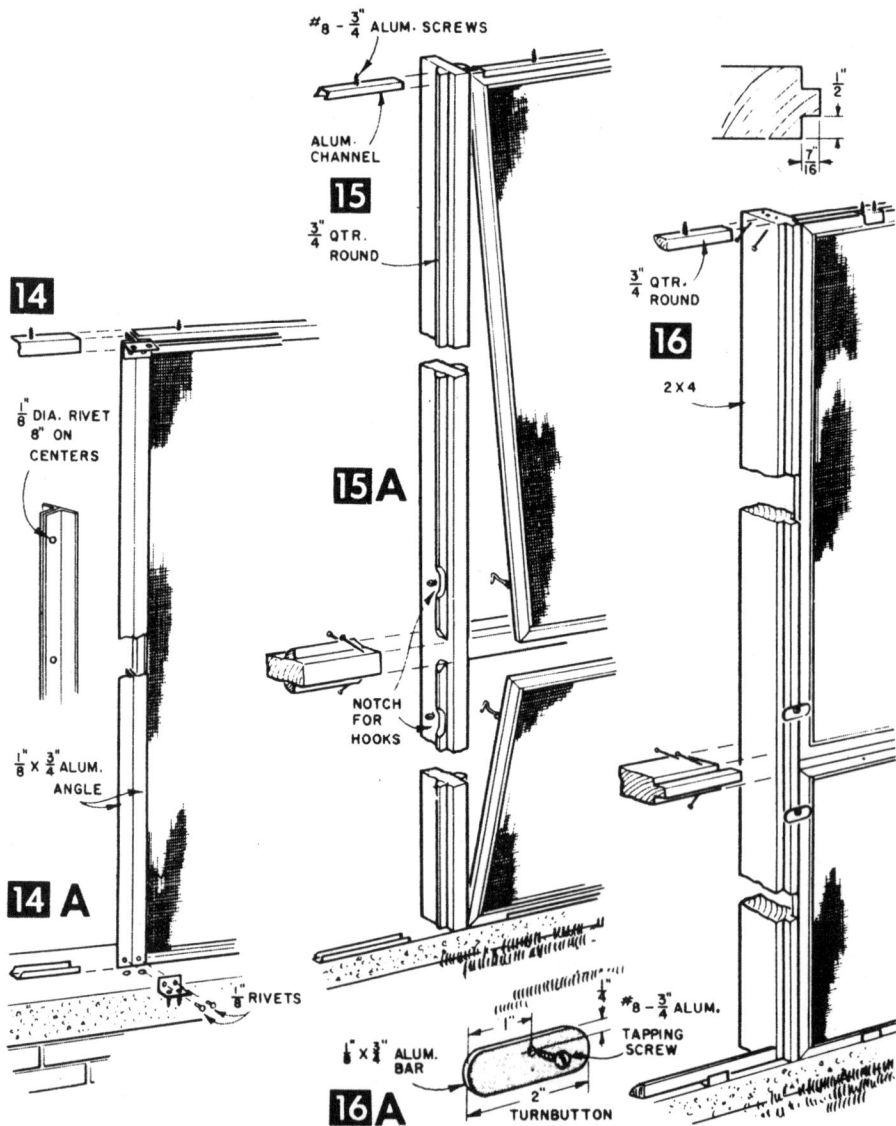

#8 - ¾" ALUM. SCREWS

ALUM. CHANNEL

15

¾" QTR. ROUND

15 A

NOTCH FOR HOOKS

¾" QTR. ROUND

16

2 X 4

1 ½"
7/16"

16 A

⅛" X ¾" ALUM. BAR

#8 - ¾" ALUM. TAPPING SCREW

TURNBUTTON

17

17 A

FILL IN
BETWEEN
PROJECTIONS

3/4" ANGLE
TRIMMED TO 3/8"

17 B

1/8" RIVETS

1/8" x 3/4" ANGLE

ALUM.
CHANNEL

18

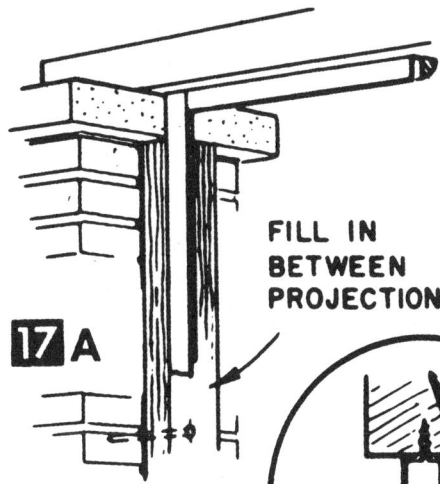

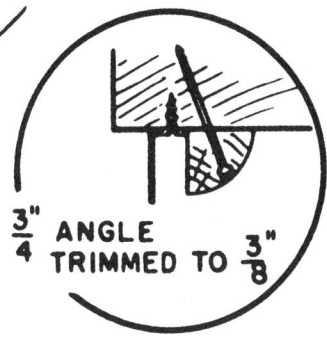

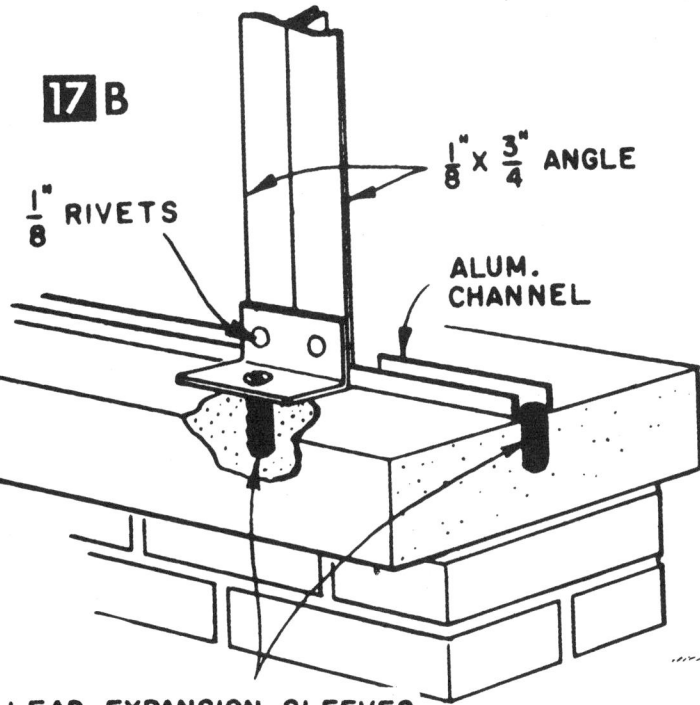

LEAD EXPANSION SLEEVES

SCREENS FOR STUB-WALL PORCHES

Screening-in an existing porch with stub walls may be more of a problem than adding full-height screens between floor and roof. Where posts and stub wall are stone, stucco or brick, consider using aluminum parts for holding the screen panels in place as indicated in Fig. 14. Along the sides, you may have to use a wood filler strip between post and aluminum angle. Where the post surface is rough, uneven or tapered, run a heavy bead of caulking compound between angle and post. Quarter-round molding and 1/8 x 3/4 x 3/4-inch aluminum angle form a recess at the top deep enough to take screen panels before they drop down into the channel along the bottom. Channel section is the same channel used for reinforcing the screen panels and can be screwed into lead expansion sleeves, the same as the angle clips holding T-section in place. Use No. 8 x 3/4-inch aluminum screws and 3/8 O.D. x 3/4-inch lead sleeves in 3/8-inch diameter holes. A carbide-tipped masonry bit in a portable electric drill makes short work of these holes into the masonry cap.

Many wooden porches have a wood rail between posts with an open lattice or pickets between top and bottom rails. Here you can fill in the areas between the top of the upper rail and the underside of the roof with screen panels. Vertical meeting rails can be 2 x 4's (Figs. 15 and 16). To cover the areas between rails, make separate panels and slip them into place between a top recess and a channel along the bottom (Fig. 18B). These screen panels can be fitted on the outside or inside of the lattice or picket section. Along the bottom between lower rail and porch floor, cut sections of embossed aluminum sheet and screw them to lower rail.

Two and three-story apartment build-

SCREENS SHOULD MEET
ON PICKET

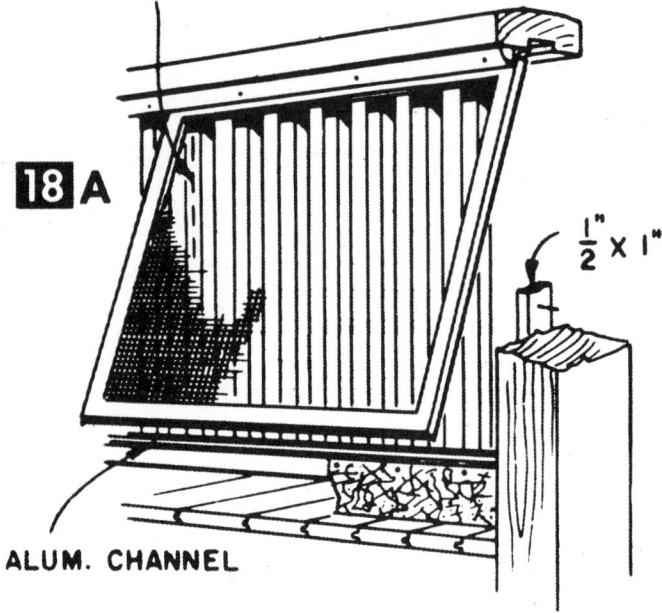

18 A

½" X 1"

ALUM. CHANNEL

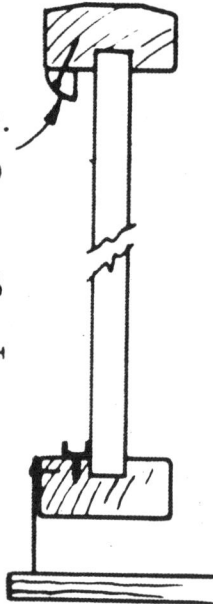

¾" QTR.
ROUND

18 B

SECTION
THROUGH
PICKET
RAILING

19 A

SECTION
THROUGH
SOLID
RAILING

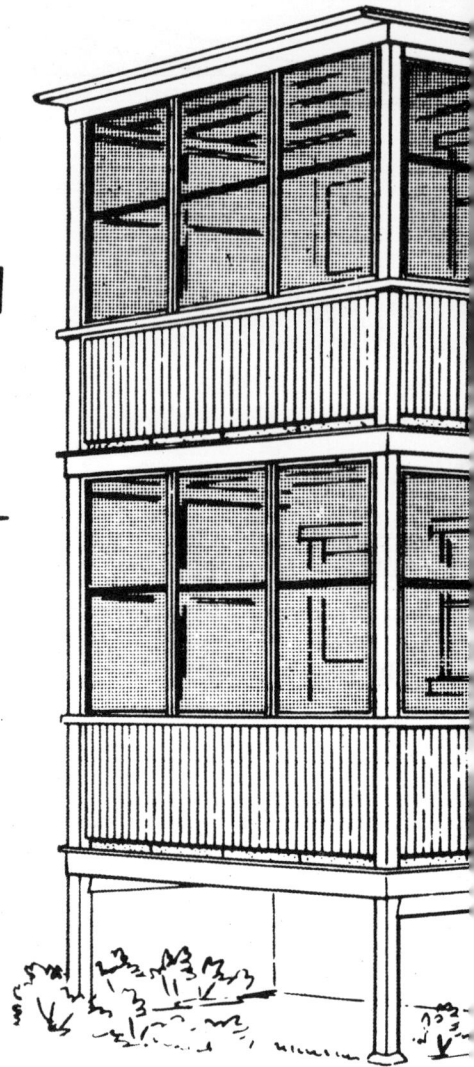

19

SCREEN

ALUM. CHANNEL

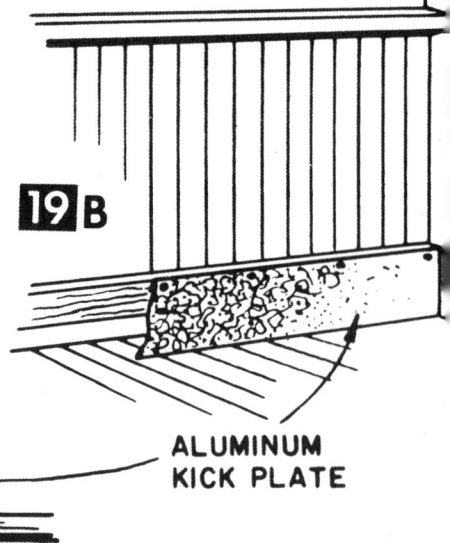

19 B

ALUMINUM
KICK PLATE

ings or multiple homes often have back porches that could be screened-in for added living convenience (Fig. 19). Many times the stub wall is covered with tongue-and-groove lumber that doesn't require screening. If this partial wall should be of open construction, you can add panels on the inside like those shown in Fig. 18A. Build in the vertical meeting rails with the top recess and bottom channel designed to permit inserting or removing screens and storm sash from the inside. Screw on strips of embossed aluminum sheet to lower rail to cover lower opening (Fig. 19B).

Frame and hang the screen or combination doors according to Fig. 30.

20B SPLIT SCREENS

20

20A
FULL-LENGTH SCREENS
WITH SASH SECTION BRACES

MOUNT CHANNEL ON ₵ OF SECTION

SPLIT SCREENS

20C

CUT CHANNEL TO CLEAR

3/4" ALUM. ANGLE 6" LONG

21

INSERT PANEL OR SCREEN

21A

#6 x 3/8" TAPPING SCREWS

GUSSET FOR ODD ANGLE CORNERS SHEET ALUM.

21B

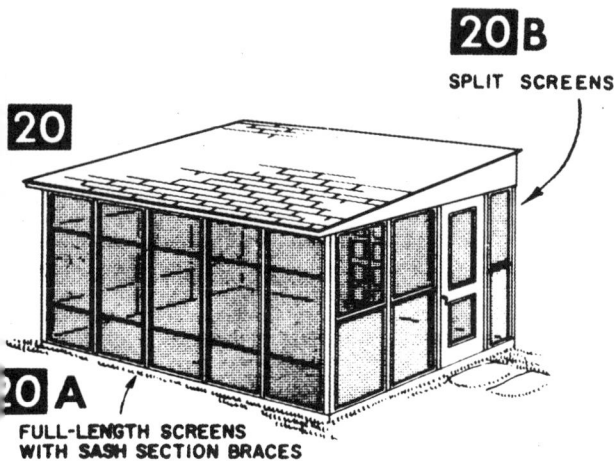

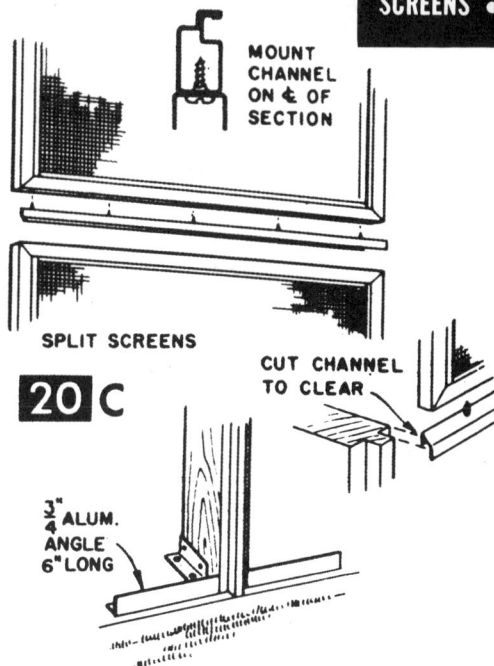

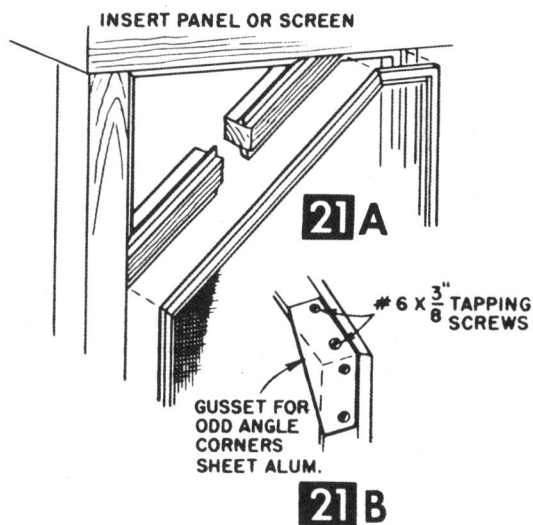

FULL-HEIGHT SCREENS FOR PORCHES

Porches or breezeways with a clear space between floor and roof may be screened-in a number of different ways. Fig. 20 shows two methods for adding full-length screens without horizontal meeting rail. This system would be desirable in areas where screen panels are removed during the winter to prevent snow from drifting into corners. When these screens are removed, only the posts and short angle clips along the floor remain and snow can be swept out easily. In Fig. 20A screen panels extend from floor to roof beam and are made from 8- or 12-foot lengths of screen section. Two sash section braces across width reinforce vertical frame members. In Fig. 20B two panels cover the full height and are joined at the center with a channel brace (Fig. 20C). Screen hooks or turnbuttons along the side are all that's necessary to hold both types of panels in place.

Horizontal meeting rails built in between vertical meeting rails permit using smaller panel sizes and protect screens from damage at chair height. Follow details for adding horizontal meeting rail as shown in Figs. 15 and 16. Separate screen panels fill upper and lower areas. If your porch framing happens to include diagonal braces at the top of posts, fabricate screen panels with a corner cut off to match the angle of the brace. Attach reinforcing gussets cut from doubled aluminum sheet or flange of 1/16 x 1 x 1-inch angle behind screen section joints as in Fig. 21B. On older homes, edges of these angular braces are often decorated in fancy designs. Probably the

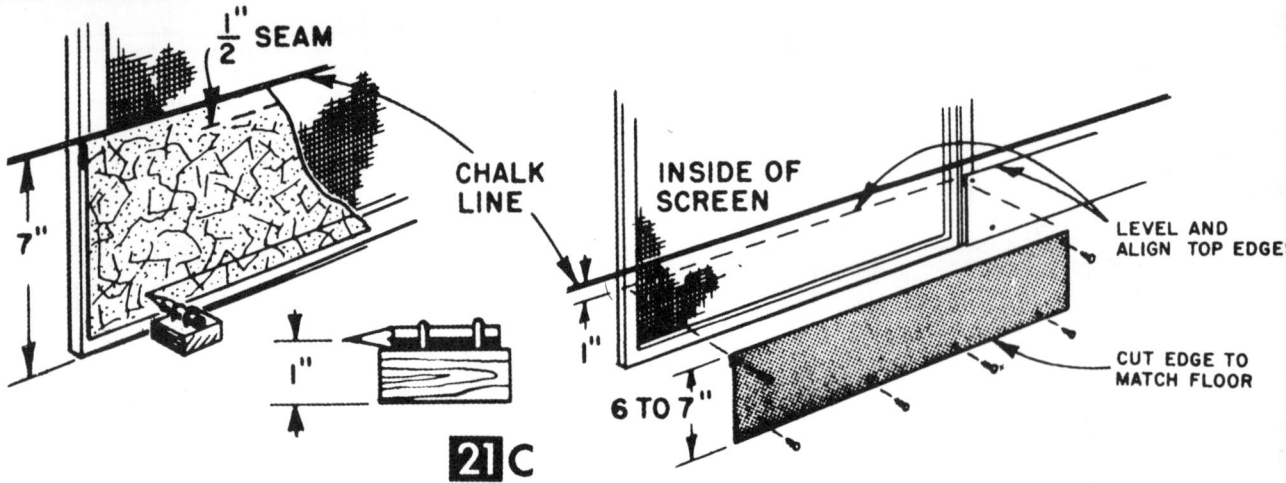

½" SEAM

CHALK LINE

7"

1"

INSIDE OF SCREEN

6 TO 7"

LEVEL AND ALIGN TOP EDGE

CUT EDGE TO MATCH FLOOR

21C

best approach if you encounter such braces is to set the screen panels out far enough to fit over the outside surface of the braces.

Breezeways can be screened-in with full-length screens using the same methods shown in Figs. 20 and 21. You can also build in a louvered stub wall as shown in Fig. 22.

If the breezeway runs between either a house or garage with beveled drop siding, you'll want a straight side to start working from. Stand a 2 x 2 vertically in place along the drop siding and mark locations for notches to fit the siding. Fit the notched 2 x 2 to the siding and lag screw or nail it in place. If you plan to use rabbeted 2 x 4 meeting rails, rabbet the edge of this notched 2 x 2 before nailing it in place. You can add a quarter-round molding to the edge later if you use that method for attaching screen panels. When fitting vertical meeting rails, use a level to plumb it in position so screen panels will fit squarely. If you add louvers, limit distances between vertical meeting rails to 36¼ inches. Prefabricate the louver assembly and fit it in between the breezeway floor and a horizontal meeting rail (see Fig. 23). Frame and hang the door as shown.

2X2" NOTCH TO FIT SIDING

LOCATE AND SECURE BASE OF VERTICAL MEETING RAIL AND PLUMB

22A

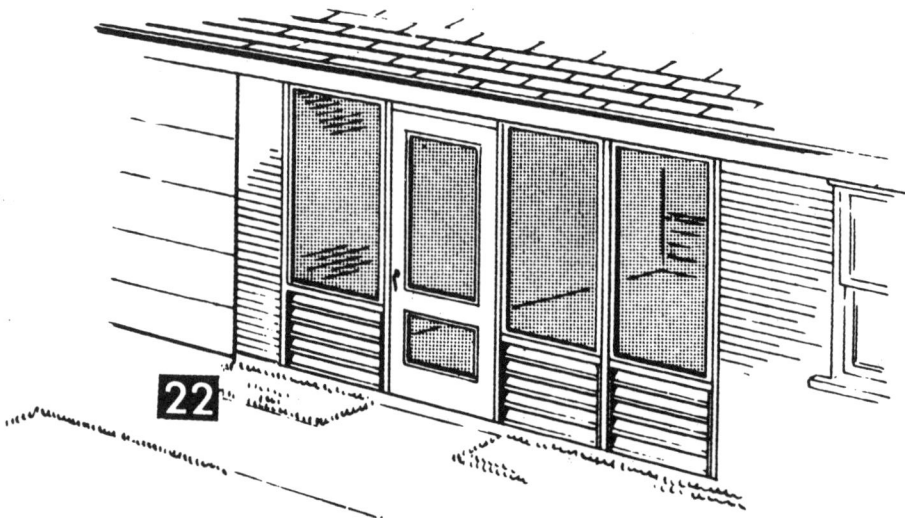

22

23

HORIZONTAL RAIL

ALLOW 1/16" TO 1/8" CLEARANCE, TOP AND BOTTOM FOR RIVETS

1/8" RIVETS OR #8-32 X 1/4" MACHINE SCREWS

1/8"

3"

1/4"

1/16" X 1" X 1" ANGLE

3" TO 3 1/2" EQUAL SPACING

1/8" RIVETS OR #8-32 X 1/4" MACH. SCREWS

LOUVER HEIGHT

3 1/2"

1/2" CHANNEL

CONCRETE FLOOR

1/8"

FLASHING STRIP

LEAD EXPANSION SLEEVE

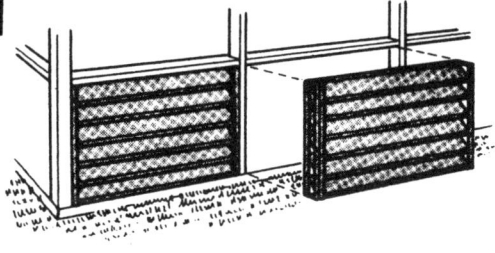

24

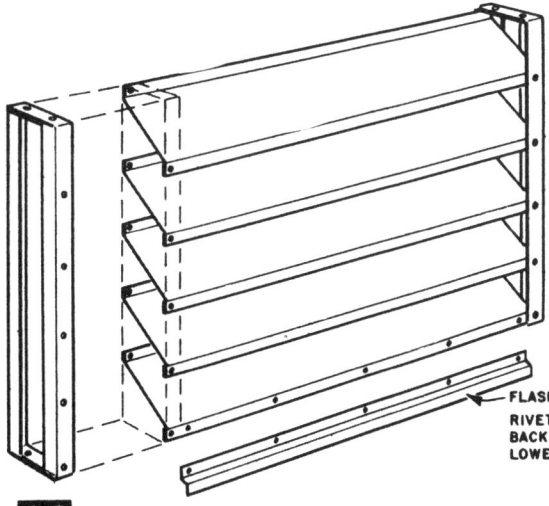

FLASHING— RIVET TO BACK SIDE OF LOWER LOUVER

25

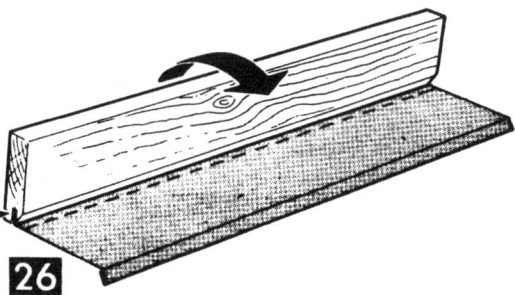

SAW CUT 1/2" DEEP

26

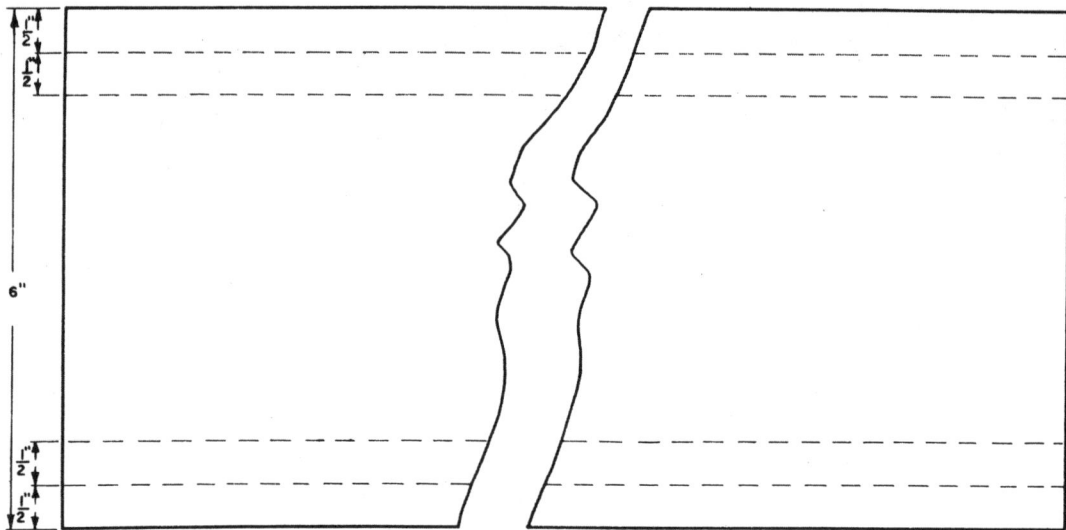

27 LAYOUT FOR LOUVER PANEL

28 END PIECE — 4 REQUIRED

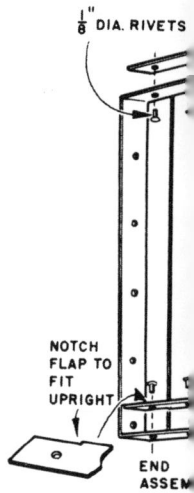

29

BUILD YOUR OWN LOUVERS

Louvers for stub walls across porches or breezeways provide ventilation that can be left open in the rain and reduce the height of screen panels. Making the louvers out of aluminum saves you the problem of painting, and you won't ever have to worry about rust. The aluminum louver shown in Figs. 23 and 24 fits snugly under a 2 x 4 horizontal rail. Screws through the angle frame at each end fasten the louver to vertical rails at each side. A 1 x 1-inch angle along the top and inside forms a recess into which a panel slips before resting in the channel along the back (Fig. 23).

To make your own louvers from Do-It-Yourself Aluminum, follow the layout in Fig. 27. Length of louvers is limited to 36 inches by the sheet size available, but you can make them shorter to fit your porch plan. Bend a ½-inch seam along both sides as in Fig. 26. Bend seam edges again to match the angle shown in Fig. 23. Lay out the end pieces (Fig. 28). Bend up the ends for the end frame and cut out notches

to clear the angle side (Fig. 29). It may be necessary to trim the ends of the bent flanges if the bend radius isn't sharp to meet the 3-inch dimension inside the angles (3⅛ inches outside). Lay out and centerpunch rivet locations before assembling the end frames. C-clamp end assembly together, and drill ⅛-inch holes for the rivets. Clip about 1/16 inch off the end of ⅛-inch diameter x ¼-inch rivets before riveting end assembly (Fig. 29). C-clamp the louvers with a ½ x ½ inch strip of hardwood under each flange of the louver. Drill through the end frame angle and the flange of the louver 11/64 inch diameter and assemble with No. 8-32 x ¼-inch aluminum machine screws. You can also assemble louvers with ⅛-inch diameter rivets using a steel bucking bar back of the head on the inside. If you plan to use storm sash insert in addition to screens, rivet flashing strip to lower louver to drain water over edge of porch floor. Once you get the hang of it, you can make a 6-vane louver in about two hours.

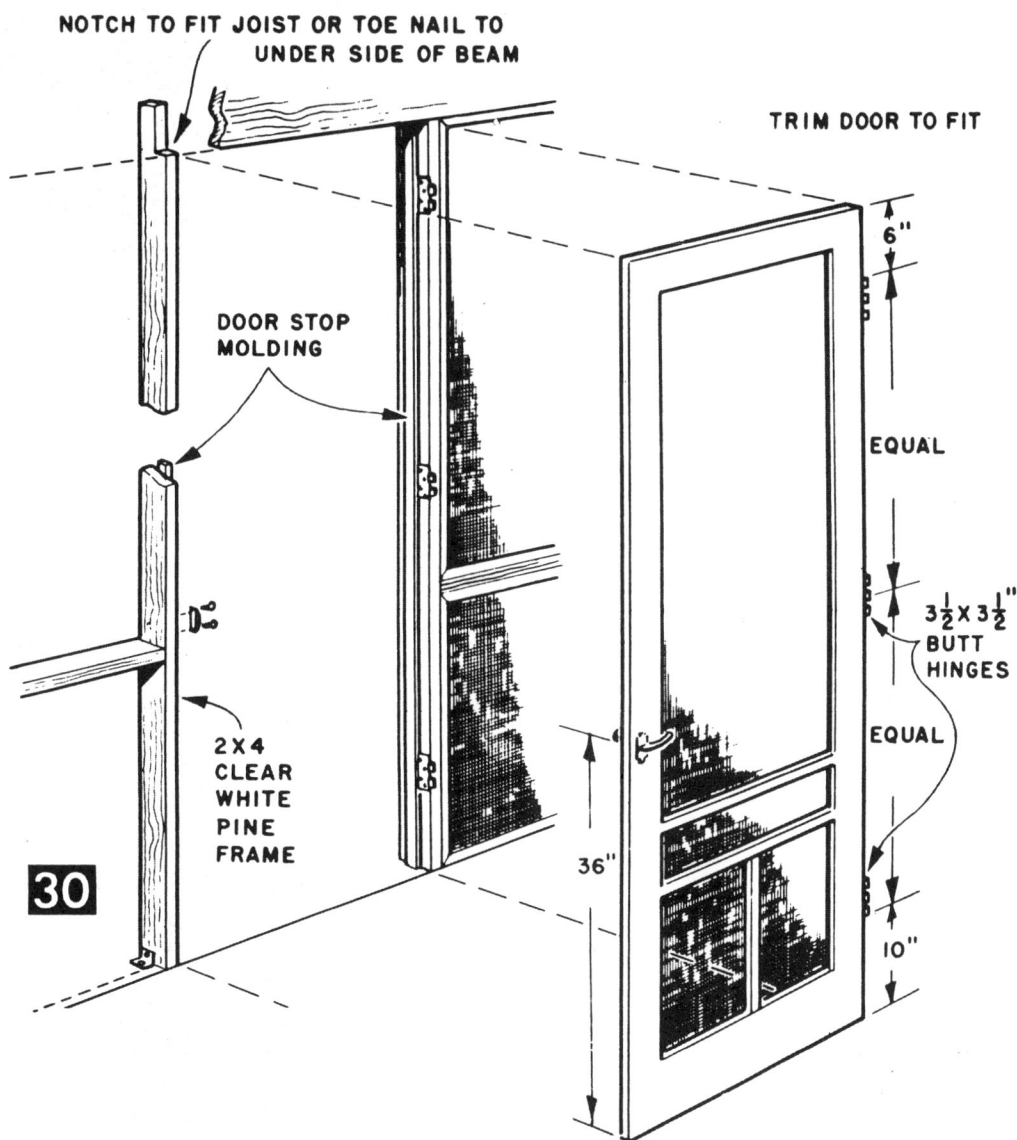

NOTCH TO FIT JOIST OR TOE NAIL TO UNDER SIDE OF BEAM

TRIM DOOR TO FIT

DOOR STOP MOLDING

2 X 4 CLEAR WHITE PINE FRAME

6"

EQUAL

3½ X 3½" BUTT HINGES

EQUAL

36"

10"

30

FRAMING AND HANGING SCREEN DOORS

There's no need to rough frame a door opening and add jambs around the inside of the frame as is commonly done for interior doors. Instead of structural lumber set 2 x 4's of clear trim lumber, such as straight-grained pine. Plumb the door frames carefully to maintain the correct size opening. At the top, notch frames to fit the side of roof beam or toenail it to the beam's underside. Fasten the bottom end in place with aluminum angle clips. Simply screw into a wood floor with No. 8 x ¾-inch aluminum screws or screw into ⅜-inch O.D. lead expansion sleeves set in ⅜-inch drilled holes in a concrete slab floor.

Mark the screen door to fit the opening and plane to fit if necessary. Mortise three 3½ x 3½-inch butt hinges into the edge of the door and frame as shown in Fig. 30. Nail door stop mold along both sides and across the top. Set the nails and putty after priming all wood parts. Finish with two coats of exterior paint. Set the door latch 36 inches above the floor level as shown in the instructions packed with the latch you buy. If you plan to convert your porch with storm sash inserts during winter, buy a combination screen and storm door. All-aluminum combination doors are also available with metal jambs that can be applied to your framed opening. Follow instructions packed with the aluminum doors when framing the opening. •

Screen Door Panel

By F. V. Rodgers

Modernize the entrance to your home and increase your summer ventilation with an inexpensive aluminum screen door panel.

Replace the glass panels in your storm door with an aluminum screen when warm weather comes.

MODERNIZING the entrance to your home and increasing your summer ventilation with an aluminum screen panel for your wood storm door is a simple and inexpensive project that can be tackled and completed in less than a day.

Instead of replacing the entire door each summer, you merely remove the heavy wood storm section and replace it with a light airy aluminum screen panel. This aluminum screen panel can be adapted to your wood storm door through the use of specially designed Do-It-Yourself Aluminum screen framing.

The aluminum screen panel is designed to be put up from inside the house. Special combination fasteners or simple aluminum strips lock the panel securely in place. These fasteners cannot be tampered with from outside the door.

Aluminum framing for these screen panels is easily assembled with corner locks, and screening is installed and stretched into position with an aluminum spline provided with the framing. Both of these simple assembly methods eliminate the need for nuts, bolts, corner braces and other special hardware and tools.

Begin the construction of your aluminum screen panel by removing the storm section from your wood frame door. This panel is usually removable as a separate section, or glass panes can be removed and an opening can be cut out for the screen panel. Measure the height and width of the opening in the storm door before you mark the aluminum framing. (Remove the special spline from the aluminum framing by using the tang end of a file or a putty knife. Slide the putty knife or tang along the length of

Cut screen framing members to desired length. Miter corners and insert corner locks to assemble.

Assemble screen frame and cut aluminum screen cloth to same size as outside dimensions of the frame.

the groove to lift out the spline without bending or kinking.) Mark your framing members $\frac{1}{16}$ inch shorter than the height and width measured in the storm door opening. Scribe a 45-degree angle in from these marks and be sure that the framing member is held in the proper position. The spline groove must be on the inside perimeter of the assembled framing for proper alignment of screening.

Using a fine-tooth hacksaw or coping saw, cut framing members along scribe lines. Smooth and remove burrs and sharp edges with a small file, sandpaper, or pocket knife. Assemble prepared framing members to check fit in door panel and to mark screen frame for slots to hold combination fasteners before screening is inserted. A rubber mallet or plastic-headed hammer is used to drive the corner locks into the end of one frame member. Insert corner lock into other end of frame member and secure by driving home. In this fashion secure corner locks in the ends of both top and bottom frame members and join to sides. Completed screen frame (without screening) is inserted into door frame opening to check fit. The frame should fit tight to effectively keep out insects. While the aluminum frame is in place in the storm door opening, you can mark the door frame for the type of fasteners you prefer.

Two types of fasteners—combination and aluminum strips—are described in this project. The combination fasteners can be purchased from your local lumber dealer or woodworking shop. Combination fasteners consist of a screw with a square shank (no threads), a tongue of metal and a round collar to hold the countersunk

Using a putty knife, form screen into groove, starting at corner and proceeding down side as shown.

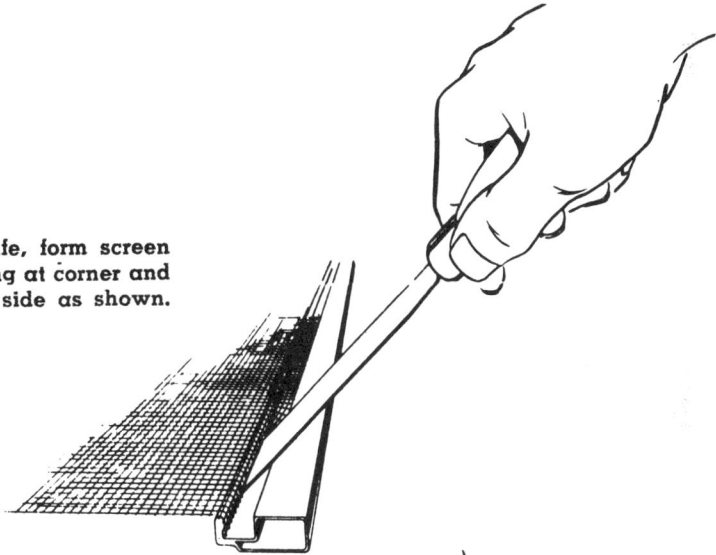

Use a hammer and a block of wood to drive spline into the groove, anchoring screen in frame.

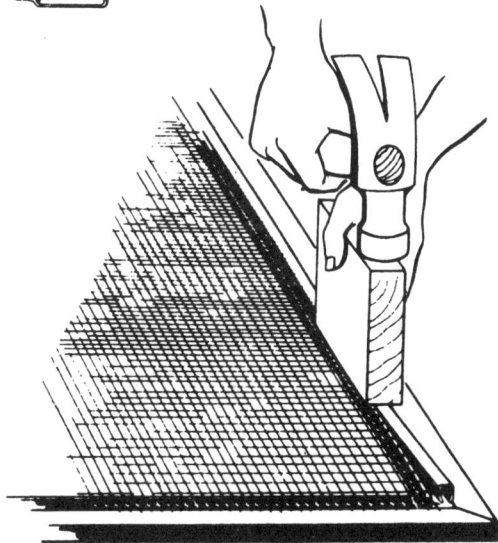

screw in place. To insert the combination screw fasteners, mark the door frame 3 inches to 5 inches above the center on the left and right sides, ¾ inch in from the opening. In the same manner, mark the center at the bottom of the opening. Drill ½-inch-diameter hole ⅝ inch deep to countersink screw head and collar. In the center of the ½-inch hole drill a ¼-inch hole the depth of the screw shank. (Screw shank will have to be cut with a hacksaw if the door frame is less than ¾ inch thick.) Determine the depth and length of the slot for the metal tongue by inserting screw through square opening in tongue and placing this unit in drilled screw hole. Turn screw head left and right to measure sweep of tongue and mark on door frame. Mount a 3-inch or 4-inch circular saw in power hand tool to cut tongue slot to proper depth and length indicated on door frame. This slot should be located ⅜ inch back from outside (face) of the door frame in the panel opening.

Install the combination fasteners by inserting the metal tongue into the slot until the square hole lines up with the screw hole; secure by placing square shank screw into hole through square opening in metal tongue and lock in place by countersinking round collar over rim projecting on screw head.

Replace screen frame in door opening and mark aluminum frame by rotating screw head. Metal tongue will be forced against aluminum frame and will mark proper position for cutting slot in framing member to receive the metal tongue and lock frame in place.

Simpler fastenings can be made from L-shaped aluminum flat corner braces by cutting them into strips. For this method, mark wooden door frames as described above. Position your aluminum strips and

The completed aluminum screen panel is placed in door from inside house and secured with fasteners.

Cut L-shaped aluminum flat corner braces into strips to make simple fasteners to hold panel.

Countersink the strip fasteners enough to hold firmly; secure with flat-head aluminum screws.

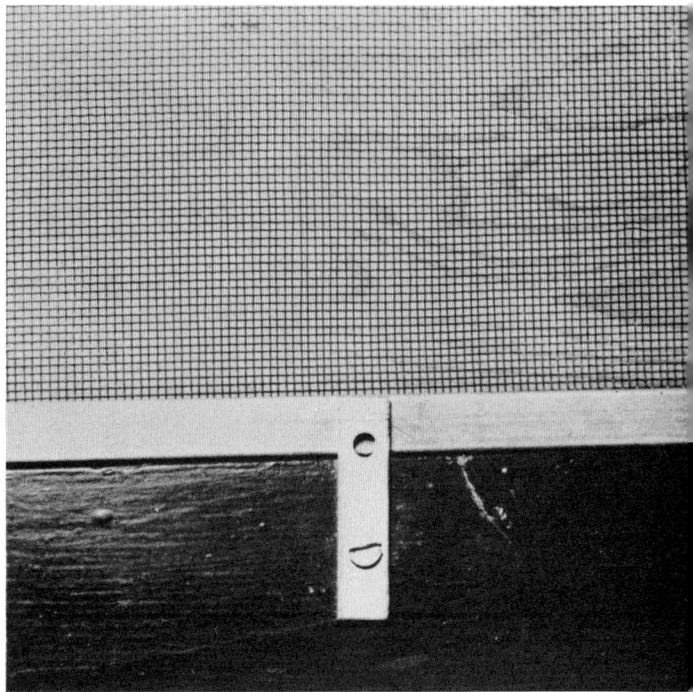

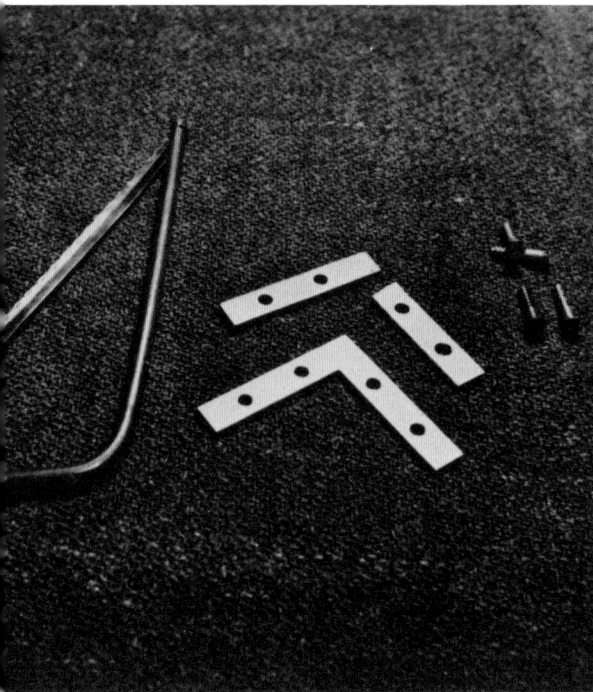

mark around them to countersink strips $\frac{1}{16}$ inch to hold firmly. Remove the aluminum strips and cut out grooves with ¼-inch wood chisel. Re-position the aluminum strips and secure in place with flat-head aluminum screws.

Remove the aluminum screen frame from the door and place on a cleared surface, groove side up, to install screen cloth. Place the aluminum screen cloth on the frame and cut to the same size as the outside dimensions of the frame. Cut carefully between two wires to insure a straight and square piece. Keeping the screen cloth square with frame, line up screen edge with outside edge of spline groove at one end and one side. Place some wooden blocks or tools on top of screen to hold in place. Using a putty knife or tool for forming screen into groove, start at one corner and proceed down long side of the frame. The screen cloth is to fit down the inside

edge of the groove only. Complete the operation along one side of the screen, then cut off excess screen cloth along a line even with the outside edge of the spline groove on the adjacent leg. Replace the edge of the screen cloth that has been formed to lay in the spline groove and drive the spline into the groove over the screen cloth. Use a hammer and a block of wood. Be sure that splines have been measured and cut to form butt joint assembly at corners.

Following the same procedure, form the cloth on the two short sides of the aluminum frame. Cut off the excess screen cloth and insert the splines.

Before you replace the aluminum screen panel, carry your modernization project a step further. Sand and smooth the wood storm door, then paint with liquid aluminum. Allow sufficient time for the paint to dry, install your new screen panel and secure with the fasteners. •

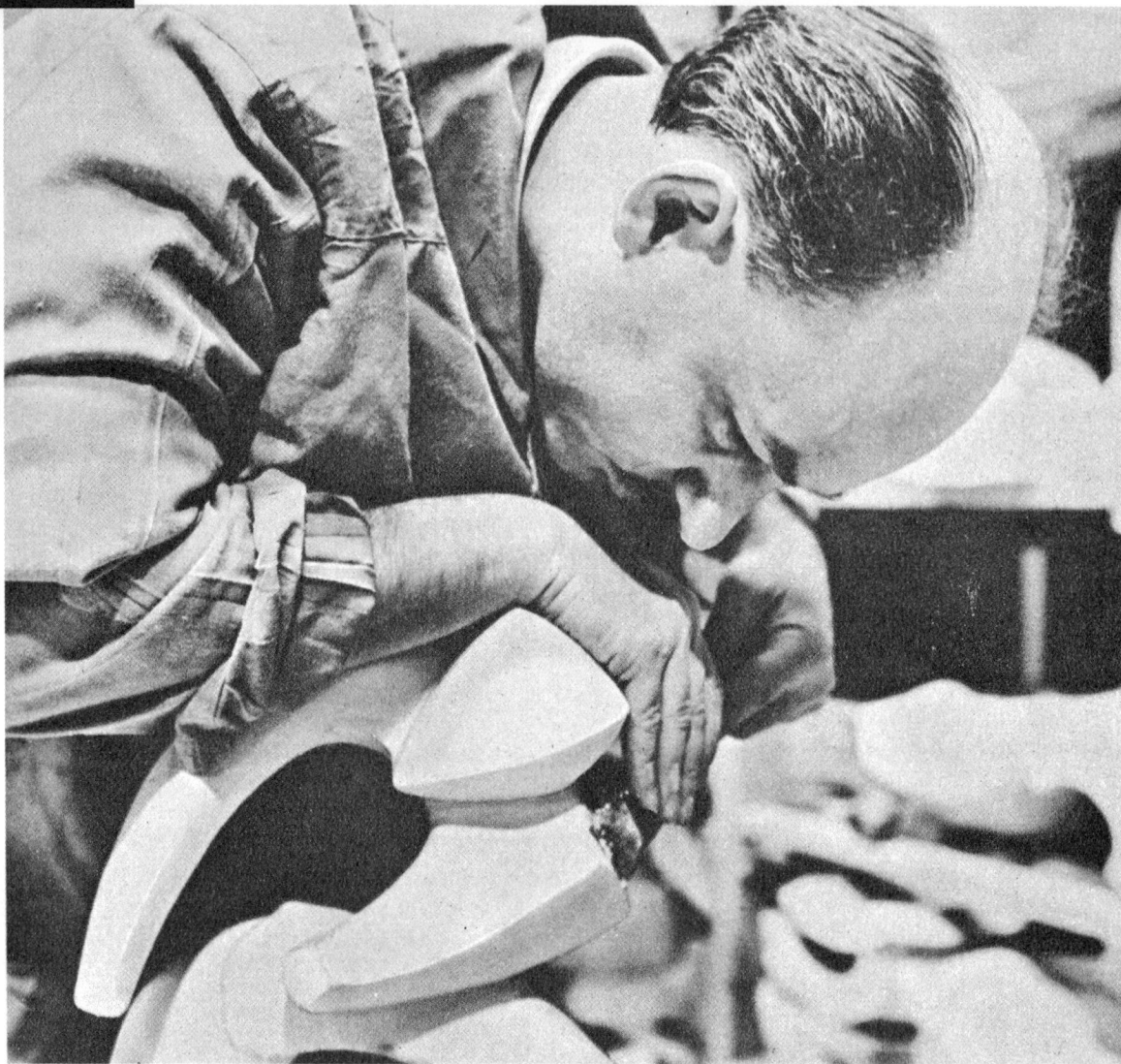

Sculpting

Here is the true test of your clay-working and artistic craftsmanship.

Modeling tools are necessary for effective sculpting after preliminary shaping. Below is a selection of wooden tools that can be purchased or made. At right: five basic tools every sculptor should own.

SMALL WIRE TOOL—ABOUT 4¾" LONG

WIRE TOOL—ABOUT 7½" LONG

HARDWOOD TOOL—ABOUT 7" LONG

HARDWOOD TOOL—ABOUT 5" LONG

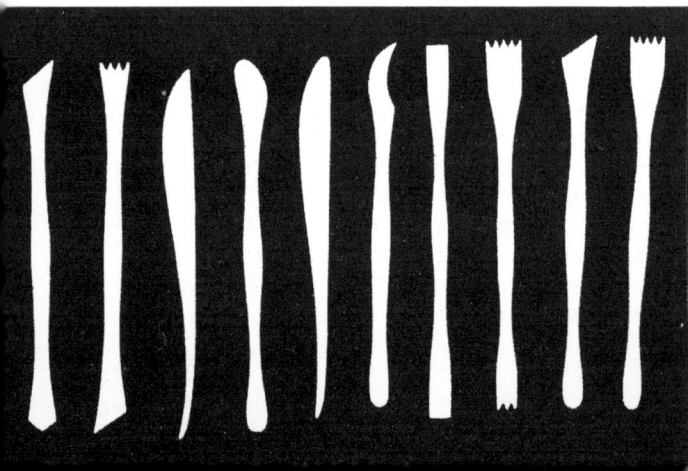

HARDWOOD TOOL—ABOUT 5" LONG

Be sure that your clay is plastic enough to be readily worked with the fingers. Remove excess clay before using tools, as this simplifies detailing. Paring knives, scrapers and a spatula are useful devices.

I N SCULPTING, you will find each of the previous steps helpful in aiding you to develop a flair for this form of ceramic work.

In preparation for sculpting it will be necessary to consider the different problems that will project themselves in this type of work. The size of the piece to be formed will, of necessity, have a direct bearing on the type of material to be used.

In forming a large piece it is necessary to have the body of the clay plastic enough to work and yet firm enough not to squash down or dunt from its own weight. In a small piece not too much attention will be necessary to these considerations since the weight of a small piece is not too vital a factor. Most prepared clays for sculpture work are reinforced with other materials, which serve two purposes. One is to prevent dunting and the other is to prevent cracking or warping during the drying process. The principal material added to the clay used for this process is grog. Grog is actually clay which has been fired and crushed. This crushed matter is then passed through various sized sieves and packaged according to size. Grog for sculpting may be as coarse as a No. 10 mesh; ths would be equal to a fairly coarse gravel, or it may be as fine as a No. 30 mesh, which would be a little bit finer than sea sand. The grade to be used and the quality should be based on the size of the piece you are going to construct. A larger piece will require more and coarser grog proportionately than will a small piece. Percentage of grog when mixed with clay may range as much as 50% of your plastic body.

If the figure is to be bent or supported in unusual positions a leather consistency is required to keep clay from sagging. Revolve the piece frequently to view it from all angles as you shape front and back.

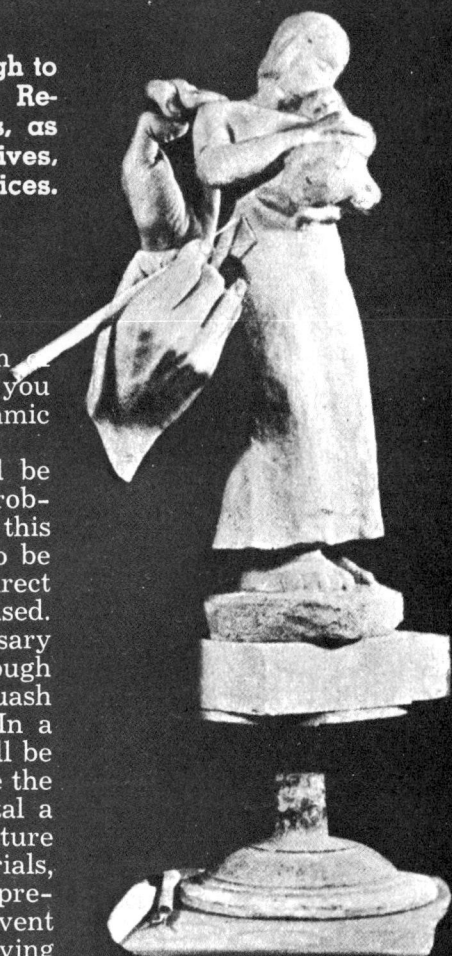

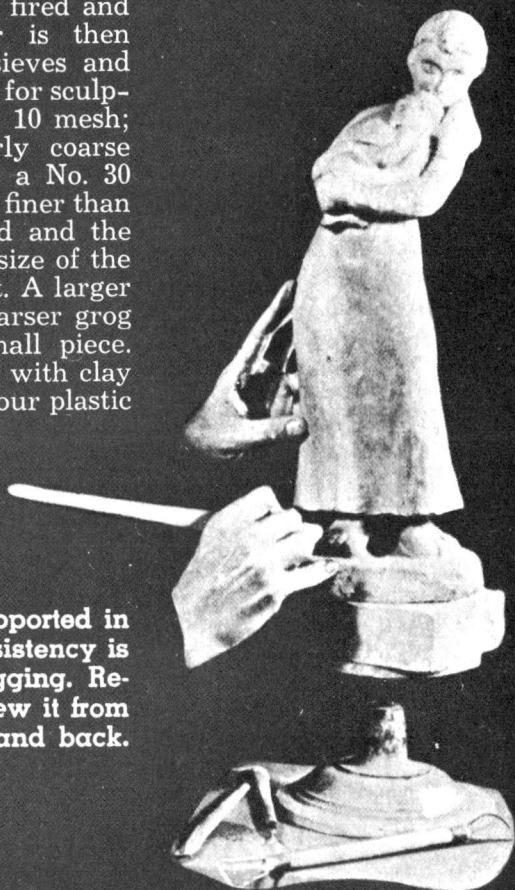

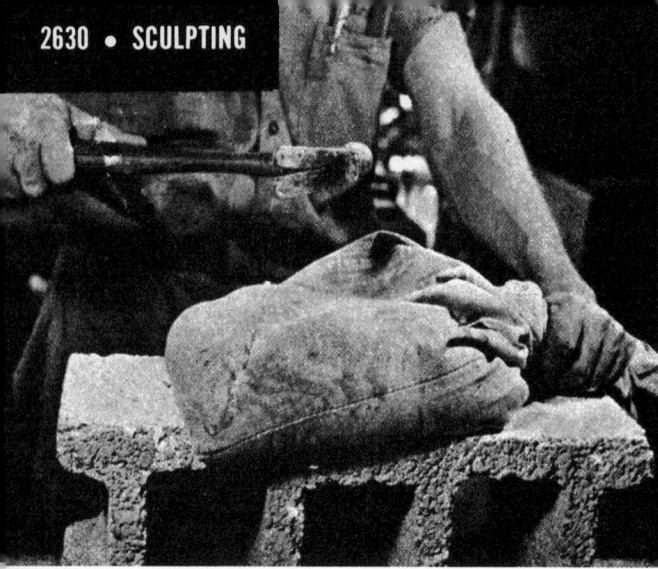

Grog is mixed with clay to prevent cracking and/or warping in sculptured pieces. To make grog, put a piece of unglazed, fired bisque ware in a burlap bag and crush it to bits with flat side of hammer.

Next, place the clay on the back side of a piece of oilcloth and make it flat with a rolling pin. A mass of clay should be small enough to be readily wedged. Proportion of grog should be above 15%.

How to Use Grog

Grog is obtainable from most brickyards. These yards crush up their breakage and sell this broken material according to the size. You may prepare your own grog by crushing up any clay object which has been fired but unglazed. This is best done by putting a piece of bisque ware into a heavy canvas or burlap bag, placing the bag upon a rock or other hard surface and striking repeated hammer blows against the middle of the bag, thereby crushing the contents within the bag between the blows of the hammer on one side and the underlying surface on the other side.

In mixing the grog with clay it-is advisable first to approximate the size of the piece you are going to create and its weight. Weigh out the proportionate amount of grog between 15% and 50%. Divide your mass of clay into sections small enough to be wedged individually. In front of each piece of clay, put the portion of grog you are going to use. This will aid in mixing your materials. Roll out the piece of clay on the reverse side of your piece of oilcloth. Make this piece ¼" thick and scatter grog over the entire surface; fold in half and roll the plastic clay in its own pile of grog. Repeat this same process with the same piece until its own pile of grog is completely imbedded in the clay. Perform the same operation with the remaining clay and grog. Wedge this material thoroughly (see chapter one for wedging).

Another method of mixing grog clay is to mix the clay flour and grog together thoroughly in their dry state in the proportions required for the size piece you are going to form. To this dry mixture add about 25% water by volume. Stir with a strong wood stick and cover tightly; allow to stand at least 24 hours before using. If more water is required, add it before wedging. If the clay should be too moist, dry it out on a plaster bat until it is plastic, and then wedge it.

As at left, sprinkle the grog over the rolled-out clay. The clay should be about a quarter of an inch thick and the grog should be placed over the whole surface. If you desire, buy grog at brickyards.

Press the grog into the plastic clay with rolling pin, moving it back and forth vigorously. Another method of mixing in grog is to take clay flour and add grog to it, then reduce the batch with water.

It is important that the grog be evenly distributed throughout the clay. To this end, fold the clay on itself, as at left, and repeat the flattening out process over and over, using rolling pin technique.

Pounding with the fist is a good way to help work the grog into the clay. The grade and quality used depend on the size of the piece to be sculpted. A larger object will require more and coarser grog.

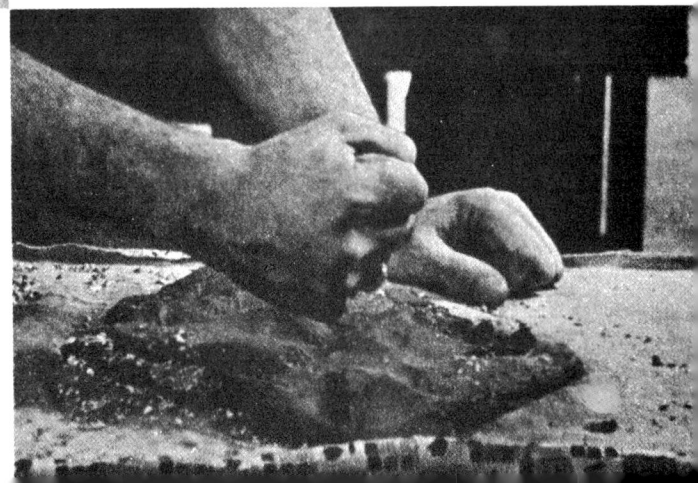

A substantial amount of detail work enters into the modeling of figurines. Suggestion, rather than slavish accuracy, however, should guide you in facial features and hair, as these will be painted in later.

Molding Figurines

Among the most suitable types of clay for sculpture work, particularly if it is to assume fairly large proportions, are terra cotta, Jordan and Monmouth.

In making a figure from a solid piece of clay it is advisable to determine first the general outline and in so doing divide the figure into its most prominent and least prominent parts, based on volume. For example, one of the most popular figures is the figurine of an old woman in native costume with a bundle of balloons over her shoulder. In considering the construction of the figure the most prominent part would be the lower portion with its billowing skirt topped by a broad waist. The second most prominent part of this figure is the torso, which includes two arms, a short bull-like neck, and a proportionately small, round head. The outline of these parts can be made from lumps of clay barely shaped, and if the clay is very plastic, no slip will be required in joining the sections. When the outline proportion is partly shaped, the lumps of clay are assembled. Their mass should be placed on a plaster bat which has been soaked in water.

The general shape will be larger than the finished piece, since clay will be carved off in forming the piece and since the piece will shrink as it dries.

With a wire tool, outline the skirt. Take off and add clay to obtain the right outline. Revolve the piece frequently while you are working so that you may view it from all directions and work the front and rear together. Observe from all angles until you are satisfied that you have achieved what was in your mind's eye when you began. If you have difficulty in visualizing the folds of the skirt, it would be a good idea to form a wire circle approximately the size of the waist. Drape a piece of soft cloth around the wire circle, holding it up and noticing the way the folds of cloth drape. This can be used as a model for you to copy the folds of the skirt. In forming the torso, define sharply the indentations which will represent the division between the body proper and the arms. Be sure to outline the suggestion of the bosom as it would appear under a coarse fabric forming the bodice of a peasant costume. For the face and head start with oval or egg shape and fashion, with suggestion rather than accuracy, nose, lips, eyes, and other facial details. Remember that these features will probably be painted in later.

Such details as a head scarf will eliminate the necessity of defining the ears, neck cords, and even parts of the neck line.

Do not let the figure dry out while you are working on it. In between your working sessions, cover the piece with a damp cloth or plastic material. Keep the piece either in an old icebox or under a crock or a can.

When the piece is entirely completed, but still in its leather stage, use a spoon or a knife to hollow out the solid object. It should be hollowed out to a wall thickness of between ½″ and ¾″.

In order to eliminate the necessity of hollowing the piece, you may, if you wish, make a wad of newspaper and wrap your starting clay around the wad of paper. Proceed as directed to sculpt your piece, shaping it as explained in the foregoing paragraphs. When this piece is fired in the kiln, the paper will burn out, leaving the piece hollow. A later chapter covers firing preparations and techniques.

Large pieces may also be sculptured from outlines or forms built up by the coil method.

In making shapes with elongated, unsupported areas, like the barrel of a horse or a dachshund, it is wise to construct your piece on an armature. An armature is a device made of supporting material such as wood, or wood combined with wire or paper, upon which clay forms are supported while being modeled. If you use a wooden armature it will be necessary to expose a portion of the armature so that it may be burned out in the bisque firing. If, on the other hand, you use a wire armature, it should be removed before the firing. If it cannot be removed, the piece should not be fired. •

Examples of the sculptor's art show wide diversity of subject matter and treatment available to the hobbyist, from portrait-busts to whimsical animals.

1. How to build a septic tank: Lay out proposed size of excavation using plank framework as a guide. This will also prevent caving in at edges.

4. After pouring, smooth the tops of the walls with a wood float as shown in photo at left. Below: Allow at least 48 hours for concrete to set.

sewage disposal

No public sewer line? You can buy a septic tank ready for installation or you can build your own.

IN locations where the public sewer line is not available, a private system will have to be constructed for the disposal of house sewage. Cesspools and septic tanks are the usual alternatives and the septic tank is much to be preferred. In many places it is the only method which is permitted because of the danger of water and stream contamination from cesspools.

The septic tank operates on the principle of reducing waste matter to liquid and evaporating it in the open air through a leaching field. The solid matter in the waste drops to the bottom of the tank in the form of sludge. Septic tanks can be purchased complete and ready to be installed or they can be built on the site out of poured concrete or cement blocks.

The tank should be located 15 or 20 feet from the house and away from lot lines and water supply wells. It should have a capacity of 500 to 600 gallons or at least 100 gallons for each person in the household. A typical 500 gallon tank would measure about 3 feet wide, 6 feet long and 5 feet deep.

House waste is carried to the septic tank by tile or iron pipe which is tightly sealed

2. Since the concrete is poured between the earth and your form, be sure that the latter is built carefully to assure uniform wall thicknesses.

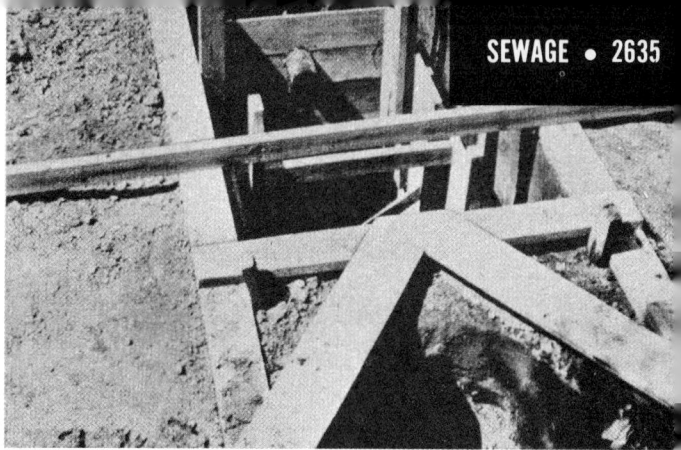

3. A completed form before pouring concrete. Note that both the inlet and outlet sewer pipe connections have already been built into the form.

5. When form is removed, cast cover slabs. Measure off size of tank and make separate forms. Slabs may be bought if your tank is standard size.

6. Completed septic tank itself. System must now be completed with installation of sewer pipe and distribution box. Sketch below explains set-up.

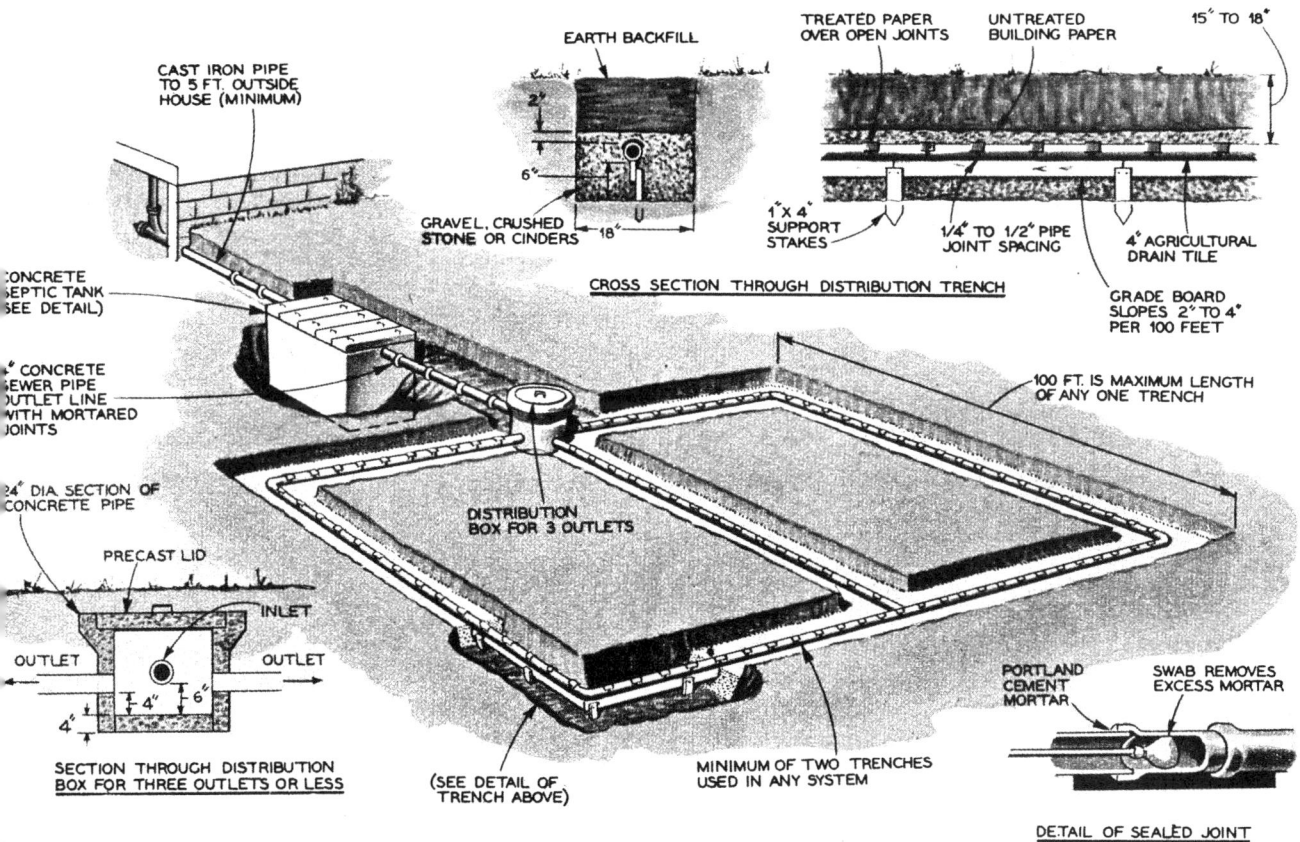

CAST IRON PIPE TO 5 FT. OUTSIDE HOUSE (MINIMUM)

EARTH BACKFILL

TREATED PAPER OVER OPEN JOINTS

UNTREATED BUILDING PAPER

15" TO 18"

GRAVEL, CRUSHED STONE OR CINDERS

CROSS SECTION THROUGH DISTRIBUTION TRENCH

1" X 4" SUPPORT STAKES

1/4" TO 1/2" PIPE JOINT SPACING

4" AGRICULTURAL DRAIN TILE

GRADE BOARD SLOPES 2" TO 4" PER 100 FEET

CONCRETE SEPTIC TANK (SEE DETAIL)

4" CONCRETE SEWER PIPE OUTLET LINE WITH MORTARED JOINTS

100 FT. IS MAXIMUM LENGTH OF ANY ONE TRENCH

24" DIA. SECTION OF CONCRETE PIPE

PRECAST LID

INLET

DISTRIBUTION BOX FOR 3 OUTLETS

OUTLET

OUTLET

SECTION THROUGH DISTRIBUTION BOX FOR THREE OUTLETS OR LESS

(SEE DETAIL OF TRENCH ABOVE)

MINIMUM OF TWO TRENCHES USED IN ANY SYSTEM

PORTLAND CEMENT MORTAR

SWAB REMOVES EXCESS MORTAR

DETAIL OF SEALED JOINT

SEWAGE DISPOSAL SYSTEM FOR LARGE ACREAGE OR SMALL FARMS

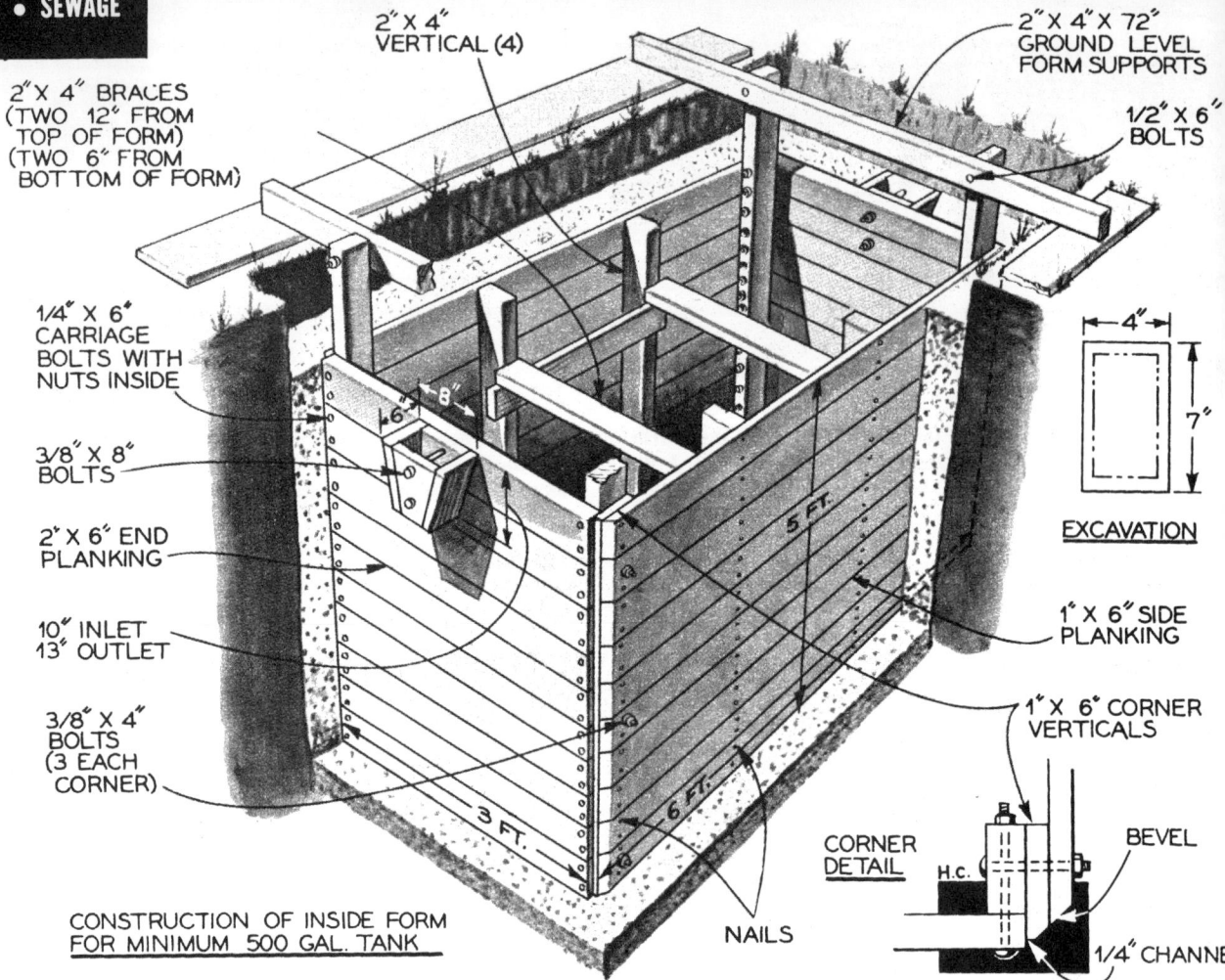

2" X 4" VERTICAL (4)

2" X 4" X 72" GROUND LEVEL FORM SUPPORTS

2" X 4" BRACES (TWO 12" FROM TOP OF FORM) (TWO 6" FROM BOTTOM OF FORM)

1/2" X 6" BOLTS

1/4" X 6" CARRIAGE BOLTS WITH NUTS INSIDE

3/8" X 8" BOLTS

2" X 6" END PLANKING

10" INLET 13" OUTLET

3/8" X 4" BOLTS (3 EACH CORNER)

5 FT.

3 FT.

6 FT.

EXCAVATION

1" X 6" SIDE PLANKING

1" X 6" CORNER VERTICALS

CORNER DETAIL

H.C.

BEVEL

1/4" CHANNEL

NAILS

CONSTRUCTION OF INSIDE FORM FOR MINIMUM 500 GAL. TANK

at the joints. It enters the tank through a tee fitting extending below the scum line of the liquid. The top opening of the fitting extends above the scum line to allow venting. The bottom of the tank should slope to one low point for better accumulation of insoluble matter or sludge. After some time the sludge has to be removed to keep the tank operating properly. The tank cover must be constructed to form a tight seal, but entrance must be allowed for when cleaning is necessary.

After the bacteria action in the tank has acted on the waste—a process that takes about 24 hours—the liquid is drained off to a leaching field for evaporation. The outlet of the tank is similar to the inlet, but the lower part of the tee fitting extends four inches deeper into the liquid. The outflow pipe is tightly sealed for about 15 feet and on a downward slope emptying into a distribution box. From this point the sections of pipe are open-jointed to allow flow of the liquid into the field.

The leaching field consists of a layout of several pipe lines placed about 20 inches below the surface in beds of gravel and sandy soil. The joints of pipe are covered

Cesspool construction. Place sand at the base before laying blocks.

Insert and cement the inlet pipe through row of concrete blocks.

Tamp sand around the blocks you proceed. Cement block end

3/8" REINFORCEMENT BARS (3 PER SLAB)

EMBED IRON HANDLES

BEVEL TWO EDGES

3 1/2" X 12" X 48" CONCRETE COVER SLAB (7)

CAULKED JOINTS

7"

12"

SCUM

3"

12"

4 FT.

10"

18"

INLET SEWER LINE

OUTLET SEWER LINE

6" THICK POURED CONCRETE WALLS AND BOTTOM

LENGTH 6 FT. (WIDTH 3 FT.)

SLUDGE

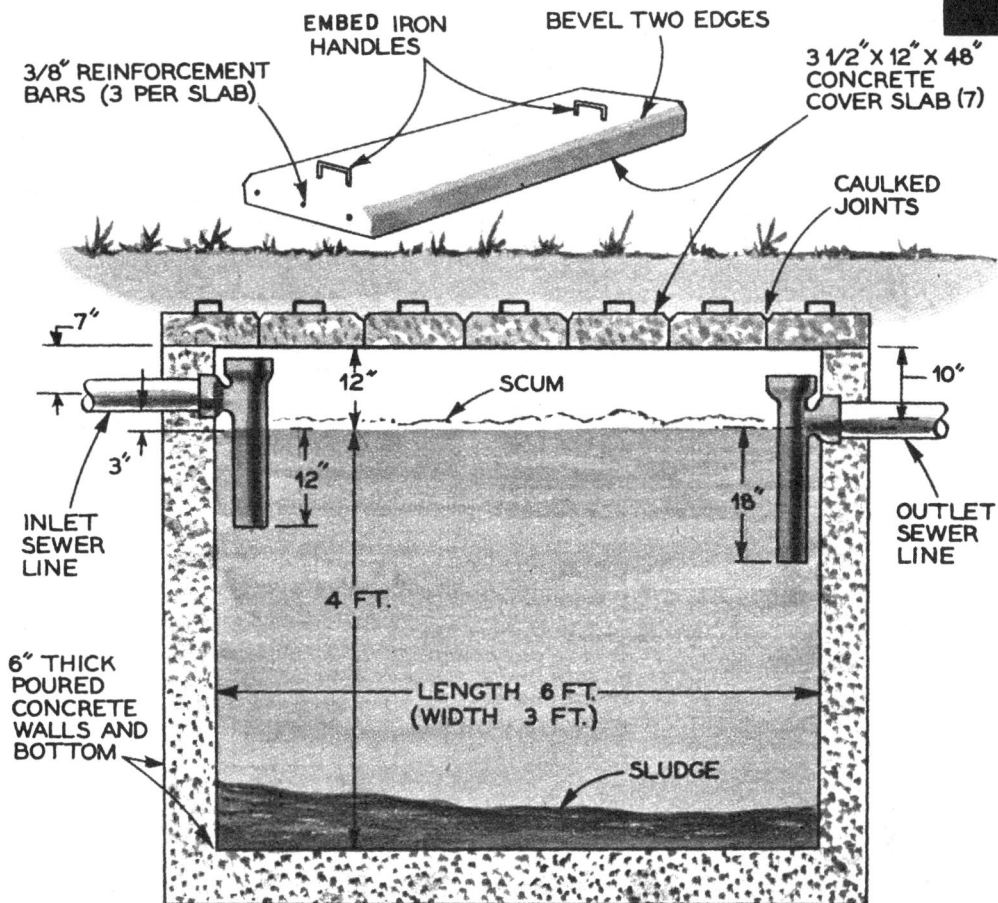

SECTION THROUGH 500 GAL. CONCRETE SEPTIC TANK

on top with tar paper and straw on top of which the soil and sod is replaced. The rows of pipe should be about 12 feet apart and a 500 gallon tank will require about 350 feet of leaching pipe. A typical layout for such a field is at top of page 2639.

When sloping the pipe and placing the septic tank, a grade downward from the house must be provided for a drop of 1 inch for every 10 inches of travel. The outlet pipes should be

Required Septic Tank Capacities

No. of bedrooms in dwellings	Maximum number persons served	Nominal liquid cap. in gallons	Recommended dimensions			
			Inside width	Inside length	Liquid depth	Total depth
2 or less	4	500	3 ft. 0 in.	6 ft. 0 in.	4 ft. 0 in.	5 ft. 0 in.
3	6	600	3 ft. 0 in.	7 ft. 0 in.	4 ft. 0 in.	5 ft. 0 in.
4	8	750	3 ft. 6 in.	7 ft. 6 in.	4 ft. 0 in.	5 ft. 0 in.
5	10	900	3 ft. 6 in.	8 ft. 0 in.	4 ft. 6 in.	5 ft. 6 in.
6	12	1,100	4 ft. 0 in.	8 ft. 6 in.	4 ft. 6 in.	5 ft. 6 in.
7	14	1,300	4 ft. 0 in.	10 ft. 0 in.	4 ft. 6 in.	5 ft. 6 in.
8	16	1,500	4 ft. 6 in.	10 ft. 0 in.	4 ft. 6 in.	5 ft. 6 in.

Keep filling in around the blocks as you decrease diameter of unit.

Top layer of tongue-and-groove cesspool blocks are cemented.

Heavy duty lid can take weight, may be used in driveways, etc.

ARCHED BLOCKS ARE
LAID UP IN MORTAR

4" SEWER
INLET PIPE

NOT OVER 24"

24"

40"

15 FT. TO
HOUSE

BLOCKS ARE
SPECIAL
TONGUE
AND GROOVE
APPROVED
CESSPOOL
BLOCKS

4" POROUS
BACKFILL

4 FT.

12 FT.

LOWER ROWS
LAID UP
WITHOUT
MORTAR

POROUS SOIL

OPEN BOTTOM

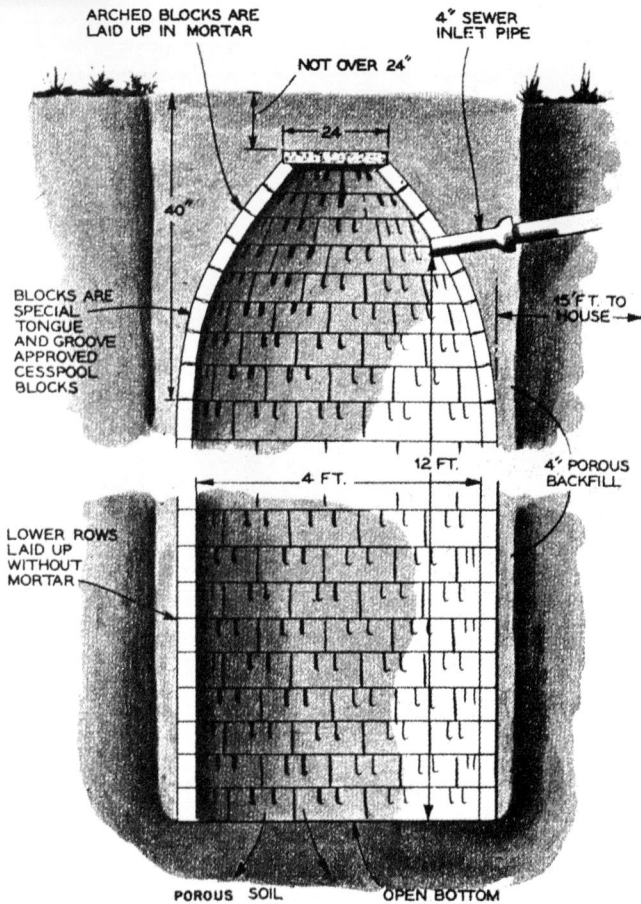

graded downward 1 inch for every 20 inches of travel. The distribution pipes in the leaching field can be only slightly dropped—not over 3 inches for every 50 feet of travel.

When there is no municipal sewer system, a grease trap is absolutely essential with any type of sewage disposal arrangement. If allowed to flow into a cesspool or septic tank, grease will clog up or waterproof the soil so that the liquid matter will not drain away.

A system to prevent backflow during storms is also important. When street sewers have become gorged by torrential downpours the sewage level may rise to a point several feet above the basement level, thus presenting the risk of a serious backflow. A good drainage system should be installed to pump the overflow out to a convenient storm water conductor line.

All storm water, sanitary and floor drain lines should be of cast iron, pressure-tight to prevent the development of hydrostatic pressure under the basement floor. •

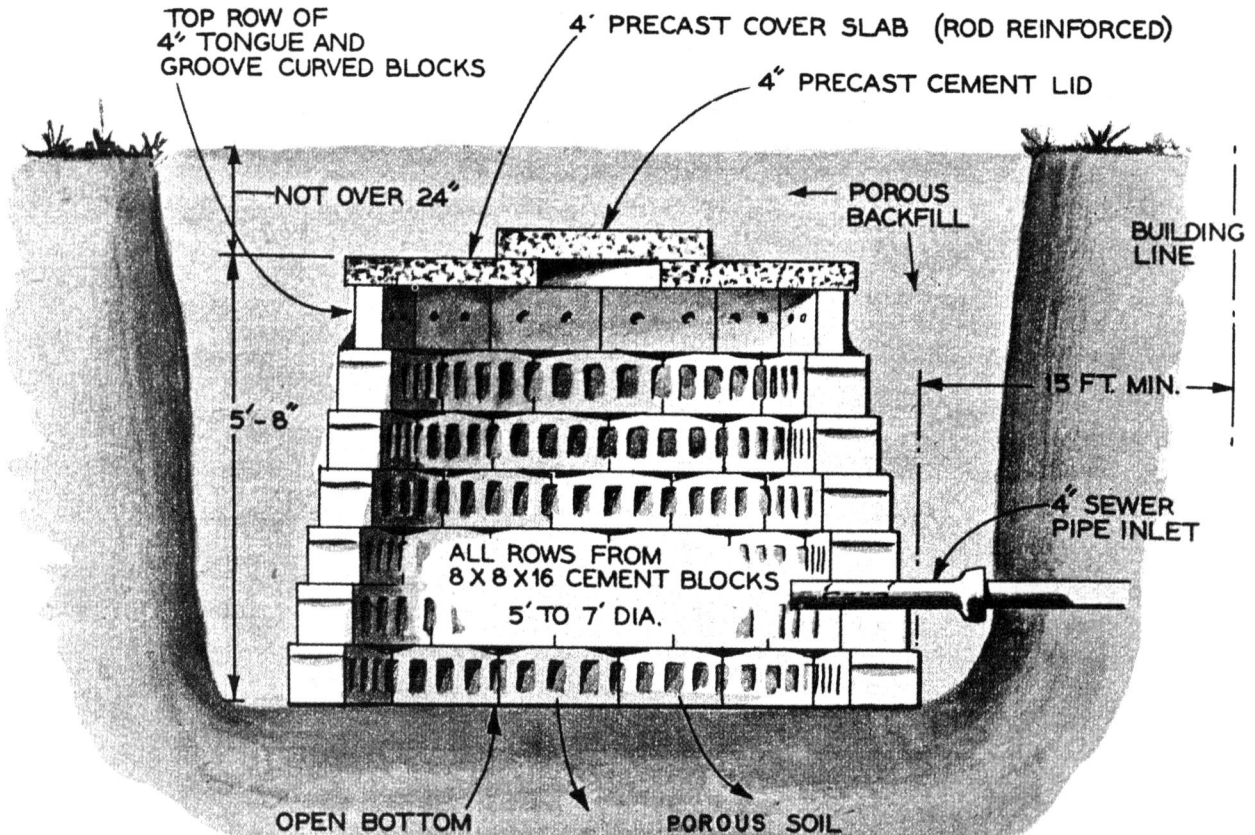

TOP ROW OF
4" TONGUE AND
GROOVE CURVED BLOCKS

4' PRECAST COVER SLAB (ROD REINFORCED)

4" PRECAST CEMENT LID

NOT OVER 24"

POROUS
BACKFILL

BUILDING
LINE

5'-8"

15 FT. MIN.

ALL ROWS FROM
8 X 8 X 16 CEMENT BLOCKS
5' TO 7' DIA.

4" SEWER
PIPE INLET

OPEN BOTTOM

POROUS SOIL

TWO TYPES OF CESSPOOLS IN WHICH
ACCUMULATED SEWAGE SEEPS THROUGH
OPEN HOLES IN BLOCKS, AND DISPERSES
IN ALL DIRECTIONS THROUGH THE SOIL

Above is a cross-section showing side view of a septic tank. Note that the bottom slopes to a low point for accumulation of sludge. At right above is a schematic lay-out of a distribution box and a leaching field as seen in plan. Rows of pipe are approximately 12 feet apart, placed 20 inches under surface and covered with gravel.

A system to prevent backflow from public sewers is shown below. By dividing the home drainage system into four separate units, with appropriate control valves, surplus drainage from areaways and from the foundation flows to an overflow sump pump and is then passed out to a convenient storm water line. Use pressure-tight pipe.

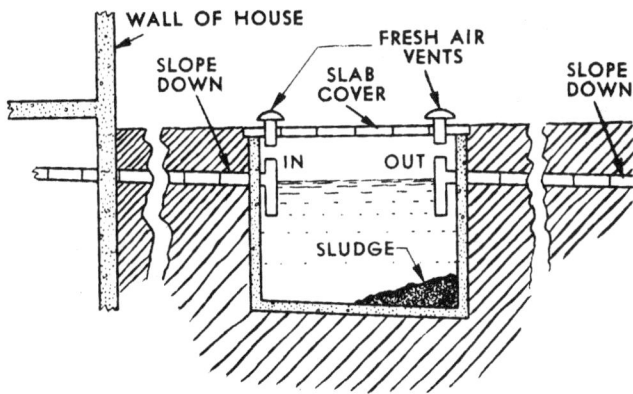

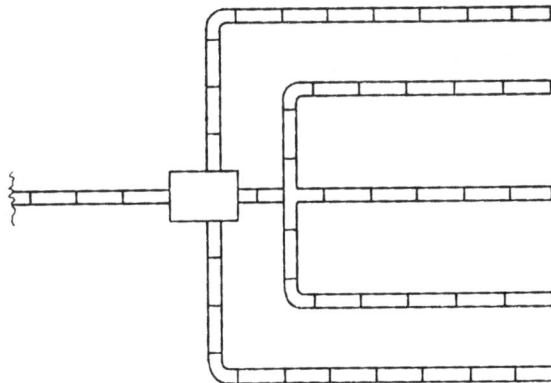

Dimensions of Clay Sewer Pipe

American Society for Testing Materials
(From Tentative Specifications C13-32T)

Internal Diam. Inches	Laying Length Feet	Inside Diam. at ½ In. Above Base of Socket Inches*	Depth of Socket Inches	Minimum Taper Socket	Thickness of Barrel Inches	Thickness of Socket
4	2	5⅞	1¾	1:20	½	The thickness of the socket ¼ in. from its outer end shall be not less than three-fourths of the thickness of the barrel of the pipe
6	2, 2½	8⅛	2¼	1:20	⅝	
8	2, 2½, 3	10⅝	2½	1:20	¾	
10	2, 2½, 3	12⅞	2½	1:20	⅞	
12	2, 2½, 3	15¼	2½	1:20	1	
15	2, 2½, 3	18⅝	2½	1:20	1¼	
18	2, 2½, 3	22¼	3	1:20	1½	
21	2, 2½, 3	25¾	3	1:20	1¾	
24	2, 2½, 3	29⅜	3	1:20	2	
27	2½, 3	33	3½	1:20	2¼	
30	2½, 3	36⅝	3½	1:20	2½	
33	2½, 3	39⅞	4	1:20	2⅝	
36	2½, 3	43⅝	4	1:20	2¾	

*When pipes are furnished having an increase in thickness over that given in last column, the diameter of socket shall be increased by an amount equal to twice the increase of thickness of barrel.

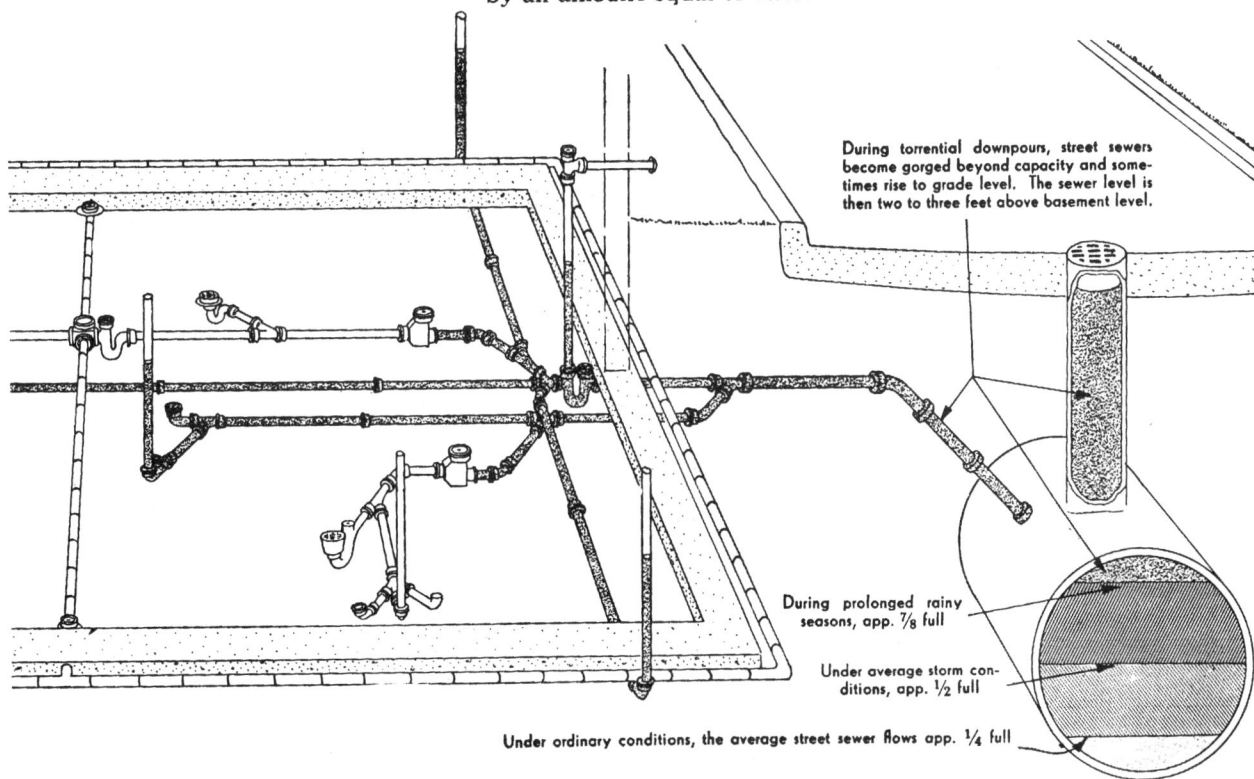

During torrential downpours, street sewers become gorged beyond capacity and sometimes rise to grade level. The sewer level is then two to three feet above basement level.

During prolonged rainy seasons, app. ⅞ full

Under average storm conditions, app. ½ full

Under ordinary conditions, the average street sewer flows app. ¼ full

China Closet— Sewing Center

The primary purpose of this furniture is to store and display chinaware and silver, but a housewife can quickly turn it into a sewing workbench.

By Henry Clark

Finished cabinet features open shelves for dishes, three drawers, hidden sewing center, and commodious storage space for materials.

Two simple movements of hands, and sewing machine and work surface are exposed, ready for a housewife to begin her sewing.

With sliding work table pushed forward, the large bin in back is exposed. In center, below, is space for three linen drawers, and on each side are compartments for dry goods storage.

THIS CHINA CLOSET serves up dinner plates from its china shelves, stores linens in its three spacious drawers, hides away the silver in a hidden drawer, and has two other commodious compartments for dry goods, trays, vases, etc. Yet, with two quick motions of the arms, a housewife has at her immediate disposal a sewing center complete with machine, threads, accessories, and a large materials bin. She can sew anything from small items with simple seams, to large, complex draperies.

All this and more, to keep the housewife happy. Should she suddenly be interrupted by company, she won't fluster a bit since she merely shoves the whole mess into the wide bin in back, pushes the sliding work table to the rear, and folds the machine ledge shut. The company would never be the wiser. Behind that closed panel lies her busy sewing project ready to be resumed as soon as the company leaves. Whole patterns could be slid into the bin intact since this area is roughly 18 by 48 inches. The housewife could likewise serve up a complete dinner without once exposing her clutter of cuts, folds and loose ends. And all this is accomplished in the comfort of the dining room, since the primary purpose of the piece is to display and store chinaware and silver.

Actually, the sewing machine unit might be hinged onto any cabinet in any room, folding away the same easy way.

Drawer construction is of the rabbet and butt joint method, and bottom panels slide into dadoes.

The drawer rails are simple, doubling as sectional walls. Masonite panels seal off compartment sides.

Screw through front face of ledge makes portable machine secure and allows for quick removal.

China cupboard is an individual unit and sets over the sewing center top, secured by screws.

A 1x2-inch facing goes around front edges, and can be made to receive a sliding door.

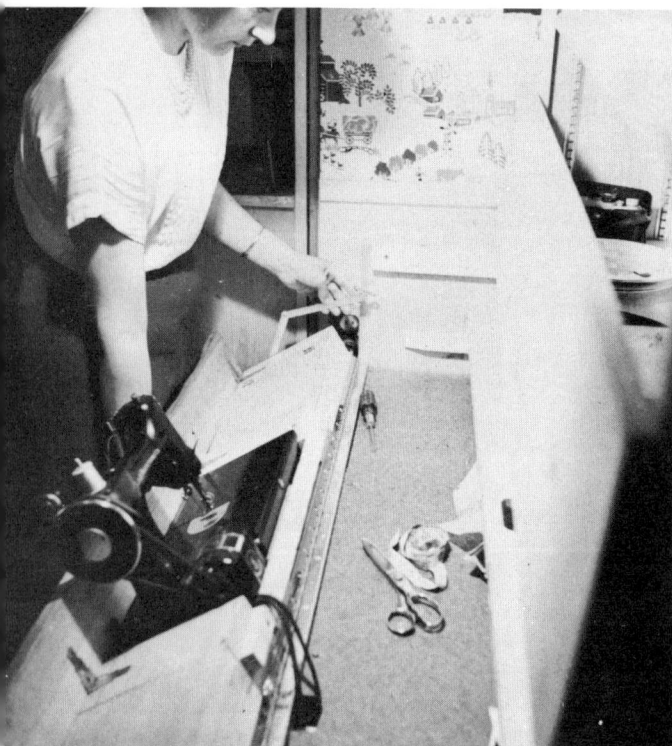

Piano hinge and brass brackets hold ledge. Fold brackets to tuck machine ledge away.

If your china cabinet has an 8-inch drawer section at top, this unit can be built right into that section, solving the problem of how to set up your wife's portable sewing machine on a permanent basis. One screw under the ledge permits quick removal for taking the machine on vacations, if needed. On the other hand, should she ever give up sewing, the machine folding ledge can be unscrewed, and the area filled with drawers.

Here's one certainty. This project, if started from scratch, will win the handy man his wife's undying gratitude. Those "company" features will be blessed many times.

The unit described in this article was built around a Singer portable which is as compact as sewing machines come. However, the same folding technique could be employed on a larger machine by juggling with the hinge locations. (Do this on drawings, first.) Choice of wood is up to the builder. Starting with the lower cabinet, we used stock sizes of select white pine, butting together 9-inch and 12-inch stock for the lower cabinet sides, joining butt with 1x2-inch cleats along the top edge and at the bottom to support the flooring.

A 1x12-inch panel was screwed across the top, and to it was attached a piano hinge to take the 1x10-inch panel which becomes the hinged lid. Rough 1-inch stock is used at the floor which now joins the two sides into a "box" unit. The back is ⅛-inch Masonite or plywood, secured to cleats set inside the back edges. This eliminates making rabbets, an optional task. A toe board was sunk into its notch to complete the base. Cleats may be buried under the floor to help support it, if desired.

Build the machine ledge next, following the drawings for procedures if not for dimensions, depending on the type of sewing machine you have. Cut the face panel first, on which is placed the machine for trial setting, and build the spool compartments around it. These will be 1x2-inch stock forming a wall at front, sides and rear, except that portion behind the machine. This is done to keep the panel narrow for neatness when folded away. Too wide, it becomes un-

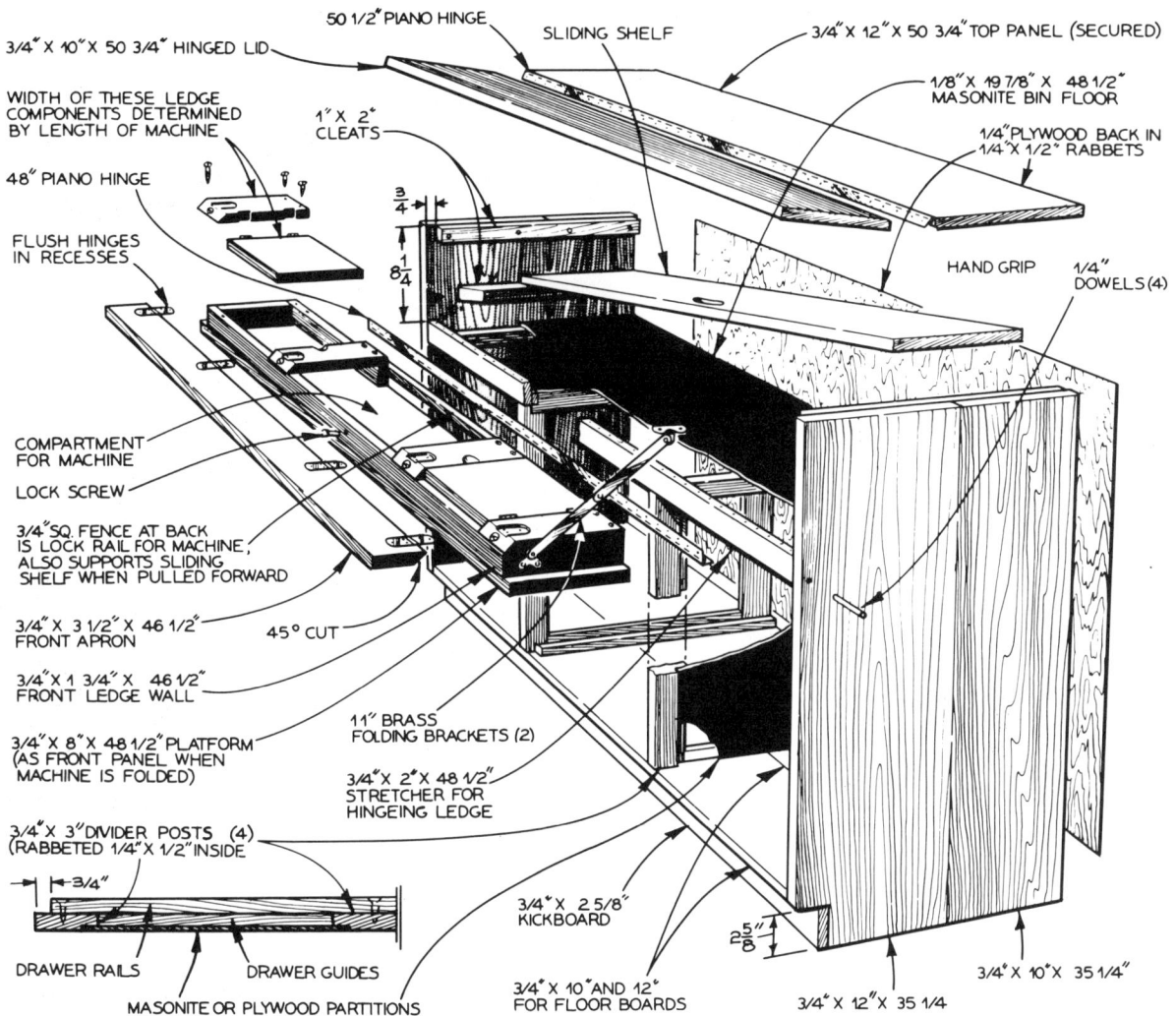

3/4" X 10" X 50 3/4" HINGED LID

50 1/2" PIANO HINGE

SLIDING SHELF

3/4" X 12" X 50 3/4" TOP PANEL (SECURED)

1/8" X 19 7/8" X 48 1/2" MASONITE BIN FLOOR

1/4" PLYWOOD BACK IN 1/4" X 1/2" RABBETS

WIDTH OF THESE LEDGE COMPONENTS DETERMINED BY LENGTH OF MACHINE

1" X 2" CLEATS

48" PIANO HINGE

FLUSH HINGES IN RECESSES

HAND GRIP

1/4" DOWELS (4)

3/4

8 1/4

COMPARTMENT FOR MACHINE

LOCK SCREW

3/4" SQ. FENCE AT BACK IS LOCK RAIL FOR MACHINE, ALSO SUPPORTS SLIDING SHELF WHEN PULLED FORWARD

3/4" X 3 1/2" X 46 1/2" FRONT APRON

45° CUT

3/4" X 1 3/4" X 46 1/2" FRONT LEDGE WALL

11" BRASS FOLDING BRACKETS (2)

3/4" X 8" X 48 1/2" PLATFORM (AS FRONT PANEL WHEN MACHINE IS FOLDED)

3/4" X 2" X 48 1/2" STRETCHER FOR HINGEING LEDGE

3/4" X 3" DIVIDER POSTS (4) (RABBETED 1/4" X 1/2" INSIDE)

3/4"

3/4" X 2 5/8" KICKBOARD

DRAWER RAILS

DRAWER GUIDES

MASONITE OR PLYWOOD PARTITIONS

3/4" X 10" AND 12" FOR FLOOR BOARDS

2 5/8

3/4" X 12" X 35 1/4

3/4" X 10" X 35 1/4"

gainly both in looks as well as handling. A ¾-inch-square cleat at the rear of the machine supports it when folded and also doubles as sliding shelf support when this is slid forward to butt the ledge of the machine.

The ledge-top panel should be one piece, if it is to be stained, in order to maintain a uniform grain. This will come from a 1x12-inch panel. Use a saw table to rip the 45-degree bevel cut and six other cross cuts for the spool and accessory bin lids. Mortise the top surface for four flush hinges to take the narrow "apron" which must fold back, as shown. The reason for the 45-degree bevel becomes apparent after folding the machine away several times. Do not attempt any other cut, unless you work it out well on paper. We spent days on this fold. (There's a 90-degree alternate,

but watch it. It's a tricky proposition.)

Secure the full-length stretcher between cabinet sides with dowels and with a 48-inch piano hinge. Secure the machine ledge on top of this, holding it with a few screws only, for making tests. Two brass folding brackets on each end of the ledge support it when open for use. Top fitting of these brackets is mortised into the edge cleat for flush fit of top lid when closed.

Before securing the piano hinge, place the cleats for supporting the Masonite materials bin bottom and furnish two rails for the sliding shelf to ride on. Wax this well. Provide a hand hold on the sliding shelf. With bin bottom set in, and sliding shelf on rails, secure the rest of the piano hinge screws, and this section is complete.

Feed the wires from machine to foot

Several ¼-inch dowel pegs are driven into the ledge bin for racking up thread spools. Flush platform hinges over to prevent snags.

The working center is quickly put away and hidden simply by folding the machine ledge up into the bin, then closing lid over it.

The convenient drawers of the cabinet can hold all the table and kitchen linens without exposing the functional sewing section.

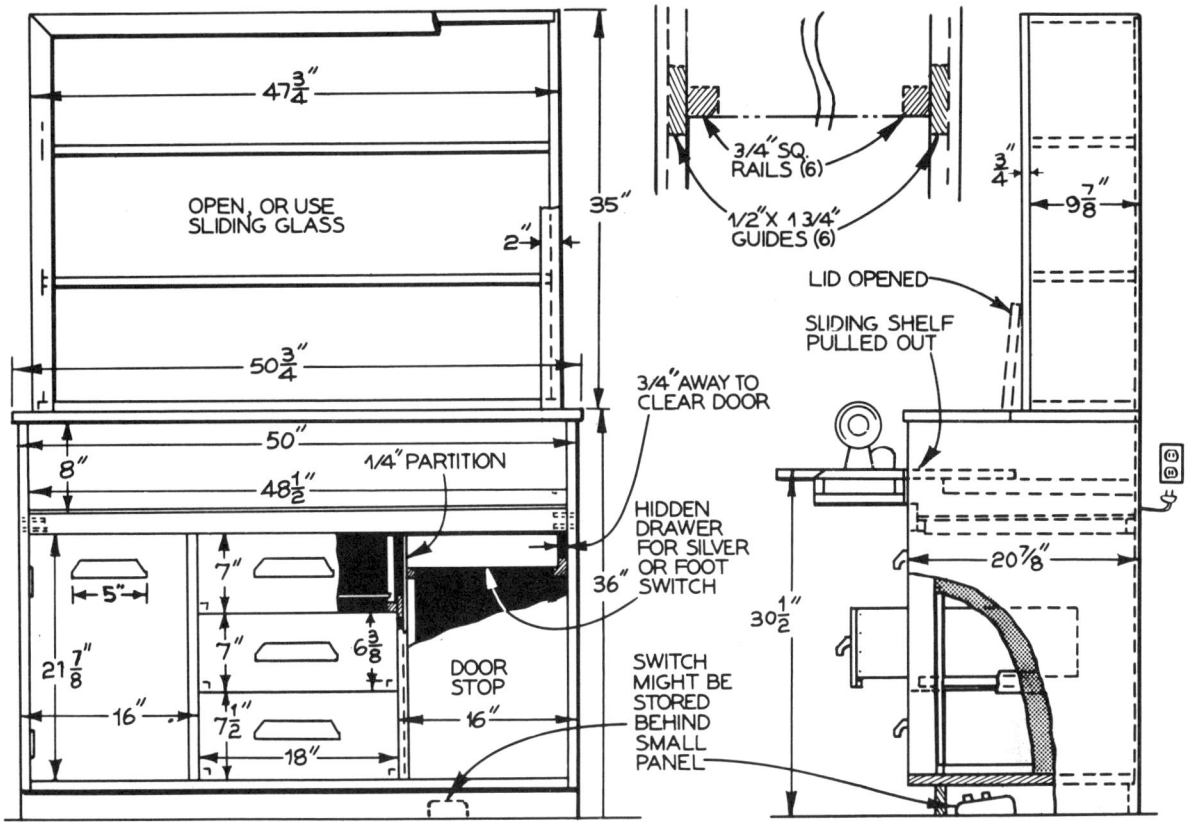

OPEN, OR USE SLIDING GLASS

47 3/4"

35"

50 3/4"

2"

3/4" SQ. RAILS (6)

1/2" X 1 3/4" GUIDES (6)

3/4"

9 7/8"

LID OPENED

SLIDING SHELF PULLED OUT

50"

8"

48 1/2"

1/4" PARTITION

3/4" AWAY TO CLEAR DOOR

HIDDEN DRAWER FOR SILVER OR FOOT SWITCH

36"

5"

7"

7"

6 3/8"

7 1/2"

21 7/8"

16"

18"

DOOR STOP

16"

SWITCH MIGHT BE STORED BEHIND SMALL PANEL

20 7/8"

30 1/2"

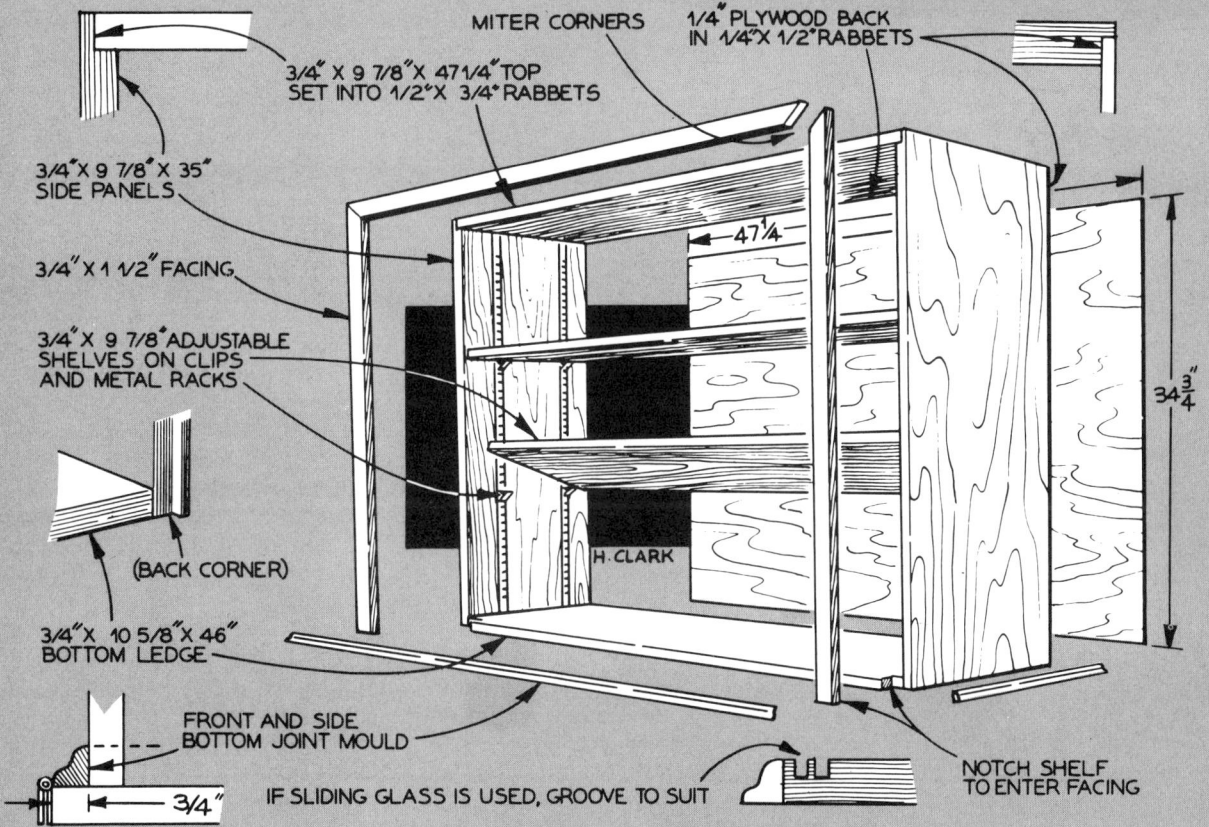

MITER CORNERS

1/4" PLYWOOD BACK IN 1/4"X 1/2" RABBETS

3/4" X 9 7/8"X 47 1/4" TOP SET INTO 1/2"X 3/4" RABBETS

3/4" X 9 7/8" X 35" SIDE PANELS

3/4" X 1 1/2" FACING

3/4" X 9 7/8" ADJUSTABLE SHELVES ON CLIPS AND METAL RACKS

47 1/4"

34 3/4"

(BACK CORNER)

H. CLARK

3/4" X 10 5/8" X 46" BOTTOM LEDGE

FRONT AND SIDE BOTTOM JOINT MOULD

3/4"

IF SLIDING GLASS IS USED, GROOVE TO SUIT

NOTCH SHELF TO ENTER FACING

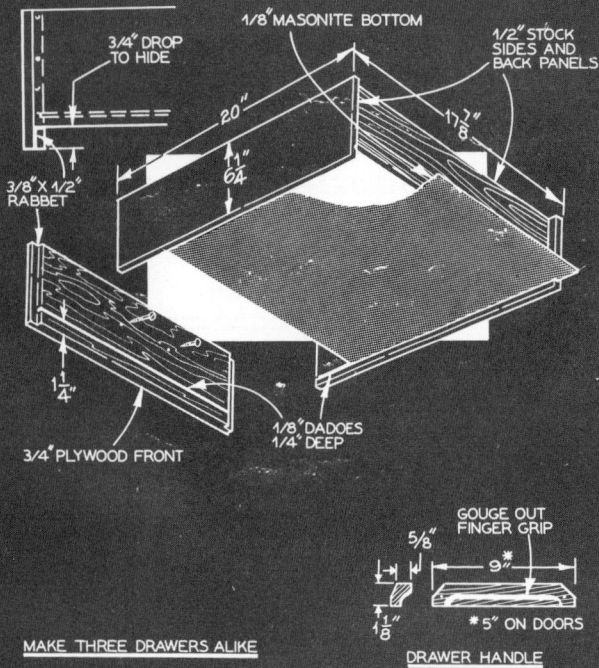

3/4" DROP TO HIDE

1/8" MASONITE BOTTOM

1/2" STOCK SIDES AND BACK PANELS

20"

17 7/8"

1"/64

3/8" X 1/2" RABBET

1 1/4"

1/8" DADOES 1/4" DEEP

3/4" PLYWOOD FRONT

MAKE THREE DRAWERS ALIKE

GOUGE OUT FINGER GRIP

5/8"

9"

1/8"

1/4"

*5" ON DOORS

DRAWER HANDLE

switch and wall plug as best suits your purpose. Switch can be tucked in the compartment, or behind the toe board, with access door. There is room under the roof of the materials bin for additional flat drawers to contain the many gadgets and accessories made for sewing machines.

The large, lower cabinet is now partitioned with 1x3-inch verticals, rabbeted on one edge for the compartment wall of Masonite or plywood. Drawer rails are ¾-inch square stock backed up with ¼-inch flat stock as guides. Doors are set flush with the cabinet front faces, and they are mounted on 2-inch brass hinges.

The hidden silver drawer runs on ¾-inch square rails also, but one side is built away from the wall ¾ of an inch to clear the door when sliding out. It likewise sets in just enough to let the door close over it. The silver drawer and three other larger drawers are constructed with simple joints. (See drawings.)

The china closet is made last. Two verticals of 1x10-inch stock, with rabbets at top and bottom edges, form the

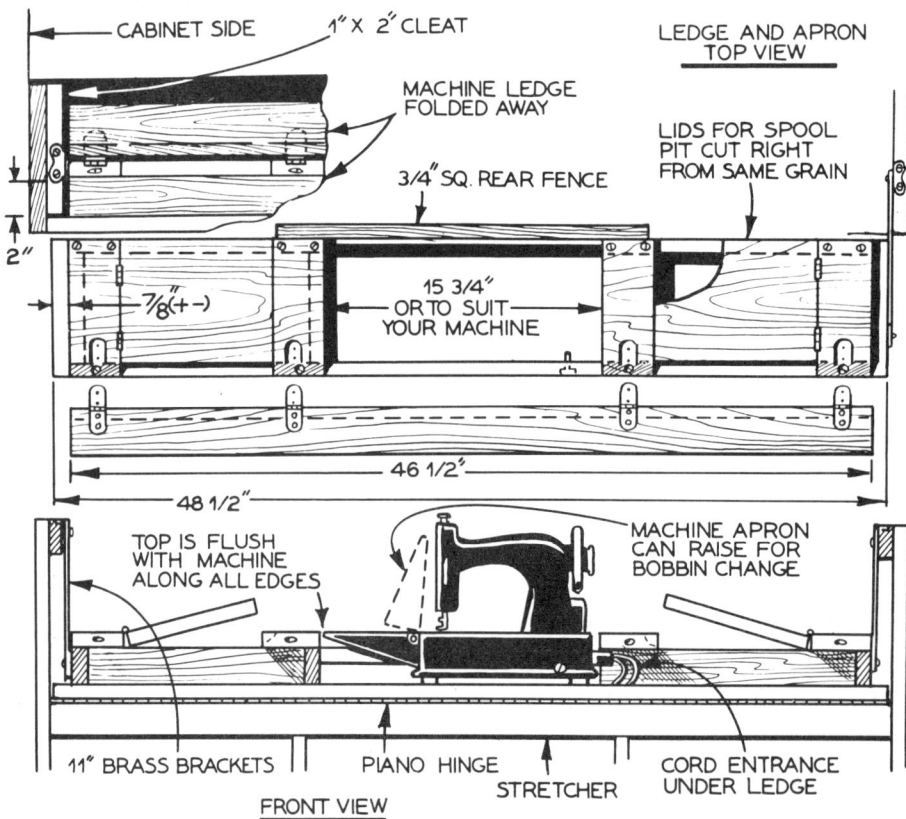

CABINET SIDE

1" X 2" CLEAT

LEDGE AND APRON TOP VIEW

MACHINE LEDGE FOLDED AWAY

3/4" SQ. REAR FENCE

LIDS FOR SPOOL PIT CUT RIGHT FROM SAME GRAIN

2"

7/8"(+-)

15 3/4" OR TO SUIT YOUR MACHINE

46 1/2"

48 1/2"

TOP IS FLUSH WITH MACHINE ALONG ALL EDGES

MACHINE APRON CAN RAISE FOR BOBBIN CHANGE

11" BRASS BRACKETS

PIANO HINGE

STRETCHER

CORD ENTRANCE UNDER LEDGE

FRONT VIEW

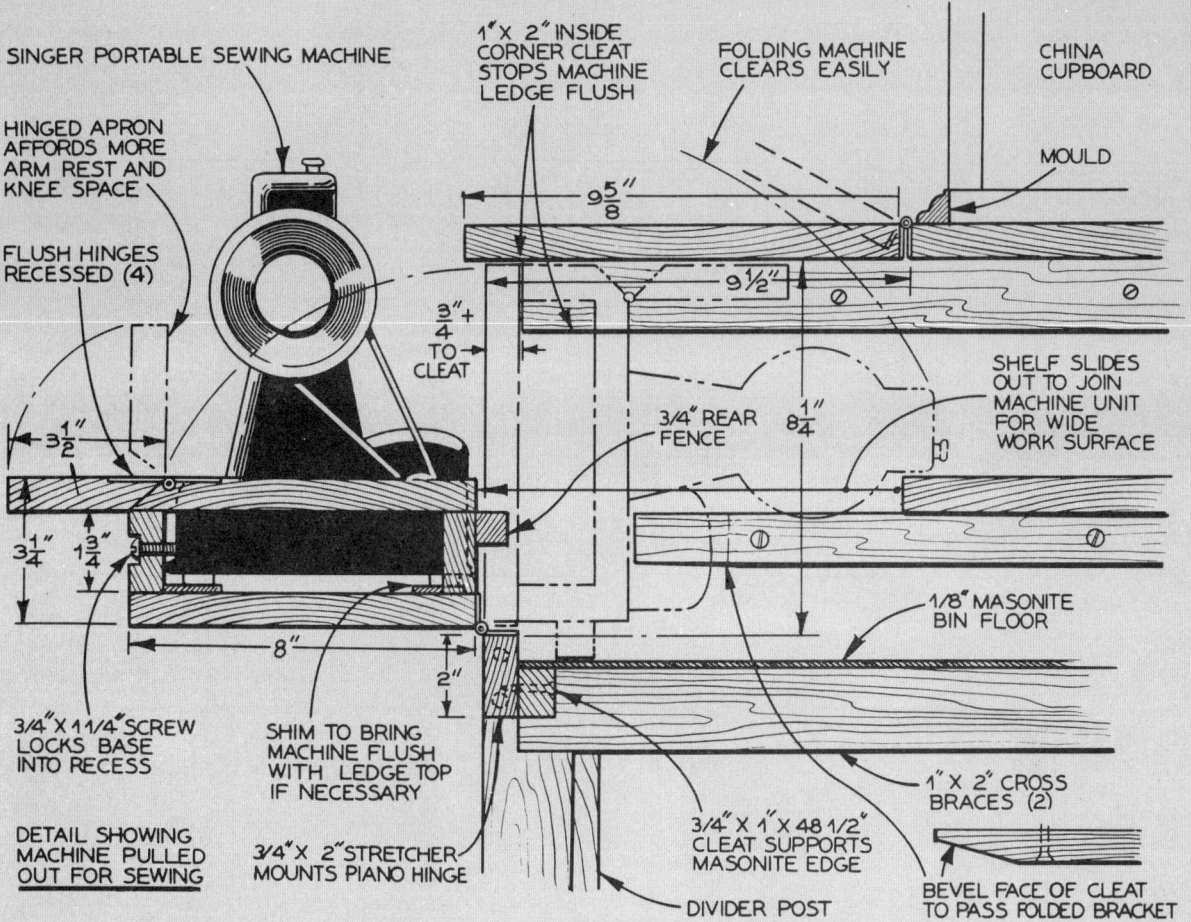

SINGER PORTABLE SEWING MACHINE

1" X 2" INSIDE CORNER CLEAT STOPS MACHINE LEDGE FLUSH

FOLDING MACHINE CLEARS EASILY

CHINA CUPBOARD

HINGED APRON AFFORDS MORE ARM REST AND KNEE SPACE

MOULD

FLUSH HINGES RECESSED (4)

$9\frac{5}{8}$"

$9\frac{1}{2}$"

$\frac{3}{4}$"+ TO CLEAT

3/4" REAR FENCE

$8\frac{1}{4}$"

SHELF SLIDES OUT TO JOIN MACHINE UNIT FOR WIDE WORK SURFACE

$3\frac{1}{2}$"

$3\frac{1}{4}$" $1\frac{3}{4}$"

8"

2"

1/8" MASONITE BIN FLOOR

3/4" X 1 1/4" SCREW LOCKS BASE INTO RECESS

SHIM TO BRING MACHINE FLUSH WITH LEDGE TOP IF NECESSARY

1" X 2" CROSS BRACES (2)

DETAIL SHOWING MACHINE PULLED OUT FOR SEWING

3/4" X 2" STRETCHER MOUNTS PIANO HINGE

3/4" X 1" X 48 1/2" CLEAT SUPPORTS MASONITE EDGE

BEVEL FACE OF CLEAT TO PASS FOLDED BRACKET

DIVIDER POST

side panels. The rear edges are also rabbeted to take the ¼-inch plywood back panel. Choose a mild grain plywood since this piece is broadly exposed. Face off this "box" with 1x2-inch stock trim strips, mitered at the top corners. Screw in four metal strips to take adjustable height metal clips. This is optional, and you may want your shelves fixed. Set them in dadoes, in that event.

This unit can be left open or glassed in with sliding panes, set in your choice of dadoes or channel rollers. Unit is then set atop the sewing cabinet and secured with screws from inside the cabinet roof. Conceal the joint with appropriate trim molding.

With the machine secured into its recess with the lock screw, the ledge is swung up and shut, the weight of the machine keeping it closed without further catches. Lower the top lid, and the entire unit is concealed. Place drawer and door handles to suit your motif and decor. •

Spool compartment is located at right side of the machine. Accessories drawer slides out without obstruction from machine ledge.

sewing console

Construct a complete sewing corner in your home with this cherry and walnut unit which doubles as a desk.

IF your wife has been complaining about a decent place to sew, here's the answer. A simple, modern design gives this cabinet the room, storage space and stability to reduce her complaints to a memory. The large top provides an ideal place to write letters or spread out business books and papers.

Use cherry wood for the top and most of the other outer sections. It's a good, hard wood. It doesn't dent easily yet is easy to work. Walnut for the drawer fronts and runners of the side chest, as well

Clamping the table top together. Watch pressure; too much will squeeze the glue right out.

Underview of the table top shows the sliding fabrics basket and the beveled cross beam to receive legs.

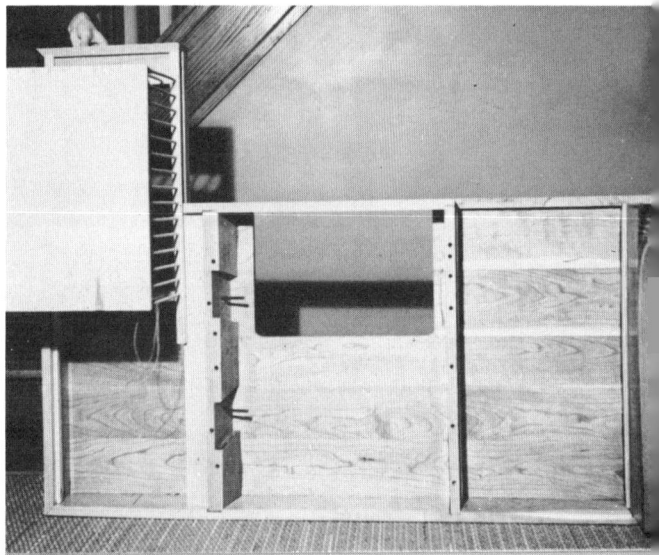

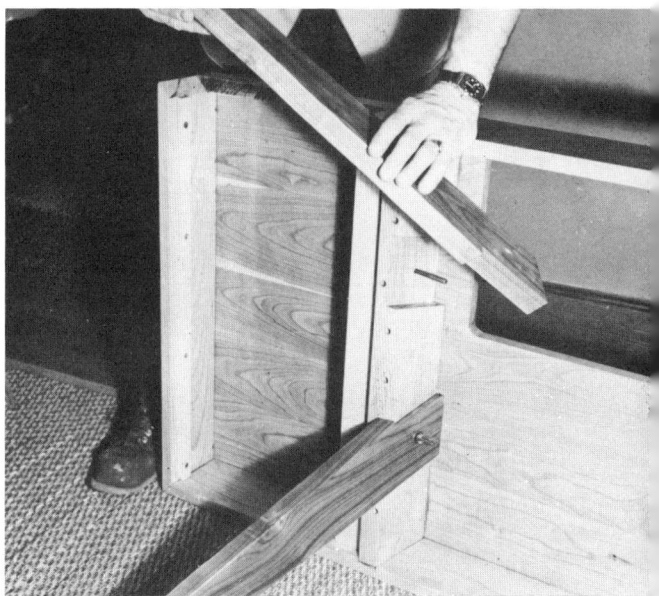

Spraying Fabulon on with a tank cleaner sprayer. Wet sanding and No. 0 steel wool give it a sheen.

Bolting the notched legs to the cross beam. Their unique design insures firm support for the unit.

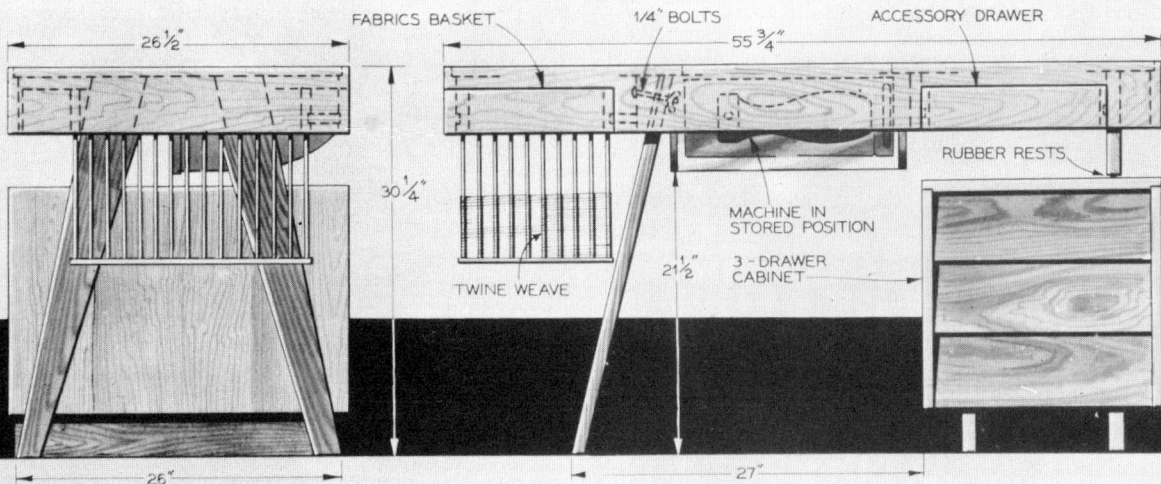

FABRICS BASKET   1/4" BOLTS   ACCESSORY DRAWER

26½"

55¾"

30¼"

RUBBER RESTS

MACHINE IN STORED POSITION

21½"

3 - DRAWER CABINET

TWINE WEAVE

26"

27"

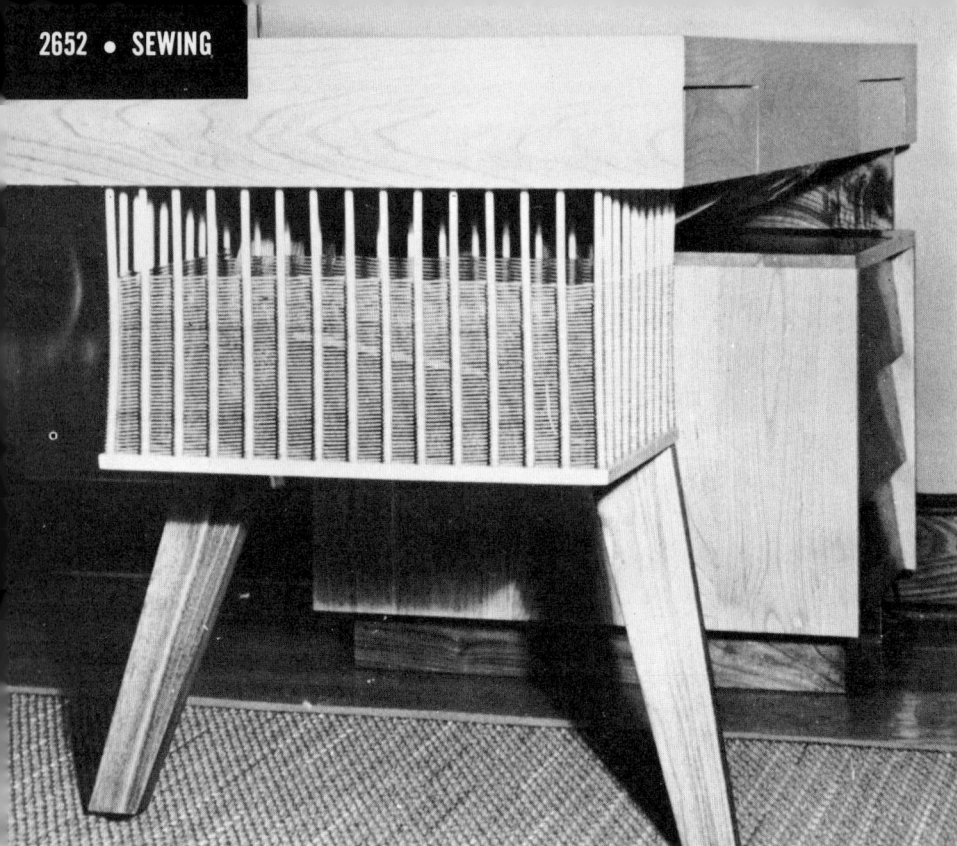

Finished top is neat and compact. Side view of the finished console showing fabric basket.

Looking up at the machine through Plexiglas dust cover. Form is curved to give greater leg room.

Passing the twine in between the dowels on the fabrics basket. A tedious job but the result is neat.

The finished basket. Notice the mitered end to meet the side apron and spool section of No. 16 nails.

Inserting 4½-in. ledge to support front edge of the machine. When not in use, use 11-in. cover.

as for the legs of the console, provides a contrasting, dark accent. All the woods and materials will cost a little over $40. It takes approximately 70 hours to put together but is well worth the effort.

Start on the top first. Glue two boards together for a width of 11¼ in. and just a little over 56 in. long. Cut out the section for the machine as shown in the diagrams and save that piece. It will serve as the cover when the machine's not in use. Then glue several other boards to the first two to get a width of 25½ in. If you haven't worked with cabinetmaker's clamps before, be careful. Too much pressure will squeeze the glue right out and too little won't give you a snug fit.

While the top is in the clamps, glue the cross beams to the underside and save yourself some time by letting them both dry simultaneously. Then insert the 2-in. No. 9 screws as pictured in the diagram. Oak was used for the cross beams and drawer sides but, naturally, you may use whatever wood is available to you. Rubber stops on the underside of the cabinet rest leg reduce vibration and also help retard any creeping tendency the machine in use might induce.

The aprons are next. With them in place, the project begins to take shape. Cut the aprons to dimensions shown making ⅜x¾-in. rabbets along the top edges to receive the table top. Miter the four corners to a 45 degree angle and cut $\frac{3}{16}$-in. dadoes in the front and rear aprons for the cross members. Glue them solidly to the top and you are ready for the legs.

Note the notch design of the legs. It makes for a good snug fit and gives good stability. Secure to the cross beam with ¼-in. bolts.

Putting the fabric basket together is interesting. The many doweled drawer, while certainly not the largest sec-

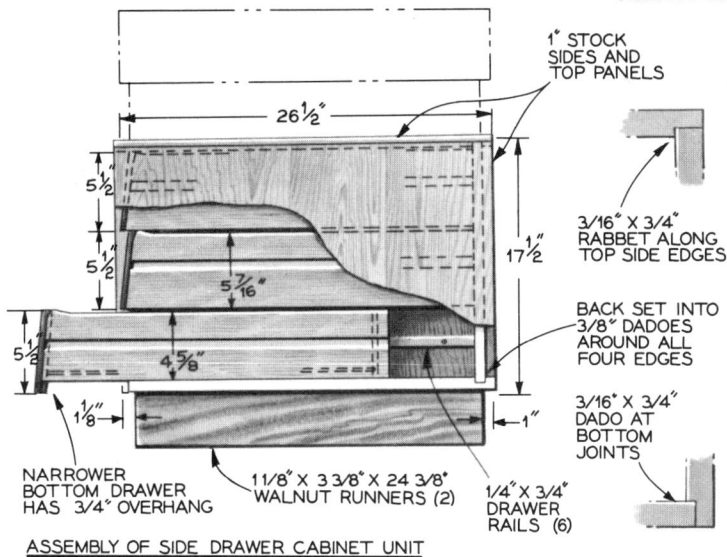
ASSEMBLY OF SIDE DRAWER CABINET UNIT

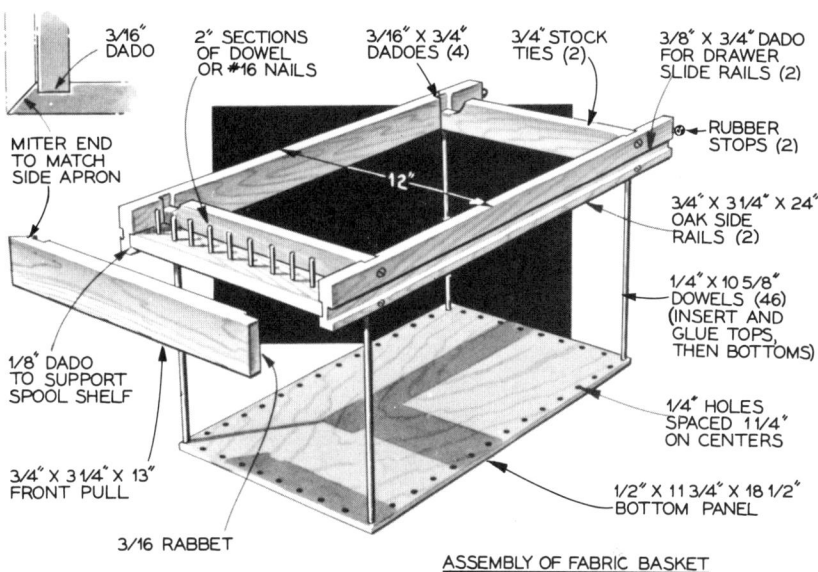
ASSEMBLY OF FABRIC BASKET

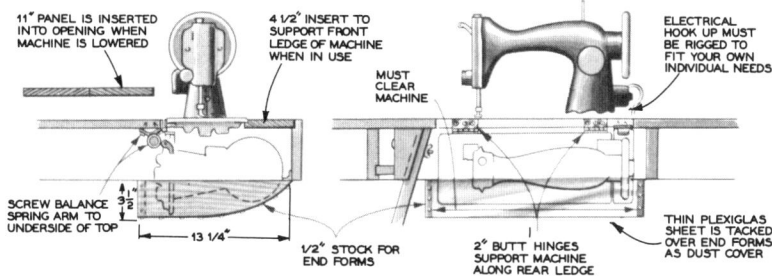

tion of the console, becomes a real eye-catcher when complete. The oak side rails of ¾x3¼x24-in. stock are cut with ⅜x¾-in. dadoes for the drawer slide rails. Insert a small piece of dowel into the rear of each of the side rails to take rubber stops. It takes the annoyance out of slamming the drawer shut with a loud bang. Cherry for the front pull is used to maintain the decor, and remember to miter the end of the front to match the side apron. You can make the spool section using either ¼-in. dowel sections or No. 16 nails. It's neat and efficient and

Left: The completed side drawer cabinet. Right: Tray of the accessory drawer showing removable sections. Far right: Front view of the console.

Front view of cabinet showing bottom drawer. Screws of drawer front are countersunk, plugged.

The three finished drawers showing Masonite bottoms. Note finger recesses at center of angled fronts.

saves your helpmate the bother of looking all over for that spool of thread. Using ¼-in. dowels, cut them 10⅝ in. long, 46 of them, and insert and glue to the top first, then glue to the bottom panel. There will be less chance of any of them setting crooked that way (see diagram). Lacing the dowels with twine can become a little tedious, but the resulting effect is really striking.

Complete the accessory drawer and the major portion of the job is finished. Oak was used again for the sides and cherry for the front. Cut a ¼-in. sq. dado in the front for a ¼x½-in. insert to support the tray. The latter tray support also requires a ¼-in. sq. dado. You might use the little space underneath the tray for papers or patterns. Use ¾-in. beveled stock for the three main divisions of the tray.

All other sections plus the sides, rear and bottom of the tray are made from ¼-in. stock. The sections are movable from ¼-in. dadoes which enables you to enlarge any compartment necessary by simply removing the divider. Cut ¼x⅛-in. dadoes for the ⅛-in. Masonite bottom. This tempered Masonite was also used for the bottoms of the small cabinet drawers. It's strong and easy to work with. Use a fine tooth saw in cutting the Masonite, however, for a rough cut might either split the Masonite or leave it with many ragged edges.

The side drawer cabinet with its dark walnut runners and drawer fronts lends a pleasant note of contrast as well as serving as a very functional piece. Two of the three drawers, you'll notice, are quite deep and will provide plenty of storage space. The bottom drawer, just a bit shallower,

has the same front of 5½ in. which results in a ¾-in. overhang. To make the drawers easy to pull out, dado the drawer slides ¼ in. by just a little more than ¾ in. Note the ¾-in. slant from the perpendicular given to the drawer fronts and the finger recesses at the center. Screw the fronts to the ½-in. oak sides using Plastic Wood or plugs.

Cut the top and side panels of the cabinet from 1-in. stock making a $\frac{3}{16}$x¾-in. rabbet along the top side edges. Set the back in firmly by cutting ⅜-in. dadoes in the panels all around.

Setting the machine in is fairly simple. Instead of the regular cabinet hinges set in the top that you most often see in these consoles, 2-in. butt hinges that come apart were used. With these hinges, the hinge pin can be slipped out at any time and the machine removed easily if need be. Secondly, the hinges are not visible from the top as are cabinet hinges. One half of the hinge is screwed to the edge of the table top. The other half is locked in place with the set screws on the machine itself. Details here, naturally, will depend on your machine. •

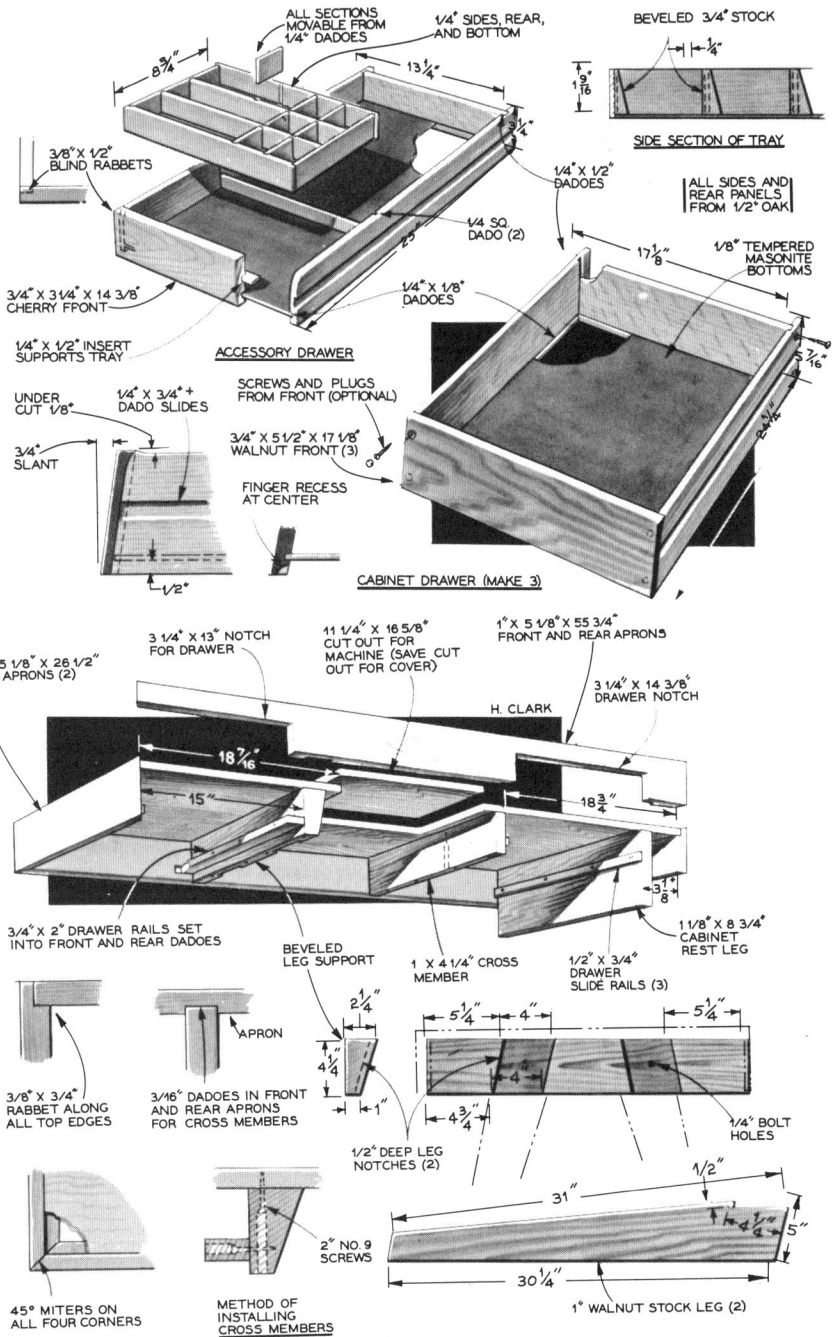

ALL SECTIONS MOVABLE FROM ¼" DADOES

¼" SIDES, REAR, AND BOTTOM

8¾"

13¼"

BEVELED ¾" STOCK

¼"

$\frac{9}{16}$"

SIDE SECTION OF TRAY

3/8" X 1/2" BLIND RABBETS

¼" X ½" DADOES

ALL SIDES AND REAR PANELS FROM ½" OAK

3¼"

¼ SQ. DADO (2)

25"

⅛" TEMPERED MASONITE BOTTOMS

17½"

3/4" X 3 1/4" X 14 3/8" CHERRY FRONT

¼" X ⅛" DADOES

ACCESSORY DRAWER

1/4" X 1/2" INSERT SUPPORTS TRAY

UNDER CUT ⅛"

1/4" X 3/4" + DADO SLIDES

SCREWS AND PLUGS FROM FRONT (OPTIONAL)

3/4" X 5 1/2" X 17 1/8" WALNUT FRONT (3)

$\frac{5}{16}$"

24¼"

¾" SLANT

FINGER RECESS AT CENTER

CABINET DRAWER (MAKE 3)

½"

3 1/4" X 13" NOTCH FOR DRAWER

11 1/4" X 16 5/8" CUT OUT FOR MACHINE (SAVE CUT OUT FOR COVER)

1" X 5 1/8" X 55 3/4" FRONT AND REAR APRONS

1" X 5 1/8" X 26 1/2" SIDE APRONS (2)

3 1/4" X 14 3/8" DRAWER NOTCH

H. CLARK

18$\frac{7}{16}$"

18¾"

15"

3¼"

3/4" X 2" DRAWER RAILS SET INTO FRONT AND REAR DADOES

BEVELED LEG SUPPORT

1 X 4 1/4" CROSS MEMBER

1/2" X 3/4" DRAWER SLIDE RAILS (3)

1 1/8" X 8 3/4" CABINET REST LEG

3/8" X 3/4" RABBET ALONG ALL TOP EDGES

3/16" DADOES IN FRONT AND REAR APRONS FOR CROSS MEMBERS

2¼"

4¼"

1"

APRON

5¼"

4"

5¼"

4¾"

4"

½" DEEP LEG NOTCHES (2)

¼" BOLT HOLES

45° MITERS ON ALL FOUR CORNERS

METHOD OF INSTALLING CROSS MEMBERS

2" NO. 9 SCREWS

31"

½"

4¼"

5"

30¼"

1" WALNUT STOCK LEG (2)

Sewing Cabinet

It also makes a fine end table and may be used as a stand for a TV receiver

Standing 19¾″ high, the sewing cabinet is constructed of wood and aluminum and is smart looking. Note spacious drawers.

YOU don't need to be an experienced cabinetmaker to make this useful, contemporary sewing cabinet which can also serve as an end table or television stand. The drawers are simple box construction. The cabinet stands 19¾″ high and is made from wood and aluminum, a combination that is a smart new trend in furniture. To finish plywood edges, cement on a strip of wood trim sold by the roll. The legs are wood dowels, covered with wood trim and do-it-yourself aluminum tubing. The first three drawers are 3″ high, the bottom drawer is 6″ high. These may be used for storing sewing supplies (directions for fitting drawers with half rounds to separate spools of thread are given later). If you don't need any spool storage, you may prefer to omit the half rounds. Refer to the diagram as well as the Bill of Materials for exact material requirements.

CABINET SIDES, BACK AND FRAMING: Bevel the front edges of each side (see detail). Nail sides to back. Screw ¾″ x ¾″ pine to sides and back, flush with top edges (see detail). Screw ¾″ x ¾″ pine to sides and back, flush with bottom edges. Temporarily nail scrap strip of wood across top front to each side for a brace.

DRAWERS: Nail ¾″ x ¾″ quarter round at both ends of inside drawer front. Nail drawer sides to drawer back; nail sides to ¾″ x ¾″ quarter round on drawer front. Screw hardboard drawer bottom to sides and back. Nail ⅜″ x ⅜″ strip to drawer front under hardboard. To make spool dividers in top drawer, glue ½″ half rounds from front to back, spaced ¾″ apart for small spools and 1″ apart for large spools. Divide the second and third drawers as desired, using ½″ pine nailed through drawer back and bottom and toenailed to drawer front. (In toenailing, you angle nail at a slant.) Drill holes for knobs. Note: measurements for top three drawers are shown on diagram. Bottom drawer measurements are: front, 6″ high, sides, 5″ high, back, 5″ high. Bottom drawer is constructed in same way as other drawers.

To fit drawers, hold top drawer flush with top of sides, draw pencil line along each side of cabinet the length of the drawer bottom. Nail runners temporarily, one on each side, along both lines with bottom of runners flush with lines. Place

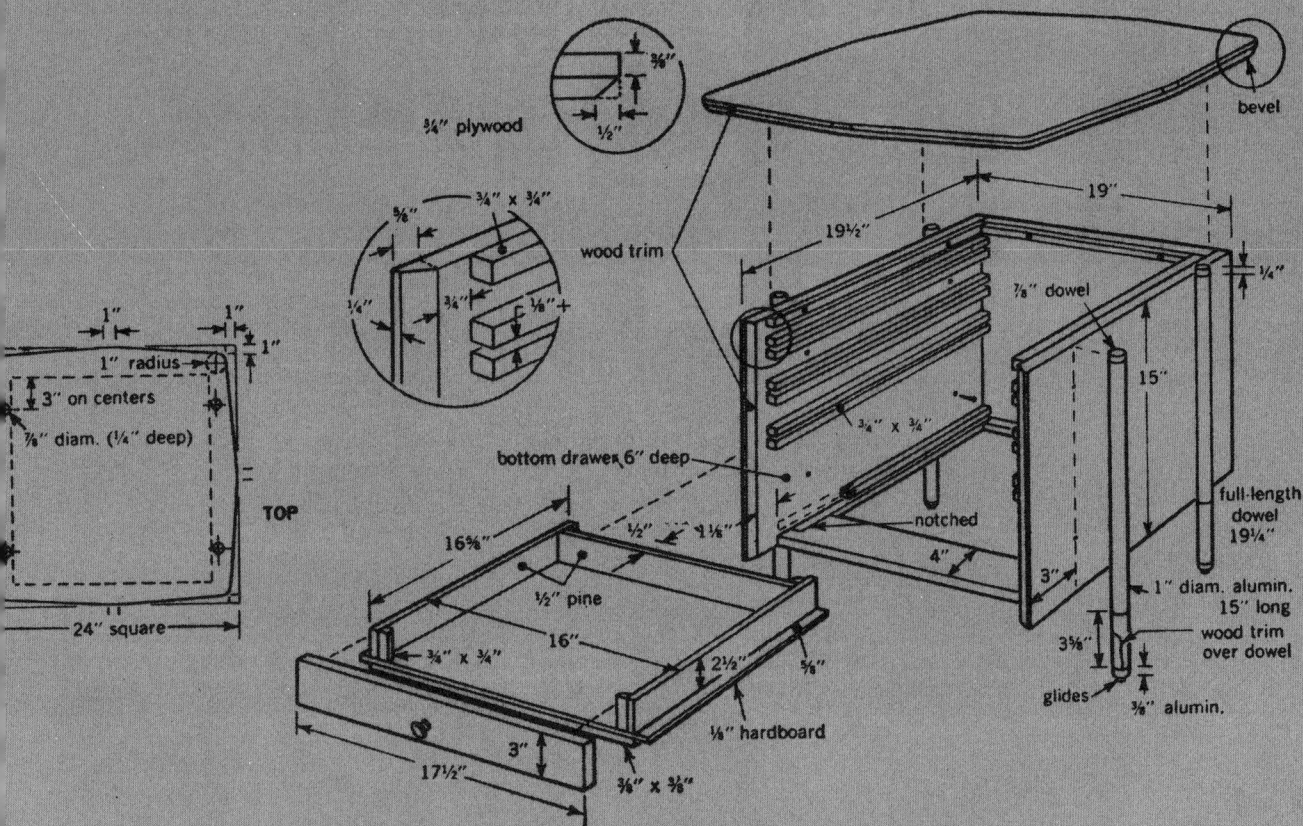

strip of ⅛" hardboard and thin strip of cardboard on top of each runner. Then place top runners (one on each side) over cardboard and temporarily nail top runners to cabinet sides. Remove hardboard strip and cardboard, slide in drawer to test positioning of runners. Make adjustments if necessary, then glue and nail in place and screw to sides. Attach remaining runners using same method.

LEGS: File edges of aluminum tubing smooth. Drill hole at top of 15" length of tubing, insert dowel, nail tubing ¼" from top of dowel. Drill hole in ⅜" length of tubing and nail flush with bottom of leg. Hammer glide to leg end. Drill holes through cabinet sides into legs; screw legs in place. Following diagram, drill holes in top for legs.

TOP AND TRIM: Bevel edges of top (see detail). Following manufacturers' directions, cement wood trim to edges of top, front and back edges of sides, and legs between tubing. Fit legs into holes in top. To attach top, drill holes at slight angle through ¾" x ¾" framing strips at top of sides and back. Screw top in place.

FINISHING: Fill with wood filler where necessary. Sand with fine sandpaper. Apply one coat of shellac, thinned 50-50 with alcohol, sand lightly and apply one coat of varnish. Rub down with steel wool. Apply coat of paste wax and polish with soft cloth. Attach the silver knobs to the drawers. •

Bill of Materials

¾" walnut plywood for cabinet top, back sides, and drawer fronts. ¾" x ¾" pine for cabinet top and bottom framing, drawer runners. ½" pine for drawer sides, backs, dividers. ¾" x ¾" quarter rounds for drawer reinforcements. ⅛" tempered hardboard smooth on both sides for drawer bottoms. ⅜" x ⅜" pine for drawer front supports. ½" half rounds for spool dividers. ⅞" wood dowels for legs. 1" do-it-yourself aluminum tubing for leg trim. 1" walnut veneer wood trim for plywood edges and leg trim. Four 1" diameter silver knobs. Four ½" furniture glides. Contact cement; finishing nails; screws; wood filler, white shellac; alcohol; spar varnish; fine sandpaper; No. 0000 steel wool; and paste wax.

Improve Your Home Climate

Noticeably lower summer temperatures result from a full planting of trees and shrubs around the home. The high shade trees help keep the house roof from absorbing the full force of the sun's rays.

Take an inventory of your home weather conditions and make plans to improve them. Your inventory might include these problem areas:

1. Hot rooms that soak up day heat. You want: cooler indoor living.
2. Scorching outdoor surroundings. You want: comfort for outdoor living.
3. Glare from walls, ground, pavement. You want: soft light.
4. Stagnant, sultry air pockets. You want: refreshing breezes.
5. Windswept areas. You want: shelter from harsh winds.
6. Problem spots where tender plants winterkill. You want: better growing conditions.

THE WEATHER that is influenced across continents by jet streams, polar ice caps, volcanic eruptions and sunspots is also influenced in home landscapes by a grassy lawn, a single tree, a pool of water, a concrete driveway or a short line of evergreens.

The green leaves of plants have protected men and their families from hot sun all the generations of humanity. They have given shelter from bitter winds, cooled and humidified the air and have helped maintain a healthy balance in the air between the oxygen and carbon dioxide content. Today, the leaves of living plants assume a major role in making modern living more comfortable and healthful and in providing an attractive environment.

Plants improve living, working and playing conditions in four important ways: they block out the glare of the sun, convert

A double purpose is served by this planting which provides pleasant shady spots in the summer and, at the same time, helps to moderate the harsh effects of winter in an otherwise wide open lawn area.

much of the sun heat into new plant tissues, humidify dry air and permit air circulation to carry off excess heat. No man-made material can do all these comforting things —and provide the added attraction of natural, restful beauty!

Here is a list of the ways in which home landscape plants can influence and control weather.

COOLING THE HOME: Structural materials of the house may absorb the heat of long summer days and radiate it toward the sweltering family for hours later. House roofs will be kept cooler when they are shaded by trees. The most cooling trees are those planted south or southwest of the home, so their beneficial shadows will fall on the house during the hottest summer hours, usually between 11 A.M. and 4 P.M.

Tree shadows are the shortest about noon, depending on the observance of daylight saving customs. A tree needed for noonday shade must be quite near the home, perhaps closer than some horticulturists would approve. All gardens should be planned so as to be practical as well as pretty, so if a tree is needed within a few feet of the home, plant it there! Provide its roots with deep, rich soil, annual deep fertilizing and occasional deep watering so they will not be tempted to stray among the footings, foundations or floor slabs. And be quick to prune lower branches which might chafe the walls or roof of the home.

A study of the "shadow path" of a stake in the lawn will be helpful in locating the trees most efficiently. Shadows will vary with the season and the latitude.

The choice of desirable shingle-shading trees is a wide one in all sections of the continent. Improved varieties of the honey locust have joined the maples, oaks, planes, lindens and elms as worthy of consideration.

House walls which absorb too much heat will be more comfortable in the shadow of small, spreading trees, like flowering varieties of crab apples, dogwoods, cherries and hawthorns. Large shrubs like honeysuckles, mock oranges, nandina, crepe myrtle and firethorn will be enjoyed for their coolness and their flowering or fruiting beauty. Where space is limited, they may be espaliered to a thin layer of house-hugging branches.

Vines in a wide variety will cool sunny walls with bursts of beauty. They will be most efficient when an air space of up to 6 inches separates the trellis from the house.

COOLING THE YARD: Large trees are the envy of the folks in barren housing developments who must retreat into the narrow moving shadow of the house itself for gasping relief from the summer sun. Family budgets and available stock in nurseries may restrict the purchase of desirable shade trees of mature sizes, but they need not prohibit all tree planting. Shorter lived trees often grow rapidly, and they will give comforting shade while some of the slower, more durable trees are developing.

Small trees and groups of shrubs will absorb a lot of sun, and their cost may be less than that of larger trees. Borders or sun screens of these plants can be planned to let cool breezes filter through.

Arbors, pergolas and other structures can be erected near almost any cooking, living or play area, and they may be covered in a season or two with rapid-growing vines that will also be enjoyed for their flowers, foliage or fruits.

Rich, thick turf is a lovely and cool part of all outdoor living areas. The recommendations of local turf experts should be followed to keep the lawn vigorous in midsummer. In many regions, the healthiest, coolest and greenest lawns are cut at least 1½ inches high, and provided with one inch of water each week of the hot season.

Pools or streams of water near the patio or terrace will absorb heat, and will humidify the air. They provide a real cooling feeling psychologically, especially when the sound of trickling water is pro-

A combination of high slat fences and trees shield this concrete play area which would otherwise become unbearably hot from the direct rays of the sun. Pleasant breezes can still filter through.

Left: A good point to remember is that solid patios will absorb and radiate the summer heat. Here, the patio stones are interplanted with the groundcover to lower the temperature.

In warm tropical areas, Florida, for example, the shade of tall trees, a grassy lawn and a heat-resistant pebble drive are most welcome in landscape (right).

vided by a circulating pump. Their ability to support ornamental fish and aquatic plants is enjoyable and they do not need to be costly.

REDUCING HOT GLARE: Light and heat reflected from exterior walls, pavements and driveways can make otherwise convenient living areas unpleasant.

Vines may be trained on wall trellises to change the glare into a flowering and delightful background. The use of lawn strips, and the planting of flowers or shrubs will reduce the temperature and the underfoot glare of a paved terrace. Pots, boxes and other planters can be used where plants cannot be put directly in the ground. A sunny lawn can often be twenty or more degrees cooler than an equally sunny pavement.

A single tree with feathery foliage may be planted through a hole in the paved area itself, if its roots are given the fertilizer, moisture and air which they require. The same treatment could be used for a single tall-growing shrub or other specimen plant such as a flowering fruit tree.

A low hedge of inexpensive shrubs will be a welcome divider between driveways and outdoor living areas. For example, a 2-foot hedge, 8 feet away from the guest

who is seated with eyes 3½ feet above the ground, will block out 16 feet of glaring pavement.

In the snow zones, these hedges should be away from the driveway so they will not drift snow or be broken by the piles of shoveled or plowed snow.

Thick lawn turf not only eliminates glare but absorbs the heat and gives off cool humidity on the hottest summer day. The most cooling lawns are those with the most healthy and thickest grass plants. Good lawn care makes for better living.

MOVING STAGNANT AIR: Outdoor living areas will be more comfortable when they are crossed with the prevailing breezes. Evergreens, shrubs and vines will supply air circulation at the same time they provide privacy and flowering or foliage beauty. Solid architectural barriers may be needed as a desperation measure, but the cooling, growing beauty of living plants will often do the job better.

Landscapes located on a slope can take advantage of currents of cool air which flow downhill, like water.

WIND BARRIERS: Harsh winds will be filtered down to breezes by windbreak plantings. Homes exposed to severe winter

blasts of wind will have reduced fuel bills when tall evergreen plantings dull the cut of the wind.

Summer living outdoors along the shore or in the mountains is sometimes restricted to the hours when the wind is calmed. Humans share with some favorite summer flowers a dislike for harsh winds, and both will be happier when groups of shrubs or trees grow up to provide shelter and background beauty. Local nurserymen will suggest the best windbreaking plants for local use.

Windbreaks will be most effective for a distance of three times their height, although the wind velocity at ground level may be reduced as far away as ten or fifteen times their height.

Living areas on a hillside which are troubled by uphill blasts may require only a low deflecting planting to tilt the wind over the heads of the family.

SNOW DRIFTS: Winter observation will show where the storms pile the most drifts of snow and where the ground is swept the cleanest. When the snow piles high across the driveway or walks, there can be considerable physical exertion or expense in its removal.

Plantings of evergreens or thick shrubs will stack much of the wind-driven snow into drifts on their leeward side within a distance of six times their height. Plantings for snow breaking must be set quite a distance from the area to be shielded, and they should be located after careful study of the property in wintertime.

When the probable location of the snow-break has been determined, it is wise to test it with a length of wooden snow fence for one winter before installing the more attractive landscape plants.

Also consider the effect of large evergreens in winter landscape planning. If they shade walks or driveways, the snow and ice will remain underfoot or under tire, longer than in sunnier spots.

Vines on a trellis, extending along and out from the wall of the house, help to lower the inside temperature and provide some shade for the outdoor living area.

A new house will receive the full effect of the summer sun and winter wind unless builder has left a tree or two. First job, as was done here, is to plant them.

Left: A roof made of timbers and hung with bamboo panels casts shade at home exhibit. A device. of this kind may be an excellent idea in newly developed area that completely lacks grown shade trees.

PROTECTING YOUR PLANTS: Harsh winds and bright sun cause more winter damage to landscape plantings than low temperatures. Windbreak groups of plants can be unobstrusive guardians for many of the borderline plants that are favorites in all regions. Immediate local conditions—within the garden itself—often determine whether a borderline plant will survive or die during a cold winter.

Alternate freezing and thawing of the soil will kill more perennials than severe cold spells. A snowbreak planting which guides the wind to drop its insulating snow cover on the garden will be a valuable addition to the landscaping.

Some scientists are concerned by the reduction in vegetated areas while world wide combustion of coal, oil and gas is increasing tremendously. Warnings have been expressed that large amounts of carbon dioxide may replace some of the oxygen in the earth's atmosphere. In the process of growth, green-leaved plants have the happy function of absorbing carbon dioxide and releasing oxygen—just the opposite process of breathing. If worldwide combustion continues to increase and areas of vegetation decrease, the breathing of humans may be made more difficult.

It has been estimated that one human being requires annually all the oxygen produced by 150 square meters of plant leaves in active growth. If a maple leaf has an area of 50 square centimeters, it will require a treeful of 30,000 of them to provide the oxygen needed annually by a single person—two trees for each married couple and a forest for a moderate-sized city.

Massive air pollution by carbon dioxide is being studied like that caused by radioactive substances, and it will be given even more publicity in the near future.

Landscape plantings will not bring tropical balminess into the temperate zone, but they can be planned so as to bring new human comfort into almost any home grounds. •

modern

Simple hand tools, a few hours of work is all that's involved in making this 32-inch square project.

FOR THOSE fancy dishes, art objects, knickknacks and similar treasures, what could be nicer than a display in this modern, handsomely designed shadow-box knickknack shelf. This is a project you can toss off in a spare evening and beautify your home with for countless evenings (and days) to come. It goes well in the living room, dining room, bedroom and den—even in the kitchen.

You can make it of plywood or solid wood to blend in with the other furniture in the room. Screws and glue hold it firmly together and a handsaw is all you'll need to cut out the pieces.

The first step in construction is to cut the top, bottom, and two horizontal shelves (A) from ¾-inch thick wood. These sections should measure 7x30½ inches. From the same ¾-inch wood, cut two 7x32-inch vertical sides (B) and two 5x30½-inch vertical partitions (C).

Tack or clamp the two middle shelves (A) together, making sure

knickknack shelf

What better way to display the small treasures you've collected over the years than in this handsome, functional knickknack shelf?

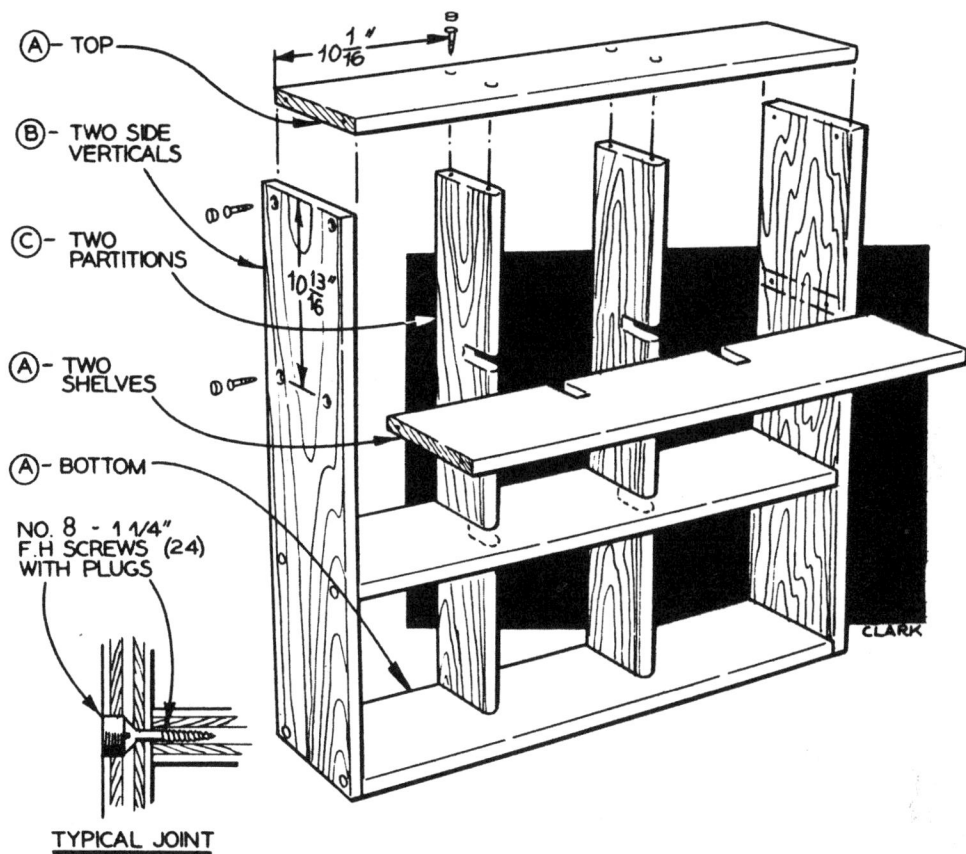

Ⓐ- TOP

Ⓑ- TWO SIDE VERTICALS

Ⓒ- TWO PARTITIONS

Ⓐ- TWO SHELVES

Ⓐ- BOTTOM

$10\frac{1}{16}''$

$10\frac{13}{16}''$

NO. 8 - 1 1/4" F.H SCREWS (24) WITH PLUGS

CLARK

TYPICAL JOINT

Using coping saw, notches are cut in two shelves (A) which have been tacked together temporarily.

Similarly, cut notches in vertical partitions (C) and round off the leading edge of each partition.

Horizontal shelves and vertical partitions are assembled by interlocking of their notched edges.

To assemble outer frame, use both glue and flat-head screws; cover screws with wood plugs; sand.

Fit shelf assembly into frame; edges of shelf assembly should align with guide lines on frame.

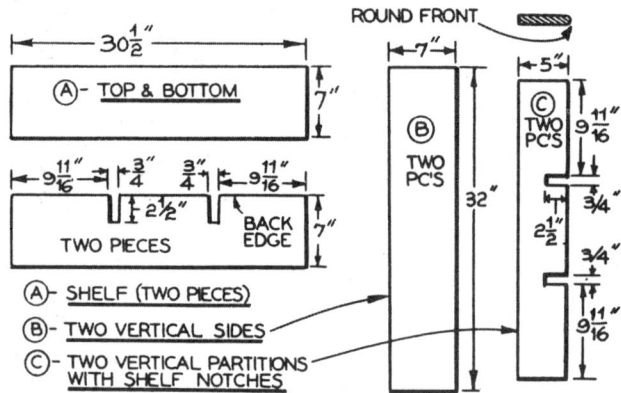

A- SHELF (TWO PIECES)
B- TWO VERTICAL SIDES
C- TWO VERTICAL PARTITIONS WITH SHELF NOTCHES

that all edges are flush. Then cut out two notches in the back edges as shown in the drawing, each notch measuring ¾ inch wide by 2½ inches deep, and located $9\frac{11}{16}$ inches in from each end. By clamping the two shelves together, you can cut the notches in both pieces simultaneously and thus insure perfect alignment when assembling the shelves.

In the same manner, tack or clamp the two vertical partitions (C) together and cut a pair of similar corresponding notches in the front edges, of the same dimensions as above. Again, locate the notches $9\frac{11}{16}$ inches from the ends.

Take pieces (C) apart and round off the front edges to a full radius as shown. Across the inside surfaces of top and bottom pieces (A), mark guide lines to indicate where partitions (C) are to be attached. These lines should be made $9\frac{11}{16}$ inches from each end of both pieces

(A), with a second parallel line marked ¾ inch in from each of these lines. Centered in the middle of the ¾-inch space between each pair of guide lines, drill two $\frac{3}{16}$-inch screw holes; the first hole should be 1¼ inches from the back edge, and the second hole 3 inches from the front edge. These holes should be counterbored to a depth of $\frac{5}{16}$ inch to allow for covering the screws with ½-inch-diameter long-grain wood plugs.

On the inside surfaces of sides (B), draw similar pairs of ¾-inch-spaced guide lines, $10\frac{7}{16}$ inches from each edge. These locate the position where the horizontal shelves (A) are to be attached. In the middle of the ¾-inch space between each pair of guide lines, drill and counterbore a set of screw holes as you did for pieces (A). Locate one hole 1¼ inches from the back edge, and the other 1¼ inches in from the front edge. Similarly-spaced screw holes

Finally, fasten knickknack shelf together with flathead screws covered with long-grain wood plugs.

should also be drilled and counterbored along the top and bottom edges of each side, ⅜ inch from the short edges.

Before assembly, sand all pieces smooth. Then assemble the horizontal shelves (A) with vertical partitions (C), interlocking them by their notched edges. Next, assemble both side (B) with top and bottom (A). Use glue and 1¼-inch No. 8 flathead screws. Cover the screws with ½-inch long-grain wood plugs, and sand flush.

Insert the shelf and partition assembly into the box frame. Align all shelf and partition edges with the corresponding guide lines drawn on the inside surfaces of the sides and top. Fasten the assembly together with 1¼-inch No. 8 flathead screws and cover all screws with long-grain wood plugs. •

MATERIAL LIST

¾" plywood, 30"x72"

24 flathead screws, 1¼" No. 8

24 long grain wood plugs or dowels, ½"

Wood glue

Sandpaper (preferably garnet paper), Nos. 1, 2/0, 4/0 (Use coarse paper for rounding only.)

provincial knickknack

Early American furniture styling with its simple, functional good looks can be happily combined with modern pieces for a charming, restful effect.

Treasured china takes on added beauty against antique stain on knotty pine.

HERE'S a simple period piece which is as easy to make as falling off the proverbial log. A transparent finish, as shown here, will add immeasurably to its beauty, especially on a pine-paneled wall.

The only drawing you'll need to make is one of the end piece (B). Use a piece of paper or cardboard at least 9x26 inches, cover it with 1-inch squares, and copy the lines of the small drawing on page 87. This full size layout can then be fastened to the wood. A coping or hand scroll saw can be used to cut out the end pieces. Use this same paper template to saw out short center piece (L).

Mark guide lines for the shelf ends on the inside of end pieces (B). Next, scribe centerlines between each pair of guide lines and transfer these centerlines to the outside of the end pieces, to give you the location of the screws.

shelf

ALL PARTS
3/4" THK. KNOTTY PINE

ASSEMBLE WITH
1-1/4"- NO. 8 FLT. HD. SCREWS
COVER WITH LONG GRAIN PLUGS

B

A

C

D

F

DRAWER SIDES & BACK
3/4" THK.
BOTTOM 1/4" PLYWOOD

L

E

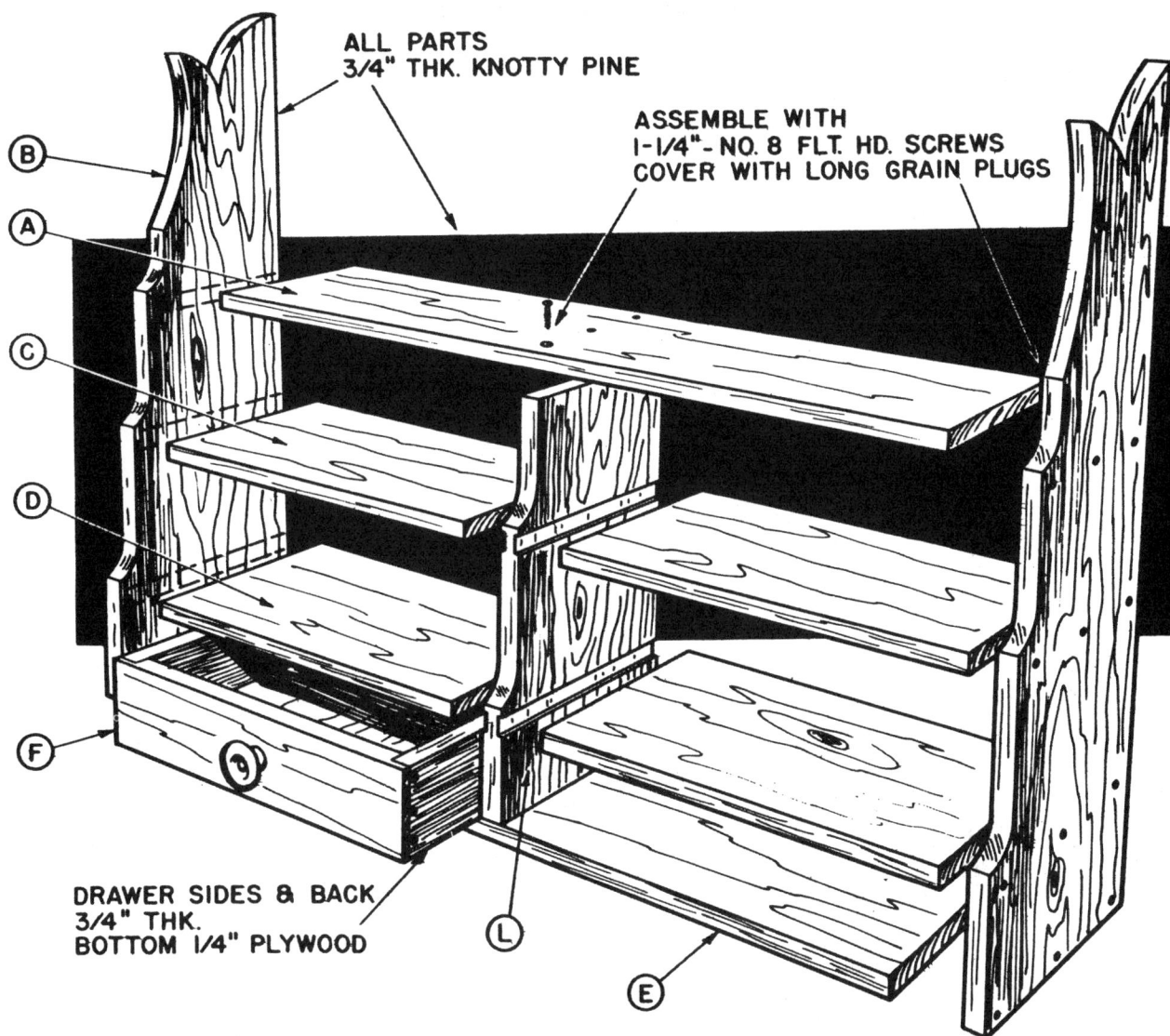

Sides (B), center partition (L) are cut on jigsaw with cardboard template tacked on as a guide.

Temporarily tack sides and center partition together, place in vise, file all edges at one time.

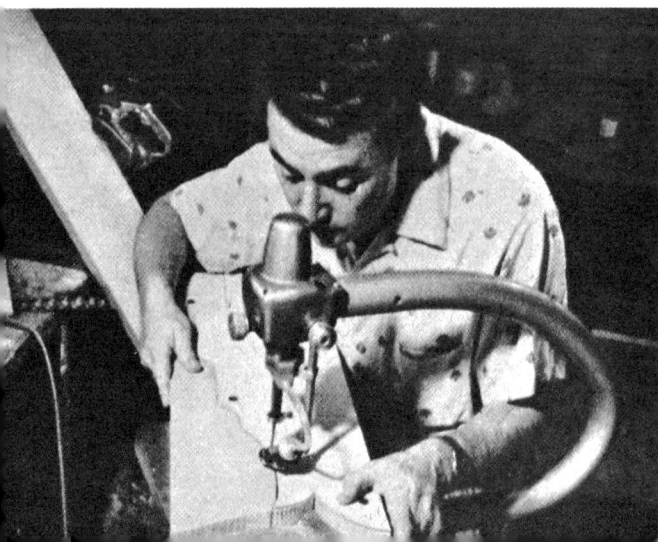

First attach top, bottom shelves to center partition and add sides, then put in middle shelves.

Middle shelves (C) and (D) fit into 3/16x¾-inch grooves dadoed into piece (L); use glue, toenail.

If you use three screws, space the holes equally apart and drill them ½ inch in diameter and $\frac{5}{16}$ inch deep. Then drill shank holes for the screws in the center of these holes, all the way through the board and exactly on the centerline.

File and sand to secure clean, smooth edges on pieces (B) and (L). By fastening them in a vise, you can file all three of the jig sawed pieces at once and transfer the guide lines from the end pieces to center partition (L). This gives you the location of the shelves on the center piece and of the dado grooves into which they will be fitted. Cut out the shelves next. They will be of three different widths, 7, 8, and 9 inches. Notice that the top and bottom shelves are both 30 inches long while pieces (C), (D) are each only $14\frac{13}{16}$ inches in length. After you have rough-sanded these shelves to eliminate major defects, check their thickness at the ends. Cut dado grooves $\frac{3}{16}$ inch deep in the center piece so that the shelf ends will fit tightly into them.

Draw guide lines on the bottom of the top shelf and on the top of the bottom shelf, to give you the location of the screws which fasten these shelves to the center partition. Again, ½-inch and $\frac{3}{16}$-inch holes are to be drilled at the centerlines on the outside of each of these two long shelves.

Begin assembly of the knickknack shelf by fastening the 30-inch long top and bottom shelf to the center partition with glue and screws. Mount the end pieces on the shelf ends in the same manner. Make sure that all back edges are flush as you assemble these pieces. Next to be installed are the small shelves (C) and (D).

For the entire assembly you can use 1¼-inch No. 8 flathead woodscrews or 6d finishing nails, plus glue. If you use finishing nails set the heads ⅛ inch below the surface of the wood and fill the holes with matching putty.

Make the two drawers in the following manner. Cut and fit the two drawer fronts in place leaving only $\frac{1}{16}$-inch space on all sides. Rabbet both ends of each drawer ½x¾ inches as shown in detail drawing Z. Cut and fit the drawer sides so that they are ¼-inch shorter than the space between the front edge and the solid backpiece. Then mark and saw the dado grooves in the drawer sides. Make these as wide as the thickness of your drawer bottom stock. Cut the drawer back so that it fits between the two sides and atop the bottom.

Finally, assemble the drawers with glue and screws or finishing nails. Either 1½-inch No. 8 flathead woodscrews or 4d finishing nails will be satisfactory. Insert the drawer bottom after the frame has been assembled and nail it to the drawer back. •

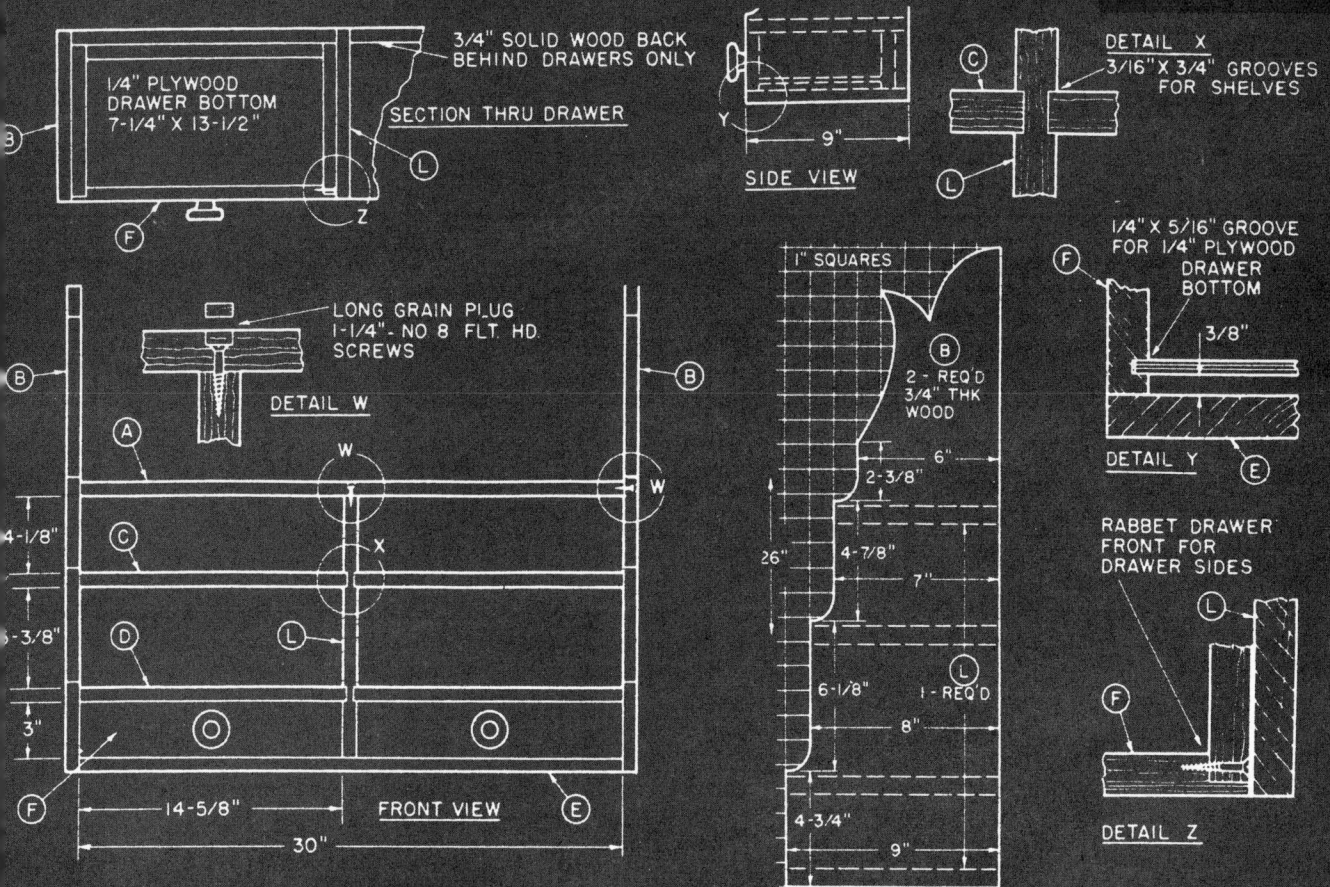

1/4" PLYWOOD DRAWER BOTTOM 7-1/4" X 13-1/2"

3/4" SOLID WOOD BACK BEHIND DRAWERS ONLY

SECTION THRU DRAWER

SIDE VIEW

DETAIL X
3/16" X 3/4" GROOVES FOR SHELVES

LONG GRAIN PLUG
1-1/4"- NO 8 FLT. HD. SCREWS

DETAIL W

1/4" X 5/16" GROOVE FOR 1/4" PLYWOOD DRAWER BOTTOM

3/8"

DETAIL Y

1" SQUARES

2 - REQ'D 3/4" THK WOOD

6"

2-3/8"

26"

4-7/8"

7"

6-1/8"

1 - REQ'D

8"

4-3/4"

9"

RABBET DRAWER FRONT FOR DRAWER SIDES

DETAIL Z

4-1/8"

6-3/8"

3"

14-5/8"

FRONT VIEW

30"

MATERIAL LIST

1/4" plywood (drawer bottoms), 8"x30"

2 pieces 1" solid wood, 10"x10 ft.

2 drawer knobs, preferably porcelain

4 dz. flathead screws, 1 1/2" No. 8 or 1/2 lb. 6d finishing nails and 1/4 lb. 4d finishing nails

Handful headnails, 3/4"

Sandpaper (preferably garnet), Nos. 1, 1/2, 2/0

Glue, matching putty

Last, fit drawers into place. Drawers can be assembled with woodscrews or finishing nails, glue.

Solid 3/4-inch wood back pieces are fitted in behind drawer sections; cut them to fit in snug.

scrolled wall shelf

The Chinese motif of this shelf makes it ideal for displaying a collection of Chinese figurines or other prized knickknacks.

THE pattern of the scrolled cut-outs in this decorative wall shelf give it a definite Chinese motif. You can use the shelf to display a collection of Oriental figurines or other knickknacks.

If you want to finish the shelf natural, make it of maple or cherry wood. Pine or birch will do should you want to paint or enamel it in a satin-finish black.

All stock used is ¾ inch thick, except for the back panel which is ¼ inch thick. By making a rabbet along the inside back edges, you could substitute a mirror for the wood panel for added effect.

If you use panel stock, be sure to seal all exposed edges so the core stock does not show. For a neat appearing job, sand all surfaces thoroughly before applying the finish. Because of the weight of the shelf, it is recommended that metal hanger plates be used to support it. They should be at least ⅝ inch wide by 1¼ inches long. •

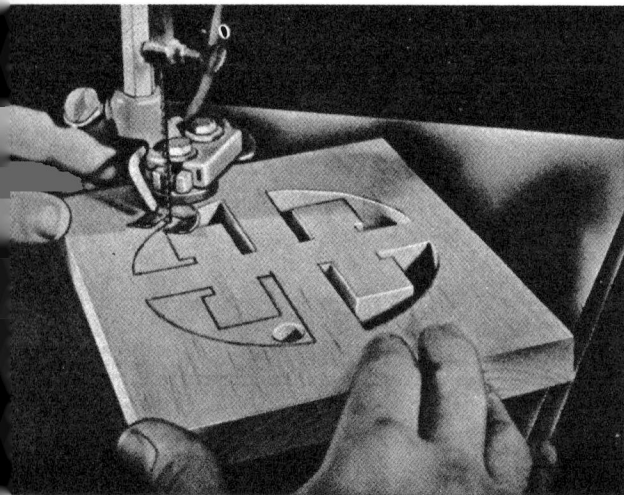

Make templates of the scroll designs, transfer to wood stock, then cut out on the scroll saw.

BILL OF MATERIAL

Qty	Part	Dimensions
1	Back	¼"x15⅝"x41⅝"
2	B (Top and Bottom)	¾"x6½"x42"
2	D	¾"x6½"x1¾"
2	E	¾"x6½"x10¾"
2	H (Sides)	¾"x6½"x14½"
1	J (Center Shelf)	¾"x6½"x22"
2	K	¾"x6½"x3½"
2	L	¾"x6½"x1½"
2	M	¾"x6½"x1¼"
2	N	¾"x6½"x3"
2	P (Shelf Supports)	¾"x6½"x7½"
2	R	¾"x6½"x16¼"
16	Splines	⅛"x5"x7/16"
2	Metal Hangers	⅛"x¾"x1¼"
14	Flat Head Wood Screws	No. 8 x 1¼"

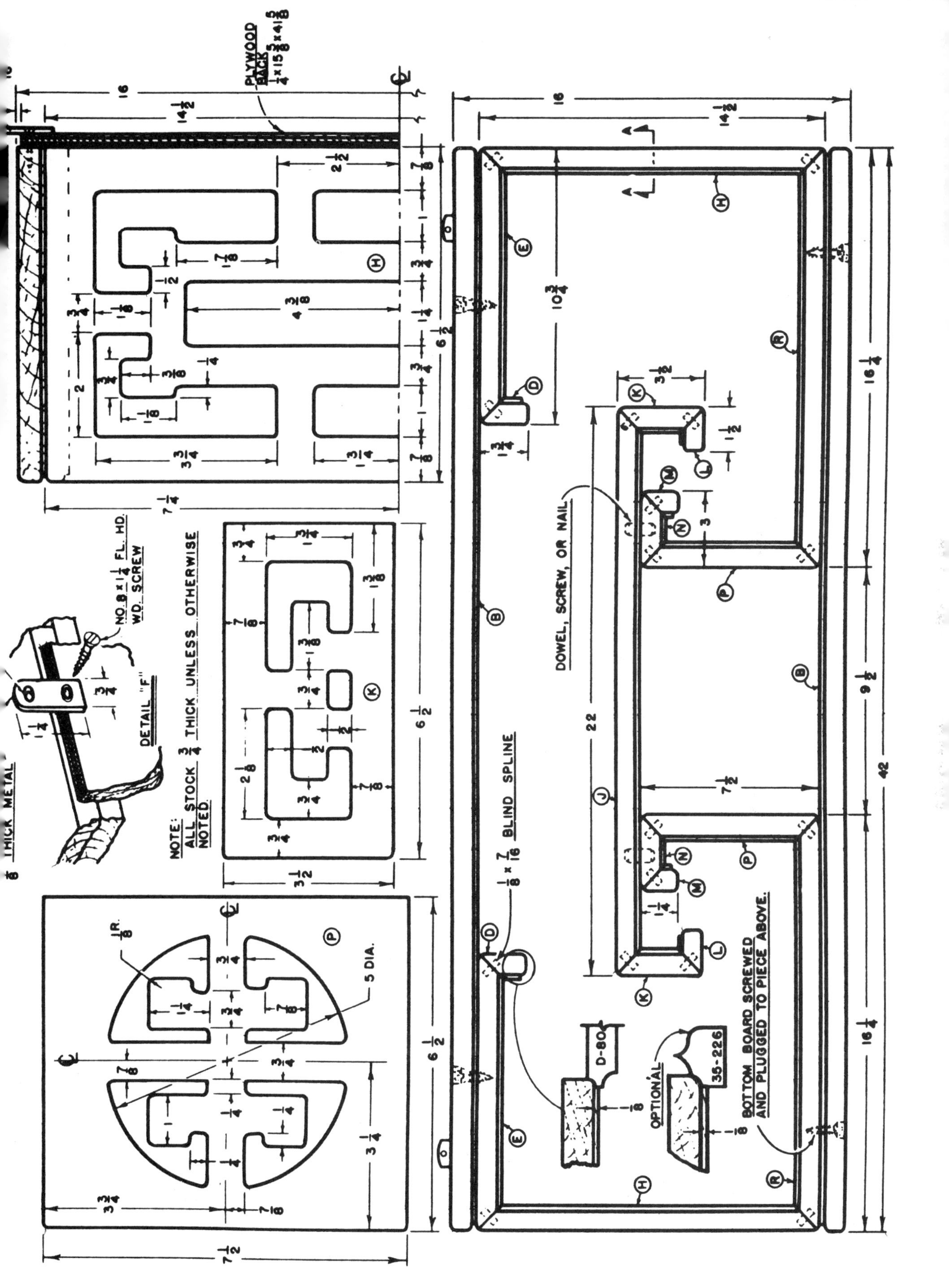
PLYWOOD BACK 1/4 x 15 5/8 x 41 5/8
THICK METAL
NO. 8 x 1 1/4 FL. HD. WD. SCREW
DETAIL "F"
NOTE: ALL STOCK 3/4 THICK UNLESS OTHERWISE NOTED
5 DIA.
DOWEL, SCREW, OR NAIL
1/8 x 7/16 BLIND SPLINE
D-80
OPTIONAL
35-226
BOTTOM BOARD SCREWED AND PLUGGED TO PIECE ABOVE.

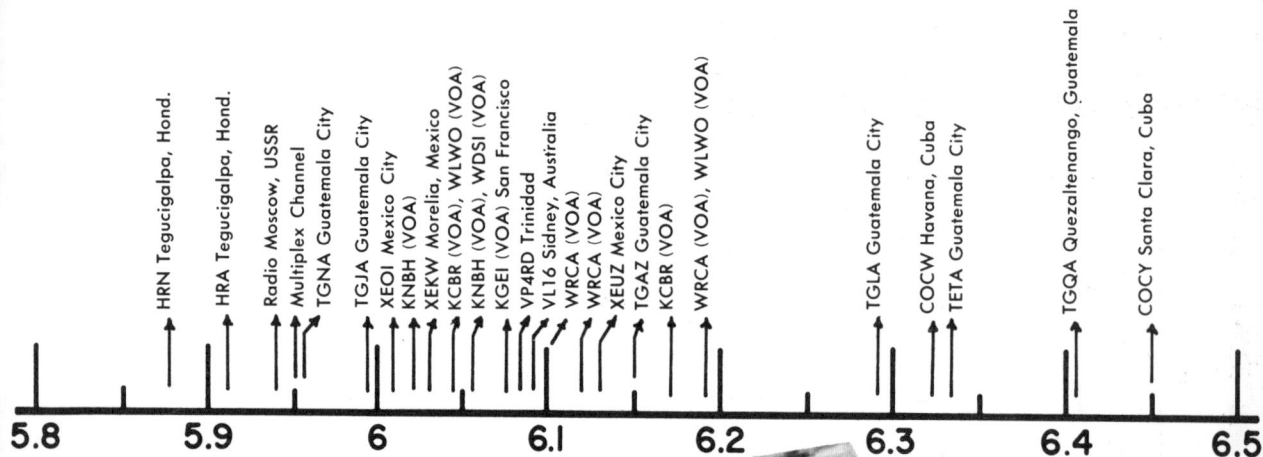

Frequency scale (MHz):

Station	Frequency
HRN Tegucigalpa, Hond.	
HRA Tegucigalpa, Hond.	
Radio Moscow, USSR	
Multiplex Channel	
TGNA Guatemala City	
TGJA Guatemala City	
XEOI Mexico City	
KNBH (VOA)	
XEKW Morelia, Mexico	
KCBR (VOA), WLWO (VOA)	
KNBH (VOA), WDSI (VOA)	
KGEI (VOA) San Francisco	
VP4RD Trinidad	
VL16 Sidney, Australia	
WRCA (VOA)	
WRCA (VOA)	
XEUZ Mexico City	
TGAZ Guatemala City	
KCBR (VOA)	
WRCA (VOA), WLWO (VOA)	
TGLA Guatemala City	
COCW Havana, Cuba	
TETA Guatemala City	
TGQA Quezaltenango, Guatemala	
COCY Santa Clara, Cuba	

5.8   5.9   6   6.1   6.2   6.3   6.4   6.5

El 49'er
Short Wave Converter

For Short-wave Listeners—a two-transistor unit that pulls in 49-meter band on a standard radio. By Don Stoner, W6TNS

YOU can eavesdrop on the world with a handful of parts that would easily fit in the space occupied by a pack of cigarettes. Transistors, of course, are the answer to such high degrees of miniaturization.

The "49'er" is a two-transistor crystal-controlled converter for the 49-meter short-wave band that occupies less than five cubic inches! The device will convert this band so that it may be received on a standard broadcast radio. The compact feature makes

PARTS LIST

R1—470,000 ohms, ½ watt resistor
Capacitors (low-voltage types)
C1,C2—20 mmf tubular or disc
C3—.005 mf disc
C4—100 mmf tubular or disc
L1—70 turns, #38 enameled or cloth covered wire, tightly scramble wound on ¼" slug tuned form, modified per text (J. W. Miller #4311)
L2—10 turns, #38 wire, wound over coil L1
L3—Same as L1
L4—Same as L2
L5—170 turns, #38 wire, tightly scramble wound on ¼" slug tuned form, modified per text (J. W. Miller #4315)
L6—60 turns, #38 wire, wound over coil L5
Q1,Q2—SB100, 2N247 or OC171 transistors (see text)
S1—SPST slide switch
B1—Three penlite cells (RCA VS034A or equiv.)
Misc.—Crystal 6.5 to 7.5 mc., plastic box 2¾"x3¾"x 1½", 2/56 hardware. Circuit board available from Semiconductors 'N' Stuff, Box 288, Alta Loma, California.

Crystal oscillator circuit using Q1 beats with incoming 49-meter signal in Q2 circuit and converts it to BC band.

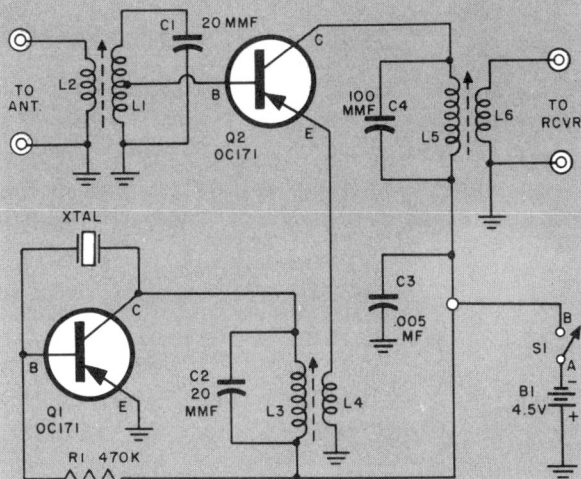

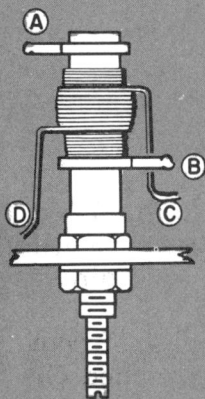

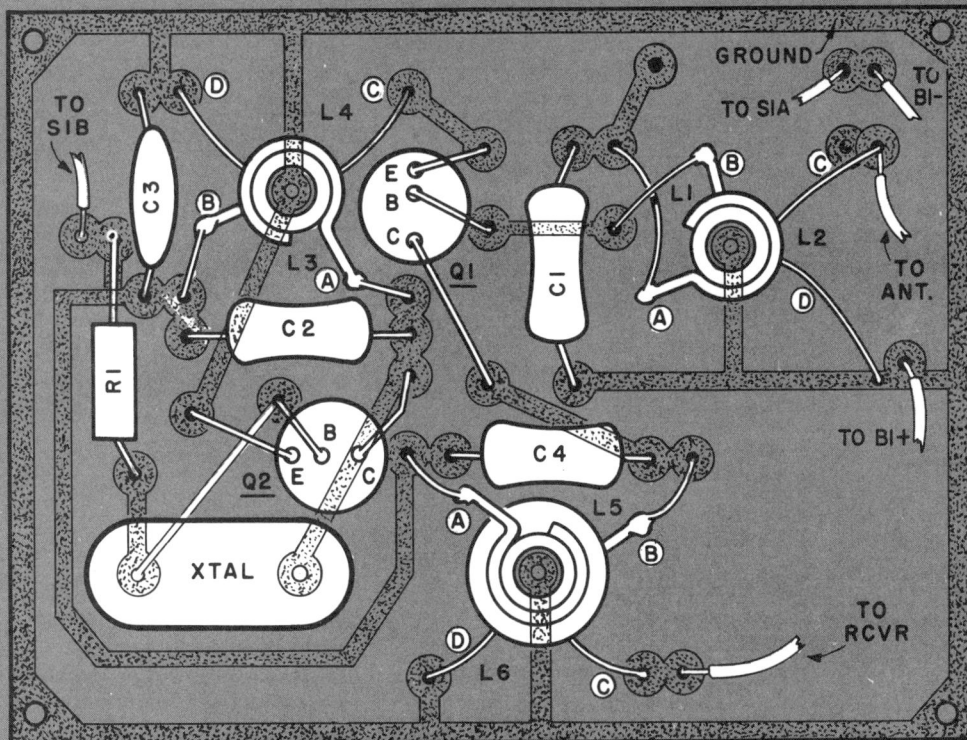

Arrangement of components on printed-circuit board. Shading indicates conductive areas. Point-to-point wiring may be used instead of board, if desired.

2676 • SHORT WAVE

Neatness of layout is inherent with use of etched circuit board for all components except batteries.

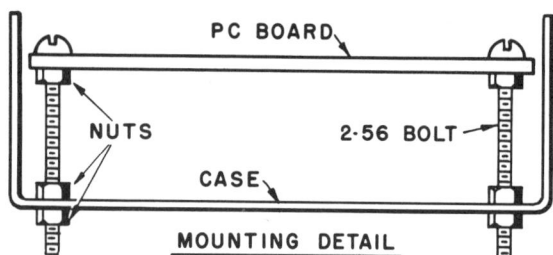

Fig. 1 Cutaway view of printed circuit board mounting. Four bolts are used as grounds.

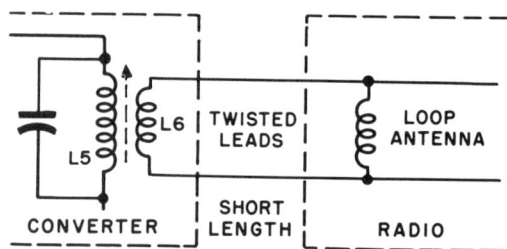

Fig. 2. Method of connecting converter to radio with loop antenna. L6 ground is removed.

it ideal as a shortwave adapter for your car radio.

Operation—The antenna is connected to coil L2. Signals arriving at the antenna are coupled to coil L1 which is tuned to the 49-meter band or about 6.5 mc. This coil also serves to match the antenna to the base of transistor Q2.

The oscillator energy, necessary for the superheterodyne process, is generated by transistor Q1. The oscillator produces a tiny crystal-controlled signal which mixes with the incoming station. The *difference* frequency between the two signals is within the receiving range of the broadcast radio to which it is connected.

To understand how this occurs, assume that a signal is received on 6 mc. This beats or heterodynes with the crystal (in the unit shown it happens to be 6.925 mc). The difference frequency, then, is .925 mc or 925 kilocycles which can be picked up near the center of the broadcast band (550-1600 kc). With a crystal frequency of 6.925 mc, the radio can tune stations between 6.375 and 5.325 mc. Other crystal frequencies will shift the receiving range accordingly. More about this later.

Construction—The majority of components are installed on an etched circuit board to aid in duplicating the converter. The board, in turn, is mounted in a small plastic box, which also contains on-off switch S1 and the three penlite cells B1.

The first step in building the "49'er" is to prepare the coils. Unfortunately no suitable coils exist for shortwave transistor circuits, and commercial coils must be modified. The Miller coils are very tiny and therefore ideal for the miniature converter.

Coil L1 is modified by winding 10 turns of #38 wire immediately under existing coil. One end of the new winding connects to terminal B (see pictorial) the other is soldered to the metal coil form base.

This produces a coil with a tap (terminal B) and the other two terminals are A and the coil base which is automatically grounded when mounted on the board. Cement this winding in place and then wind an additional 10 turns of #38 over the top of the original coil. This winding is L2 and about 1″ of wire at both ends should be left free. Next, wind 10 turns of #38 over winding L3. This additional winding becomes L4. Leave both ends of this coil free, also.

Modify coil L5 (A and B) by adding 40 turns over the top of the winding. This coil is shown as L5 (C and D) in the schematic.

Next, solder the transistors, capacitors, resistor, crystal, and coils directly to the circuit board, in that order. Use a pencil iron to avoid overheating the board and grip the transistor leads with a long-nose pliers to remove heat from the junctions. All the components are mounted on the board on the side opposite the printed wiring. The shield lead on the OC171 should be cut short and bent out of the way.

The circuit board is mounted in the box as shown in Fig. 1. Be sure to drill holes in the plastic box slowly or it will crack. The board's mounting bolts serve as the ground terminals. All wires to the various terminals and the battery should be connected before the board is installed. The input terminal (from the antenna) is marked S1A, and the output eyelet is S1C.

Testing—Connect a 0-10 ma meter across the terminals of S1 (with the switch off) and measure the transistor current. It should be between 6 and 9 ma. Touch the top terminal of the oscillator coil L3/L4. If the current rises noticeably it indicates the oscillator circuit is working properly. If the current is slightly higher than normal, or if you do *not* note an increase when you touch the coil, adjust the slug of the coil until a dip in current is noted. Once this position is found, the coil need not be adjusted further.

To check performance, connect the converter to the antenna terminals of your receiver, and an antenna exceeding 20 feet to the input terminals of the converter. By tuning across the band you should receive shortwave stations. Adjust the slugs of coils L1/L2 and L5/L6 for the loudest signal strength. If you also hear broadcast stations, it indicates your receiver does not have adequate shielding.

You may also use the converter with radios having a built-in loop antenna system by connecting it as shown in Fig. 2. Connected in this manner it eliminates pickup from the loop. Note that the ground end of L6 must be disconnected from the circuit board.

Notes—The crystal determines the frequency at which the shortwave stations appear on the radio dial. Any crystal between 6.5 and 7.5 mc will allow you to receive the 49-meter short-wave band. The exact frequency is not at all critical.

If you would like to pick up other bands, the crystal and coils will have to be changed. A detailed explanation of how to accomplish this will be found in the *ARRL Amateur Radio Handbook.* Complete coil and crystal data is given. Any PNP type transistor with a 30 mc alpha cutoff will work in the circuit. The printed circuit plate specified in the parts list need not be used, a perforated board with flea clip terminals will work as well. •

THE 49 METER BAND

Location of the 49-meter broadcasting band shown in diagram on page 2674. The stations shown have the strongest signals on the West Coast, although there are many other weaker ones. The European stations, in particular, should be well received on the East Coast. Voice of America stations (VOA) are quite prominent because of their high power. The best time to receive stations on the 49-meter band is around sunrise.

Stall Shower Door

Here's a welcome improvement! A rustproof, mildew-proof stall shower door designed to replace that bothersome shower curtain.

HERE'S a welcome improvement for the shower stall or ready-built shower cabinet. It is designed to replace the bothersome shower curtain with rustproof, mildew-proof aluminum and Fiberglas.

Begin by determining size door needed. This will vary of course with your particular shower installation, so overall dimensions shown on the plan may not suit your needs; change as required. Be sure to leave enough space on sides for hinge and door-latch stop angles. Height of door should leave about 6-inch space at top for air and steam circulation. Bottom should be close to sill so that water will stay inside shower.

Begin construction by cutting screen extrusion to size for sides, top and bottom, with channel facing in. Miter corners 45° on circular saw or with miter box and hacksaw. The standard screen-frame corner locks require a bit of modification—the extra web of metal inside the corner angles should be cut or filed away as shown in the photo. Determine location of latch and stiffener strips and drill inside of frame for self-tapping screw attachment of front strip ends and door pull.

The Fiberglas panel is next cut to size. The edges should be covered with rubber tape for a tight seal where panel fits into channel in frame. Caulking compound may be substituted for tape if desired.

The frame is now assembled around the panel using the concealed corner angles.

The latch assembly comes next. This is hung on both sides of the panel and joined to stiffener strips running across door.

Make back plate first. This is slotted across center for rod handle. Make latch strip and join handle to it. Peen rod stock flush with latch. Next cut lengths of "Y" stock for latch slides. Also cut filler strips which go between slides and back plate. Now clamp slides and filler strips in place on back plate with latch in position. Space so that latch slides easily. Drill through slides, filler and back plate for rivets. It is a good idea to drill one hole, add rivet, then repeat for others so that holes are properly aligned.

The front plate is made to match back plate and handle slot. At this point it would be advisable to cut handle slot in Fiberglas panel before final assembly of latch. Use front plate for pattern.

Make front and back stiffener strips now. Note that back strip also has filler strip to bring strip up level with back plate. Bend front strip to fit inside frame edges. Back strip lays flat across frame sides.

Assemble all latch and strip parts on

The extra lip on the inside of each corner lock will have to be cut out to adapt for the project.

Assemble mitered frame members around Fiberglas door panel, securing with concealed corner locks.

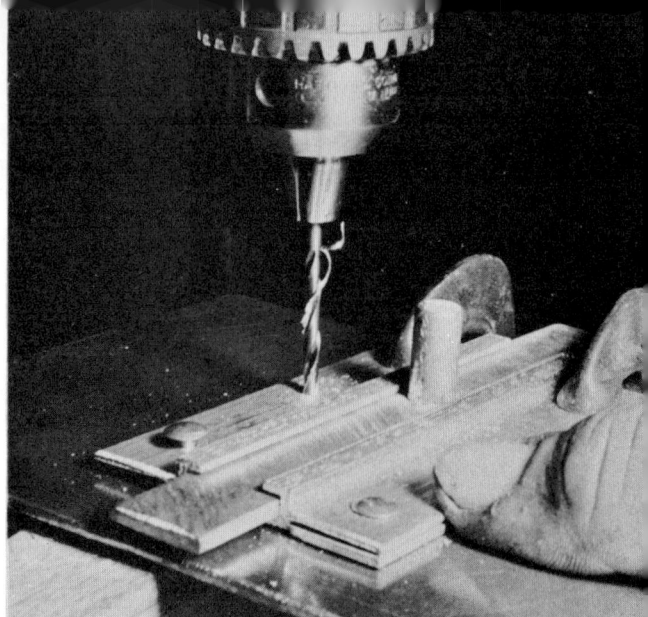

Begin latch assembly by clamping sliding handle and slides in place against slotted back plate.

Drill holes for rivets through latch-strip slide, filler bars and back plate, then rivet together.

Drill one hole at a time, add rivet, then repeat process so that all holes are properly aligned.

Attach latch unit to shower door. Latch strips should be spaced so that latch slides smoothly.

Add a short length of ⅜-inch rod at top and bottom of back side of door for hinge pivots.

panel; clamp and drill for rivets. Any length rivet may be used since they can easily be cut to suit thickness of metal layers. It is best to get rivets slightly longer than necessary and cut down as needed.

Add ¾-inch angle for door pull at front plate. Short lengths of ⅜-inch rod are shown for hinge pivots at top and bottom.

These mate with short section of angle which serves as pivot holder. The pivot holder is attached to stall sides with metal or masonry screws according to construction of your particular shower stall. A length of angle fastened to stall side serves as door stop; locate so latch engages rear face. •

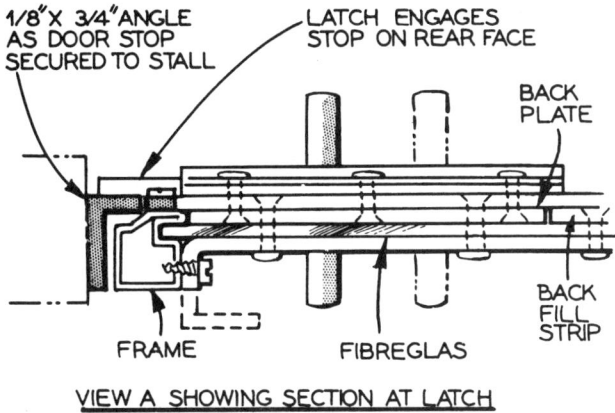

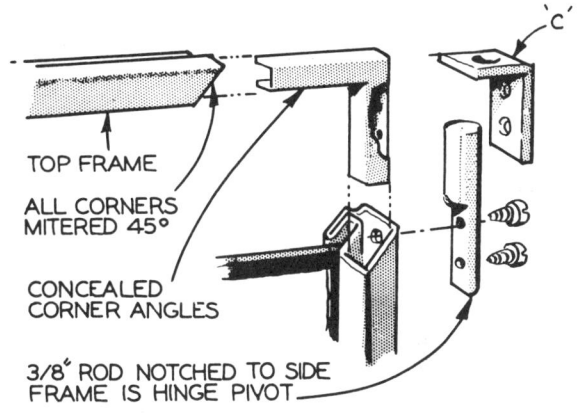

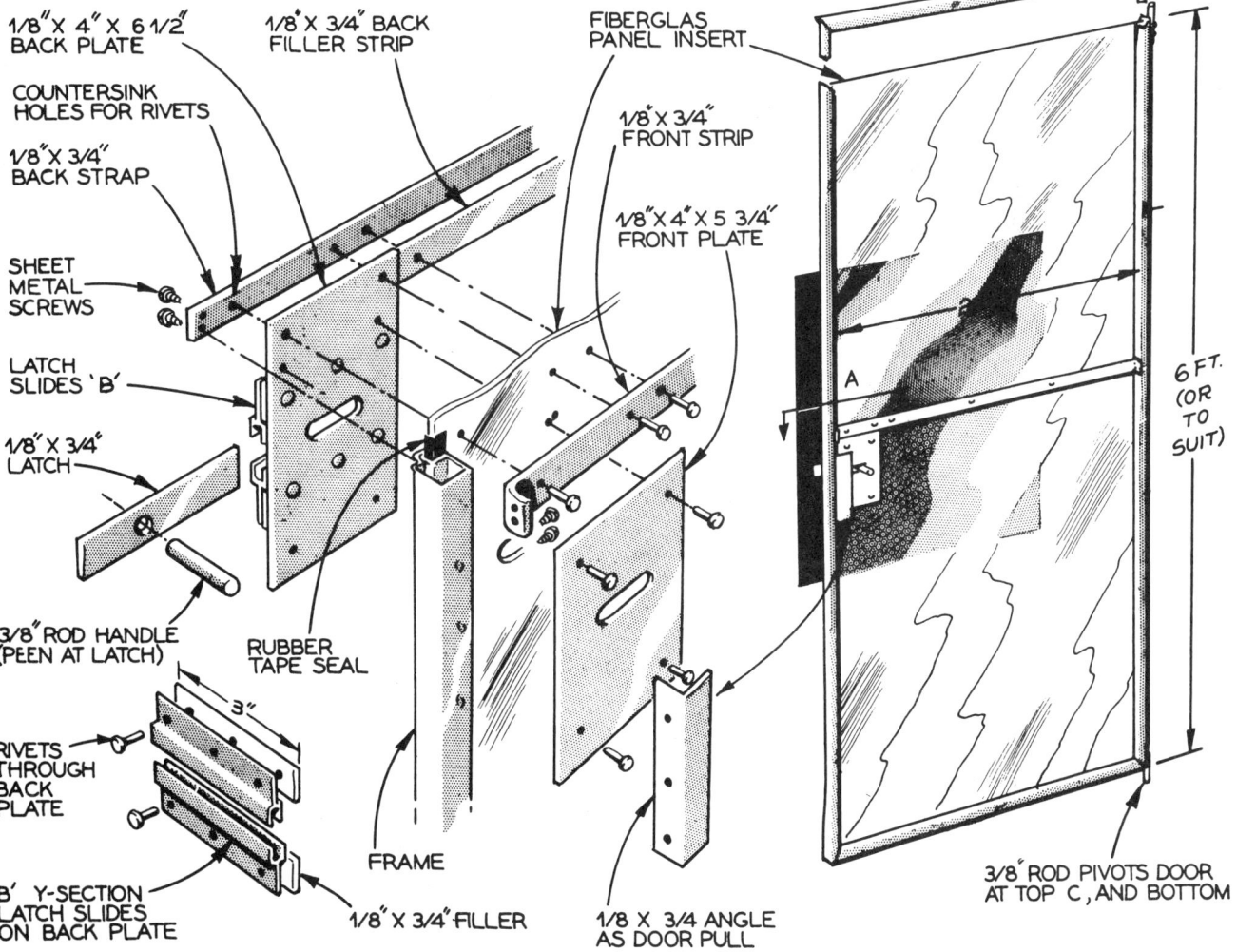

1/8" X 3/4" ANGLE AS DOOR STOP SECURED TO STALL

LATCH ENGAGES STOP ON REAR FACE

BACK PLATE

BACK FILL STRIP

FRAME

FIBREGLAS

VIEW A SHOWING SECTION AT LATCH

C

TOP FRAME

ALL CORNERS MITERED 45°

CONCEALED CORNER ANGLES

3/8" ROD NOTCHED TO SIDE FRAME IS HINGE PIVOT

1/8" X 4" X 6 1/2" BACK PLATE

1/8" X 3/4" BACK FILLER STRIP

FIBERGLAS PANEL INSERT

COUNTERSINK HOLES FOR RIVETS

1/8" X 3/4" BACK STRAP

1/8" X 3/4" FRONT STRIP

SHEET METAL SCREWS

1/8" X 4" X 5 3/4" FRONT PLATE

LATCH SLIDES 'B'

1/8" X 3/4" LATCH

A

3/8" ROD HANDLE (PEEN AT LATCH)

RUBBER TAPE SEAL

6 FT. (OR TO SUIT)

RIVETS THROUGH BACK PLATE

3"

'B' Y-SECTION LATCH SLIDES ON BACK PLATE

FRAME

1/8" X 3/4" FILLER

1/8 X 3/4 ANGLE AS DOOR PULL

3/8" ROD PIVOTS DOOR AT TOP C, AND BOTTOM

rustic shutters

IT'S no trick at all to tack up panels or lath beside your windows and call them shutters. But if you take pride in your domicile, why not spend a few profitable hobby hours and turn out something that you'll enjoy for years to come?

Let's see how easily these distinctive shutters can be made. If you happen to have some old grainy boards in the garage, you've got a head start. All you'll need in addition are some dowels, leftover paints and varnish and a few ordinary tools.

Fairly soft woods, such as pine or redwood, are preferred for this job. If you do not have V-rustic siding in 8-inch width, take some old 1x12-in. stock and saw to the desired length. To secure the proper length or height, measure from the middle of the sill to the inside edge of the top window frame. •

Before attaching the scored 1x12-in. pieces that serve as elements of one shutter, cut out half of proposed design from the adjoining edge of each.

To make studs, hold length of ⅝-in. dowel in vise, round end with rasp, cut off rounded tip and insert brad. Finished stud is seen at the extreme right.

HINGES FINISH
NAILED TO
WINDOW CASING

5/8" DOWEL
'STUDS'

BRAD THROUGH
ROUNDED DOWEL
SECTION TO
SIMULATE STUDS

SCORE 'V' NOTCHES
(OR BEVEL AT JOINTS)

4"

H.C.

8½"

26"

3½" 2½"

1¼" 1¼"

CATCHES FROM
1/2" STOCK

GOUGE OUT
NOTCHES
TO INDICATE
NATURAL
WEAR

3/4" STOCK SHUTTER (2)

24"

1" SQUARES ON 3/4" STOCK

KNOTS AND GRAIN
SCRIBED INTO WET
PAINT WITH DRY BRUSH

OUTLINE FOR HINGE LEAF

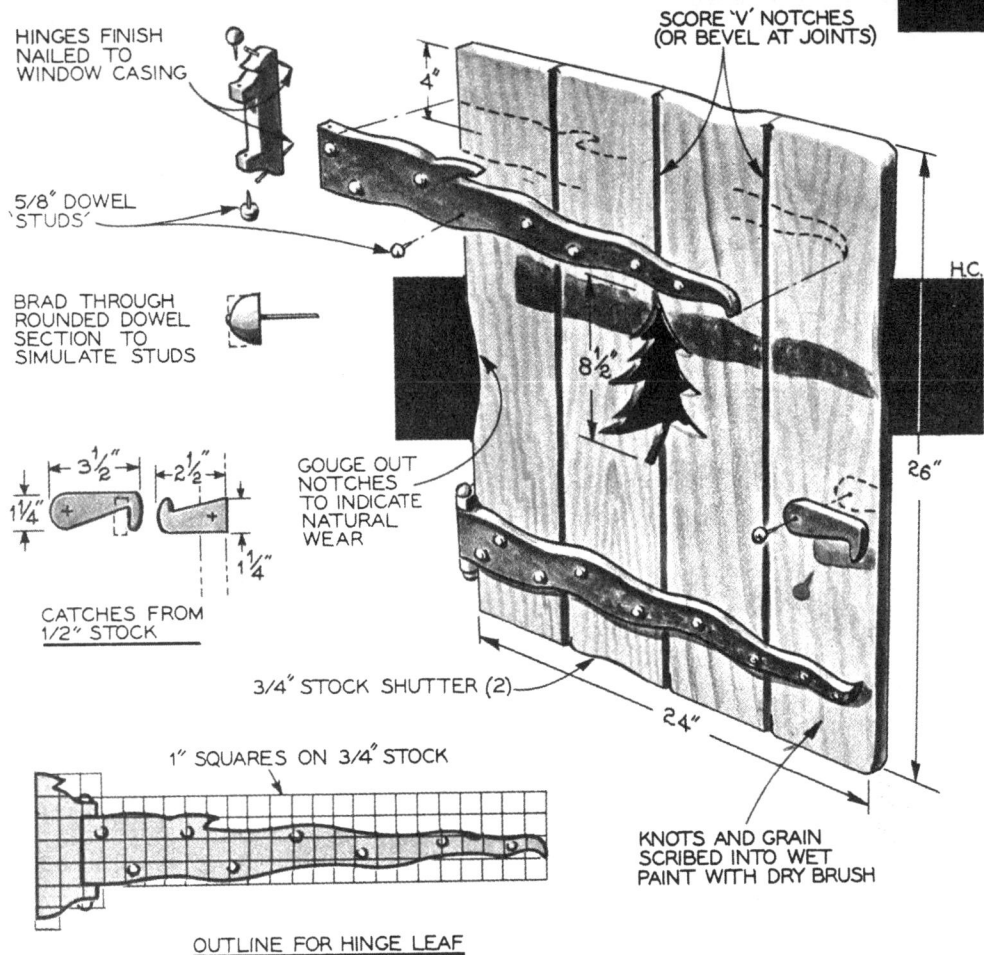

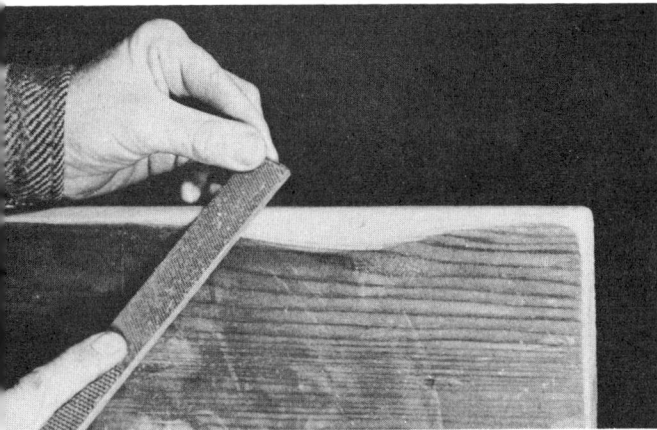

Roughen some of the outside edges at random to achieve that rustic appearance. Use progressively finer rasps, then sand smoothly to ease painting.

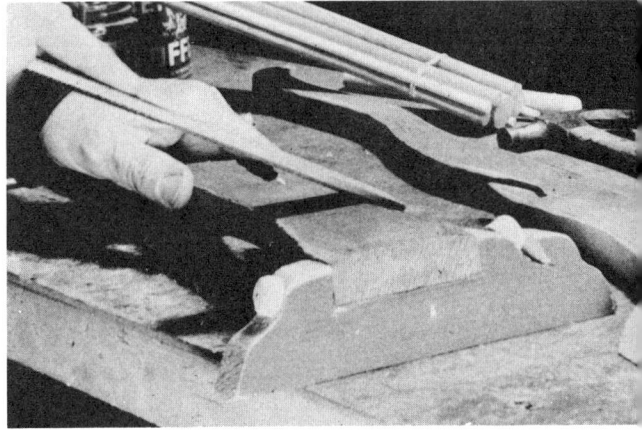

A jig like this will simplify the shaping of your custom-made hinges. General outline to be followed is indicated in diagram at top of the page.

After undercoat is applied, brush on thin coat of spar varnish. The cutout design is then edged with enamel. Orange was color used in this case.

In all cases shutters are proportioned to windows as much as possible. This one was made wider to correspond with a long narrow stretch of glass.

As raised storage shelf, unit is mounted atop the 72-inch-long Sliding-Door Cabinet.

sideboard-
bed cabinet

Build this piece as a back rest and storage cabinet for a couch, as a raised or floor-level storage shelf, or omit legs and mount it on a wall.

THE flexible design of this handsome piece enables you to use it in several ways, depending on your own furnishing demands: (1) it can be built as a snug floor cabinet that can be used in conjunction with a studio couch or bed. The bed slides under the unit and may be drawn out a night. (2) By substituting an alternate leg assembly for the two side legs employed in the Bed Cabinet, you can either place the cabinet on the floor, where it will serve as a convenient sideboard, or else set it on any large cabinet; it was designed with a sliding door cabinet in mind similar to the one shown above. (3) You can

1 1/2 FINISHING NAILS   DOOR SLIDES   SEPARATOR   REAR BRACE

1 1/4" NO. 8 SCREWS

CHOICE OF ANGULAR LEGS
– OR FULL LENGTH SIDE LEGS

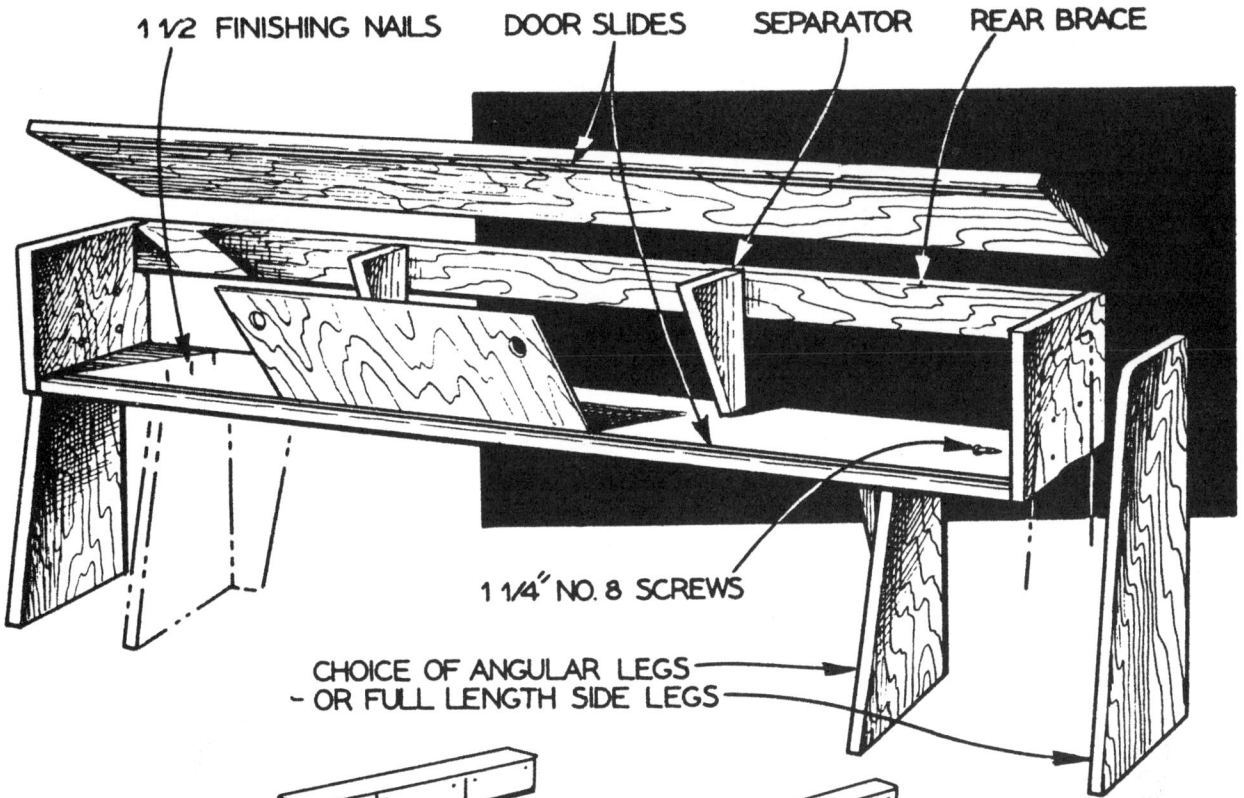

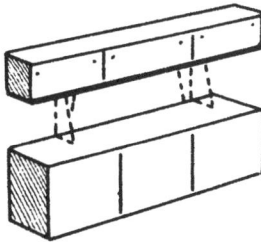

AS WALL CABINET
WITH OR MINUS LEGS

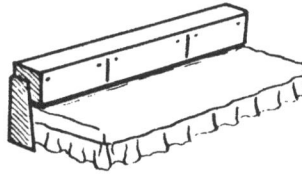

AS USED OVER COUCH
OR DAY BED UNIT

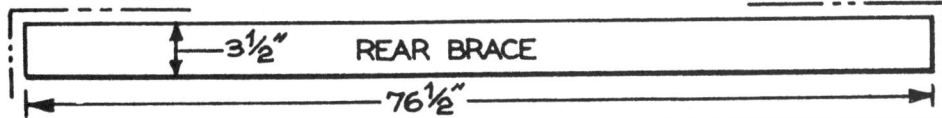

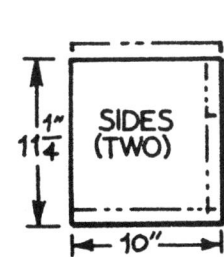

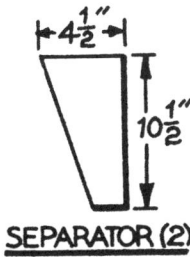

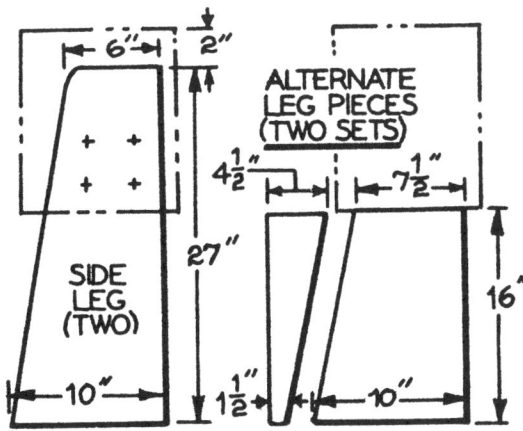

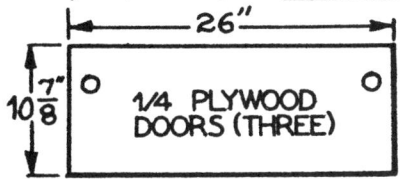

TOP PANEL   78"   10"

7/16"

5/16" DIVISIONS
FOR SLIDING
DOOR GROOVES

REAR BRACE   3 1/2"

76 1/2"

BOTTOM PANEL   10"

1/4"

SIDES
(TWO)   11 1/4"   10"

SEPARATOR (2)   4 1/2"   10 1/2"

ALTERNATE
LEG PIECES
(TWO SETS)

ALL PARTS
FROM 3/4"
PLYWOOD
EXCEPT DOORS

6"   2"

SIDE
LEG
(TWO)   27"

4 1/2"   7 1/2"

16"

1/4 PLYWOOD
DOORS (THREE)   26"   10 7/8"

10"   1 1/2"   10"

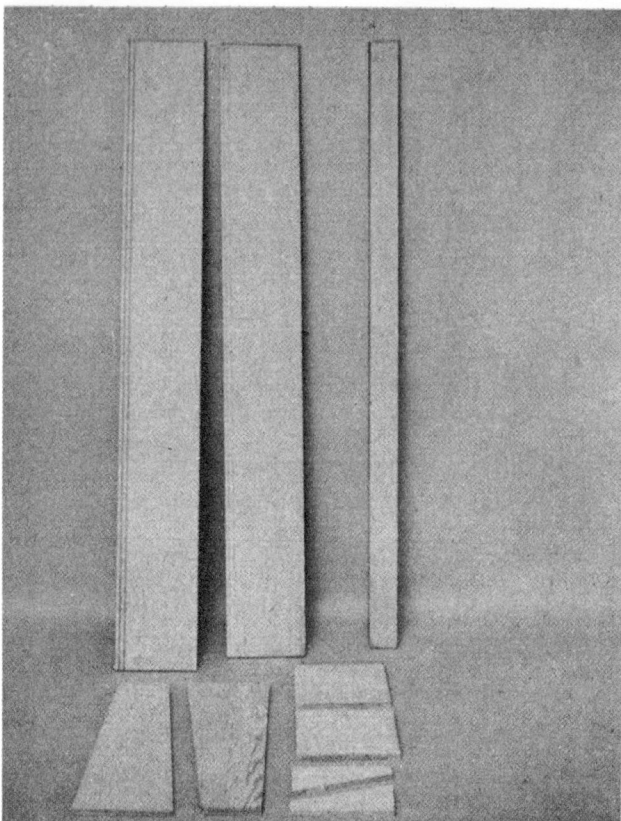

BILL OF MATERIALS

Note: All lumber, unless otherwise specified, is ¾" plywood.

1 Top . . . . 10"x78"
1 Bottom. . . . . 10"x76½"
2 Sides . . . . 10"x11¼"
1 Brace . . . . .3½"x76½"
2 Separators . . . . cut as shown
2 Side Legs (Bed Cabinet only) . cut as shown
4 Leg Elements (Sideboard only). cut as shown
3 Sliding Doors (¼" plywood) . . . 10⅞"x26"
1½" Finishing Nails . . . . ½ lb.
Glue
8 Flathead Wood Screws . . . . . 1¼" No. 8

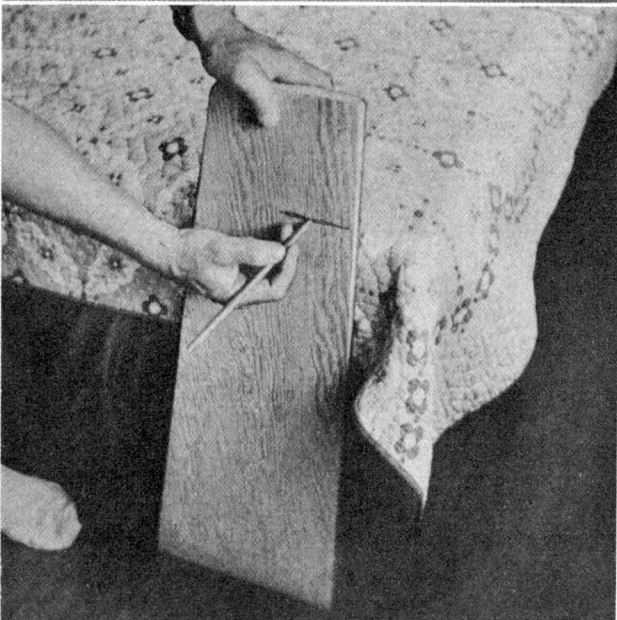

Assembly photos are for Bed Cabinet. Add 1 inch to bed height; indicate this dimension on legs.

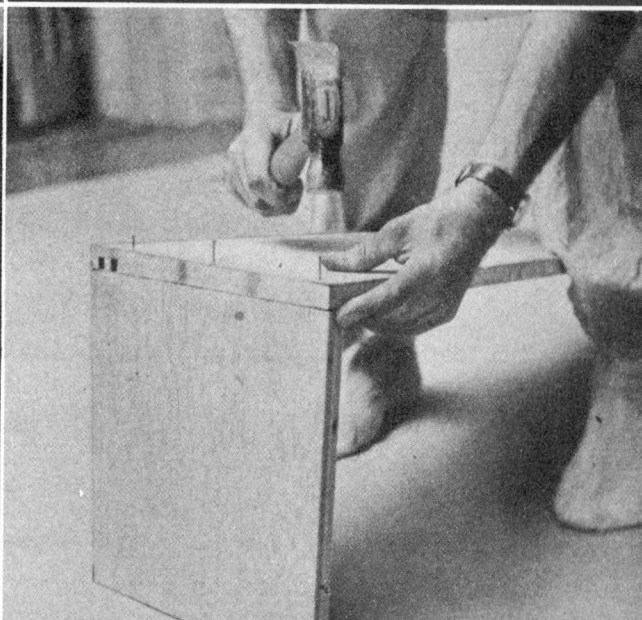

Nail top panel to both sides. Notice that top extends to outside edges of 10x11¼-inch side pieces.

make it without either type of leg assembly, and mount it right on your wall.

You'll note that the top and bottom panel each have two grooves to accept the sliding doors. Note, also, that the top grooves are deeper than those on the bottom; this permits installation of the doors after completion of the entire unit. If you have these grooves cut at a lumber yard, they'll probably be cut to extend to the ends of both panels, which means that you'll have to plug them up later on. If you have your own circular saw, however, you'll be able to make "blind" grooves that will not extend to the very ends of the panels.

The assembly photographs shown concern